Karen M. Raddatz

FORM
IN
MUSIC

Order gave each thing view.
Shakespeare

The poet's eye, in a fine frenzy rolling,
Doth glance from heaven to earth, from earth to heaven;
And as imagination bodies forth
The forms of things unknown, the poet's pen
Turns them to shapes, and gives to airy nothing
A local habitation and a name.
Shakespeare

I am seeking always . . . the coherent and living
expression of my musical ideas.
Roger Sessions

PRENTICE-HALL INTERNATIONAL, INC., *London*
PRENTICE-HALL OF AUSTRALIA, PTY., LTD., *Sydney*
PRENTICE-HALL OF CANADA, LTD., *Toronto*
PRENTICE-HALL OF INDIA (PRIVATE) LTD., *New Delhi*
PRENTICE-HALL OF JAPAN, INC., *Tokyo*

FORM
IN
MUSIC

An examination of traditional techniques
of musical structure and their application
in historical and contemporary styles

WALLACE BERRY

Professor of Music
University of Michigan

Prentice-Hall, Inc., *Englewood Cliffs, New Jersey*

Library of Congress Catalog Card Number: 66-12872

Current printing (last digit):
17   16

Printed in the United States of America

32920-C

To my mother,

and to the memory of my father

FOREWORD

*S*ince music is an <u>art that exists in time</u>, the intelligent listener must face the problem of relating the successive manifestations of the musical discourse to those already heard, and ultimately, through familiarity, to those yet to be heard. Music acquires its meaning through the interaction of all its parts. The unprepared listener is seldom aware of these interactions and may even be unable to identify the protagonists of the musical drama. He listens to music as a succession of individual moments, of greater or lesser beauty, never discovering the larger structures that give these moments meaning.

The study of musical form has been all too often an establishing of textbook patterns, averages of common practice to which few actual compositions conform. In a sense, every piece of music creates its own form out of its individual materials. Comparison of two sonatas by the same composer is likely to reveal more significant differences than similarities; only in the most general sense do the works of different composers agree. It is essential to consider the larger dimensions, which make it possible to categorize ; but it is equally important that the individual differences, the unique solutions, be specially considered in the analysis of many works.

In the pages that follow, Wallace Berry has systematically examined the structure of music, mainly instrumental, in the light of historical orientation and aesthetic necessity. He turns the beam of his inquiry upon every facet of the form, illuminating as he penetrates to the essentials. From the smallest elements of music — figure, motive, phrase — he proceeds in an orderly fashion to the most complex musical organizations — sonata, variations, fugue. He ranges widely through the literature of all periods. His terminology is unequivocal; though not always traditional, it may well become standard.

A careful and thorough study of this book will abundantly reward the reader, especially if he brings himself to acquaintance with the vast treasury of music unlocked here, by reading, playing, and listening. I can imagine no more congenial guide through the storehouse than Dr. Berry.

HALSEY STEVENS
University of Southern California

PREFACE

What is form in music? It is the sum of those qualities in a piece of music that bind together its parts and animate the whole. It is the product of intellectual control over the musical ideas which bring a composition into existence. It is a discipline through which the inherent power of the musical materials is realized and directed to an end that is convincing and seemingly inevitable. It is all of these; yet, the complexity of any comprehensive answer is indicated by the fact that books like this are written.

The primary purpose of these studies is the exposition of fundamental principles of musical form, illuminated by illustration of the techniques by which they are applied. While one cannot, alas, describe music with recourse to its own explicit and inexhaustibly rich language of notes, the theorist must conduct his study of musical form with constant, probing reference to musical works of clear, but challenging form. That is the reason for the number of musical quotations and citations in these chapters and for my pausing at frequent intervals to take a careful look at the makings of form in complete examples. Observations are shown, I hope with the consistency I have desired, to be based on significant musical practice.

When music theory speaks of *traditional forms,* its reference is to established models of musical structure which were brought to consummate realization in the eighteenth and nineteenth centuries, and which show remarkable viability today. Most formal studies in musical form have as their basis of subject matter the literatures which reflect the broad principles of these forms.

As is apparent from the table of contents, this book approaches the question of musical coherence through a systematic investigation of traditional forms, and is thus adaptable to the usual advanced music theory course variously designated "Form and Analysis," "Analytical Techniques," or "The Analysis of Music." Overemphasis on surface structure at the expense of more critical and decisive elements of form in much recent music education has produced a reaction against the study of traditional forms in many places, but there survives a just appreciation of their importance as flexible and proven frameworks for the solution of structural problems, and as monuments to human invention and artistic evolution.

I believe that the study of traditional forms is useful and valid so long as it proceeds beyond surface identification and classification into the penetrating analysis of *all* aspects of form in significant works — unorthodox as well as conventional. Such analysis must pursue every detail of form, recognizing that over-all "surface" design is only a basis, and that the application of a traditional structural scheme is no assurance of logic, coherence, and animate substance in music. Therefore, it is crucial that analysis be directed into the investigation and best possible understanding of all relevant *principles*.

The present study is not conceived as an end. A part of the reason for singling out those forms which are the nuclei for these essays is their adaptability through changes of musical style and idiom. I choose to deal extensively with *fugue*, for example, rather than *ricercar*, which is important for more specialized study but less universal. Also excluded are vocal types like the *mass*, which have no standard musical structure. Thus, I have rejected the inclination to try to discuss all musical *genres*, with a hasty *aperçu* of the *motet*, and a page and a half on the *oratorio*, in favor of exhaustive treatment of common forms that afford vivid illustration of principles of musical logic and unity in expansive development, and which, in their immediacy, are the most useful foundation for later, more particularized research. Virtually all Western music derives unity and vitality from one phase or another of a common set of principles, whether or not a conventional total design enters into the solution of the problems of form. Hence, I have been able to draw many illustrations from such types as the oratorio, the mass, the opera, and the art song, and from a wide historical span which extends to the present moment.

The studies in this book are made with a constant awareness of the dangers of categorization which is too rigid and generalization which is too broad and insistent. At the same time, I believe that any observation of traditional practice leads to the delineation of important parallels among forms and styles, and that classification is therefore possible and reasonable — providing a background of common practice against which to regard the anomalies that are so valuable a source of instruction. Of course, the discussion of classification with respect to any given work must often be content to point the way to the structure of a rationale, while leaving particular questions unanswered. Such, I think, is one of the arts of pedagogy.

This volume is addressed to the musician — amateur or professional — who has studied basic music theory. In seeking to demonstrate techniques of form and analysis through careful and searching examination of the most tenacious forms and literatures, it does not try to be a history of those forms, nor of their rarer antecedents. In analysis, I have wanted to restrict myself to discussion of musical anatomy in preference to subjective description. ("As the little piece prances along it plays us many tricks, the most amusing of which is to wheedle us into supposing, when it cracks the whip in C major, *fortissimo*, more like a big stick than a lash, that we have regained the home key and are near the end. But not at all. This is not, for all its bluster, the true return. . . ."[1]) Indeed, had I the gifts of Sir Donald Francis Tovey, I might more easily have been enticed into the indulgence of literary fancies.

The musical examples are intended to encompass a wide variety of styles and media. The music suggested for supplementary analysis, when not listed for high intrinsic value, either has some special usefulness or illustrates some particular device or problem. I have not provided a workbook for what is to me a very important reason: the risk of stagnation in the classroom practice of dealing with the same limited frame of reference in course after course, year after year. It seems altogether feasible as well as profitable to refer to a varied selection of moderately priced editions of such indispensable items as Bach fugues and Beethoven sonatas in addition

[1]Daniel Gregory Mason, *The Quartets of Beethoven* (New York: Oxford University Press, 1947), p. 38.

to contrasting materials, some of them recent, offering stimulation and broad stylistic experience and often meeting the special needs of a specific situation. Materials for such use are listed throughout this book, and published collections and workbooks will be found to be readily available for conditions in which they are deemed essential, and for individual study. My examples from and preceding the early eighteenth century are, in many instances, drawn from the *Historical Anthology of Music,* whose two volumes are convenient and accessible as well as abundant in range of content.[2]

The exercises are specimens of projects for valuable study beyond the material of the text itself. Rare will be that situation in which the reader can turn his attention to more than a few of them, but the listing of many makes possible the choice of an area of investigation offering either special relevance or interest. Where group study is involved, several projects might be undertaken, the results of each shared with the group. In this, as in all respects, specific application of the material is left to be governed by the limitations and demands of particular circumstances.

When a concept or term seems to require explanation or when my own understanding of a term seems important to impart (unlike a word such as *mixolydian,* about which there can be little difference of understanding), I have inserted a brief footnote. Cross reference to these definitions is available through the index.

I have tried — not altogether realistically — to disavow uncertain preconceptions, to avoid unwarranted generalization, to address myself to the problems of musical form with the highest degree of terminological clarity and consistency possible in writing about so elusive a subject, and to read with my ears every musical passage to which I have given space.

The value of musical analysis which goes beneath the surface structure, having more as its end than the classification of works as rondos, ternaries, or whatever, is generally accepted in areas in which music is a serious field of study. Apart from the practical functions of analysis, I for one would make no apology in pointing to the sheer delight in discovery of all the working parts of a musical organism. But, beyond that, analysis is a vital experience for all musicians; and it is axiomatic that music has only the palest reality apart from the transmissions of its past.

Analysis is, of course, indispensable to the theorist and musicologist who must use its techniques in the evaluation of style and significance. The young composer, for whom analysis is one of the paths to skill in his own craft, too often forgets, in his impatient search for self-expression, that he must fulfill himself as a musician (if he is to write music), imbibing deeply the instructions of great musical achievements, learning intimately the principles and techniques that make a musical work a vital unit, remembering that the art he practices is never totally new, and false if it pretends to be anything but, in words of Ernest Bloch, a "balance between tradition and evolution."

The performer must, like all musicians, acquire a comprehension and ultimately an intuition of the functions and requirements of form. He must have the means to consider, when necessary, the structural functions of any problematic passage. He has to understand how tension is mounted and released in music; otherwise, how can he be an effective instrument for the realization of the musical content, and on what basis are his decisions of dynamics, tempo adjustments, phrasing, and all elements of "interpretation" to be formed?

The critic is incapable of wisdom respecting musical effectiveness and ineffective-

[2]Willi Apel and Archibald T. Davison, *Historical Anthology of Music* (Cambridge: Harvard University Press, 1949, 1950).

ness without a thorough understanding of the *reasons* behind fundamental failings that inhibit so much musical expression. And how incredible it is that the scholar whose primary concern is the aesthetics and psychology of musical communication is so often ignorant of the technical factors that make for motion, dynamic intensity and recession, dramatic effect, stability or instability, and unity and variety, some of the elements that enter into the form of music.

Finally, we must recognize the deeper enjoyment that accrues to the listener who makes an effort to understand the anatomy of music. His response to emotional stimuli, at a primitive and innocent level, is by no means unimportant; but how much his experience deepens when he can participate intellectually as well. Music has a logical, rational organization; and all the vital details brought out in analysis are meant to be heard and felt.

Correlatively, all scholars need to be reminded of the value of listening. It is in the act of listening that analysis is finally understood and confirmed, and the listening as a prelude to analysis not infrequently suggests the most fruitful avenue of approach in the study of the music's form.

I have been obliged in the present volume to avoid involvement in many of the specific applications of structural principles in contemporary styles, preferring to forego a shallow *précis* of twentieth-century techniques in favor of deeper penetration at another time, and referring the reader to other texts at appropriate points. The large number of musical examples which I have culled from works of today's composers is testimony to my acute interest in new music, and to my belief in its importance in contemporary life and education. Musical richness is diluted as much, after all, by the denial of today as by the denial of yesterday.

Many of the musical excerpts and textual quotations reprinted in this book are drawn from works or editions which are restricted by copyright, and I am indebted to the publishers and other copyright owners who have consented to my use of them.

For stimulating and challenging discussion with my colleagues at the University of Michigan — exchanges that have led me to reexamination and better formulation of not a few ideas — and to that occasional student of searching mind and relentlessly critical inquiry, I would express most earnest thanks, mentioning among the former Professors Albert Cohen, Paul Cooper, John Flower, and John Lowell. Professor Edward Chudacoff of Oberlin listened patiently and with invariably useful response to many of my inchoate ideas while this book was in its earliest stages. Dr. Arthur Daniels and Dr. Ingo Seidler lent their accustomed competence and clarity of thought to the solution of specific questions I posed. And Dean James B. Wallace of the University of Michigan School of Music assisted me in many ways.

The staff of the Music Library of the University of Michigan and those of the Libraries of the American Academy and the *Accadèmia Nazionale di Santa Cecilia* in Rome have been very helpful, and I am grateful both for their assistance and for the facilities placed at my disposal.

Professors Louise Cuyler and Halsey Stevens read the complete manuscript and made many helpful and important suggestions. My indebtedness to them is inestimable.

It is customary in the final words of his preface for an author to acknowledge the support of his wife. This is a gesture in which I, having so much greater reason than most, can scarcely fail. Her incisiveness of mind, wisdom of critical perception, and inspiriting warmth have been resources upon which I have drawn constantly through the long months in which these studies have taken form.

Wallace Berry

CONTENTS

and harmony; the melodically-harmonically-fixed variation; Motive as a fixed element; the free variation; The tone series as a fixed element in the free variation; Other fixed elements in theory and practice. Examples of theme elements in variation: Structure; Harmony; Melody; Meter; Rhythm; Color; Tonality; Mode; Tempo; Dynamic levels; Texture; Character; Treatment of the variable elements in the practice of variation. Coda; appendage of separate structure. Brahms, Quintet in B minor, Op. 115, for clarinet and string quartet, final movement. Variation principles freely applied. Double variation: variation on variation. Exercises and examples for further study.

FORM
IN
MUSIC

1

SMALLER
STRUCTURAL UNITS

*J*ust as a novel, a play, or a choreography is divided
into episodes, scenes, acts, and individual movements and speeches, so the
progress of music in time achieves form and intelligibility through the
occurrence of small groupings of sounds, each making its particular con-
tribution to the development of the whole. The small structural units which
are the building stones of music are, ideally, bound together into a logical
succession by (1) the common rhythmic, harmonic, and melodic features
which they share; (2) the techniques by which they are joined—some of
them discussed at the end of this chapter; and (3) their use in the development of accumulative points of climax (and repose) in the musical work.

Words, the smallest meaningful structural units in language, convey
distinct and intelligible impressions when purposefully combined into phrases
and clauses. The larger units (phrases, clauses, sentences, verses, paragraphs) usually relate to one another and to the whole of which they are
portions by virtue of central, significant *meaning* to which they contribute,
even though other unifying factors may be involved—as, for instance, meter
and rhyme.

Music, however, lacks discursive and concise meaning. This is not to
say that music has no meaning: it may impart a sense, a mood, an
impression of states or qualities. But it is essentially abstract, and its
structural components achieve integration chiefly by their corroboration
through *repetition,* often in varied form and new combinations, as well as
by lending appropriately to the general direction and expressive character of
the work or passage of which they are a part. Because of the abstract nature
of music it is often difficult to distinguish the individual phrases or "cells"
of the musical organism. Some guides to their identification and analysis
are discussed in this chapter.

It is from small structural units—especially the motives and phrases—that large forms evolve. Although this book will present descriptions of a number of conventional designs, the features of which are shared by multitudes of musical works, it must be recognized that these surface forms find unique application in nearly every specific example. For the form is not predetermined and then filled with musical ideas. The opposite is true: the ideas of the composer, occurring to him out of the richness of his imagination and through his mastery of the musical language, become the material from which the specific directions of the form emerge. A vital musical motive, like a living cell, has a pregnancy and energy of its own and often stimulates its own continuation; the rest is up to the composer's craft. Combining small structural units into a convincing and persuasive whole, with a balance between forces of tension and release and a sense of logical and inexorable course, requires the highest degree of technical command.

Part of the coherence of any piece of music lies in the fact that it rests upon a succession of usually regularly spaced beats, or impulses, against which the rhythmic patterns play, and in relation to which, as to one another, they enter into coherent form. These pulsations fall into groups (measures), often of the same length throughout a given piece or movement. It is the size of the measure—the number of beats—that determines the metric structure;[1] and it is the frequency of the fundamental pulsations and the amount of activity interspersed among them that determine the tempo of the music, one of the most basic factors governing its character. In some music the length of the measure changes frequently during the course of a work, and such metric change lends a quality of its own.

Metric irregularity can be a very interesting feature in music. Similarly, phrases and periods of odd numbers of measures can constitute an effective element of asymmetry in music, provided that other qualities are of commensurate effect and that intelligibility is preserved. Many composers have almost consistently written structural units of 2, 4, 8, and 16 measures. While a predictable regularity of this kind can easily dispel the listener's interest, there are of course, *many* ways of achieving contrast and asymmetry in music. The fact that thematic phrases of a Classical work are entirely of four-measure lengths may be offset by asymmetry in "free," developmental passages, and by devices like overlapping, or "elision," in the joining of adjacent units.

---

[1] *Meter* may be defined as a system whereby the span of time in music and the series of basic impulses upon which it rests are divided into units (of time) or groups (of impulses, or "beats"). It is a means of rhythmic organization in music by which the coincidence of voices and their relationship to one another and to the fundamental succession of beats can be perceived and indicated in notation. The most apparent unit of meter is the measure, or bar; the unit of measure is the beat. These units together constitute the mensural level of the metric structure, and govern its nature. On p. 17, reference is made to other levels of metric organization—*intermensural meter,* a unit of which is the measure.

Musical form invariably involves division into interrelated segments. The lines of distinction, especially between *motive* and *phrase,* are often a question of subjective impression; precise absolute definitions that will apply for all listeners in all cases are not possible. Yet there is no question of the existence of these units in music, and it is important to consider their qualities and the manner of their delineation even if we cannot always fit examples into invariable nominal categories.

The Motive

A motive, as is suggested by its etymological source, is a motivating idea in music—the small cell out of which the music evolves. The French composer, Vincent d'Indy (1851–1931), labeled the essential motives in his scores as *cellules* (cells). Also worth noting is the definition of motive given by Coeuroy: "It is an element, ordinarily short—shorter than the theme—from which the composer draws a musical development."[2]

In his study of the motive, the student can best refer to Ernst Toch's *The Shaping Forces in Music,* in which Toch describes with rare insight and sensitivity the functions of the motive: the "motive power" of a composition—reviving, animating, bridging, splicing, feeding movement. "It lives on repetition and yet on constant metamorphosis...."[3] Toch cites as an example of such a propelling force the opening motive of the first movement of Brahms' Second Symphony; this motive sounds unassuming indeed when it is first heard below the theme melody, but becomes the prime motivating force as the movement develops.

Ex. 1.1   Brahms, Symphony No. 2 in D, Op. 73, first movement.

Thus, the potential and significance of a thematic fragment may be unapparent until it is subjected to manipulation in the course of a work. In other words, a good part of the significance of a motive is, in a given

2 André Coeuroy, *La Musique et Ses Formes* (Paris: *Les Editions Denoël,* 1951), p. 19. Translated by the author.
3 From *The Shaping Forces in Music* by Ernst Toch, copyrighted 1958 by Criterion Music Corp.

example, precisely the measure of its development by the composer. Ex. 1.2 shows a motive which is announced inconspicuously in the final measures of the exposition; it would hardly be predicted that this motive would later form the basis for nearly all of the development section.

Ex. 1.2   Beethoven, Sonata in B-flat, Op. 22, first movement.[4]

The motive might be defined, then, as the smallest characteristic unit whose significance is established in development. In isolation it lacks coherence (although it may convey a particular impression) and it is principally meaningful as a stimulus to its own development and continuation. Motives are not necessarily delineated by actual harmonic cadential formulae. Often, they are punctuated by means of metric division, by rests, by articulation, or by a momentary cessation of movement on a longer note. Or, as suggested above, a motive may have integral identity which becomes apparent only in its later appearances and development, or in immediate repetition. Some of these principles are apparent in Exs. 1.3, 1.4, 1.5, and 1.6.

Ex. 1.3   Brahms, Sonata in A, Op. 100, for violin and piano, second movement.

Ex. 1.4   Aaron Copland, Symphony No. 1, Prelude.

Ex. 1.5   Mozart, Sonata in D., K. 284, third movement.

4 "Sonata" is understood to mean *sonata for piano*.

Ex. 1.6 Beethoven, Trio No. 4 in B-flat, Op. 11, for clarinet, cello, and piano, first movement.

The rhythmic anacrusis, or upbeat, is exceedingly common in the structure of a motive; it acts as a preliminary "inhalation" which sets the motive in motion.

Ex. 1.7 Paul Hindemith, Pittsburgh Symphony, first movement.
© 1959 B. Schott's Soehne/Mainz, Germany. Used by permission.

The length of a motive—how many notes it contains—depends on a number of factors, especially the tempo of the music. Obviously, in a slow succession, fewer notes will combine into a single total impression, while if the notes are faster a greater number can be perceived as a single unit. The following motive contains 12 notes in its first appearance; in subsequent extensions it incorporates as many as 21 notes.

Ex. 1.8 Stravinsky, Le Sacre du Printemps, Part I (Danse de la Terre).
Copyright 1921 by Edition Russe de Musique. Copyright assigned to Boosey & Hawkes Inc., 1947. Reprinted by permission.

If they are of distinctive quality, or if they have importance in later development, as few as two notes may constitute a motive.

Ex. 1.9 Debussy, Nocturnes, No. 1 (Nuages).
  Permission for reprint granted by Editions Jean Jobert, Paris, France, copyright owners, and Elkan-Vogel Co., Inc., Philadelphia, Pa., agents.

Of course, any musical segment is arbitrarily divisible into small fragments. But, having recognized the factors of punctuation and *significance* in our definition of the motive, we can see at once that a musical form does not necessarily fall into motivic units. In Ex. 1.10, phrase 7 is a repetition of the final motive of phrase 6, and the motive of measure 2 occurs in various forms. But for the most part, the phrase is the smallest unit of structural significance. Unity is produced by identities among the phrases (1–5, 2–6 in rhythm; 1–3, 2–4 in every respect), and by progression toward D, the final of the modal scale.

Ex. 1.10 Chorale, Ich ruf' zu Dir, Herr Jesu Christ.

Ex. 1.11 Brahms, Quartet in A, Op. 26, for piano and strings, first movement.

Motives enter into the larger musical structure by their literal restatement, by their *sequential*[5] repetition (at other pitch levels), by modification
of *rhythm*[6] or some other feature, by *imitation*[7] in other voices, by combination with other motives, and by many other devices. A few of these are
shown in Ex. 1.11, Ex. 1.12, Ex. 1.13 and Ex. 1.14.

Ex. 1.12   Mozart, Sonata in E-flat, K. 282, third movement.

Repetition and sequence:

└─ Sequential repetition of entire
   motive group

Ex. 1.13   Bartók, String Quartet No. 1, Op. 7, second movement.
            © 1949 by Rozsavoelgyi & Co., Budapest. Copyright 1954 by Edizioni Suvini
            Zerboni. Used by permission.

Rhythmic transformation:

5 A *sequence* consists of the systematic, usually regular, repetition of a basic
pattern in the same part or parts. If the pattern is a melodic one, the sequence is a
melodic sequence; if it is harmonic, the sequence is termed *harmonic*. A *total sequence*
is one in which all voices participate. When the pattern, in its repetitions, refers even
ephemerally to different key centers, it is a *modulating* (or *real*) *sequence*; when
adjustments are made in the repetitions to preserve the original key feeling, it is
called a *nonmodulating* (or *tonal*) *sequence*. Frequently the repetition in a harmonic
sequence is strict to the extent that the actual positions and distributions of the
harmonies of the basic pattern are reproduced exactly. For an unusual example in
which the duration of the pattern changes in its repetitions, see Ex. 11.29. Many
examples of sequence will be found in this book. (See footnote, p. 182.)
6 *Rhythm* has so many facets and properties (see pp. 316–18) that it defies
brief definition. It might be described, in a very general way, as that quality in music
which results from and consists of patterns formed by successive musical sounds of
varying durations, tension-levels (difference of pitch and real or implied tonal-harmonic
function), and degrees of stress. On the basis of this concept, it would be concluded
that a succession of "equal" musical sounds does not produce rhythm.
7 *Imitation* is the contrapuntal device by which a particular musical idea is
stated in one voice, then taken up in another, usually at a new pitch level but sometimes "at the unison." Rarely, the material is simultaneous in both parts ("time
interval" of zero), one a variation of the other. If the imitation is precise in its
duplication of the intervals and rhythms of the original, it is said to be *strict* (real);
otherwise it is *free* (tonal—see Chapter 11 for real and tonal fugal answers and other
types of imitation).

Ex. 1.14 Schubert, Der Einsame, Op. 41.

The figure

It will be useful to make a distinction between that kind of fragment which is of thematic and developmental significance in a work and that which is used accompanimentally or episodically. The latter is a *figure*. The episodic figure is sometimes found in the connective passages—the transitions, although these passages are often based upon motives from the thematic groups which they bridge. Example 1.15 and Ex. 1.16 will illustrate accompanimental and episodic figuration. The figures quoted here are of

Ex. 1.15 Mozart, String Quartet in C, K. 465, third movement.

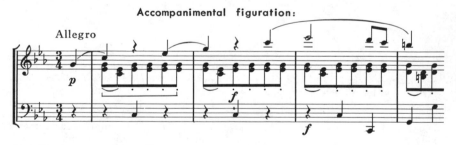

Ex. 1.16 Beethoven, Trio in G, Op. 1, No. 2, for piano, violin, and cello, fourth movement.

secondary importance, hardly to be equated with a motive, which might be the basis for nearly an entire movement.

The common cadence forms

Structural units larger than the motive commonly end with a formula called a *cadence*: a punctuation, a progression conveying a sense of close or of interruption in the rhythmic motion of the musical line.

We should now define briefly the standard cadence forms, classified according to their harmonic composition. The harmonic composition of a cadence, in addition to a host of other factors, has much to do with the impression of finality which it imparts; thus, some types are relatively conclusive in effect (especially the authentic cadences) while others are tentative and incomplete (especially the half-cadence). It is of importance to consider each cadence not only in its broad classification, as outlined below, but also as to its strength or weakness on its own particular terms. The same cadential harmonic formula can be affected in its degree of finality by a number of subtle factors, such as the voicing and metric positions of the harmonies, the use of *nonharmonic*[8] dissonances, the direction of linear parts, and many other circumstances. Variations of these kinds, within the classification of *perfect authentic cadence*, are shown in Ex. 1.17. The consideration of the cadential qualities is an exceedingly vital aspect of musical analysis.

Ex. 1.17

(a)   (b)   (c)

As suggested in Ex. 1.17, the perfect authentic cadence consists of a tonic harmony preceded by its dominant. When the authentic cadence is "perfect," the tonic harmony is in root position, with the root occurring in the upper voice as well. When the root is absent from either of the outer

---

[8] *Nonharmonic tones* are foreign to the harmony against which they sound. Theorists differ in their classifications of these (especially with regard to the *appoggiatura*) and the reader should if possible consult several basic theory sources. In Chapter 12, the concept of a *nonharmonic chord* is presented in connection with examples from works of Debussy.

voices, the authentic cadence is said to be "imperfect." An *imperfect authentic cadence* is illustrated in 1.18.

Ex. 1.18   Mozart, String Quartet in D minor, K. 421, second movement.

I in the position
of the 3rd

A cadence in which the penultimate harmony is not the dominant (usually **I, II,** or **IV**) and in which the final harmony is not the tonic is called a *half-cadence*. The half-cadence, in the vast majority of instances, is a cadence ending on the dominant. Examples follow.

Ex. 1.19   Brahms, String Quartet in C minor, Op. 51, No. 1, first movement.

⑨ The symbol in measure 2 of Ex. 1.19 denotes that the harmony is a sub-dominant seventh chord in which the *fourth scale degree* is raised. Since the symbol is an abstract one without relationship to a specific key, the raising of the scale degree is represented with a sharp even though in a given context (e.g., the key of E-flat) the raising might involve the natural form of an originally flatted note.

The above-mentioned symbol is used from time to time in this book in addition

Ex. 1.20   Schubert, Du bist die Ruh, Op. 59, No. 3.

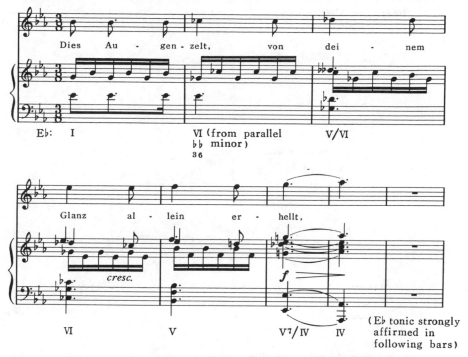

A tonic cadence in which the final harmony is preceded not by V, but by IV, or occasionally II, is known as a *plagal cadence*. Distinction may be made, as in the case of the authentic cadence, between perfect and imperfect forms. A plagal cadence, in the context of eighteenth- and nineteenth-century styles, gives the impression of elision in the harmony, since the normal V, following the IV, is omitted.

Ex. 1.21   Tchaikovsky, Symphony No. 5 in E minor, Op. 64, third movement.

---

to the usual signs for other common chromatic functions (A6, N6, and that of the secondary function, seen in Examples 1.19, 1.20, and 1.22, and defined in footnote 14 of the present chapter). Ex. 1.19 (like Ex. 1.22) also illustrates a secondary function twice removed: a dominant of the supertonic of the submediant—V/II/VI (see also footnote 1, Chapter 7).

Sometimes the dominant, as the penultimate harmony in the cadence, will progress to a harmony other than its normal resolution, I. In such cases the tonic substitute is often VI, or IV₆. Or the dominant may turn in any of a number of other directions: for example, to a dissonant form of the tonic. This formula is called a *deceptive cadence*.

Ex. 1.22   Brahms, Symphony No. 1 in C minor, Op. 68, second movement.

A cadence is said to be *elided* when it marks, at the same time, the end of one structural unit and the beginning of another. The continuity of the music is hastened and the feeling of punctuation obscured; the impression is that something (usually a measure of pause in some, though not all, of the voices) has been left out.

Ex. 1.23   Mozart, Sonata in F, K. 280, first movement.

One of the common devices for extending a phrase or other unit is to turn away abruptly at the moment the ear expects the prepared cadence. An *avoided cadence* is illustrated in Ex. 1.24.

Ex. 1.24   Mozart, Sonata in F, K. 280, first movement.

In the absence of functional harmonic relationships (harmony support-ing the impression of a key center), a cadence may—as is often the case in twentieth-century music—be achieved by the rhythmic device of pause on a longer note, by an actual rest, or by a descent in the melodic line. Or there may be a sense of harmonic resolution in the arrival upon a relatively consonant harmony. The harmony may be functional, of course, without being of traditional construction—i.e., in triads and seventh chords. In turn-of-the-century French and other impressionist music, as well as in more recent works, the basic harmonic scheme is often traditional and functional, especially at cadence points, despite the ostensible "freedom" of the har-monic movement around the basic scheme (see Ex. 12.8). Ex. 1.25, Ex. 1.26, and Ex. 1.27—cadential passages from Bartók's First String Quartet—illustrate some of the above points.

Ex. 1.25 quotes the final measures of the Quartet's first movement. The longer note-values, the falling motive, the diminishing dynamic level, the thinning of the texture, and the consonance of the final intervals are some of the factors establishing the movement's final cadence.

Ex. 1.25   Bartók, String Quartet No. 1, Op. 7, first movement.
© 1949 by Rozsavoelgyi & Co., Budapest. Copyright 1954 by Edizioni Suvini Zerboni. Used by permission.

Ex. 1.26, a quotation from the second movement of the Quartet, shows a cadence achieved by an abrupt stop, rest, and change of material. The music is made to stop suddenly in the midst of heightening tension of rising pitch, dissonance, rhythmic activity, and intense dynamic level.

Ex. 1.26 Bartók, String Quartet No. 1, Op. 7, second movement.
© 1949 by Rozsavoelgyi & Co., Budapest. Copyright 1954 by Edizioni Suvini Zerboni. Used by permission.

Of course, many cadences of a conventional order are found in the work, despite the generally unsettled and ambiguous tonal context of the whole. An example may be seen in the measure before rehearsal no. 9, a cadence on the dominant in A.

Finally, Ex. 1.27, from the third movement, is a cadence in which tonic feeling is strongly conveyed by the insistence upon the note E (preceding bars have dwelt upon its leading-tone, D-sharp). There is no rest here, but an abrupt abandonment of the syncopated motive after a high degree of momentum has been developed. The fact that the formation of the motive is not triadic does not weaken the sense of E as a tonic note.

Ex. 1.27 Bartók, String Quartet No. 1, Op. 7, second movement.
© 1949 by Rozsavoelgyi & Co., Budapest. Copyright 1954 by Edizioni Suvini Zerboni. Used by Permission.

The phrase

If the motive is comparable to a prepositional phrase in language (or to other syntactical units of 2 or 3 words), the musical *phrase* may be compared to the clause, which, whether or not it is complete enough to warrant a period at its close, contains at least a subject and a predicate.

Morris defines the phrase by comparing it to a clause in speech, as above, and states that it "comes to a stop (and is to that extent self-subsistent) yet cannot stand by itself."[10]

[10] R. O. Morris, *The Structure of Music* (London: Oxford University Press, 1956), p. 10.

Although a phrase is normally incomplete—i.e., needs the corroborating and complementary statement of further phrases—it does have a distinct beginning, a clear course of direction, and an ending (cadence).

The length of the phrase cannot be specified for it varies widely, depending on such factors as the tempo of the music, the occasional deliberate avoidance of cadence, and (as in the case of the motive) the perceptive capacities and responses of the listener. Often in traditional music, especially that of the late eighteenth and nineteenth centuries, the phrase occurs in even-numbered two-measure multiples and is very commonly four measures in length—or two in a slow tempo, eight in a very quick tempo. But by no means is this to be taken as a rule for even the Classical period. In considering measures of phrase length, meter is also a factor: a two-measure unit in 12/8 has the same actual "length" as a four-measure unit in 6/8, if the eighth note is of the same value.

The phrase is often composed of a two-measure motive in sequence (Ex. 1.28). In such a case, marked cadential punctuation after two measures will lead many analysts to the conclusion that each two-measure segment is a "phrase." The quoted example is in moderate tempo, and there will be less than universal agreement as to whether the phrase is two or four measures long.

Ex. 1.28   Beethoven, Sonata in B-flat, Op. 22, fourth movement.

While most phrases have important harmonic and other characteristics, it is usually the melodic-rhythmic features which are of primary effect and immediacy, both to the ear and to the eye. In the majority of cases, then, the analyst will find the phrase's beginning, progress, and end most readily apparent in the line of the primary melody, which is frequently in the highest voice.

Like the motive, the phrase often begins with an anacrusis. Here again, the approach from weak to strong—the sense of inhalation to exhalation (*arsis, thesis*)—is a generative one; the upbeat affords a "push" that sets the phrase in motion.

Ex. 1.29   Beethoven, Sonata in D, Op. 10, No. 3, first movement.

Occasionally, the upbeat may be considerably prolonged, constituting an elaborate preparation for the first strong downbeat in the phrase.

Ex. 1.30 Beethoven, Sonata in B-flat, Op. 22, first movement.

Many phrases are of irregular length—3, 5, or 7 measures, for example. This disruption of perfect symmetry has been discussed earlier as more than a rare exception even in the works of the Classical composers.

Ex. 1.31 Mozart, String Quartet in F, K. 590, third movement.

Or the irregular phrase may be a basically symmetrical one which has been extended in some manner. There may be internal extension by repetition of a pattern within the phrase (Ex. 1.32), extension by repetition of the final pattern (Ex. 1.33), extension by avoidance of cadence (Ex. 1.24), or the opening motive may be repeated (Ex. 1.34). In the latter instance the feeling may be that the phrase actually begins with the second statement of the motive and is therefore regular in length.

Ex. 1.32 Haydn, Symphony in B-flat, No. 102, first movement.

Ex. 1.33   Brahms, Trio in C minor, Op. 101, for piano, violin, and cello, first movement.

Ex. 1.34   Mozart, Sonata in E-flat, K. 282, second movement.

It may be valuable to note again the clear relationship between the asymmetric phrase and the asymmetric measure. Just as beats are grouped into measures to form a primary level of "meter," measures group into larger units to form "intermensural meter" (see footnote, p. 304). Thus, the asymmetric quality of a 5/4 measure is, on another scale, comparable in effect to a five-measure phrase.

Repetition of the phrase

Phrases normally combine into periods or phrase-groups, both to be discussed presently. Occasionally, however, the phrase is simply repeated, possibly with variations in color, dynamics, texture, etc., or with minor changes in the notes themselves, but with the essential melodic and harmonic outlines left unchanged. A *repeated phrase* should not be confused with any of the larger structural units.

Ex. 1.35   Beethoven, Sonata in D, Op. 10, No. 3, first movement.

The repeated phrase may be in sequence.

Ex. 1.36   Beethoven, Trio No. 9 in E-flat, Op. Posth., for piano, violin, and cello, second movement.

The period

The period is a pair of consecutive phrases, the second ending with a cadence which is more final and positive in effect than that of the first. Usually the two phrases are in parallel construction—i.e., of the same motivic material, although this is not always the case. The first phrase (*antecedent*) has an interrogative, tentative character as compared to the second (*consequent*), which is more affirmative in effect. This kind or relationship is achieved, for the most part, by the contrast of cadences: by far the commonest cadential relationship is that of dominant (half-cadence) ending the first phrase to tonic (authentic cadence) ending the second. Ex. 1.37 illustrates this usual type of period structure.

Parallel construction in period form is often a correspondence in motivic material between measures 1 and 5, 2 and 6, and 3 and 7, if the period is eight measures long. (See Ex. 1.37.)

Ex. 1.37   Beethoven, String Quartet in B-flat, Op. 130, second movement.

But the two phrases are not necessarily in parallel construction. The well-known theme which opens the second movement of Beethoven's Sonata in C minor, Op. 13, is an example of a period in which the two phrases lack actual motivic correspondence. Unity is achieved in the Beethoven theme by the cadential relationship implicit in period form, as well as by such factors as the complementary melodic curves, common accompanimental patterns, consistency of character, common tonality, regularity of length and consistency of rhythmic motion. Ex. 1.38 is another instance of period form without parallel construction (and without the frequent symmetry of equal division).

Ex. 1.38   Robert Jones, What If I Seek for Love (Book of Ayres, 1601).

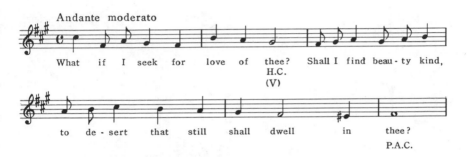

Goetschius' characterization of the middle cadence as "never anything more weighty than a semi-cadence"[11] is curiously expressed in view of his definition of the semi-cadence as "any deviation from the formula of the perfect cadence." Coeuroy speaks of the middle cadence as "a transient point of repose on the dominant,"[12] excluding examples having the antecedent-consequent relationship with, for example, an imperfect authentic cadence at the end of the first phrase.

Ex. 1.39   Mozart, Sonata in F, K. 332, first movement.

11 Percy Goetschius, *Lessons in Music Form* (Bryn Mawr, Penn.: Theodore Presser Co., 1904), p. 70.
12 Coeuroy, *La Musique et ses Formes* (Paris: *Les Éditions Denoël*, 1951) p. 26. Translated by the author.

The period may or may not be entirely in one key. *Modulation*[13] in the first phrase is likely to be transitory, usually better analyzed as a half-cadence in which the dominant is associated with its *secondary dominant*[14] (Ex. 1.40); stronger modulation in the antecedent results in an *incipient binary* (Chapter 2). The second phrase may modulate to the dominant or to another key, ending on a tonic cadence in that key (Ex. 1.41).

Ex. 1.40   Beethoven, Sonata in C, Op. 2, No. 3, fourth movement.

[13] *Tonality* is the system of musical organization around a particular note (the tonal center, or tonic) toward which all functions within the tonal system ultimately point. It may be argued that some such tonal organization is common to nearly all music, but tonality is the most important single structural force in music of the eighteenth and nineteenth centuries and, to a large extent, in that of the seventeenth and twentieth as well. *Modulation* is change of reference in a musical passage from one tonic to another; various degrees and types of modulation are discussed at appropriate points.

[14] The harmony in measure 4 of Ex. 1.40 is identified as a dominant to the dominant—a *secondary dominant,* with F-sharp, its third, as a *secondary leading-tone.* If the harmony occurred in a context of G major rather than C, it would be a *primary dominant,* the F-sharp a *primary leading-tone.* Hence, the "correct" analysis depends upon the recognition or nonrecognition of modulation. To outline further a basic terminology in this connection, we may say that measure 2 of the example is at a dominant *harmonic level,* and measures 4–5 are at a *secondary* dominant *tonal level* (or in a "secondary tonal region"). If the G tonic were strongly established and confirmed, it would become a *primary tonal level.* Actually, the reference to G is so fleeting that C is felt as the primary tonal level of the entire passage, G a secondary level toward which the progression ephemerally "leans" because of the occurrence of F-sharp. All of this terminology comes into use in later portions of this book.

Ex. 1.41   Brahms, String Quintet in F, Op. 88, first movement.

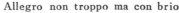

The period relationship can also be observed at lower structural levels, as suggested by Ex. 1.28. The following example does not constitute a period (since its halves are not phrases) ; however, the antecedent-consequent principle is clearly implied in the relationship of the two motives.

Ex. 1.42   Mozart, Sonata in E-flat, K. 282, second movement.

Enlargement of the single period

Just as the most frequent length of the phrase is four measures, the period is most often twice that length. The majority of the examples quoted above have been eight measures in length, with the two phrases of equal size.

A single period may, in a faster tempo, be longer. The following is a sixteen-measure period of two eight-measure phrases.

Ex. 1.43   Beethoven, Sonata in C, Op. 2, No. 3, third movement.

Strictly speaking, Ex. 1.43 represents a type of period which is longer than the norm (in number of measures) only by virtue of its tempo and meter; it is not an enlarged period. Similarly, where no extension is apparent, a period of five, six, or seven-measure phrases cannot be said to be "enlarged."

Ex. 1.44   Bartók, Mikrokosmos, Book II, No. 62.
        Copyright 1940 by Hawkes & Son (London) Ltd. Reprinted by permission.

There are, however, various ways in which the single period is actually enlarged. (1) Either phrase may be repeated. An example, too long for quotation, is the opening theme of the third movement of Beethoven's Sonata, Op. 13. Here, the consequent phrase is not only repeated but extended to more than twice its normal length. (2) Either phrase may be extended, as just suggested. Another example is the opening theme of Mozart's Sonata in G, K. 283, whose consequent phrase is extended two measures beyond the "normal" terminal point, measure 8. Ex. 1.45 illustrates a period in its symmetrical form, and in its extended form (b) as Schubert actually wrote it. (3) There may be two or more antecedent

Ex. 1.45   Schubert, Frühlingsglaube, Op. 20, No. 2.

phrases (Ex. 1.46), or, more rarely, additional consequent phrases. Ex. 1.47,

Ex. 1.46   Thomas Ford, Come, Phyllis (Musicke of Sundrie Kindes, 1607).

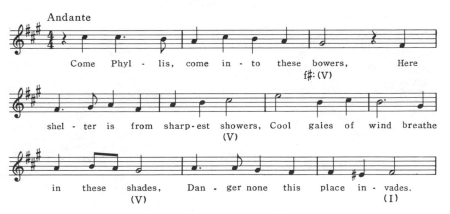

whose first antecedent phrase is not quoted, includes two consequent phrases, both ending in strong cadences on the tonic.

Ex. 1.47 Irish Folk Song, Bendemeer's Stream.

The double period

In a double period the bipartite structure is expanded so that the antecedent element is of two phrases, as is the consequent part, with a perfect authentic cadence delayed until the end of the final phrase. Frequently all four phrases share the same, or very similar, motivic material; *especially the first and third phrases may have motives in common.*

Since the two "periods" which comprise the double period exist in the same relationship as the two phrases of a single period, an incomplete cadence ends the first two-phrase element, as well as the first and third phrases. The entire form may be tonally homogeneous or, as in the single period, modulation to a related key may be carried out in either the antecedent or consequent part. In the former case, a type of incipient binary results (Chapter 2). A typical double period is shown as Ex. 1.48.

Ex. 1.48 Mozart, String Quartet in B-flat, K. 458, fourth movement.

Analogy is made by Goetschius to a four-line stanza in poetry.[15] The final line ends in a period in the example quoted below—the period being analogous to the perfect authentic cadence, the most emphatic punctuation in traditional music. Each line in the example is of four feet: a parallel to

[15] *Lessons in Music Form,* p. 80.

the common four-measure phrase and sixteen-measure double period. The rhyme scheme parallels the frequent correspondence between the first and third, and second and fourth phrases of the double period. Obviously, further analogy could be drawn between the couplet and the period. The example is from "The Definition of Love" by Andrew Marvell (1621–1678).

> And yet I quickly might arrive
> Where my extended soul is fixt,
> But Fate does iron wedges drive,
> And always crowds itself betwixt.

An example of a double period with an imperfect authentic cadence at the middle point is given below. This theme has an incipient binary feature—a concept explained in Chapter 2—in the internal modulation. There is an unusual degree of correspondence between the first and fourth phrases, with a rounded total effect. All four phrases have nearly identical rhythmic structure.

Ex. 1.49   Beethoven, Symphony No. 7 in A, Op. 92, second movement.

Irregular phrase lengths in an enlarged double period are seen in Ex. 1.50. The final phrase of the Tchaikovsky theme is substantially extended.

Ex. 1.50   Tchaikovsky, Symphony No. 4 in F minor, Op. 36, second movement.

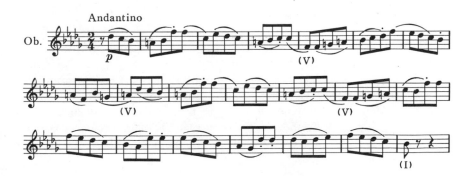

Repetition of the period

Sometimes a period is repeated immediately, in which case there may be minor changes of orchestration or setting. In such a repetition, there is no change in structure or material, and the resulting pattern is antecedent-consequent-antecedent-consequent. The two consequent cadences are harmonically equivalent. In Ex. 1.51, the two periods are in strict correspondence except for changes in dynamics and orchestration, and omission of the nonharmonic C in the second perfect authentic cadence. The repeated period should not be confused with the double period, in which the final cadence is harmonically superior to all of the preceding cadences.

Ex. 1.51   Haydn, Symphony No. 102 in B-flat, first movement.

The phrase group

Two disparate phrases, both of which end on the dominant, obviously constitute neither a period nor a repeated phrase. Such a succession of phrases would be described as a *phrase group,* or part of a phrase group. A phrase group lacks the correspondence and antecedent-consequent cadential pattern of period form. Example 1.52 is from measures 10–26 of the *Cavatina* movement of Beethoven's Quartet, Op. 130. The movement begins with a period with considerably elongated consequent phrase. A phrase group begins at measure 10.

Ex. 1.52   Beethoven, String Quartet in B-flat, Op. 130, fifth movement.

   A succession of phrases ending in perfect authentic cadences also forms a phrase group, as in Bach's[16] harmonization of the chorale *Auf dass wir also allzugleich* (from Cantata No. 176, *Es ist ein trotzig und verzagt Ding*). When a series of phrases ending in incomplete cadences is followed by a phrase with tonic cadence (Bach's Aria, *Mein Verlangen*, measures 31 ff., from the Cantata No. 161), the analyst must judge whether the final tonic is a complement to and affirmation of the preceding incomplete cadences—forming a period with several antecedents—or merely part of a phrase group in which such correspondence is absent. Many factors enter into this evaluation: the number of phrases involved, tonal stability or fluctuation of the passage, the proximity of the phrases, motivic correspondence, and the lengths of the phrases.

   Phrase groups are relatively rare, although somewhat more common in pre-Classical and recent music. In works of the late eighteenth and nineteenth centuries phrase groups are primarily seen in developmental and episodic passages, although they are not unheard-of in expository thematic complexes (opening of Mozart's Sonata in C, K. 279).

Irregular examples

   It should be recognized that the structural units as defined in the preceding pages—phrases and combinations of phrases—are not always to be found.

   Music may, for example, fall into isolated motivic fragments interspersed among the larger units or repeated developmentally. The concentra-

---

16 When the family name is used without given names or qualifying initials, it refers to Johann Sebastian (1685–1750).

tion upon short motives and figures contributes to the unstable character of many developmental passages.

Ex. 1.53   Beethoven, Sonata in F minor, Op. 2, No. 1, first movement.

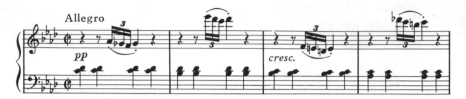

Phrase- and motive-divisions usually overlap among the several voices of a musical texture in passages which are *polyphonic*.[17] This is illustrated in Ex. 1.54, a transitional section, in which motives of varying sizes overlap, sometimes in imitative fashion, so as to obscure all "seams" and to impart a feeling of forward movement without definite punctuation. This quality is, of course, basic to music of a consistently polyphonic style.

Ex. 1.54   Mozart, String Quartet in D minor, K. 421, first movement.

Composers often adopt a type of rhetoric in which traditional phrase divisions are suppressed in the interest of a more prose-like structure, as in Ex. 1.54. There is important and valuable contrast in the greater degree of obscurity of cadence and asymmetry of phrase and motive which charac-

---

[17] *Polyphony* is that texture in which two or more distinct voices proceed relatively independently, none of them, on the average of the whole, subordinate or accompanimental to the others. Imitation is common in polyphonic textures as a means of achieving unity among the voices. The chief, but not only, means of asserting the individuality of the voices is rhythmic differentiation.

terize these anomalous examples. Such passages, however, are best understood against the background of "normal" phraseology.

The joining of structural units

Major sections of a work or movement sometimes come to a complete stop, followed by a rest and then a continuation into the following section. However, the maintenance of motion over the cadences within such major divisions—and often the joining of the major divisions themselves—is always significant and of interest. Without skillful bridging of the various structural units a work becomes disjointed and fragmentary. The methods by which the composer achieves an effect of cadential punctuation without a full stop in the musical flow are numerous, and the careful analysis of these methods is always instructive.

Consecutive structural units may be joined simply by drawing them into the closest proximity, causing the new unit to begin concurrently with the end of the one preceding. This has been illustrated in connection with the elided cadence, Ex. 1.23.

At the point of cadence, a motive of the succeeding phrase may be introduced as a means of establishing a palpable connection between the two units.

Ex. 1.55   Bach, Christmas Oratorio, Part III, No. 31 (Alto aria: Schliesse, mein Herze).

Rarely, a new section enters before the preceding part has ended; the entry of the new material may even be concealed within the framework of the cadence ending the preceding section. A justly celebrated example, representing a highly ingenious if rather uncommon procedure, is the "hidden entry" of the reprise of the theme in the first movement of Mozart's G minor Symphony.

Ex. 1.56   Mozart, Symphony No. 40 in G minor, K. 550, first movement.

The most common method of joining two structural units is that of filling in the measure of the cadence with a figuration or line of some kind. This does not obscure the cadence, and affords a continuation of rhythmic activity, often in a single voice.

Ex. 1.57   Bartók, Mikrokosmos, Book II, No. 66.
            Copyright 1940 by Hawkes & Son (London) Ltd. Reprinted by permission.

For further examples, and for a full and perceptive discussion of this problem, the student is again referred to Toch's *The Shaping Forces in Music,* Chapter 11.

Exercises

A thorough understanding of the material of each chapter is necessary before completing the exercises suggested below. The study of the text may be aided by specific questions provided to test the thorough understanding of the material, although such questions are not included here.

The activities suggested at the end of each chapter, most of them in the nature of research, will consolidate and illustrate the principles learned by reference to the literature itself, and will prove of inestimable value. It is not assumed that all of the exercises will be undertaken; benefit will derive from the completion of any number of these assignments. Various types of exercises can, at times, be divided among the members of a group with a common sharing of the results, or the exercises may be taken as specimens upon which further projects are to be developed.

1. Look for examples of the structural units discussed in Chapter 1. Do not limit yourself to the literature of any single period. Include examples of irregular proportions.

2. Try writing each of the following—at least the melody, with appropriate cadential harmonies indicated below the melodic line.
   a) a 4-measure phrase
   b) a 5-measure phrase
   c) an 8-measure period, a half-cadence at the middle *first Phrase = 4 Second = 6*
   d) a 10-measure period, the second phrase extended
   e) a 12-measure period, with two antecedent phrases *3 4 meas. phrases*
   f) a double period *4 4 meas. Phrases*
   g) other types of small structural units discussed in the text *poly. overlapping motives*

3. Prepare in considerable detail an examination covering the material in Chapter 1. Include examples for analysis.

4. Try to find (or invent) passages in language—poetry or prose—which compare, in structure and meter, and cadential punctuation, to specific specimens of phrase and period which you have found.

5. Classify the cadences of a particular piece or movement, according to the cadential forms discussed in Chapter 1.

6. Find examples of consecutive phrases and other structural units. Consider how they are joined—how the cadential points are bridged, as discussed in the text. Try to imagine another way of accomplishing the same effect.

7. Develop an analysis of the first 24 measures of Beethoven's Sonata in E minor, Op. 90. Do you feel that the half-cadence at measure 16 is a period division? Classify the cadences and identify the key levels. What elements of symmetry do you observe? Would you describe the passage as a phrase group or an enlarged period?

8. Prepare an analysis of phrase and period structure in the folksongs "Arkansas Traveler" and "Blue Bells of Scotland."

2

BINARY

*A*n almost invariable principle in the forms of traditional music has been division, by one or more strong cadences, into two or more contrasting and related sections. Such segmentation is, as suggested in Chapter 1, an aid to coherent organization.

A piece or movement in which there are no major divisions and in which thematic and tonal homogeneity prevails is sometimes called a *unisectional* form. But such a form is best described with respect to the internal structural units which are its components. The terminology set forth in Chapter 1, identifying various kinds of phrase combination, is more precisely descriptive of the internal composition of unisectional form.

Two-part form (binary), which may constitute an entire movement, is a magnification of the period and thus a larger manifestation of the antecedent-consequent idea. However, the two portions become, in themselves, periods or phrase groups, and the half-cadence of the antecedent element usually becomes a modulation or strong reference to the dominant key. In fact, the period may be regarded as an embryonic basis for single-movement sonata form (Chapter 6), which is the ultimate evolution of binary form.

The incipient binary

It is often difficult to establish a distinct line of separation between the enlarged period, or double period, and binary form (see Ex. 1.49 and Ex. 2.1). Only two criteria apply: (1) the condition of modulation to the dominant or other related key in the first part, and (2) the size of each part.

Where the first of these criteria is concerned, it is often difficult to say that a modulation is or is not in effect, since the perception of modulation is largely a subjective problem. A period in which the antecedent phrase ends with a dominant preceded by its secondary dominant may be considered by some analysts to contain a modulation to the dominant key (Ex. 2.5). Thus, where modulation is a factor, the choice of terminology often cannot be made with insistence. As illustrated in the discussion of Ex. 1.49, an *incipient binary* is a period with special qualities, and both terms can be relevant to a single example.

In general, a single appearance of the leading-tone of the "new key" (or the single appearance of the cancellation of the previous leading-tone) is insufficient to convey an impression of modulation. Whether two or more occurrences of an accidental effect such change depends on a host of factors: tempo of the music, rhythmic quality of the accidentals, whether the accidentals are harmonic or nonharmonic, and others.

As to the second criterion, that of proportion, one can establish a distinction only by the arbitrary specification that a full binary form is necessarily of a certain size. Although the problem is largely a semantic one, it is reasonable to give a different, qualified name to a two-part form of 8 or 16 measures as compared to one of 50 or 100 measures. We may assert, then, that in full binary form each of the two parts is composed of *more* than two phrases (hence probably more than 8 measures) and that the cadence ending the first part represents a modulation to the dominant or other related key.

A TWO-PART FORM IN WHICH EITHER OF THESE CONDITIONS IS PRESENT, BUT NOT THE OTHER, MAY BE DESIGNATED AN *INCIPIENT BINARY*. Such a sub-classification is appropriate because of the existence of examples (2.1, 2.2) in which relatively strong modulation lends something of binary character to what would otherwise be simple period form, and further examples (2.3) which, despite the absence of any hint of modulation, are inflated far beyond the period norm.

In either sense, incipient binary form is properly regarded as significantly distinguished from, although clearly related to, simple and enlarged period form, having rudimentary properties of full binary form. The two types of incipient binary, as defined above, are represented in Figure 2.1, after which some examples are cited.

In Ex. 2.1, the two divisions are single phrases, repeated, the first 8 measures long and the second extended to 10 measures. Yet there is a substantial feeling of modulation to C minor at the end of the first phrase: the E–flat introduced in the seventh bar makes it difficult to feel the final measure as a dominant harmony in the original key of F minor. An example of this kind, in which the proportions are those of a period, but in which there is considerable sense of modulation at the middle point, is an incipient binary of the first type.

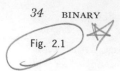

Fig. 2.1

INCIPIENT BINARY

First type, composed of 2-4 single phrases with
modulation

One or two phrases

Part I

Auth. cadence in
related key

One or two phrases

Part II

Auth. cadence in
original key

Second type, composed of multi-phrase sections
with no modulation (analogous to very
enlarged period)

More than two phrases

Part I

Cadence (usually V) in
original key

More than two phrases

Part II

Auth. cadence in
original key

Ex. 2.1   Beethoven, Sonata in F minor, Op. 57, third movement.

A further example of this type of incipient binary is quoted as Ex. 2.2.
Here, each ·of the two parts is 4 measures long, but of *two 2-measure phrases*.

Each half is a period. The designation *incipient binary* is again based on the small dimensions (individual sections of two phrases or less) and the strong reference to a new key—here, the relative major—at the middle point.

Ex. 2.2   Beethoven, Sonata in G, Op. 79, second movement.

An example of incipient binary of the second type, in which larger proportions are in evidence (a total of 7 phrases, excluding the codetta: a first part of 12 measures and a second part of 16) without indication of modulation at the conclusion of the antecedent part is the *Air* from Bach's Partita No. 6 in E minor. The half-cadence ending the first part is shown as Ex. 2.3.

Ex. 2.3   Bach, Air from Partita No. 6 in E minor.

An example like the Bach *Air* is obviously closely allied to, but more extensive and digressive than, the normal enlarged period.

We may now investigate a few examples which lie at the borderline between incipient binary and enlarged period. Ex. 2.4, Prelude in E minor, Op. 28, No. 4, by Frédéric Chopin (1810–1849) is an example of a single period of unusual dimensions. The first cadence occurs at measure 10 (extended into measure 12). It is clearly a cadence on the dominant of the original key. Up to this point, the motion of the accompaniment and of the restless, active chromatic harmonies precludes any feeling of cadence. Thus, the first 10 measures constitute a single phrase, enlarged. The same is true of the second part, 13 measures in length, ending on the tonic. The Prelude is better identified as an enlarged period because it embodies neither of the features of binary form as established in the definition stated earlier, while clearly incorporating the period concept of antecedent and consequent parts.

Ex. 2.4 Chopin, Prelude in E minor, Op. 28, No. 4.

Occasionally, the analyst may come upon a specimen which, while definitely in two parts, defies classification on any of the bases outlined above. Such an example is the variation theme from the second movement of Beethoven's Sonata in F minor, Op. 57. It conforms to neither condition of binary as now defined: it is neither a double-period nor a repeated period; it is entirely homogeneous tonally and the two principal cadences are perfect authentic types. It is best described simply as two periods. A similar example is the trio of the third movement of Beethoven's Quartet in B–flat, Op. 18, No. 6. In this case, a 4-measure codetta in B–flat minor is appended.

In Ex. 2.5, "modulation" at the end of the first half is extremely doubtful. The single E-natural does not convey a sense of change of key center; thus, the first half ends on the dominant of the original key with the E-natural acting as its secondary leading-tone. Here, both by specifications of length and tonality, the example is best designated a period. If the proportions were the same, but the reference to the dominant key stronger, as in Ex. 2.1, the form would be an incipient binary.

period

Ex. 2.5   Mozart, Twelve Variations on an Allegretto, K. 500, theme.

(V/IV)

Binary form: the first part

In binary form, the first part, often ending with a double-bar and repeat sign, may be as little as a phrase or period (incipient binary), or it may be a double period, enlarged period, or a group of phrases.

The modulation, which we have established as a usual characteristic of binary form, normally occurs early enough so that the cadence is felt to be a tonic in the new, related key. There may be a sequence of *passing modulations*[1] leading to this point. The key in which the first part ends is very often the dominant, when the example is in the major mode, and the relative major, if the example is in minor. Exceptions to the principle of major to dominant are exceedingly rare (Ex. 2.6), but the minor occasionally goes to its dominant rather than to the relative major (Ex. 2.1).

---

[1] A *transitory modulation* is one in which a new center is not firmly established and continued.

The *passing modulation,* a type of transitory modulation, is a fleeting, intermediate tonal reference in a process leading ultimately to a *full modulation* to a key other than that out of which the process began. (Note that, in such a situation, the basic key is in disintegration. A secondary V, in contrast, is related to a particular harmonic function *within a stable, prevailing tonal system,* and is a tonal reference too slight—i.e., secondary—to be perceived as a modulation of any degree.)

A *false modulation,* a second type of transitory modulation, is the brief emergence of a new primary tonic, followed by a return to the original key level. Unlike the secondary V, it is a strong enough tonal reference (probably several appearances of the new leading-tone) to be felt as modulation—a disruption of the original tonic.

The retentive power of a particular tonic in a specific example varies, of course, from listener to listener, so that tonality is subject to varying individual interpretation, but the distinctions made here and at many points in this book are nonetheless functionally significant.

Goetschius speaks of an "introductory phrase."[2] Such a feature is extremely uncommon, although in the following example the opening segment, as marked, is introductory, with the form proper beginning at measure 5. Only portions of the first part, modulating exceptionally to the mediant key of A minor, are quoted. Another rare example of the introductory phrase is seen in No. 9 of the Schumann *Papillons,* Op. 2. This example is binary in form after the first eight measures, which are introductory.

Ex. 2.6 Schubert, Sonata in A minor, Op. 42, third movement.

Often the material centers in a particular motive, with the same basic idea prevailing, in development of various kinds, throughout the form.

Ex. 2.7 Handel, Allemande from Suite IX in G minor.

Sometimes the texture is fugal (Chapter 11), as often in the *gigues* of Bach suites and partitas.

---

[2] *Lessons in Music Form,* p. 85.

Ex. 2.8   Bach, Gigue from French Suite No. 1 in D minor.

The cadence ending the first half commonly forms a strong and decisive punctuation, most often a perfect authentic cadence in the new key. It constitutes a pronounced interruption and is followed by a clear sense of resumption.

Ex. 2.9   Froberger, Plainte from Suite in A minor.

The second part

The structure of the second part of binary form may be comparable, even identical, to that of the first. Often it is a phrase group in which there is somewhat free development of the common motive. Frequently the second part is longer than the first, and more freely modulatory within the range of closely related keys. The diagram in Ex. 2.10 illustrates the greater length and more fluctuant quality of the second part. Those tonal levels indicated in parentheses are very fleeting references to related keys. The tonal range consists of tonic, relative major, subdominant, and dominant minor.

Binary form in which the second part is longer than the first is termed *asymmetrical binary* as opposed to *symmetrical* binary form, in which the two parts are of equal length. (The binary with a longer first part is a rarer asymmetrical type.) There may be considerable difference in the relative lengths; three-part form results only when the example ends in a systematic reprise of the first part (at least its principal elements) in the tonic key. A perfectly symmetrical example is the *corrente* from Bach's Partita No. 5—

Ex. 2.10 Geminiani, Concerto in C minor, Op. 2, No. 2, for strings, fourth movement.

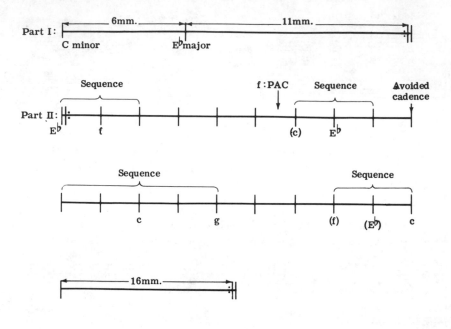

32 measures in each section—or the theme for Bach's *Goldberg Variations,* in which each half is made up of two periods totalling 16 measures.

The fourth Partita contains interesting examples of asymmetrical binary—for example, the *allemande,* which has 24 measures in Part I and 32 in Part II. In the same Partita, the *sarabande* is extremely asymmetrical: its proportions are 12–26. One can see in this movement some of the principles of later single-movement sonata form in emergence. Not only is there a developmental quality in the opening measures of the second part, but in measure 17 in Part II there is a return of the original material, abbreviated, in the tonic key.

During Part II of binary form, the tonic key returns, again early enough so that it is strongly established and reaffirmed before the final cadence. Ex. 2.11 is from another Bach suite movement—a relatively short, very asymmetrical example. There are 24 measures in all (8–16), the second part exactly twice the length of the first, but lacking the ternary feature of thematic restatement. The quoted excerpt shows the point of modulation back to the tonic key (measure 11 of Part II; measure 19 of the whole); this is preceded by passing references to E, b, and e, in addition to a strong reference to the key of D.

The aspect of the form discussed above—that of the departure from the original key level and the return to it in the final bars—is exceedingly significant and characteristic. Binary form has in this sense a ternary quality:

Ex. 2.11   Bach, Courante II from English Suite No. 1 in A.

there is a rounding of the form in its tonal implications, if not in segmentation and contrast of thematic materials.

There is nearly always a strong motivic correspondence (parallel construction) between the two divisions of binary form, lending a pervasive unity to the entire structure. Often, the second part begins exactly like the first (Ex. 2.7), except for probable difference of key, and the authentic cadences ending the two sections are frequently identical in harmonic and melodic formula.

Ex. 2.12   Hindemith, Ludus Tonalis, Interludium between second and third fugues.
Copyright 1943 by Associated Music Publishers, Inc., New York. Used by permission.

Occasionally, especially in eighteenth-century examples, the parallel construction described above is realized by the use of an inverted form of the common motive at the beginning of the second part. Ex. 2.13 shows such a motive and its inversion; the second quotation (inversion) is the beginning of Part II.

The diagrammatic designation for binary form is often given as *AB*. It can now be seen that this representation is not altogether accurate; the use of the letter *B* usually denotes a substantial change of character, of materials, of texture—none of these likely in binary form. The rule is a second part which is simply a new arrangement of the motives of the first,

Ex. 2.13   Bach, Gigue from French Suite No. 2 in C minor.

having the same rhythmic pace and the same ideas, even though it may be more fluctuant tonally (AA′).

In the majority of cases there is no exact correspondence between the tonic passages at the beginning and the end, although the introduction of the original key in the second part may be a momentary recapitulation of the first gestures of the opening. If there is a more extensive reprise, the form is a "rounded binary" or, better, "incipient ternary," discussed in Chapter 3.

The codetta

Frequently the form ends with a short closing section or *codetta* (from the Italian *coda,* meaning "tail") commonly only a few measures in length. The codetta (rarely a coda—the distinction to be considered later) appears as an appendage at the end: it is set off by a premature, marked cadence in the key in which the section is to end, and the ensuing material adds a stamp of finality to the form. Ex. 2.14 shows a deceptive cadence setting off a codetta of 2½ measures. The example is taken from measure 22 of the second part of the movement; it closely parallels the corresponding point in the first part.

Ex. 2.14   Bach, Allemande from French Suite No. 3 in B minor.

In the usual binary form, which is of relatively small proportions, the codetta is unlikely to be more than an elaboration and confirmation of the final tonic. There may be a final appearance of the characteristic motive or motives or simply a flourish of cadential harmonies. Ex. 2.15 is typical in

length and substance. It is the codetta to the first part of a binary movement
in B–flat; the second part contains no corresponding codetta.

Ex. 2.15   Handel, Allemande from Suite XIII in B-flat.

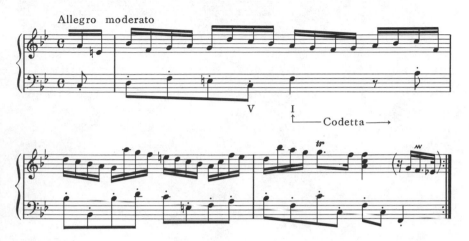

In Ex. 2.16 from Karl Philipp Emanuel Bach (1714–88), the 8-measure
codetta recurs in the second part in precisely the same form except for the
difference of key. In the identification of a codetta it should be remembered
that the section which it concludes comes first to a tentative cadence, in
which the expected tonic harmony is somehow weakened or avoided, with
the codetta following as an affirmation of that cadence. Otherwise, there is
no codetta.

Ex. 2.16   K. P. E. Bach, Prussian Sonata No. 1 in F, third movement.

Ex. 2.16 (continued).

Later: V   I

Rarely, a codetta may be in two distinct parts. It is clear in Ex. 2.17 that the *final* section (set off by the perfect authentic cadence at measure 72) is matched by the preceding material. The two segments are obviously divisions of a larger unit, since they are exactly parallel in construction and material. This is a two-part codetta. The quotation is from Part I of the total form.

Ex. 2.17   D. Scarlatti, Sonata in E minor, K. 263[3] (Longo 321).

Andante

codetta

m.72

Bach, Sonata No. 2 in A minor, for violin alone, third movement

The outline of one complete example will serve to summarize in a specific representation the features of binary form as discussed in this chapter.

[3] Index established by Ralph Kirkpatrick in his book, *Domenico Scarlatti* (Princeton: Princeton University Press, 1953).

In Ex. 2.18 principal points of punctuation are marked as authentic or half-cadences. Simple periods are concluded by the authentic cadences in measures 8 and 19.

The passage following the beginning of measure 8 and extending to the perfect authentic cadence in G at measure 11 is modulatory, taking the music to the expected dominant key level for the conclusion of Part I.

Ex. 2.18   Bach, Sonata No. 3 in A minor for solo violin, third movement (in C).

Ex. 2.18 (continued).

The early part of Part II is, as so often, the most modulatory area in the form;[4] its various key levels are indicated in the quotation by identification of the first dominant of each. The passage touches the relative minor, and its dominant and subdominant levels.

Following the authentic cadence at measure 19, there is a *motive-group*. The four motives of which it is composed are of exactly the same length; the specific ways in which they are related and contrasted should be studied with care. The final phrase (from the anacrusis to measure 24) achieves the tonic key and a strong perfect authentic cadence in that key, for the conclusion of Part II and of the entire form.

The reader should observe the manner in which Bach maintains rhythmic motion, even through subordinate cadences, arresting it only at the two primary cadences. The strongest of the subordinate cadences (measure 8) is attenuated by reiteration of the tonic root; another authentic cadence (measure 19) is weakened by the *appoggiatura*[5] F–sharp. Additional urgency and drive are produced by a prevalence of *dissonant*[6]

[4] This passage is further illustration of a pregnant binary feature mentioned before—the often fluctuant nature of the beginning of Part II, in which one sees in incipience the development of single-movement sonata form (Chapter 6).

[5] An *appoggiatura* is understood here as a nonharmonic tone (of whatever preparation and resolution) which has rhythmic stress. Thus, it occurs *on the beat*—the beat understood as the place where stress is felt in the particular context of meter and tempo. In an appoggiatura figure, the resolution tone is rhythmically weaker (lighter) than the nonharmonic tone. (See Walter Piston, *Harmony,* 3rd ed., New York: W. W. Norton and Company, Inc., 1962, pp. 85–7.)

[6] A *dissonance* is considered here to be a relationship among tones (two or more either in melodic succession or in harmony) which, in the context of a particular style, conveys a feeling of instability and gives rise to the expectation of progression into a resolution. It might be argued that in a tonal system the only "perfect" harmonic consonance is the tonic triad, its root emphasized by its presence in the most exposed voices—the highest and lowest (position of the octave)—and the only "perfect" melodic consonance the tonic note itself. But, with rhythmic support in particular contexts, lesser resolutions can be accepted by the ear as final. (See also p. 193 for mention of specific classifications of dissonance in tonal music.)

harmony, and imperfect positions of tonic harmony, as well as by the use of *chromatic harmony*[7] in the final phrase (IV_7–V_7/V in measure 24).

$$\begin{array}{cc} \flat & \flat \\ 3 & 6 \end{array}$$

Additional study should be made of the recurrence of characteristic motives which lend unity to the form, in the midst of contrasts of rhythm and tonal level. Further analysis would note, too, the rise and fall of secondary high points of pitch within each part. Thus, in Part I, there is ascent through g′, c″, e″, and g″ to a″, followed by controlled descent (in a shorter time) to the g′ of the cadence.

Significance of the repeats

It is now obvious that the two parts which make up binary form are often repeated—followed by double-bars and repeat signs—in the actual examples cited. The question may properly be raised as to the effect upon the structural outlines of the form, which we have described as being in *two* parts, when such repeats are practiced.

The over-all outlines of the surface structure are not affected by the repeats, which normally include *retransitions*[8] so that motion is uninterrupted (Ex. 2.18). That is simply to say that in a general sense AA is the equivalent (except in length) of AA AA, and AB the equivalent of AABB. While it might be argued that the resultant form is in 4 parts, it is undeniable that the significant division is still at the "middle" point. AABB is thus a two-part form in which each part is repeated, with its proportions but not its general design affected. It is not suggested that the question of size is without consequence: few would argue that a repeated phrase is the equivalent of a single phrase, or a repeated period of a single period.

The problem is more complex when one considers the tonal outlines of the usual binary form. The symbols TD DT represent the most common tonal relationships in the two parts of binary form. It seems absurd to argue that TD DT is the equivalent of TDTD DTDT. Despite the literal nature of the repeats, *the frequency of tonal digression and return has been multiplied in a way that can hardly be said to have no effect upon the form.* The problem is difficult and one does not face it constructively by summarily dismissing its implications, as does Morris: "Another point that musicians have

---

[7] A *chromatic harmony* contains notes which are foreign to the diatonic scale of its key and mode. (See also *chromatic progression* and *chromatic modulation*.) Principal categories of chromatic harmony are the secondary dominants and other secondary functions, exchanges of mode (e.g., use of II in a major context), and

$$\flat \atop 6$$

other much-used altered harmonies like the augmented-6th chords and the Neapolitan 6th.

[8] A *retransition* is, as fully developed later, a bridge passage (transition) preparing the return of previously stated material—a connective link leading back to material already featured.

determined by general consent (italics mine) is that the internal structure of a movement is not affected by the repetition of the constituent sections."[9]

In practice, both of performance and of composition, the repeats are not always used. Even when indicated, they are often ignored in performance and sometimes, illogically, one is ignored and the other observed. When repeats are practiced, binary form is magnified, and its tonal outlines altered, as discussed above.

The rounded binary

A two-part form in which part of the opening section is formally and substantially returned, in its original key, in the final bars of the second part, is sometimes termed "rounded binary." Preference is given here, however, to the synonym "incipient ternary" and the form is discussed thoroughly at the beginning of the following chapter.

Ex. 2.19   Mozart, Variations on Come un agnello by Sarti, K. 460, theme.

Exercises and examples for further study

1. Compose a small binary that includes at least a melody line and an indication of cadential formulae.

[9] *The Structure of Music,* p. 23.

Outline due: Jan 7th

2. Look for examples of the following:
   a) incipient binary
   b) full binary form
   c) a codetta in a binary example
   d) binary in which the first part modulates to a key other than the dominant
   e) a binary illustrating parallel construction, including parallel cadential patterns in the two parts
   f) asymmetrical binary form

3. Take one example of full binary form and outline its structure according to the procedure followed in this chapter with relation to the Bach Solo Violin Sonata movement.

4. Diagram a hypothetical example of binary form to show its basic features and tonal levels; incorporate into it a reasonable anomalous feature of some kind.

5. Answer the following questions concerning a binary example of your selection, or you may refer to one of the examples mentioned in the text.
   a) What is the basic key?
   b) Where is the modulation to the key in which the first part ends?
   c) Characterize each cadence as to its form.
   d) Write out the principal motive or motives on which the music is based.
   e) Describe the structure of each of the two main parts.
   f) Is there a codetta? What is its length? What is its content?
   g) What are some of the techniques for joining individual structural units within each part—for keeping up a constancy of motion and obscuring "seams"?
   h) Is the form symmetrical?
   i) Locate the modulation in which the basic key returns in the second part.
   j) Are there other modulations than those to and from the principal keys?

6. What opportunities for variety do you feel are implicit in binary form?

7. Look for examples of binary form in one or more of the following sources:
   a) suites and partitas of Bach
   b) suites of George Frideric Handel (1685–1759)
   c) eighteenth-century sonata and concerto movements
   d) keyboard pieces of Henry Purcell (1659–95) and his English contemporaries

8. What unusual element of asymmetry is often found in binary sonatas of Domenico Scarlatti (1685–1757)?

9. Examine the binary slow movement of the Piano Sonata in D (Peters No. 7) of Franz Joseph Haydn (1732–1809). Why does it end on the dominant of the tonic key?

10. In each of the examples of Béla Bartók (1881–1945) cited below, carefully compare Parts I and II.

11. The text of Chapter 2 refers for illustration to many examples of binary form—examples that may be used for further analysis. Additional works are listed on the next page, and the reader is urged to study binary form in as many of them as he can.

Bach, Prelude No. 22 in B-flat minor from the *Well-Tempered Clavier,* Book I
Sinfonia (Three-Voice Invention) No. 6 in E

Bartók, *Mikrokosmos,* Book II, Nos. 42 and 51; Book III, No. 69

Ludwig van Beethoven (1770–1827), String Quartet in C minor, Op. 18, No. 4, trio of third movement
Variations on a Theme of Diabelli, Op. 120, theme
String Quartet in G, Op. 18, No. 2, second movement, measures 29–52
Sonata in D, Op. 28, trio of third movement
Sonata in G, Op. 79, last movement, measures 1–16

Johannes Brahms (1833–97), Waltz in G-sharp minor, Op. 39, No. 3

François Couperin (1668–1733), harpsichord pieces *L'Aimable Thérèse, L'Anguille* (an incipient binary), and *Les Tricoteuses*

Haydn, Sonata in E-flat (Peters No. 12), trio of second movement and theme of last movement
Symphony No. 73 in D (*La Chasse*), trio of third movement

Paul Hindemith (1895–1964), *Ludus Tonalis,* Interludes preceding Fugues 3, 6, and 12

Wolfgang Amadeus Mozart (1756–91), Variations on a Theme of Salieri, K. 180, theme
Eight Variations on a March from *Mariages Samnites* by Grétry, K. 352, theme
String Quartet in E-flat, K. 428, trio of third movement (unusual tonal plan)

Jean-Philippe Rameau (1683–1764), harpsichord piece *L'Entretien des Muses*

D. Scarlatti, Sonata in E minor, K. 263 (Longo 321)
Sonata in E, K. 46 (Longo 25)

Franz Schubert (1797–1828), Sonata in A minor, Op. 42, second movement, measures 1–32

3

Jan. 10

SIMPLE TERNARY

ince music passes in time, consisting of con-
tiguous events, the faculty of memory is necessarily engaged in its perception.
As an aid to tying together the successive components, it has been customary
to use the device of recalling a particular, significant idea after its initial
appearance. Thus, a theme or motive, A, may be repeated immediately—
creating a relationship of perfect identity between two contiguous segments—or it may be repeated after a contrasting idea has been introduced
(ABA).

Repetition of some kind—of melodic motive, of rhythmic pattern, of
cadence, of key level—has been a factor in each of the forms and structural
units discussed so far, with the exception of the motive, which may lack
obvious and significant pattern repetition except for the succession of
evenly-spaced pulsations, if that. A motive is so small that the mere tem-
poral proximity of its parts is enough to relate them. Repetition of motive
in period forms is clearly implicit in the idea of parallel construction, discussed in Chapter 1. In binary form, the use of a characteristic motive
throughout both divisions constitutes the principal technique of repetition.

Of course, repetition is not necessarily literal and precise; the recurrence
of a musical idea may involve many modifications of the original pattern
while preserving its essential identity.

The concept of *ternary* structure is that of repetition (or return) after
digression, conveniently represented by the symbol ABA, or ABA' when the
return is a modification of the original statement. This principle was discussed briefly in connection with the tonal levels of the standard binary
structure (Chapter 2): statement of original key; digression into related
key(s); return to original tonal level. The further retracing of this principle
to the period forms is evident, although the contrasting levels are usually
harmonic rather than tonal in the case of the smallest forms.

The idea of repetition after digression, the basis for ternary (or tripartite) form, is very old. It can be seen, for example, in the *da capo* principle of certain forms of the past five centuries (the fifteenth-century Spanish *villancico* is an early type) and in such early musico-poetic forms as the medieval *virelai,* which includes the succession ABBA.

A famous example of early sixteenth-century ternary form is the *chanson, Faulte d'argent* by Josquin des Prez (1450-1521). This piece falls into three nearly equal sections with a codetta at the end (measure 64). The third part is recapitulative.

Ex. 3.1   Josquin des Prez, Faulte d'argent.

Reprinted by permission of the publishers from Archibald T. Davison and Willi Apel, *Historical Anthology of Music: Oriental, Medieval, and Renaissance Music* (Cambridge, Mass.: Harvard University Press, copyright, 1946, 1949, by the President and Fellows of Harvard College).

Beginning of Part I, 24 measures:

Beginning of Part II, 21 measures:

Restatement (Part III), 21 measures:

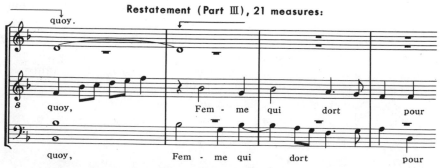

Our basic definition of ternary form will involve the following features: (1) three parts or sections; (2) a clear relationship between the first and third parts, so that the third is felt to be a return of the first; and (3) contrast—tonal, thematic, textural, developmental, or any combination of these—in the second part.

Significance of tripartition as a structural principle

The practice of making a musical statement, following it with a contrasting statement, and then restating the original material is, when carried out convincingly, an extremely satisfactory solution to the problems of unity and variety in musical form. The possible variation of the material in its return in the third part is a further treatment of the same problem—at once a provision for both requirements. The digressive material of the second part must, of course, be complementary to that of the first (therefore like it in many respects) and, while contrasting, never contradictory.

The recapitulation of original thematic materials in a third section—a conscious relating of events, separated in time, for the purpose of binding the whole into a perceptible and logical unity—is often described as a "rounding" of the form. The flanking of a middle section with two similar outer parts circumscribes the material, containing it in time. Ideally executed, ternary form conveys the logic and unity of a circular form. It is the most significant, fundamental achievement in the history of musical structure, as viable now as ever before. Most of the more highly developed traditional forms are in one way or another a manifestation or extension of the ternary principle. A twentieth-century illustration of that principle is shown in Ex. 3.2 by Anton Webern (1883–1945).

Ex. 3.2 Webern, Variations for Piano, Op. 27, first movement.
Copyright 1937, Universal Editions. Used by permission.

Ex. 3.2 (continued).

Modified Restatement (Part Ⅲ), at m. 37:

Partition without reprise; other types of multiple segmentation

Tripartition in music does not necessarily mean a sequence of sections in the pattern ABA, although that pattern is apparent in the vast majority of tripartite examples. For instance, there may be three sections with no contrasting part—that is, three identical or nearly identical sections (or a larger number), as is the case in many *strophic* songs. There may be minor variations to fit the changing text of each stanza, but the pattern is clearly AAA or AA′A″, etc. Folk songs of this type are very numerous. Examples of strophic art songs are Schubert's *An Mignon, An die Musik,* and *Der Fischer.* In each of these the music of the basic song is repeated unchanged. *An Mignon* lacks repetition altogether within the stanza itself and is in that sense irregular. Each stanza of *Der Fischer* is a double period, and therefore not without internal repetition.

A further example of strophic art song, Schubert's *Der Schiffer,* recalls essentially the same music with each stanza, but in variation. The stanza consists of a period, a repeated phrase, and another period.

In Ex. 3.3 only a single stanza is quoted for examination of its structure at the most basic level. The anomalous feature is the succession of phrases in the pattern ABCDE. There is repetition of motive, but no repetition of phrase. Another example is the well-known "God Save the King," consisting of a series of two-measure phrases having mainly rhythmic correspondences.

Ex. 3.3 American Folksong of English origin, "Lord Lovel."

Thus it is conceivable that a three-part piece might proceed without digression and formal reprise. Chopin's Prelude, Op. 28, No. 9, is in three parts, each based on the same theme—an example of instrumental *strophic form*. Each section begins in E, and the total form conveys no feeling of departure and return.

Another example in three sections (ABC), with some sharing of motives but no real reprise, is the first part (*Premier Acte*) of François Couperin's (1668–1733) *Les Fastes de la Grande et Ancienne Ménestrandise,* a work for harpsichord. It is assumed, in all such cases, that the various sections or phrases will share common motives and be related in a number of ways; a series of *totally* contrasting sections would never result in convincing form. When, as in the Couperin, the form is composed of strongly contrasted sections related only by the sparse occurrence of common motives, it is said to be *additive*. Additive procedures are rare in musical form.

Theoretically, several additional arrangements of three sections are possible—AAB, ABB, etc.—and if the number of sections is greater, the number of possible arrangements increases at the same time. There is irregularity, although no lack of reprise, in Claude Debussy's (1862–1918) *La Fille aux Cheveux de Lin*, Prelude No. 8 from Book I. This work is outlined as Ex. 3.4.

Ex. 3.4   Debussy, La Fille aux Cheveux de Lin.
Permission for reprint granted by Durand et Cie., Paris, France, copyright owners, and Elkan-Vogel Co., Inc., Philadelphia, Pa., agents.

Ex. 3.4 (continued).

Another Debussy Prelude using segmentation and repetition in an irregular manner is *Voiles,* No. 2 of the first book. Here, the various sections follow the pattern ABCDA.

In this study we will adopt the generally accepted definition of the term "tripartition," embodying the concept of statement-digression-restatement. It is in this sense that the ternary idea is universally significant and extremely widely practiced.

The incipient ternary

Incipient ternary form (mentioned in the preceding chapter as "rounded binary form") occurs most commonly as a minor section within a larger form.

The general, definitive characteristics of incipient ternary form are three. (1) The form is in *two* principal parts, of which the second is identical, or nearly identical, to the first in length, admitting the possibility of a slightly longer second part in asymmetrical types. (2) The second part contains, in its closing measures (before the codetta, if there is one), a formal return of part of the principal thematic material of the first section. In many cases only one of an initial two phrases is brought back, sometimes slightly extended. (3) The close of the first part, like that of binary form, is most often in a related key.

Thus, incipient ternary form demonstrates its relationship to binary form in its proportions—division into two major sections of comparable length—and in its tonal structure—modulation away from the tonic key at the end of the first part, return to the original tonal level in the second part. The second part includes the contrasting elements, of whatever degree, and the token gesture of reprise.

Ex. 3.5   Brahms, Liebeslieder Walzer, Op. 52, No. 4.

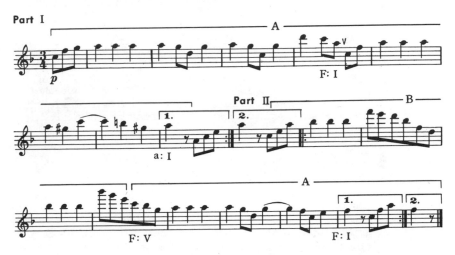

It is apparent in Ex. 3.5, of which only a single line is shown, that the feeling of thematic return in the final measures is entirely possible even when there has not been pronounced motivic contrast preceding it. The opening phrase of the second part uses the motive of Part I, while treating it differently and establishing mainly dominant harmonic feeling.

There are occasional examples of incipient ternary in which the second and third features included in the above definition are present, but whose proportions are on the borderline between binary and ternary. For example, the first 22 measures of the second movement of Beethoven's Sonata in D, Op. 28, suggest incipient ternary form by virtue of the modulation to A minor at the end of Part I, even though the over-all proportions are 8–8,6. (Note that the second part is lengthened by extension; there is reprise of *only one phrase,* but it is six measures long as compared to the original four.)

In Ex. 3.6 incipient ternary form is implicit in the equal proportions of the two parts and the clear feeling of reprise at the end. But the first part ends in the original key, so that the third characteristic given in the definition is inapplicable. All three examples (3.5, 3.6, and the excerpt from Beethoven's Op: 28) can be characterized as incipient ternary forms, even though only the first one (Ex. 3.5) conforms to the stereotype in all three respects. Examples 3.5 and 3.6 are symmetrical specimens; the example referred to in the text of the preceding paragraph is asymmetrical.

Ex. 3.6 Spilman?, Flow Gently, Sweet Afton.

Analysis of any of the following examples will clarify further the nature of incipient ternary form: trio of the second movement of Chopin's Sonata in C minor, Op. 4 (proportions 16—8,8; keys of E–flat minor and G–flat); Beethoven, Bagatelle, Op. 119, No. 4 (8—4,4; in A and E); first sixteen measures of the Mozart Concert Rondo for piano and orchestra, K. 382 (8—4,4; entirely in D; two periods whose consequent phrases are identical); Robert Schumann (1810–56), *Album for the Young*, Op. 68, No. 2 (16—8,8; in G and D); and Mozart, Sonata in A, K. 331, theme of the first movement variations (8—4,6; entirely in A; the single phrase of the reprise enlarged by two measures).

Simple ternary form further defined

It is characteristic of simple ternary form to have three sections (as opposed to the two of binary and incipient ternary) of which at least the first and third are of comparable proportions. Occasionally the second part is, while large enough to establish a moment of change, considerably smaller than the flanking sections. (See the trio of the second movement of Mozart's String Quartet in G, K. 387. The proportions are 25–8–25, the final section, the reprise, longer than the corresponding part in incipient ternary form. There is an irregular modulation to the dominant minor at the end of Part I.)

We may recall at this point that definitions of all the small forms (binary, incipient binary, and incipient ternary) discussed so far have involved consideration of *tonal structure and relative proportions* of principal sections. To continue on this basis, we may extend our definition of simple ternary form to note that Part I often ends in the original key, with an authentic cadence. Part II is in some way a digression, as explained at the beginning of this chapter. Finally, and most basically, the third section is a return, possibly with some variation, of the first part. Ex. 3.7, of the proportions 8–8–8, illustrates all the above points defining simple ternary form.

Ex. 3.7 Beethoven, Sonata in B-flat, Op. 22, third movement.

In exceptional examples (like the Mozart excerpt referred to in the first paragraph of this section) we may speak of ternary form even when Part I ends in a related key—a vestigial binary trait—provided there are three sections rather than the two of the incipient type. An example of simple ternary having three nearly equal parts (20–22–20), with modulation to the dominant at the end of Part I, is Bach's Two-Voice Invention No. 6.

Ex. 3.8 Bach, Two-Voice Invention No. 6 in E.

The basis for discussions like the above, and their justification, is that specific designations, or labels, *must be used* in the analytical description of music and the classification of musical works that have common structural features. The meanings of such labels should be established as clearly as possible, although there are cases, to be sure, in which no one can wisely insist upon the exclusive applicability of a given term. The question of binary as opposed to ternary features, specifically having to do with questions of tonal structure and relative proportions, is taken up again in Chapter 6 in connection with single-movement sonata form.

Simple ternary form, like incipient ternary, occurs in art music commonly as part of a larger form, although it is not infrequently the organizational principle underlying a complete piece. Very often the first part is repeated, as a means of impressing it upon the listener before contrast is introduced or simply as a survival of binary practice. Often the combined second and third parts are repeated as well, giving the formula A:||:BA:||.

Ex. 3.9 Haydn, String Quartet in B minor, Op. 64, No. 2, third movement (first violin only).

For clarity and convenience, if not for historical significance, a clear line can be traced from period to incipient binary to binary, thence to incipient ternary and simple ternary form. It will be useful to pause long enough at this juncture to review the individual features of these forms and, especially, those qualities which are carried forward from the smallest to the largest of them.

The following chart will aid such a review. For obvious reasons the many variants discussed in the text are omitted and only the prototypes are represented. Neither repeats nor codettas are shown, and the symbols at cadences indicate the most probable arrival harmonies. The symbols *R* and *T* refer to related and tonic keys, respectively.

Fig. 3.1

SUMMARY OF SMALL FORMS

PERIOD   A   (Antecedent phrase)   A'or B   (Consequent phrase)

T:V   T:I

INCIPIENT BINARY (1)

More than two phrases

A   *used on A material*   B (on A)

T:V   T:I

(2)

One or two phrases

A   B (on A)

R:I   T:I

Related Key Modulation

Comp. due → **BINARY**

More than two phrases

A   B (on A)

R:I   T:I

INCIPIENT TERNARY

A   B   A

R:I   T:I

TERNARY

A   B   A

T:I   R ——————→ T:V   T:I

The first part

Very rarely, the first part begins with a short introductory gesture— conceivably as much as a complete phrase.

Ex. 3.10   Ernst Křenek, Twelve Short Piano Pieces, Op. 83, No. 4.
Copyright, 1939, by G. Schirmer, Inc. Reprinted by permission.

The first part is entirely homogeneous in material, being based throughout on a common motive or set of motives, and it is usually also homogeneous in key. Here, of course, the basic material of the form is presented; and the later reprise of this material in the tonic key is the form's fundamental structural basis. Ex. 3.11 shows the main motivic substance of Part I of a simple ternary. The first section actually continues to measure 20, and is involved throughout with the material shown here. In this work, the entire ternary form takes up 46 measures of the complete movement. Ex. 3.13 is also useful for study in this connection.

Ex. 3.11   Brahms, Sonata in F minor, Op. 5, second movement.

The form of Part I may, like that of binary form, consist of a group of motives or phrases, or some variety of period form—simple period, double period, or enlarged period. Rarely is it a single phrase. Ex. 3.12 is very common in form, consisting of a period of two regular phrases. The quoted excerpt, together with its immediate *tutti* repetition, constitutes Part I of a small ternary.

Ex. 3.12 Mozart, Piano Concerto in B-flat, K. 595, third movement.

An example of an opening section in which a phrase group occurs is found in the *Menuet* from *Le Tombeau de Couperin,* a suite for orchestra by Maurice Ravel (1875–1937). Measures 1 to 8 consist of two phrases which do not form a period.

As already indicated, and as is borne out, for instance, in Ex. 3.7 and Ex. 3.12, Part I normally ends with an authentic cadence in the tonic key. (For an example of a first part ending in a new key, see Ex. 3.8 and its explanatory paragraph.) In many cases, especially in the late eighteenth and early nineteenth centuries, the first part is followed by a repeat sign with two endings. Occasionally, however, especially in more recent examples, Part II follows immediately without the repeat of Part I. In Ex. 3.13 not only is there no repeat, but Parts I and II are joined by an elided cadence.

Ex. 3.13 Elgar, Enigma Variations, Op. 36, opening theme.
      Reproduced by permission of Novello & Co., Ltd.

↑
End of Part I,
beginning of Part II

In simple ternary form, no transition is usual between Parts I and II, but now and then the first part moves imperceptibly, by dissolution,[1] into Part II. In this regard, the student may examine the Chopin Prelude in G-sharp minor, Op. 28, No. 12. Part I begins with an 8-measure phrase. At the repetition of this phrase (measure 9) the music moves off into a long, digressive, modulatory middle section, with a reprise at measure 41. Thus, the form is ternary despite the absence of clear cadential separation between Parts I and II.

The second part

The principal structural function of the second part is to provide contrast—a sense of departure as a prelude to the restatement of the original thematic material in the tonic key. In the simple ternary, the second part is frequently based on the same motivic material as Part I. In such cases there will be contrast of general melodic contour, of texture, of key, or of some other kind. In most cases there is at least contrast of key level. If the original tonic persists, there is likely to be harmonic contrast in the use of secondary functions (Ex. 3.9), dominant prolongation, or other means.

In Ex. 3.14, the basic motives are carried into Part II, but they are turned into different melodic effect and the tonal level is changed.

[1] The *dissolution* of a musical unit is its failure to continue to an expected conclusion—to pursue its previously established or implied direction. Often the material disintegrates into thematically insignificant figuration, or it may stop at a certain point, wander off by repeating a fragment of itself at different levels, possibly reaching a tentative cadence, or avoiding a cadence altogether. Ex. 4.17 is a particularly clear illustration.

Ex. 3.14   Ravel, Le Tombeau de Couperin, Menuet.

Permission for reprint granted by Durand et Cie., Paris, France, copyright owners, and Elkan-Vogel Co., Inc., Philadelphia, Pa., agents.

An imaginative composer has infinite possibilities for variety in the second section; yet, a part of the composer's problem is to achieve variety without introducing what might be felt to be contradictory elements—for example, extreme changes of rhythmic motion and pattern. In other words, in the small dimensions of the form under discussion, the middle section ideally offers contrasting attitudes and substance which are at the same time complementary to Part I. Of all the possibilities of variety, change of key is the most common in the traditional ternary.

Again, the most likely key relationships are tonic to dominant or relative. Examples of each, including one irregular relationship, are shown

Ex. 3.15   Schumann, Album for the Young, Op. 68, No. 3.

in Ex. 3.15, Ex. 3.16 and Ex. 3.17. In each of these examples, the end of Part I and the beginning of Part II are shown.

Ex. 3.16   Schumann, Papillons, Op. 2, No. 3.

Ex. 3.17   Schubert, Die Liebe hat gelogen.

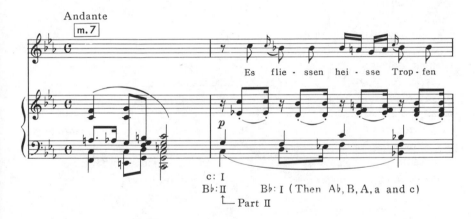

Other tonal relationships are possible (see Ex. 3.20). In Chopin's Prelude No. 15 in D–flat the middle section is in the parallel enharmonic minor. Of course, the question of modulation does not apply where *atonal*[2] examples are concerned (Ex. 3.2 and Ex. 3.10).

The form of Part II is occasionally as short as a single phrase, more often it is a phrase or motive group. It is most commonly comparable in

---

[2] Theoretically, *atonal* music lacks a tonal center; it is a style in which the composer seeks to avoid formulations of melody and harmony that would give tonal prominence to any note over the remaining eleven. Musicians differ as to the degree to which this is possible, and the degree to which it is achieved in practice. Certainly tonal feeling can be obscured and negated, whether or not it can be extinguished.

length to Part I. Because the second part often ends on dominant harmony (T:V),[3] in anticipation of the return, period form is very uncommon. (A rare example may be seen in the trio of the second movement of Haydn's Sonata in G, Peters No. 11, whose middle section is settled in B–flat.) An example of Part II as a single phrase, in this case of four measures, is seen in Ex. 3.9. The *Menuet* from Ravel's *Le Tombeau de Couperin,* cited above, affords a good example of a second section constructed as a phrase group (measures 9–24).

Rarely is a new theme introduced in the middle section of a simple ternary. An exception to, this principle is in the scherzo of Beethoven's Sonata in A, Op. 2, No. 2. Measure 19 of this movement has a new theme in G–sharp minor.

The character of the second part, even in simple ternary, is often of particular interest, being more tentative, less settled, less likely to be punctuated with firm cadences than either of the flanking sections. This is especially true in a Part II which is a motive or phrase series in sequence. (See, in addition to Ex. 3.18, the theme of Mozart's Ten Variations on an Air of Gluck, K. 455.)

Ex. 3.18   Chopin, Prelude in D-flat, Op. 28, No. 15.

The end of the contrasting middle section is of especial importance. This is true primarily in more extended ternary forms, but is not to be ignored in smaller types. The second part may close with a strong cadence in the contrasting key, with the third part beginning directly. This means,

---

3 *T:V* denotes "dominant of the tonic (fundamental, or original) key."

of course, that the final harmony of Part II normally functions as a logical
pivot point[4] into the return of the tonic key.

Ex. 3.19   Tchaikovsky, Symphony No. 6 in B minor, Op. 74, second movement.

Part II may dissolve (by the disintegration of one of its formal units)
into a retransitional passage which prepares the return of the original
material and tonal level, or such a retransition may follow a cadential ending of the second part.

Ex. 3.20   Beethoven, Bagatelle, Op. 119, No. 1.

Part I beginning:

End of Part II:

---

[4] *Pivot point* is understood here as the point to which the previous key center
is maintained, and the point from which the new center is felt—hence, the point
of tonal change. Often it is a harmony which is common to both tonal systems, the
new key approached through a diatonic progression. (See *chromatic modulation* and
chromatic progression, pp. 109–10 and 125.)

Ex. 3.20 (continued)

It is also possible for the second part to contain within itself, without any disruption of its formal structure, a modulation back to the original key. The example from which Ex. 3.21 is taken is of the proportions 4–7–7, forming part of a larger form. As is not unusual in freer styles, the music is characterized by loose joints, and very tentative cadences.

Ex. 3.21 Debussy, Suite Bergamasque for piano, Menuet.
Permission for reprint granted by Editions Jean Jobert, Paris, France, copyright owners, and Elkan-Vogel Co., Inc., Philadelphia, Pa., agents.

The question of transition (here, retransition) arises in this context for the first time. It is useful and interesting to consider the three types of preparation involved in the function of retransition—the introduction of the return of important material. (For reference to examples of surprise returns, in which conventional preparation is lacking, see Chapter 6, pp. 199–200.)

(1) Tonal preparation: introduction of the key level of the forthcoming material.

(2) Thematic preparation: anticipation of the motivic material of the forthcoming section.

(3) Harmonic preparation: not separable from tonal preparation, but often involving statement, even prolongation, of a dissonant harmony to underscore and intensify the expectation of the approaching section.

As an example of retransition, necessarily brief because of the limits of the form under discussion, Ex. 3.22 illustrates all three principles of preparation: the modulation is indicated; motives appearing in the thematic preparation are bracketed; the five measures of dominant harmony, finally yielding to the tonic of B–flat, make up the harmonic preparation. Of course, it should not be assumed that all three factors are applicable in all cases.

Ex. 3.22   Mozart, String Quartet in B-flat, K. 458, second movement.

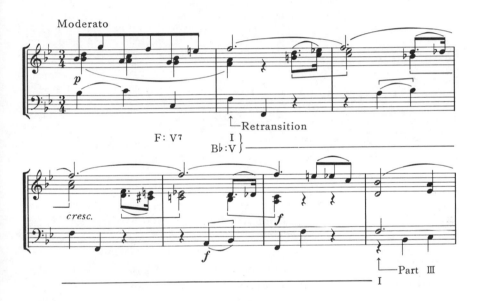

A notable example of harmonic preparation of unusual intensity and effect occurs in the scherzo (second movement) of Beethoven's Sonata in A–flat, Op. 26. At the preparation (measure 25) of the return of Part III of the simple ternary there are no fewer than 20 measures of dominant prolongation.

The third part

In the restatement in Part III, the almost invariable rule is the return of the tonic key, usually before the beginning of this section. Ex. 3.23, from Brahms' String Sextet, Op. 18, is highly exceptional in this respect. Only key points are shown. Part I is 10 measures long and Part II is

Ex. 3.23 Brahms, String Sextet in B-flat, Op. 18, third movement (trio).

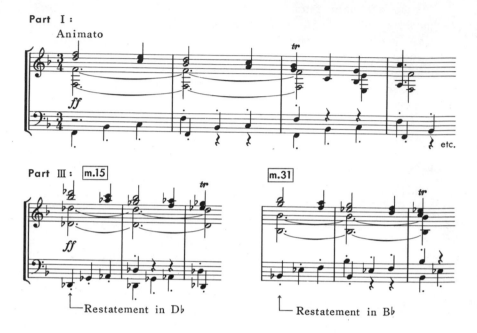

uncommonly brief (measures 11–14). Measure 15 begins a restatement which is at the same time elaborately developmental. This section is 26 measures long, returning to the key of F only three measures before the end of the trio (at measure 38).

All possibilities relevant to the structure of Part I will apply to Part III. The return may be a literal *da capo*, as in the Beethoven Bagatelle, Op. 119, No. 3. However, now and then (more often in larger ternary forms) the material of the first part is varied in some way in its return. Theoretically, any aspect of the material—structural, harmonic, melodic, rhythmic, coloristic, textural, etc.—is subject to change. In practice, however, the

Ex. 3.24 Beethoven, Allegretto für F. Piringer (Kinsky-Halm Wo O 61).

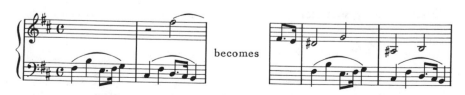

return in simple ternary form is more often quite literal, with variational possibilities generally limited to changes in accompanimental motion, slight embellishments of the theme melody, or excisions or extensions. A few of these possibilities are illustrated in Ex. 3.24 and Ex. 3.25. A further type of treatment is seen in Examples 3.8 and 3.10 in which the first and third parts are in double counterpoint.[5]

Ex. 3.25 Bartók, Mikrokosmos, Book V, No. 128.
     Copyright 1940 by Hawkes & Son (London) Ltd. Reprinted by permission.

An abbreviated return is found in Beethoven's Bagatelle, Op. 126, No. 5, whose proportions are 16–16–8. Haydn often develops the basic material after the feeling of return is established; an example of this is the second movement of the Sonata in G (Peters No. 11) after measure 29. For a final example the reader may look into No. 3 of the Schumann *Papillons*, Op. 2, in which the theme is made into a canon in Part III. It should be repeated that the possibilities for variation are limitless.

The third section in simple ternary form, when modified, affords our first example of a very useful principle in musical form, that of variation. Some elements of the original thematic material are retained, lending unity in the relating of the two sections; other features of the material are subjected to variation, supplying contrast.

When all three sections of the form are of identical length, the example is described as *symmetrical*. An example of asymmetrical simple ternary

[5] *Contrapuntal inversion* is the exchange of position between two (or more) voices. If voice *A* is initially above voice *B*, in the contrapuntal inversion voice *B* will occur higher than voice *A*. The interval of inversion is most often an octave or 15th, occasionally a 12th or 10th, in traditional styles. Other intervals of inversion are common in more recent times. Two voices capable of such inversion constitute *invertible counterpoint*, or *double counterpoint*. If three voices are involved, they are in *triple counterpoint*. (See Chapter 11, p. 388, for more complete discussion.)

form is shown as Ex. 3.26. Symmetrical examples are very easy to find. The proportions of the Haydn excerpt quoted here are 8–16–8, the second section a developmental motive group modulating to the dominant key and back.

Ex. 3.26   Haydn, Symphony No. 82 in C, second movement.

Part I :

Part II :

Part III :

etc., as above

  Part III normally ends with a strong authentic cadence, or with a codetta. However, when the simple ternary is part of a larger form, there may be a dissolution or transition leading into the following section.

The codetta

  A codetta may or may not occur at the end of Part III (or Part I, since it, too, usually ends with an authentic cadence). The concept of the codetta has already been explained (see Chapter 2) as the final section, set off by the latest clearly perceptible cadence in the key in which the section closes. A codetta in simple ternary form would obviously be very brief, and not likely to be sectional because of the limited size of the total form. (See pp. 44 and 99–100, for discussion of the sectional codetta.)

Ex. 3.27 is a quotation of a rare codetta ending Part I of a simple ternary; Ex. 3.28 shows a codetta at the close of Part III of a different example. In the Beethoven, the same material, extended to 9 bars, is used as a codetta to the complete ternary, whose proportions are 16–20–34, codettas included. The final section is a good basis for study of variation and extension in the return. The second movement of Haydn's Sonata in G (Peters No. 10), measures 8–10, affords another example of a codetta to Part I.

Ex. 3.27 Beethoven, Trio in G, Op. 1, No. 2, for piano, violin, and cello, third movement.

Ex. 3.28 Mussorgsky, Pictures at an Exhibition (The Ox-Cart).

Brahms, Ballade in G minor, Op. 118, No. 3, measures 1–40

The diagrammatic representation included as Ex. 3.29 summarizes graphically the features of simple ternary form as discussed. It is of the most usual type—an excerpt from a larger form. Indications of the main divisions and materials, as well as phrase and motive analysis, are given. Cadences and key levels are shown, together with other important features. The conclusion, as noted, is upset by transitional movement into the next part of the piece. Here, the melodic G becomes the root of a dominant seventh-chord, treated enharmonically as an augmented-sixth to lead into the key of B, an unusually remote level for the next section in the larger form.

Individual features of the work should be studied with the complete score at hand. Brahms uses the opening motive as the thematic basis for Part II, varying it tonally, and in dynamics and articulation. Another striking feature is the enormous energy which propels the music over the joint linking Parts II and III: *crescendo*, chromatic harmony (augmented-sixth on E–flat, again as a device of modulation), *syncopation*,[6] accent, extension of the anacrusis and upward drive in pitch, and the cadential elision itself. The irregularity of 5-measure phrases in the opening period,

---

[6] When attention is drawn (by duration, or by dynamic emphasis) to points in the meter which are normally relatively weak, so that a sort of rhythmic counterpoint to the basic pulse is effected, the result is described as *syncopation*. "Weak" points are normally beats other than the first of the measure, although other points than the first beat (e.g., the beginning of the second half of a symmetrical measure) may have relative prominence in slower tempo. When a particular voice is syncopated, the natural metric organization is usually left undisturbed in the remaining voices, although the entire texture may be set in opposition to a previously established meter.

and the asymmetry of the total form, add to the interest of the music. The reader is urged to continue the analysis of *all* factors making for unity, contrast, and vitality in these 40 measures.

Ex. 3.29 Brahms, Ballade in G minor, Op. 118, No. 3, first 40 measures.

⑦ A *pedal point* is a note (in traditional music usually the root of I or V) sustained or reiterated in a particular voice while the harmony changes above, below, or around it. Strictly speaking, it is dissonant to at least one of the harmonies to which it is coincidental. Most often it occurs in the bass. If it is in the top voice, it is called an *inverted pedal;* an *internal pedal* if in one of the middle voices.

Incipience of the rondo principle

We have reached a convenient point for anticipation of the rondo principle in musical form (the subject of Chapter 5). Ternary designs of a larger scope are identified by some theorists (for example, Goetschius) as a species of rondo. But a rondo is characterized by a pattern of several recurrences of the opening thematic material, and a single restatement is not adequate to establish either the principle or the feeling of the rondo design. As will be developed fully in Chapter 5, we take the position that a rondo design involves at least three statements (two restatements) of the principal thematic material.

However, the simplest rondo form is clearly an *extension of the ternary principle:* ABA becomes ABABA or ABACA. So at this point the rondo idea is emergent, although not yet realized.

It may be noticed, in passing, that when a small three-part design is practiced with the most usual pattern of repeats (AABABA) it is, in effect, even closer to rondo form.

Exercises and examples for further study

1. Try to think of as many ways as possible in which the restatement of material can be varied, without losing its original identity. How is this problem significant in ternary form?

2. Write a paragraph explaining the significance of the ternary principle.

3. Find an example among the string quartets of Mozart illustrating simple ternary form. Analyze it thoroughly according to the procedures developed in this chapter. Refer to Ex. 3. 29 as a model for your analysis.

4. Find an example of small ternary form in which Part III is not a strict duplicate of Part I. Compare the two sections minutely, and discuss the relationships and differences between them.

5. Compose at least the melody line of a small ternary according to the following plan.
   Part I: A period of irregular length in the key of D.
   Part II: A related motive in sequence followed by a single phrase with a cadence on the dominant of D. Begin this section in B minor and arrange it to lead back to D.
   Part III: An abbreviated form of Part I. Be sure that it is adequate to balance the form. Follow it with a short codetta, possibly modeled after an example you have studied.

6. Study each of the examples in Chapter 3 (those from which musical quotations are made). Consider precisely what each of them is intended to illustrate.
   Try to find additional examples in the music of the eighteenth, nineteenth

and twentieth centuries to illustrate some of the same features of simple ternary form. Do this with as many of the examples as possible.

7. Examine the simple ternary form of Schubert's song, *Schäfers Klagelied*. Why might this be described as a musical "arch" form?

8. Study the methods by which simple ternary form dissolves into the subsequent section of the total form in some of the slow movements of sonatas of K. P. E. Bach. An example is the second movement of his *Württemberg Sonata No. 6.*

9. A few supplementary references to simple ternary form will point the way to further study. In addition to the following, the examples cited in this chapter can form the basis for independent analysis. A vast, general source can be found in movements with trios (scherzos, minuets) of symphonies, sonatas, and chamber works of the eighteenth and nineteenth centuries; individual sections of such movements are very often in simple ternary form. After observing the outlines of the total form, examine the means by which the composer unifies its parts, introduces contrast, maintains interest and vitality, joins sections, and prepares tonal and other changes. List individual, striking features in at least one or two specimens.

Bach, English Suite No. 6 in D minor, both *gavottes*
Beethoven, Bagatelles
    Variations in F, Op. 34, theme
Brahms, Symphony No. 2 in D, Op. 73, third movement, measures 1–32
    Waltz in E, Op. 39, No. 2
    Waltz in E minor, Op. 39, No. 4
F. Couperin, *Les Bacchanales* for harpsichord, No. 1, *Enjouements Bachiques*
Zoltán Kodály (b. 1882), Piano Pieces, Op. 3, Nos. 2, 4, and 7
Ernst Křenek (b. 1900), Piano Pieces, Op. 83 (Which are ternary in form?)
Mozart, Twelve Variations on a Minuet by Fischer, K. 179, theme
Schubert, *Am Strom* (song)
    Sonata in E-flat, Op. 122, second movement, measures 1–20
Schumann, *Album for the Young*, Op. 68 (Which are ternary in form?)
Igor Stravinsky (b. 1882), Concerto for violin and orchestra, arias—second and third movements
Peter Ilyich Tchaikovsky (1840–92), Symphony No. 5 in E minor, introduction to first movement, measures 1–37

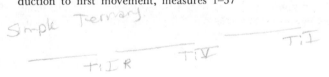

4

COMPOUND TERNARY

*T*he significance and wide application of the principle of tripartition in music, emphasized in the preceding chapter in connection with the simple ternary, is further attested by the common occurrence of a ternary structure of broader and more intricate design—a structure which we shall call *compound ternary form.*

The important features of contrast and unity, and of the distribution and equilibrium of unifying and contrasting features, are evident here in an expanded pattern; the possibilities of variety and diversity in compound ternary form are greater than in any of the forms discussed so far, and with a wider framework a new flexibility emerges. Of course, this is not to say that the realization of these qualities is necessarily more successful in practice in compound ternary form.

Ernst Toch discussed the importance of ternary form persuasively and succinctly:

> To it [the principle of tripartition] most of the forms can be traced, regardless of their substructures, proportions, standards, terms. ...whence we came, thither we return, after all the blooming and climaxing, after all the turbulence and trepidation. The principle of tripartition is rooted in nature..., in our very existence.[1]

Ternary forms are sometimes reasonably described as "arch forms" because of the arch-like image suggested by the progression and return implicit in the idea of tripartition. We reject, however, the term "song-form," even though it is much used, because there is no basis whatever for the implied specific reference to the literature of the song. The term "song-form" is equally inapplicable to the binary design, to which it is also often applied.

[1] Ernst Toch, *The Shaping Forces in Music,* pp. 163–4, copyrighted 1958 by Criterion Music Corp.

The use of the ternary principle through several periods of music history was pointed out in Chapter 3. *Da capo* arias of the Baroque period are sometimes in compound ternary form (examples are cited in the following pages), not infrequently too inchoate in the distribution of tonal and thematic change to conform strictly to the form as it emerged in later traditions. Still, examples of early *da capo* arias will be seen to embody the ternary principle clearly, and in many cases to approach compound structure. The reader may investigate examples in the Apel-Davison *Historical Anthology of Music,* Vol II. Examples 203, 244, and 258 by Luigi Rossi (1598–1653), Agostino Steffani (1653–1728), and Alessandro Scarlatti (1659–1725), respectively, are *da capo* arias. Even the earliest of these has a first part which may be described as an incipient binary; other examples from this period bring back, at the end of the first part, the phrase with which it is introduced, yielding a suggested simple ternary in the first section as part of an over-all larger ternary whole.

Eighteenth-century *da capo* vocal and choral forms in full-fledged compound ternary form are easier to find. An example is the alto aria, *He was despised,* from Handel's *Messiah.* Part I of this aria is a binary form in the keys of E–flat and B–flat, with a return to E–flat in its second section. Part III is, of course, a literal *da capo.* Another example is the chorus, *Ruht wohl, ihr heiligen Gebeine,* from Bach's *St. John Passion.*

Occasionally composers of the eighteenth-century suite included contrasting dance pairs, with instructions for the performer to repeat the first dance after playing the second. The indication *alternativo* (It.) or *alternativement* (Fr.) was understood to mean that the first dance of the pair was to be played again after the second, resulting in a compound ternary form, each component of which would usually be a binary. An example is the pair of *bourrées* in Bach's English Suite No. 2 in A minor. The third and sixth of the English Suites have *gavotte* pairs played in *alternativo* form, and the minuet and *passepied* pairs of the English Suites 4 and 5 are further examples of eighteenth-century compound ternary forms.

Compound ternary form, because it is a more diverse mold, makes possible genuinely contrasting moods and thematic ideas. With this characteristic of more pronounced change in Part II, compound ternary form is a popular vehicle in the nineteenth century for character pieces written for the piano by Beethoven, Schubert, Schumann, Felix Mendelssohn (1809–47), Chopin, Brahms, and many other composers, under such labels as *bagatelle, nocturne, prelude, fantasy, intermezzo,* etc. Also included among the many piano pieces of this genre are dances and dance-derived compositions of a great variety of types—waltzes, mazurkas, *polonaises,* and others. Nineteenth-century salon pieces for the piano are almost invariably in simple or compound ternary form, often the latter.

Finally, the slow movements of symphonies, sonatas, and chamber works are sometimes in compound ternary form, and the minuet and scherzo movements of the Classical and Romantic multi-movement works of these types are more often than not in compound ternary form.

The above notes are sufficient to emphasize again the universality and importance of ternary form, especially since the early eighteenth century. Specific examples are mentioned in appropriate references throughout the present chapter.

Compound ternary form

Compound ternary form can best be defined as a tripartite form in which each of the three parts, or at least one of them, is in itself a binary or ternary design of at least an incipient character. The following is a common outline for the compound ternary, the symbols T and R denoting tonic and related keys, respectively.

aba (or ab)	cdc (or cd, or c)	aba (or ab)
A	B	A
T	R	T

Part II is often centered in the parallel major or minor. Possible introductory phrase, transitions, and codetta or coda are not represented in the above.

Two observations concerning the tonal design may be useful, providing the qualification is again made that exceptions are to be found. First, each of the three parts is usually "closed" tonally—that is, each part usually begins and ends in the same key. (The second part may end in the tonic key in preparation for the return; more often its final chord acts as a direct pivot or is followed by a transitional passage.) Secondly, because of the binary or ternary design of the individual parts, there is in many cases some modulation within each of the three sections. Specific features, tonal and other, are discussed in the balance of this chapter with reference to specific examples.

It should be emphasized that the above definition provides that *at least one* of the three sections, not necessarily all of them, will be in binary or ternary form. This will be clarified by a glance at the Chopin Prelude in F-sharp, Op. 28, No. 13. Part I of this compound ternary is reproduced in its melodic outline as Ex. 4.1. It is an asymmetrical incipient binary

Ex. 4.1 Chopin, Prelude in F-sharp, Op. 28, No. 13 (principal line of Part I).

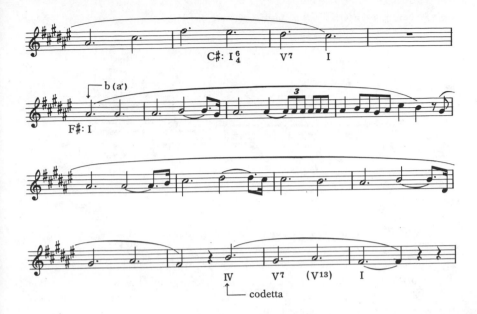

form: its first part, 7 measures, moves to the dominant key (more strongly than is apparent in the single line); there is 1 measure of transition, followed by a second part, 10 measures on the same thematic material, which returns to the tonic key. A short codetta concludes the binary. The over-all compound ternary continues with an 8-measure Part II which starts in C–sharp, the dominant key, developing a new motive sequentially (Ex. 4.2) and leading back to the original key in preparation for Part III.

Ex. 4.2   Chopin, Prelude in F-sharp (portion of Part II).

The third section is a return of only a portion (8 measures) of Part I, not leaving the key of F–sharp. A 2-measure codetta (Ex. 4.3) is appended; it includes a short reminiscence of the motive of Part II.

Ex. 4.3   Chopin, Prelude in F-sharp (final, 2-measure codetta).

In general compound ternary form is larger than the average simple ternary. But the rule is not absolute, especially in twentieth-century music, in which ternary form is a very important element. Here, strict tonal organization into smaller binary and ternary substructures is not usual. An example, which cannot be quoted, is Charles Griffes' (1884–1920) *The White Peacock,* from *Roman Sketches,* Op. 7, which must be described as a simple ternary because of the simple organization of its separate parts, which do not form 2- or 3-part designs. Yet, its proportions are quite large. Part I rests mostly on the dominant of the key of E and Part II (measure 19), extensive and fluctuant, is somewhat developmental of material of Part I. The total design is recapitulative. (The 21st measure before the end is the return to the dominant of E for the reprise, which proceeds from the next bar.)

The introduction

Although it is more likely in a larger form that some sort of introductory material will precede the form proper, the introduction is still relatively uncommon in the compound ternary. Even in the most extensive forms introductions are very frequently omitted.

The concept and function of the introduction, already presented briefly, is discussed fully in Chapter 6, with regard to single-movement sonata form, where the introduction is sometimes very significant and highly-developed. It will suffice here to point out a few examples of passages which are introductions to compound ternary forms, with mention of some possibilities of structure and quality.

Again, there may be an attention-getting device of no more than a chord or two, or a single brief motive.

Ex. 4.4 Chopin, Nocturne in B, Op. 62, No. 1.

The following excerpts, which are introductory to compound ternary examples, are slightly more extensive—the first, which is very familiar, a series of harmonies amounting to a single phrase. The imperfect plagal cadence in measure 4 is extended for 2 measures by prolonging the tonic harmony. The same phrase is used as part of the closing section at the end of the movement.

Ex. 4.5 Dvořák. Symphony in E minor, Op. 95, second movement.

Ex. 4.6 is an introduction of two short phrases, the second identical to the first except for the harmonization leading to a half-cadence in A minor. The ternary design of this Chopin Etude is apparent in its tonal structure, although it is based on similar material throughout. Only very

Ex. 4.6 Chopin, Etude in A minor, Op. 25, No. 11.

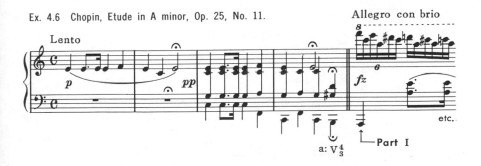

rarely does an introduction to compound ternary form exceed 8 measures in length. However, an unusually large example of the form may have a correspondingly long introduction: the second movement of the *Symphonie Fantastique,* Op. 14, by Hector Berlioz (1803–69) has an introduction of 38 measures.

Because an introductory passage is a preparation for the main body of the form, it frequently ends in an unresolved fashion, establishing at its close an air of expectancy, often by means of a half-cadence, as in Ex. 4.6. Further, the introduction may anticipate the thematic material of the form proper. Ex. 4.7 illustrates both points; it is a brief introduction (a repeated motive) to Part II of a compound ternary.

Ex. 4.7   Brahms, Sonata in E minor, Op. 38, for cello and piano, second movement (trio).

The first part

The principal thematic content is stated in Part I. Since decisive thematic contrast is usually introduced in Part II, the first section is most often of similar motivic material throughout, even when it is itself a simple ternary structure.

Several possibilities of structure exist. In most cases, the form of the first part is binary, incipient ternary, or simple ternary. Examples of ternary types are quoted below in melodic outline (Ex. 4.8 and Ex. 4.9), with the opening of Part II included in each case. A binary first part may be seen in Ex. 4.1. It will be observed that Ex. 4.8, an incipient ternary, is entirely in D–flat. Ex. 4.9 is a simple ternary. The traditional repeats are often included.

Ex. 4.8   Beethoven, Sonata in C-sharp minor, Op. 27, No. 2, second movement.

Part II (Trio)

Ex. 4.9   Schubert, Sonata in E-flat, Op. 122, third movement.

Ex. 4.9 (continued)

└─ **Part II (Trio)**

It is possible, but not usual, for the first part to be in period form or a phrase group. According to the foregoing definition of compound ternary form, this would require that Part II be a binary or ternary design, as illustrated in Ex. 4.34.

Obviously, there is often some modulation—of at least an ephemeral sort—in the course of Part I. This can be a basic factor, of course, only in music in which tonality is a pertinent structural feature, and in incipient forms a single key may prevail (Ex. 4.8). Where there is modulation, the traditional key relationships—tonic to dominant or relative—are usually in effect. Part I usually ends in the tonic, with an authentic cadence, as demonstrated in Ex. 4.8 and Ex. 4.9.

There may, at the end of the first section, be a transition of one or more measures, a feature which is treated later in this chapter in the section dealing with the integrated compound ternary form. When there is no transitional passage, the final harmony of Part I must function as a smooth pivot into the following section. This is seen in the Schubert (Ex. 4.9), in which the final harmony (E–flat: I) becomes a dominant in A–flat, leading directly into Part II.

Occasionally Part I is even larger in scope than in any of the examples cited, still forming the basis for a compound ternary, for example *ababa— cdc—ababa*. This type of compound ternary is discussed near the end of this chapter under the heading "extended compound ternary," with a few examples cited. The relationship of the extended compound ternary to a certain type of rondo will also be discussed. In some instances, Part I appears with its various component sections written out in repeats with variations, so that it takes on an unusual size. Part I of the Chopin Nocturne in B, Op. 9, No. 3, is 87 measures long, but it boils down to an incipient ternary in which individual sections are repeated in variation.

The second part

see pg. 82 for additional info. on Part II.

Part II, as in the simple ternary, has the primary function of contrast. If the themes themselves are not unlike those of Part I, there is contrast of another kind, but in most cases different motivic material is introduced. In Ex. 4.10, which shows the beginnings of Parts I and II of a compound ternary, the thematic substance changes while the imitative technique is retained.

Ex. 4.10   Chopin, Sonata No. 1 in C minor, Op. 4, second movement.

Part I

Part II (Trio)

While the second section is not predictably of any particular character in its relationship to the first, the analyst will find certain common tendencies with particular composers and specific types of works. The typical bubbling restlessness of a Beethoven scherzo often pours over into its middle section, so that the form may rely chiefly on harmonic and tonal contrast. In Chopin nocturnes, Part II will frequently represent a change of tempo. Ex. 4.11 shows an unusual change of meter in Part II, and even greater animation than the section it follows, as well as increased dynamic emphasis and urgency.

Ex. 4.11   Beethoven, Symphony No. 6 in F, Op. 68, third movement.

Part I

Part II

In most cases, however, Part II does not depart radically in basic features (tempo, meter) from Part I. A change of key is usual, although often the same tonic is retained while the mode is changed, or there may be an emphasis *on* the dominant rather than *in* the dominant. An instance of the use of parallel keys is shown in Ex. 4.12. This is especially common in movements with trio and *da capo*. Sometimes when the second section is on the same tonic with change to major or minor it is labeled *maggiore* or *minore* as the case may be.

Ex. 4.12   Haydn, Sonata in E-flat (Peters No. 3), second movement.

Part I

Adagio cantabile

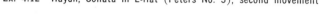

Part II

When Part II is in a different key, the original tonic is avoided until the point of preparation for Part III. Again, the traditional key relationships apply: the most usual modulations in Part II are to the relative, or the dominant or subdominant keys. An exception is shown below, as Ex. 4.13. Ex. 4.8 serves as an illustration of the unusual use of the same key throughout an entire movement.

Ex. 4.13   Bach, St. John Passion, chorus, Ruht wohl (upper part and figured bass).

Part I

(c minor)   6   6   8   6   ♭   7♭ 6   ♮
                         5   ♮   —

Part II

(Bb major)

All the possibilities of form discussed with respect to Part I are applicable here: Part II may be either a two- or three-part design or quite free in form. An example of a second part in simple ternary form is seen in Brahms' *Capriccio* in G minor, Op. 116, No. 3 (proportions of 12–14–7). A symmetrical simple ternary can be seen in Part II of the Chopin Nocturne in G minor, Op. 37, No. 1. A portion of the vocal part of a *lied* is quoted below with indications of cadential harmonies; this is a middle part of freer structure, a phrase group. The over-all form is unusual in that the ternary implications of Part I (not shown) are not actually realized until its recurrence as Part III. Thus, Part I may be represented by the symbol *ab*—(keys of G and D); Part II as a more freely designed phrase group; Part III as *aba* (keys of G, D and G). A relatively large coda is included, incorporating all of the basic material.

Ex. 4.14   Wolf, Epiphanias (No. 19 of the Goethe-Lieder).

Part II

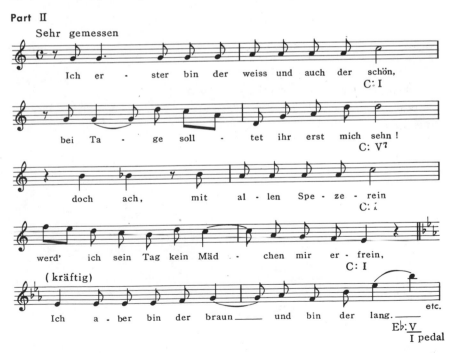

Part II is usually comparable in length to Part I. If it is identical in length, the form is symmetrical, assuming that Part I is returned at the end without change in its length. The quality of symmetry is much rarer in compound ternary form than in smaller forms. Some proportional relationships between Parts I and II are listed below.

Beethoven, Sonata in C minor, Op. 30, No. 2, for piano and violin, third movement.

Part I —48 measures
Part II—36 measures

Beethoven, Trio in E-flat, Op. 70, No. 2, for piano, violin, and cello, third movement.

Part I —56 measures
Part II—52 measures (including transition by dissolution, starting at measure 43 of Part II)

Haydn, Sonata in B minor (Peters No. 33), second movement.

Part I —22 measures
Part II—18 measures

The second part may be taken up with developmental techniques on motives of the first part. In such a case, sequential movement with tonal fluctuation is extremely likely. Ex. 4.15 shows a group of motives as they originally appear in Part I, then their development in a sequential passage in Part II. Part I in this movement is in binary form, its first part moving

Ex. 4.15   Walter Piston, Sonata for violin and piano, second movement.

Part I   m.1 and m.7

Andantino quasi adagio

Part II mm. 31–38

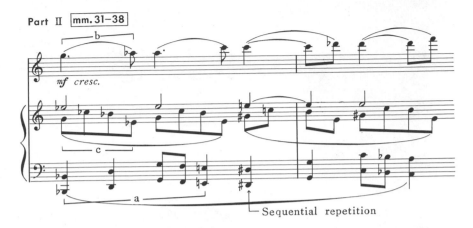

Sequential repetition

to the dominant key and its second part (using the same theme in *mirror inversion*[2]) returning to the tonic key. The second part of the binary in Part III, the recapitulation, starts in the unexpected key of F, working its way back to B minor. The student will observe that the motive labeled *a* in Ex. 4.15 is developed in its mirror inversion in Part II.

Again, the final cadence may lead directly into the next section or there may be a passage of retransition to reintroduce the tonic key and otherwise lay the basis for the return of the original material. Retransitional functions are discussed more extensively later in this chapter. If the final cadence of Part II leads directly into Part III, it is to be expected that it is itself a pivot point for change of key (Ex. 4.16), or that the change to the original tonic has already taken place. In the case of a second part in the parallel major or minor, there is no problem of modulation or tonal preparation.

Ex. 4.16   Brahms, Capriccio in G minor, Op. 116, No. 3.

Un poco meno allegro

[2] *Mirror inversion* is a variation technique, common in all musical styles, whereby a melodic idea, the original or *rectus* form, is turned in opposite directions, interval by interval. For example, the melodic progression down a 2nd, up a 5th, would move, in mirror inversion, up a 2nd, down a 5th. The inversion is said to be "strict" when each interval of the *rectus* form is duplicated exactly in the mirror. If adjustments and modifications in the intervals are made in the mirror inversion, it is said to be "free."

Ex. 4.16 (continued)

g: II⁷
↑—Part III

The third part

As is usual in tripartite forms, Part III is a restatement of the first part. It is therefore normally of the same form and of the same thematic material and key.

Frequently, especially in late eighteenth- and early nineteenth-century works, the middle section is followed by the indication *da capo* (from the beginning), denoting a precise repeat of Part I. This instruction to repeat Part I may take any of the following forms: *da capo e poi la coda* (repeat the first part and then play the coda); *da capo al fine* (repeat the first part "to the end"—to the point marked *fine*); *dal segno* (repeat from the sign 𝄋, used when the repeat of Part I is not from the first note); *da capo senza repetizione* (repeat the first part but do not observe the repeats of its separate sections; this is generally practiced in performance even when not specifically stated).

As was the case with simple ternary form, the third part, when written out, is subject to all kinds of variation treatment. This has been discussed in Chapter 3 and will be treated in subsequent chapters in connection with other forms. It will suffice here to quote from examples of compound ternary form to show a few of the many possibilities of such variation. The reader is reminded that any feature of the original material may be modified—its form, harmony, texture, etc. Embellishment of the melody is especially common.

The return may be abbreviated, Part I being recalled only briefly; often this is adequate to turn back the "arch" of the form to its base. This is what happens in the Chopin Prelude No. 13, mentioned earlier. A further example is quoted as Ex. 4.17. In this Prelude, the return of Part I (originally 27 measures long) is limited to 6 measures, at which point there is a dissolution into the final cadence. The point of dissolution is marked in the example.

Ex. 4.17   Chopin, Prelude No. 15 in D-flat, Op. 28.

Part III   Sostenuto

Ex. 4.18 illustrates the return of a theme with a new contrapuntal associate in Part III, the original theme taken into a different register with the harmony essentially unchanged.

Ex. 4.18   William Schuman, Anticipation, No. 1 from piano cycle Voyage.
Copyright 1954 by Howard Music Company. Reprinted by permission.

Sometimes an element of Part II continues into Part III, merging with the materials of the first part. This seems inevitable in Ex. 4.19, a quotation from the Mendelssohn Violin Concerto. Here, the rhythmic motion in 32nd-notes, established in the second part, is maintained well into Part III. An excerpt from each of the three parts is shown.

Ex. 4.19   Mendelssohn, Concerto in E minor for violin and orchestra, Op. 64, second movement.

The codetta; the coda

A more useful distinction should now be made between the terms *codetta* and *coda,* the former a diminutive of the latter. The coda is defined as the final section to an entire piece or movement—a section in which something more than mere cadential extension or elaboration occurs. We shall not attempt to specify that a coda is of a certain minimum length, but obviously length is a factor in the distinction between a real coda and its corresponding diminutive.

A coda must be judged as having *significant* length and substance—thematic statement or development. A codetta, on the other hand, is defined as: (1) the closing section to a major *part* in the over-all form; or (2) the closing section to the entire piece or movement when the material of which it is composed is of minor significance, serving chiefly to intensify the decisiveness of the final cadence, and of minor dimensions as well; or (3) the simple repetition of an earlier closing section (codetta) occurring within the body of the over-all form. Often the analyst must decide for himself, but he must be prepared to underscore his judgment with sound reason and logic.

Some theorists define "codetta" as the closing section for a part of a piece and "coda" as the final closing section, regardless of other factors. But this simple distinction breaks down when one considers that often (as will be remembered from preceding chapters) the two are in fact identical and it is therefore unreasonable to describe one by one term, the other by another term.

The reader may ask if there is any point in making a distinction; is it not more reasonable to apply a single term—say, *coda*—to all closing sections? The answer is that in examples in musical literatures, many of them already cited, there is a clear separation of degrees of functional significance as detailed above. This factor of significance becomes particularly apparent in Chapters 5 and 6, which deal with larger forms than have been discussed before. Of course, the experience of studying the content of a closing section, and the conclusions drawn from such study, are more important than the specific label assigned to the example under consideration. But on the basis of the distinction established here, the use of the term "codetta" in place of "coda" bears definite and important implications as to the character, scope, and content of the passage in question. Therefore, there is a point in the use of the two terms and the distinction drawn between them.

In tripartite forms, closing sections occur more commonly at the conclusions of Parts I and III than in connection with Part II, as was observed in connection with the simple ternary. An important point should be repeated here: if a closing section is attached to Part III it is often *an enlarged version of the codetta to Part I*, having a "setting-off point" which corresponds. In Ex. 4.20, the "final" tonic of the original codetta is

Ex. 4.20   Brahms, Trio in C, Op. 87, for piano, violin, and cello, third movement.

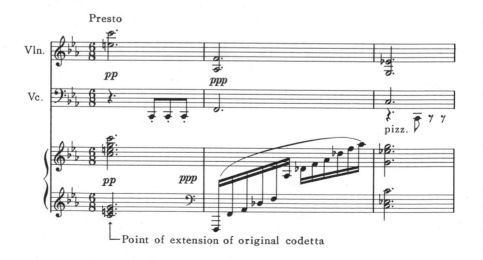

└─Point of extension of original codetta

followed, at the end of the movement, by several additional measures of chromatic cadential harmonies. The beginnings of the two codettas are identical, as the reader will see if he compares measures 52 and 161.

Ex. 4.21 illustrates a sectional codetta.[3] The various sections of the codetta are parts of a single division in the form because of their obvious thematic and structural identity. This material, unlike that of Ex. 4.20, is appended to Part I, a simple ternary form. It is set off by an elided imperfect authentic cadence, weakened by the use of the first inversion of the tonic. A similar cadence occurs four measures later. At the next cadence point, indicated in the quotation, the tonic is avoided by the use of the submediant, followed by a strong (IV–V–I) cadential formula in the final two measures.

Ex. 4.21   Mozart, String Quartet in B-flat, K. 589, third movement.

[3] See page 44 for additional discussion of this concept. The fact that codettas may be sectional must be understood in view of the definition of the closing section as set off by the *latest* cadence of the section to which it is appended.

Ex. 4.21 (continued)

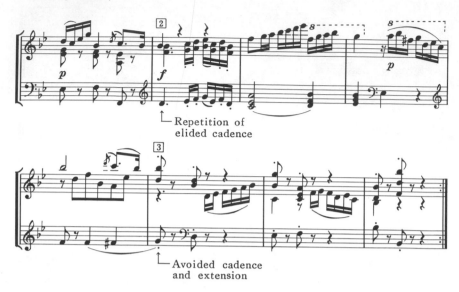

In compound ternary form the first part may end in one of three ways: (1) by a simple authentic cadence which, as a pivot harmony, leads directly into Part II; (2) with a codetta—an elaboration or extension of such a cadence, ending on the same tonic harmony; or (3) with a transitional passage which, tonally and thematically, forms a bridge into Part II. If there is a transition, it will in most cases preclude strong cadential interruption between Parts I and II, leaving the tonic key if part of its function is modulation. A codetta, on the other hand, puts a decisive stamp of finality on the section it closes.

The larger the form, the more likely it is to have a coda at its close rather than a codetta. Compound ternary form is the first in our line of discussion which occasionally has a real coda. Excerpts from such a coda are shown as Ex. 4.22. Part I of this example ends with a perfect authentic cadence in A minor (a, below). At the end of the reprise (Part III) this cadence is modified; it becomes a half-cadence (b) which is repeated three times, prolonging the dominant feeling of the cadence. At this point, the second part of the cadential formula is repeated twice (c), after which the dominant prolongation is continued through three measures of figuration (d) in piano and violin (only the piano part is shown). The basic theme of the movement returns briefly, developed in a short sequence (e). A perfect authentic cadence three measures later sets off a new section of free imitation between the two instruments (f). This leads to the final cadence, in which the tonic is repeated twice (g). Obviously this example, because of its size and the significance of its material, is a coda.

Ex. 4.22   Beethoven, Sonata in A, Op. 12, No. 2, for piano and violin, second movement.

Ex. 4.22 (continued)

Another example is found in the second movement of the Berlioz *Symphonie Fantastique,* Op. 14, which has a large sectional coda beginning at measure 256, with "seams" at measures 272, 288, 302, 320, 338, and 353, from which point there is a rapid, *stringendo* movement to the end. Another example is the third movement of Beethoven's Piano Trio in E–flat, Op. 70, No. 2; in this movement the coda, consisting of the final 24 measures, is formed of materials of Parts I and II.

Compound ternary form with da capo

Further mention should be made of that species of compound ternary form, common in the eighteenth and nineteenth centuries, consisting of a middle section often called a *trio* followed by a literal *da capo* restatement of Part I.

The term *trio* as applied to Part II of this type of ternary design is in most cases inapplicable in any strict sense, but it is so firmly established and is of such minor importance that it can be accepted and understood to have this as well as its more literal meaning. Its use stems from a Baroque practice—that of dance pairs in which the second, in a texture of three voices, was followed in *alternativo* fashion by repetition of the first, forming a ternary pattern in which Part II was literally a trio. The final movement of Bach's *Brandenburg Concerto* No. 1 in F is a case in point, actually containing two such trios, forming digressions for the rondo-like repetition of the minuet.

Ex. 4.23   Bach, Brandenburg Concerto No. 1 in F, final movement.

Trio No. 1

Trio No. 2

In sonatas, symphonies and chamber works of the eighteenth and ninteenth centuries the compound ternary form with *da capo* occurs principally as one of two middle movements in a four-movement scheme, usually the third. It is commonly a minuet with trio or a scherzo with trio. In the late eighteenth century the former is more often the case, the scherzo becoming more common in the nineteenth century. The evolution of the sweeping, sometimes very powerful scherzo (see Beethoven's Ninth Symphony) from the elegant and courtly minuet is one of the most interesting episodes in music history.

An important structural feature of the compound ternary with *da capo*, one to be emphasized here, is that it is most often characterized by decisive cadential separations between the three major divisions without bridging, transitional sections. An example is shown as Ex. 4.24; only the ends of

Ex. 4.24   Handel, Why do the nations so furiously rage?, bass aria from Messiah.

Parts I and II are quoted. This is not, of course, to say that such separations are entirely peculiar to the form with *da capo,* nor that transitions never occur in this type of ternary form (see Ex. 4.28).

A more exceptional *da capo* is shown as Ex. 4.25. Here, the close of Part II is followed by a codetta-like transitional passage which clearly re-establishes the original key of F major. The passage may be termed a *transitional codetta:* it is at the same time an emphatic cadential appendage to Part II and, in its modulatory function, a preparation for the restatement of Part I. Often, in examples with repeats, the simple expedient of first and second endings is used to effect smoother passage from one section to another.

Ex. 4.25 Pergolesi, La Serva Padrona, bass aria from Act I.

An extension of the formal design outlined here is brought about by the insertion, after the reprise of the first part, of a second trio, which is followed by a further restatement of Part I. Thus, a five-part form evolves, a rondo design. The second trio may be identical to the first, as in the Beethoven Fourth Symphony. In the third movement of this work, the pattern of repetition is as follows: scherzo, trio, scherzo, trio (identical to the first), scherzo and coda. The scherzo and trio are initially of almost equivalent lengths. The scherzo, in its final appearance, is cut to less than half its original length.

An example of a movement with two *different* trios is the scherzo of Schumann's Symphony No. 1 in B–flat, Op. 38. Its first trio, in duple meter, is in the parallel major key of D; the second, in triple meter, is in B-flat. Both restatements of the original scherzo are shortened—especially the final one, which is followed by a coda.

Bach's *Brandenburg Concerto* No. 1 (Ex. 4.23) carries the principle even further. Its final movement, a compound form, is in seven major parts: minuet, trio I, minuet (*da capo* each time), *polacca,*[4] minuet, trio II, minuet.

The repeats in the ternary with da capo

The component binary and ternary forms of the compound ternary often occur with their usual repeats, especially in the sonata movement with trio and *da capo*. Thus, in an example in which the three sections are small ternaries, the pattern of repeats might be the following. (The symbols *c* and *d* are used for Part II even though the material may be related to that of Part I.)

I	II	III
a:‖:ba:‖	c:‖:dc:‖	aba (*da capo senza repetizione*)

In a movement in which the second part, for example, is binary, the pattern might be the following.

I	II	III
a:‖:ba:‖	c:‖:d:‖	aba

It is clear that while the pattern of sectional structure and tonal change is elaborated by the repeats, the fundamental ternary design is unaltered. (See the section on extended compound ternary form near the end of this chapter.)

The use of repeats in movements of more than one trio varies considerably. For example, in the third movement of Beethoven's Fourth Symphony, the initial statement of the scherzo is in simple ternary form with the usual repeats, but no further repeats are used. In the scherzo of the First Symphony of Schumann, the first part and the *second* trio (both simple ternaries) have repeats, but no other section employs them.

Even in the more common ternary with one trio the use of repeats varies a great deal. Thus, in the Schubert Impromptu in A–flat, Op. 90, No. 4, no repeats are used in Part I, while the second part employs the standard repeats of the simple ternary form. Sometimes, especially in examples lacking the literal *da capo*, repeats may be omitted altogether, or they may be written out, frequently with variation. In Chopin's Nocturne in A–flat, Part I is an incipient ternary (*a–ba,* of which the *ba* is written out a second time without variation) ; when this material returns as Part III, the same portions are repeated, this time with variation.

---

[4] The *polacca* (It.) is a *polonaise,* discussed in Chapter 10.

Ex. 4.26   Chopin, Nocturne in A-flat, Op. 32, No. 2.

The integrated compound ternary; transition and retransition

The integrated compound ternary, like the ternary with trio and *da capo*, is a species within the general category of compound ternary forms. These two species share identical structural possibilities except that in the integrated type (1) repeat signs are less common and lacking even more in any norm of arrangement, (2) the third section is written out rather than being a *da capo* return, and (3) there is less pronounced cadential interruption at the points dividing Parts I and II, and II and III, with bridging often achieved by the use of a transitional figure or passage. The adjective "integrated" obviously will apply to any compound ternary example in which the major cadential seams are obscured by elision or transition, and in which there is a written out recapitulation involving change of some kind rather than a simple *da capo*.

A specific example, the third movement of Brahms' Symphony No. 3 in F, Op. 90, is outlined as Ex. 4.27 to show how the characteristics of the integrated compound ternary appear in a given case.

Ex. 4.27

Part I (Simple ternary)

 a—Measures 1–24. Best characterized as a double period, with half-cadences at measure 8, measure 12, measure 20, and a perfect authentic cadence at measure 24; there are motive punctuations within each phrase, as in measures 2 and 4 in the first phrase.

b—Measures 24–36. Brief development of motive

in C major and A minor, ending on half-cadence in A minor.

Transition—Measures 36–41. Anticipates motive of *a* and modulates back to C minor.

a—Measures 41–52. A single period, only half of the original statement.

Transition—Measures 52–53. Very brief link between Parts I and II, yet clearly transitional, entering abruptly on the second beat of measure 52, anticipating the harmony with which Part II begins.

Part II (Incipient ternary)

a—Measures 54–61. Phrase or 2-phrase unit, introduces key of A-flat, ends with half-cadence.

a—Measures 62–69. Same material in variation.

b—Measures 70–78. Contrast touching keys of G-sharp minor and B major, by enharmonic change, before returning to A-flat; ends on half-cadence.

a—Measures 79–86.

Transition—Measures 87–98. On material of II-b, dissolving and modulating to C minor; ends on German 6th chord in C minor, having anticipated the motive of Part I.

Part III

Measures 99–150. Same structure as Part I, but with changes of accompanimental pattern and orchestration.

Coda

Measures 150–163. Leans toward A-flat at outset but quickly reaffirms C minor; material is reminiscent of both Parts I and II in brief mounting and descending line.

Transitions may occur in the compound ternary with trio and *da capo*, although much less commonly than in forms like that cited in Ex. 4.27 and with less thorough integration. An example of a ternary with *da capo* having transitions is cited as Ex. 4.28. Here, the transition into Part II actually follows and is distinct from the strong cadential ending of Part I, rather than emerging out of it. This type of transition does not effect as high a degree of integration as, for example, those cited in Ex. 4.27.

Ex. 4.28   Brahms, Trio in E-flat, Op. 40, for piano, violin, and horn, second movement.

It will be instructive at this point to discuss and illustrate important features of some transitional passages from specimens of the compound ternary form. Transitions are normally not more than a few measures in length, in a form of this scope, and they may even be as short as a single measure or two. Ex. 4.27 illustrates a transition of a single measure, a single chord. Ex. 4.29 shows a transitional measure from a twentieth-century aria. In this aria, Part I is a simple ternary; at the end of Part I, shown in the example, an expected cadence in C is altered by the sudden leading toward D. This is followed by a transition in which *chromatic progression*[5]

[5] The theory of *chromatic progression, chromatic harmony,* and *chromatic modulation* (the latter defined on p. 125) is complex and can be treated only summarily in this context.

A *chromatic progression* is one between harmonies having no diatonic relationship, harmonies which do not coexist in any single diatonic system of key and mode. For this purpose, the harmonic form of the minor scale is considered the tonal-harmonic basis of its diatonic system. A usual characteristic of the chromatic progression is a single or multiple *chromatic inflection*—the change of one or more notes from one form (sharp, natural, or flat) to another.

A *diatonic progression* involves two harmonies deriving from any single, unaltered tonal system.

The exclusion of the melodic minor in the definition of the *basic* diatonic system takes into account that its use, extremely frequent in traditional styles, is the product more of coloristic and melodic than of functional harmonic needs. The m: $\frac{\sharp}{6}$ can be a chromatic alteration of modal interchange in the same sense as the m: $\frac{\sharp}{3}$ of the tonic cadence, or the $\frac{\flat}{6}$ of M:IV. Chromaticism can thus be a device of color as well as function—m: $\frac{\sharp}{3}$ (Picardy third) an example of the former, $\frac{\sharp}{4}$ nearly always the latter. Occurring in neither of the two principal modes, $\frac{\sharp}{4}$ is a chromatic alteration of greater severity than modal color changes of the 3rd and 6th degrees.

A few examples will help clarify the implications of the above definitions, which consider bimodality an important source of chromaticism, and which recognize the 3rd and 6th degrees as major-minor determinants, the leading-tone as having an essential function in the tonal system, and the $\frac{\flat}{7}$ as a contradiction of that system— a leaning, not necessarily modulatory, toward the relative major. M:IV-II$_{\frac{\sharp}{4}}$ is an example of a progression which is chromatic by all possible criteria. The progressions m:IV-V and m:V-I contain, by the above definitions, chromatic alterations of modal
    $\frac{\sharp}{6}$ $\frac{\sharp}{3}$
origin—interchange of major-minor features, but the *progressions* are *diatonic*, since in each case the two harmonies have diatonic coexistence in a given key, namely the parallel major.

However, when the IV contains a minor 7th, the classification is altered: the
    $\frac{\sharp}{6}$
progression is then considered chromatic since the two harmonies do *not* have a diatonic relationship in any major or harmonic minor tonal system. In the major mode, the progression involves the chromatic, modal lowering of the 3rd degree (from the parallel minor); in the minor mode, it involves the raised 6th degree (from the parallel major).

The harmonies of the progression m:III-V$_4$, the V containing the leading-tone
    $\frac{\flat}{7}$ $_3$
of the harmonic minor, would be of the same diatonic system *if that system were considered to encompass the forms of the melodic minor,* but the progression is chromatic, as the ear immediately perceives, in the light of the above definitions and by virtue of its chromatic inflection. (Footnote continued on p. 110.)

leads into the key of F, which prevails in Part II. This is a reminder that transitions are often modulatory, introducing tonal change after Part I, or restoring the original tonal level for Part III.

Ex. 4.29   Stravinsky, Persephone, aria of Eumolpe (Rehearsal No. 140).
Copyright 1934 by Edition Russe de Musique; renewed 1961. Revised version copyright 1950 by Boosey & Hawkes, Inc. Reprinted by permission.

Often a transition, instead of following the cadential close of the preceding section, occurs in lieu of such a cadence—that is, out of the dissolution of the form of the preceding section and the avoidance of the expected cadence. In Ex. 4.30, dissolution begins at the end of measure 6 of the quotation, where the motive last heard is taken up in development leading eventually into F, the key of the following section. Only a sketch of the passage is shown.

Ex. 4.30   Berlioz, Symphonie Fantastique, Op. 14, second movement.

Progressions involving augmented-6th chords are chromatic, despite the usual absence of inflection. For example, m:IV-V is a chromatic progression; diatonic coexistence of the two harmonies is not possible since the first occurs in no diatonic system.

Finally, m:I-N₆ involves a chromatic harmony, but the *progression* (i.e., the relationship) is *diatonic*: the two harmonies are diatonically related in the submediant major key, or, if the progression occurs in the major mode, in its subdominant minor. These relationships constitute a bond linking the two harmonies—a bond clearly acknowledged in the classification of the progression as diatonic.

The material of the transition may be any of a number of types, as will be discussed more thoroughly in Chapter 6. It may consist of figuration having no thematic importance. Or it may be motivically related to both of the two sections to which it forms a bridge. The logic of such a transition is apparent. Ex. 4.31 is a transition joining Parts I and II; motive *a* is from Part I, motive *b* from Part II. A transition may, of course, be related motivically to either of the adjacent sections and not to the other.

Ex. 4.31 Brahms, Ballade in G minor, Op. 118, No. 3.

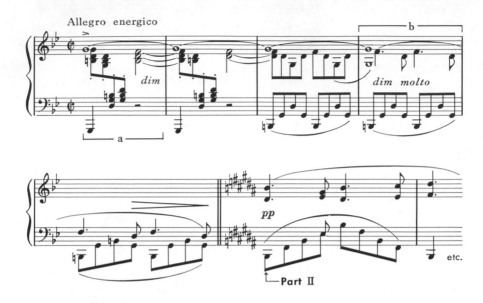

In the Chopin Nocturne from which Ex. 4.32 is taken, Parts I and II are in parallel keys. Not only is there no transition but the cadence ending Part I is actually elided to the beginning of Part II. This must be considered another kind of integration in ternary form, since it is an avoidance of cadential break.

Ex. 4.32 Chopin, Nocturne in B, Op. 9, No. 3.

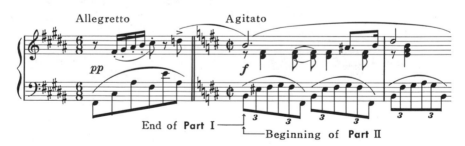

The transition into Part III was explained briefly in Chapter 3 as a *retransition* involving preparation of the original key and the original material, often characterized, especially in larger forms, by the prolongation of a point of tonal instability (V, usually) as a tension-building device. Example 4.33 illustrates the three factors of retransitional preparation:

tonal preparation (modulation to E–flat minor by *enharmonic-chromatic progression*[6]) ; motivic preparation (use in the retransition of · the steady triplet motion which is basic to Part III) ; and harmonic prolongation, consisting of four measures of dominant harmony. The *ritardando* just before Part III makes the dominant prolongation longer than it appears. The tonal relationship between Parts II and III is astounding on the surface (B minor to E–flat), but the relationship seems closer when one realizes that the E–flat minor tonic is, enharmonically interpreted, the mediant harmony in the key of B. A further illustration of this type of transition is to be seen in the Schubert Impromptu No. 4 in A–flat, also of Op. 90.

Ex. 4.33   Schubert, Impromptu in E-flat, Op. 90, No. 2.

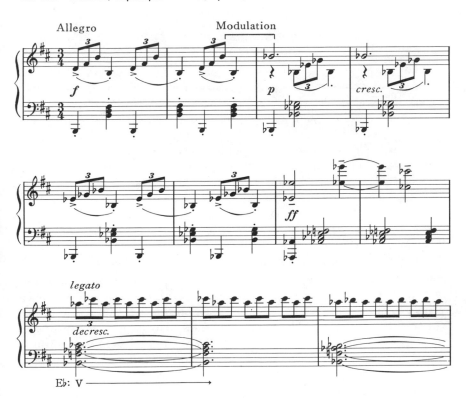

---

6 An *enharmonic-chromatic progression* is one in which there is enharmonic change (D-flat to C sharp, E sharp to F-natural) in addition to chromatic inflection. An *enharmonic-diatonic progression* contains enharmonic change but no chromatic inflection—e.g., the triad C-flat-E-flat-G-flat progressing to the triad D sharp-F sharp-A sharp, to which, with enharmonic interpretation, it is "diatonically" related. Such a progression is an important device in modulation.

Ex. 4.33 (continued)

Integrated compound ternary forms are common among nineteenth-century piano pieces and slow movements of multi-movement sonata forms.

Extended compound ternary form

The term *extended compound ternary* refers to a type in which one of the three parts is more extensive than either the binary or the simple ternary. The total effect of such a form is comparable to that of the normal compound ternary with individual parts repeated, but the extensions are usually of greater diversity and significance than direct, literal repeats.

An example of extended compound ternary form, cited for reference, is the *adagio* movement from Haydn's Sonata in E-flat (Peters No. 3). Its first part consists of five sections in the pattern *ababa,* the digression, *b,* occurring on the dominant harmony rather than in the dominant key. (See measure 17.) Part II is in the parallel minor and its relative major. The reprise, Part III, is a simple ternary, *aba,* followed by a sectional, 16-measure coda set off by a deceptive cadence.

The second movement of Brahms' Trio in E–flat, Op. 40, is another example. This is a compound ternary with trio and *da capo;* its first part, the scherzo, is even more extensive in structure than the example mentioned in the foregoing paragraph: *abacab(a),* without repeat signs. The use of parentheses in the symbol indicates that the final return of the theme is a mere suggestion, consisting of little more than a strong reaffirmation of the tonic key, after which there is a transition into the trio (Ex. 4.28).

A final example of extended compound ternary form which the student may wish to investigate is the *Queen Mab Scherzo* from Berlioz's *Romeo and Juliet,* Op. 17. In each of the above examples, Part II is larger and more contrasting than the digressions within Part I; thus, Part II gives a feeling of satisfactory balance to all of Part I. For these reasons the over-all form is regarded as ternary.

Debussy, String Quartet in G minor, Op. 10, third movement

The discussions of this chapter will be summarized and drawn into focus by Ex. 4.34, taken from Debussy's String Quartet (third movement), a late nineteenth-century example of compound ternary form. The melodic outline is given, together with indications of chief cadence points, key levels, and principal divisions in the form.

The Debussy movement is an example of compound ternary form in which only Part II is a simple ternary; Part I is a phrase group centering in the key of D-flat. Part II begins with a modal theme in C-sharp, the parallel enharmonic key, taking the form of a phrase group; at measure 21 of Part II a characteristic theme enters and undergoes rather extensive modulatory development, some of it sequential, finally dissolving into a transition which modulates chromatically back to C–sharp for the return of the original theme, now reduced to two phrases. The reprise of Part I in the over-all form is also abbreviated, the movement as a whole being extremely asymmetrical, with proportions of 23–75–17. This seems a less radical asymmetry when one remembers that the middle part is slightly faster, and in a meter of 3/8 rather than 6/8.

Ex. 4.34   Debussy, String Quartet in G minor, Op. 10, third movement.
Permission for reprint granted by Durand et Cie., Paris, France, copyright owners, and Elkan-Vogel Co., Inc., Philadelphia, Pa., agents.

Ex. 4.34 (continued)

sequential development (e – a – f# – g#)

into dissolution and
retransition

Ex. 4.34 (continued)

The Debussy movement, within each of its three major divisions, is a rewarding basis for study of similarities and subtle variations from phrase to phrase. Very striking are the variations in phrase length in Part II. The long extension of the final phrase of Part I, with its irresistible rise and fall, is effectively climactic just preceding the pronounced cadential settling before the middle section.

The means by which units are joined—by elision, by maintenance of internal movement—should be studied in the complete score. A point should be made of *listening* for all of the structural qualities, and for the unusual harmonic and instrumental colors within a framework of traditional form and tonal function.

While there is no codetta, the final cadence is broadened into a perfectly conclusive gesture. The phrase in which the theme returns in octaves is dissolved *(un peu retenu)* by continued ascent in unsettled, syncopated rhythms. At the restoration of tempo, on the steadier rhythm of the principal motive, cadential feeling is initiated: 2 measures of "dominant," 3 measures of "tonic" (see all four parts), and the final plagal progression from an altered II_7 to an imperfect tonic—reminiscent of the cadence which concludes the opera *Tristan und Isolde* by Richard Wagner (1813–83).

Relationships to the rondo

The reasoning which occasionally classifies the compound ternary as a type of "rondo" is considered to be doubtful for the same reasons as those given in rejection of the rondo designation for simple ternary form. On the other hand, the rondo principle may be said to be incipient in the compound ternary, even more extensively than in the smaller form.

When the first part of a compound ternary form is a simple ternary, a design results which is, on the surface, quite like that of the sonata-rondo form, treated in Chapter 7.

But several important distinctions set the two forms apart: (1) the extended rondo form is more often and more thoroughly integrated, the effect being one of a more continuous fabric; (2) the scope of each minor division in the ternary design (each *a*, each *b*, etc.) is normally smaller than the corresponding sections in the rondo; (3) the tonal structure of the third major division is a further distinction—the final *b* digression in the sonata-rondo is most often in the original tonic key; (4) in a genuine rondo the first contrasting section, *b,* is much more digressive both in key and material than in the ternary norm, in which *b* is usually taken from *a* so that the *aba* of Part I form a more cohesive unit than in the rondo; and (5) the middle section in the large rondo is frequently developmental, a feature not characteristic of the ternary form.

But despite the most careful attempt at clarity of definition, problems of classification persist. As an example, we may cite the final movement of Haydn's String Quartet in D, Op. 64, No. 5. This movement is normally described as a rondo (sonata-rondo, extended rondo, third rondo) and it clearly is of a design which we may represent by the symbol *aba c aba*. The *b* section is digressive in key more than in material, and when it returns in the final division it is in its original key, unlike the usual practice in sonata-rondo form. The movement is a modest one in dimensions, the opening theme, *a*, having the form of an 8-measure period. But the middle section, *c*, which is in the parallel minor, *is* fairly extensive; while it maintains a thematic relationship to the opening materials, it sets out on a vigorous, fugal scheme of development before a retransition prepares the return of *a*. While there is a pronounced cadence at, for example, the end of the initial ternary, there is marvelous integration throughout the movement in the sense that sixteenth-note motion is incessant except in the final measures. The best description of this movement, as in many other cases, is that which points out those of its features which relate it to the rondo, and those which relate it to compound ternary form. (See also Chapter 7, pp. 239–40.) Nothing is gained by insisting upon a particular classification, although much is gained *in consideration of the problem of classification,* even when it results in the decision that no major category satisfactorily suits the example at hand. Analysis of the question of classification will eventuate, if conducted with perception and in depth, in an understanding of many aspects of the form of the music.

Exercises and examples for further study

1. Find an example of compound ternary form in which no codettas are present. Try writing some codettas, limiting yourself to a few measures of cadential elaboration.

2. Try inserting brief transitional passages into an example in which the main divisions are not bridged.

3. Find a Part III which is a literal reprise. Write out the first two measures three or four times, showing possible variations on the material.

4. Write the melody line of a compound ternary of your own, showing key levels and harmony at principal cadence points.

5. Find examples of the integrated compound ternary form to demonstrate various kinds of transition.

6. Analyze the second movement of Mozart's Sonata in C, K. 330, according to the following points.
   a) Mark the three major parts.
   b) Are there codettas?
   c) Is there a coda?
   d) Outline the tonal structure by listing the key levels and telling where each appears.

e) Identify the basic motivic materials of each section.

f) Classify the cadence forms according to the terminology given in Chapter 1.

g) Consider symmetry versus asymmetry in the over-all design and within each of the sections.

h) What motivic relationships, if any, are there between Parts I and II?

7. Explain, in a paragraph of your own, the differences between simple and compound ternary forms.

8. Try writing a 2- or 3-measure introduction (chordal or otherwise, ending on the dominant) to a specific compound ternary which has none. Consider carefully what the effect of the introductory passage should be, and try to make it "set the stage" for the beginning of the form proper.

9. Find an example of compound ternary form in one of the following sources. Be prepared to discuss its important features, considering all points discussed in the chapter to the extent that they are relevant to the example you select.

a) Dances in *alternativo* form from eighteenth-century suites.

b) *Da capo* arias from seventeenth- and eighteenth-century operas and oratorios.

c) Piano pieces of the nineteenth century.

10. Consider whether either or both of the following are compound (as well as ternary) in form. Assemble the best possible arguments to support your view. If you feel that firm classification is not possible, explain why.

a) Debussy, *L'Après-midi d'un Faune,* prelude for orchestra.

b) Ravel, *Menuet* from the *Sonatine* for piano.

11. The following are suggestions for further study and are intended to supplement the many works cited in Chapter 4.

Bach, French Suite No. 3 in B minor, minuet

Bartók, Concerto No. 3 for piano and orchestra, second movement

Brahms, Concerto in D, Op. 77, for violin and orchestra, slow movement

Beethoven, Sonata in E-flat, Op. 7, slow movement (integrated)
   Symphony No. 3 in E-flat, Op. 55, slow movement

Debussy, Prelude, *Feuilles Mortes,* from Book II

Mozart, String Quartet in B-flat, K. 589, final movement

Arnold Schönberg (1874–1951), Suite for piano, Op. 25, minuet

Giuseppe Verdi (1813–1901), *Falstaff,* dance from Act III, Scene II

Hugo Wolf (1860–1903), *Nimmersatte Liebe*

5

RONDO

pg 628 Analysis

The rondo can be conceived as an expansion of ternary form in which there is a further contrasting section and a second reprise. Rondo form thus comprises a recurring theme or complex alternating with contrasting episodes, and having at least five sections as opposed to the three of ternary form.

The rondo form, like ternary, is sometimes characterized by analogy with an arch, because of its rounded design framed by the first and final statements of like thematic material. While it is often argued that the spatial, physical symbol of the arch is inappropriate and even misleading when related to music, the suggestiveness of the symbol is easy to see.

Many discussions of the rondo describe it as having a cheerful, sprightly character; indeed, it is true that such adjectives apply to many examples of the form as found in the literatures of the past three centuries. But it is better to avoid a generalization that must exclude many other examples, thinking of the rondo as a formal structure rather than as a musical expression of any particular character. Rondo form is often used as the basis for the final movement of a multi-movement work, occurring in symphonies, sonatas, chamber works, and concertos. The examples cited in this chapter will show that it is also used in individual pieces and, more rarely, in slow movements.

The application of the principles of unity and variety remains fundamental. The larger the form, the more complex the problems of balance and integration—of the distribution and equilibrium of the elements of unity and contrast.

Occasionally a composer deliberately places materials of an extremely different, seemingly contradictory character side by side for dramatic effect. Such extreme contrast occurs in Ex. 5.1. Not only are the two strongly dissimilar themes abruptly contiguous, but Beethoven has also deliberately avoided any suggestion of transition or preparation of the digressive material.

As part of the dramatic quality of the music, there is even a *crescendo* just preceding the appearance of the new section, emphasizing and intensifying the suddenness of the change. Moreover, the change of tempo and the chromatic progression have an important function in the dramatic effect. The movement as a whole is a rondo form (ABABA).

Ex. 5.1   Beethoven, Sonata in E, Op. 109, first movement.

In the following pages, particular examples of the individual parts of the rondo design will be cited and discussed. Since most of the component parts (theme, transition, coda, etc.) have been amply defined in connection with other forms, we shall emphasize in this chapter the analytical discussion of quoted passages from rondos of various periods.

Historical backgrounds of the rondo principle

There is no general agreement regarding the origin of the rondo. Discussion of what is known concerning antecedents of the rondo, and further speculation as to its origin, are beyond the scope of this book, but it will be valuable to point out some sources for study of the history of the rondo, as well as some examples of types of music and specific works that undoubtedly have a place in that history.

There is a clear analogy to be drawn between the rondo, with its series of statements of a particular thematic idea alternating with digressive themes or episodes, and that type of song which alternates between stanza and refrain. This is a familiar scheme in many songs from popular sources, some of them very ancient; and songs of this kind are sometimes cited as among the ancestors of the modern rondo.

The medieval *rondeau*, a poetic form found in many of the monophonic songs of the French *trouvères*, is a microcosmic embodiment of the principle of repetition after digression. A late twelfth-century example of one Guillaume d'Amiens is quoted below. The vertical series of letters at the side indicates the recurrences of two musical entities which are the setting for the poem. The first of these (A) is of one phrase, the second (B) two. The poetic refrain is indicated by the symbol *R*.

R	A	Vos n'aler mie si com je faz.
R	B	Ne vos, ne vos n'i savez aler,
R		Ne vos, ne vos n'i savez aler.
	A	Bele Aaliz par main se leva,
R	A	Vos n'aler mie si com je faz.
	A	Biau se vesti et mieuz se para.
	B	Bonjor ait cele que n'os nomez;
		Sovant m'i fait ele soupirer.
R	A	Vos n'aler mie si com je faz.
R	B	Ne vos, ne vos n'i savez aler,
R		Ne vos, ne vos n'i savez aler.
R	A	You do not live as I do.
R	B	Nor do you know how,
R		Nor do you know how.
	A	Fair Alice got up one morning,
R	A	(You do not live as I do.)
	A	Prettily clothed and better adorned.
	B	Good-day to her whom I dare not name;
		Often she causes me to sigh.
R	A	You do not live as I do.
R	B	Nor do you know how,
R		Nor do you know how.

The music for this *trouvère* song may be seen in the first volume of the *Historical Anthology of Music,* where it appears as No. 19e.   No. 14 of this volume contains Gregorian *responsoria* in which alternation between solo verses and choral responses is suggestive of the later rondo, as pointed out by the editors.

A further example in this same volume is the three-voiced *Deix soit* (No. 36c) by Adam de la Halle (c. 1230–1287). This piece follows the scheme ABABA and is thus, in the editors' words, "interesting as an early instance of the modern rondo, ababa, a form which did not come into general use until after 1650."[1]

An important and immediate precursor of the eighteenth-century rondo is the seventeenth-century instrumental *rondeau* with refrain and changing *couplets*. Again, we refer to the Apel-Davison *Anthology* for examples. No. 212 (Vol. II) is a seventeenth-century example of Jacques Champion de Chambonnières (c. 1597–1672), a harpsichord chaconne in which theme recurrences are separated by *couplets* to form a total of eleven parts. In the same volume, a seventeenth-century set of organ variations by Georg Muffat

---

[1] A. T. Davison and Willi Apel, eds., *Historical Anthology of Music,* Vol. I (Cambridge: Harvard University Press, 1946, 1949), p. 219.

(c. 1645–1704), No. 240, has the original theme returning after the 5th, 11th, 17th, and 23rd variations, thus conforming to the rondo principle. Somewhat later examples of *rondeau* types are Nos. 265b and 277 in the same volume; the first of these is a 7-part harpsichord *rondeau* by Couperin, and the second a 5-part *rondeau* from the opera *Dardanus* by Rameau.

Another pre-Classical example is the *gavotte* movement from Bach's Partita No. 3 in E for solo violin—a work which will be familiar to most of the readers of this book. This movement contains five statements (four returns) of an 8-measure, symmetrical rondo theme. The form may be represented by the diagram A:‖B A C A D A E A. The first digression is in C-sharp minor, the second in B, the third in F-sharp minor, and the fourth in G-sharp minor. The final statement of the rondo theme is a *da capo* repetition. The movement presents no difficulties of analysis, where its formal design is concerned, and the reader is encouraged to undertake a careful study of the score.

Rondo form further defined

The type of rondo form with which this chapter is chiefly concerned has five essential parts and might be labelled a "five-part rondo" to distinguish it from rondos of similar principle but of seven or more parts.

In this form, there are three appearances of the basic thematic material separated by two similar or dissimilar contrasting sections, called *digressions*. The form proper may be preceded by introductory material and may be followed by a closing section, a codetta or a coda. The form may but often does not include bridging passages between sections.

The usual diagrammatic symbol for this form is **ABABA**, when the second digression is built of the same theme or themes as the first, and **ABACA** when the two digressions are of different materials.

Ex. 5.2 illustrates part of a rondo of small dimensions, given here in melodic outline. It is of the type, ABABA. The rondo theme, A, is related to the digression. At the same time, there is strong tonal contrast: the digression occurs both times in the mediant major without preparation (i.e., by direct *chromatic modulation*).[2] The divisions between parts are clearly marked by double-bars and changes of key signature. In the example only the first two parts (*AB*ABA) are shown; the repetitions proceed with perfect regularity.

2 A *chromatic modulation* is one in which the new key is approached through a chromatic progression (q. v.); a *diatonic modulation* approaches the new key through a diatonic progression.

Ex. 5.2 Schubert, Der Musensohn.

Another Schubert song in rondo form (like that of *Der Musensohn*) is the first of the *lieder* on Scott's *Lady of the Lake, Raste Krieger, Krieg ist aus.* In this song, Schubert uses enharmonic change to modulate from five flats to three sharps. The reader will find it helpful to examine this additional, very clear specimen of rondo form.

Examples for discussion:

The introduction

The introduction, if present at all, may consist of anything from a single stroke to several phrases, and may be of simple, figural content or important motivic material.

In Ex. 5.3, the introduction is a mere attention-calling sounding of the dominant root, of indefinite length.

Ex. 5.3   Schubert, Impromptu in C minor, Op. 90.

The final movement of Mendelssohn's Piano Concerto in G minor begins with a 39-measure introduction before the rondo theme appears. (This introductory passage also serves to link the second and third movements, leading from A minor to G major in preparation for the rondo.) Nineteen measures of the introduction are on and immediately around the tonic six-four and the dominant in G. Except for its beginning, the introduction consists mainly of figuration. In Ex. 5.4, the chief passage of tonal and thematic change is quoted, including the strong approach to the G: I_4^6, which is introduced by a chromatically derived augmented-sixth chord. The omitted 16 measures steadfastly maintain a pedal on the dominant of G, established at the entrance of the solo part.

Ex. 5.4 Mendelssohn, Concerto in G minor, Op. 25, for piano and orchestra, third movement. Reduction by Adolf Ruthardt.

Rarely, the introduction may have broad significance in the form proper. In Ex. 5.5, the introductory material, which is quoted, extends to 18 measures, leading ultimately to D-flat for preparation of the rondo theme. In the course of the movement, the same material forms the basis for transitional passages from digression to theme and from theme to digression. It is much more episodic than either.

Ex. 5.5 Berry, Four Movements for Chamber Orchestra, fourth movement.

Ex. 5.5   (continued)

Rondo
proper

The rondo theme

The rondo theme may be a period, an enlarged or double period, a phrase group, or a small binary or ternary. When it is a binary or ternary form, the over-all design is said to be a *compound rondo*.

In a compound rondo in which the theme is a small ternary form, any digression *within* the rondo theme is of very minor importance, having a close relationship to the flanking parts and being very short. The argument here is similar to that which distinguishes between the compound ternary and the larger rondo form (see Chapters 4 and 7). The effect must be that the whole of the small ternary is bound, by length and likeness of material and tonal level, into a single unit in the over-all form.

In the final movement of Haydn's String Quartet in E-flat, Op. 33, No. 2, the first 36 measures constitute the rondo theme—a small ternary form. In this movement, the theme returns in its complete form after the first digression, but is abbreviated in its final statement. The above suggestions concerning the strong unity of the ternary theme—a unity to be viewed against the background of the two digressions and the total form—are borne out in this movement. (See also Ex. 5.28 and related discussion.)

In Ex. 5.6, the rondo theme is a period followed by two variations preceding the entry of the first digression, which appears without transition at measure 27. The two complementary phrases of the theme are quoted; the first ends with a half-cadence, the second with a perfect authentic cadence. Following the initial statement of the theme, there is an ornamental variation (Chapter 9). Two measures of the variation are shown. The second variation, also ornamental, includes an extension of one measure at the cadence. Thus, the symmetry of the initial period is not carried out in the over-all theme design. This variation, shown here by the opening of its consequent phrase (measure 22), is to be compared with measures 5 and 6 of the original period. A rondo theme of this type is unusual.

Ex. 5.6 Prokofiev, Piano Sonata No. 9 in C, third movement.

Ex. 5.6 (continued)

— Second variation (consequent phrase)

In the continuation of the Prokofiev movement, the rondo theme is reduced in size with each appearance. Thus, the second statement consists of only two periods; the final statement is a single period.

The rondo theme may end with a brief codetta. An example can be seen in the final movement of Schumann's Piano Sonata in G minor, Op. 22 (Ex. 5.17).

Transition

Often no transition is used. If present, a transition may take any of a variety of shapes, lengths, and materials. We need not review here the various possibilities as to the content of the transitional passage (see Chapter 4).

Whether the transition is modulatory may depend on the first digression. If the first digression is, for example, in a parallel key (C major to C minor), modulation is unnecessary. Or the digression may enter in a closely related key without modulatory preparation, taking the final harmony of the rondo theme as a pivot into the new key. Examples of this technique have already been seen. The finale of the Schumann Sonata in G minor, Op. 22, has no transition of any kind between rondo theme and first digression; there is a perfect authentic cadence, a *fermata,* and an immediate entry of the digression section.

The transition may begin out of a dissolution of the rondo theme, as in the final movement of the Beethoven Sonata in C, Op. 2, No. 3. A comparison of measure 4 with measure 22 will reveal how the dissolution takes place. There is at this point an abrupt substitution of a chromatic harmony which leads sequentially into G major, the key of the first digression.

Where the transition is absent, the motion of the music may be thrust forward suddenly at the theme cadence to minimize the segmenting effect of the cadential punctuation. In Ex. 5.7, the first digression enters directly at the cadence of the rondo theme, taking the original tonic as dominant in the new key. The cello and second violin parts, both *forte,* prevent any sense of relaxation. The sustained tone in the bass and the quick, pronounced forward movement in the second violin point directly into the digression.

Ex. 5.7   Haydn, String Quartet in E-flat, Op. 33, No. 2, final movement.

The Haydn rondo, incidentally, has a coda which is striking in its use of dramatic pauses and tempo change (measure 149).

In Ex. 5.8, the composer arrests the rondo theme on a strong tonic cadence, after which the music proceeds sequentially through B minor to A. The material used in the transition is based on the opening of the theme:

The A:V to which the transition leads is prolonged, moving to its secondary dominant and back to A:V, again prolonged, this time by *ritardando* and *fermata.* The digression, the beginning of which appears in the example, begins with but is not limited to material of the rondo theme in the dominant key.

Ex. 5.8 Clementi, Sonata in D, Op. 26, No. 3, final movement.

The transition may have the character of a codetta. In the final move-ment of Schubert's Sonata in A minor, Op. 143, the transition consists first of a phrase repeated with variation, confirming the initial key and strengthen-ing the cadence of the rondo theme. Then, in the final 5 measures, there is a modulation to F (see measures 45–50). The transition, at measure 31, introduces a distinctive 2-measure motive of its own. There is a good deal of emphasis on the submediant of A minor as a prelude to the modulation to F. It is suggested that the reader make a careful study of this example.

The first digression

The first digression is usually a strong contrast in material, in character, in key, in rhythmic quality, in texture or in any combination of these factors. The change of key is customary in traditional models, although sometimes there is use of the parallel major or minor. The digression is normally comparable in length to the rondo theme.

Occasionally, the digression introduces material which is an extreme contrast in all its basic attributes, as in Ex. 5.1.

More commonly, the digression affords thematic and tonal contrast while adhering to the precedent of the rondo theme in such fundamental qualities as tempo and meter. There must be justification for the presence of the contrasting materials in the same movement. Thus, certain factors will unite the digression to the rondo theme while others set it apart. This is the problem of achieving contrast while maintaining balance and unity in the form.

If the digression material is actually derived from the rondo theme, the factor of tonal contrast has special significance. Often, for example, in Haydn movements, analysis has to be made essentially on the basis of tonal outlines. In Ex. 5.9, there is strong tonal contrast, while the thematic material carries over from rondo theme to digression.

Ex. 5.9 Haydn, Sonata in C (Peters No. 21), final movement.

Rondo theme melody
(first phrase)
  Presto

End of transition

First digression

Ex. 5.9 (continued)

The possibilities of length and form are again of a very wide range. The question of size, of course, concerns the proportions of the total form. The digression may be expected to be comparable in size to the rondo theme; extreme contrast in length is unlikely. Differences in form between the rondo theme and the digression are, however, usual.

The key of the first digression is, traditionally, closely related to that of the rondo theme, entering in the dominant (Ex. 5.9) or relative key, or in the parallel key. The first digression may assert its uniqueness by the simple change of theme, while adhering to the tonal level of the beginning, venturing later in its course into other tonal areas. (See the closing movement of the Mendelssohn Piano Concerto in G minor, whose first digression enters in the basic key of G at measure 32, with modulations to follow.)

Ex. 5.10 begins without transitional preparation. It consists of a long phrase (7 measures in slow tempo), constantly moving forward, leading from F minor to E-flat. It ends on a perfect authentic cadence in E-flat, after which there is a retransition which at the last instant brings in the note D-flat over the E-flat tonic to effect a return to A-flat major, the key of the rondo theme.

Ex. 5.10   Beethoven, Sonata in C minor, Op. 13, second movement.

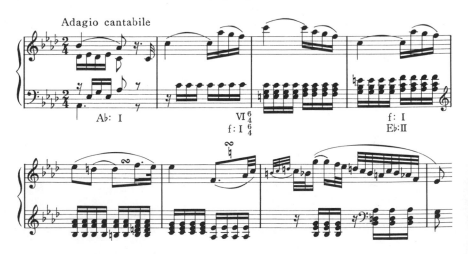

Ex. 5.11, illustrating digression, is a simple ternary form consisting of an initial period (*a,* moving from E to B) ; a group in which a 2-measure motive is repeated and varied (*b,* going to E) ; and a return of the period (*a*), entirely in E. Its motivic material is clearly derived from the rondo theme, a fragment of which appears in the example, and the same is true of the second digression. The principal contrast is one of mode—the parallel major. In fact, the entire movement is on an E tonic, which changes to the parallel major at points of digression. There are no transitions. The use of simple ternary form in the digression makes a compound form of the whole.

Ex. 5.11   Haydn, Sonata in E minor (Peters No. 2), final movement.

Retransition; the restatement of the rondo theme

Like the transition, the retransition may be from one to several measures in length. Again, its character may be purely figural or it may have thematic substance, or it may be a mere continuation of motion through the cadential seam.

Ex. 5.12 carries on the accompanying figuration of the first digression, effecting a rapid modulation for return of the rondo theme.

Ex. 5.12   Schubert, Sonata in A minor, Op. 143, final movement.

The retransition shown in Ex. 5.13 clings to the note G, the dominant root, with that note appearing first as the E-flat mediant, quickly becoming the dominant in C minor. The motive of the rondo theme is anticipated. The rests intensify the feeling of expectation of the rondo return. There is a brief dialogue between the instruments, after which the rondo theme enters almost imperceptibly. The rondo statement which follows is developmental in character, and considerably extended, but it remains in the tonic key of C minor.

Ex. 5.13   Beethoven, Sonata in C minor, Op. 30, No. 2, for violin and piano, final movement.

L— Restatement

Ex. 5.14 includes fragments of the rondo theme and the first digression (derived from the first movement in this work), thus relating to both of the sections which it links. The retransition is not shown in its entirety. It is entered by dissolution of material of the first digression (see measure 135) with a gradual emergence of the motive of the original thematic complex.

Ex. 5.14   Ravel, String Quartet in F, final movement.
Permission for reprint granted by Durand et Cie., Paris, France, copyright owners, and Elkan-Vogel Co., Inc., Philadelphia, Pa., agents.

**Motive of
Rondo theme**

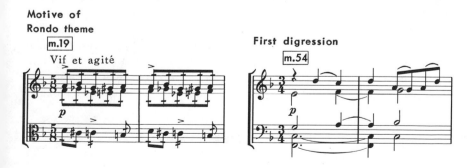

Ex. 5.14   (continued)

Part of Retransition

Another example of this type of retransition, incorporating materials of both A and B, is the final retransition in the fourth movement of Beethoven's Octet in E-flat, Op. 103, for winds. In measure 142, following the *fermata*, the reader will easily mark the use of materials of the section just past and that which is approaching.

With rare exceptions the return of the rondo theme is in the tonic key, and usually it is varied in some way. Leichtentritt speaks of this when he says that "the rondo theme is often ornamented in various ways at the repetitions."[3] Ex. 5.15 shows a small fragment of a rondo theme, and the corresponding point in its first return, to illustrate the variation technique used.

[3] Hugo Leichtentritt, *Musical Form* (Cambridge: Harvard University Press, 1956), p. 118.

Ex. 5.15   Schubert, Sonata in D, Op. 53, final movement.

The expansion of the theme by developmental procedures is illustrated in the final movement of Beethoven's Sonata in C minor for violin and piano (see Ex. 5.13). This is an excellent example for study. In the development of the theme, Beethoven concentrates on a seemingly unimportant phrase of the rondo theme, taking it into far regions with extraordinary control. The particular portion of the rondo theme developed here is omitted altogether in the final return.

An example of restatement in a key other than the tonic is seen in the Schubert Sonata in A minor, Op. 164, second movement. The rondo is in E major, with the first return of the theme in F.

The second transition

This point in the form is, of course, to be compared with the corresponding approach to the first digression. The character of the second transition depends on the character and key of the second digression, which follows it. As before, the transition may be omitted entirely.

Ex. 5.16 is a quotation from the first and second transitions in a rondo of Brahms; both transitions lead to the same digressive material (B), and both use motives of the rondo theme. Characteristic of both is a kind of rhythmic and harmonic-rhythmic "unwinding"—a part of the preparation for the approaching new thematic material. But the transitions are not alike: the first leads to the dominant key and is somewhat longer, while the second transition remains in the tonic, requiring no change of key.

Ex. 5.16 Brahms, String Quartet in G, Op. 111, fourth movement.

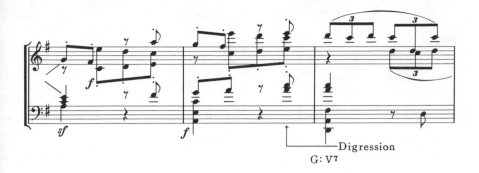

In Ex. 5.17, there are no transitions, in the true sense of the word, but the approaches to the B digression differ because the original material returns in a different key. Passages at both points are shown to make clear the alteration in approach. The codetta to the rondo theme appears as part of the first quotation.

Ex. 5.17   Schumann, Sonata in G minor, Op. 22, final movement.

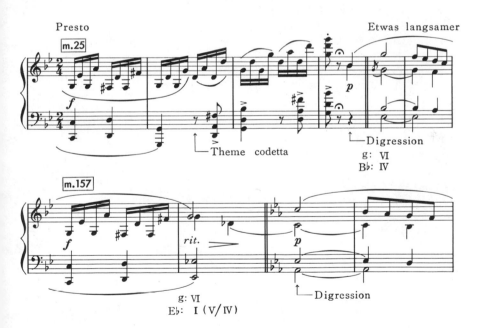

In a rondo in which the two digressions are distinctly unrelated (ABACA), the passages by which they are approached should be studied independently, since they are likely to differ in their basic features. In such a case, the manner in which the transitions are entered may be the only real basis of comparison.

The second digression as a repetition of the first

When the material of the first digression is brought back as the second digression, some variation may be introduced, although this is less common than in the case of the rondo theme, probably because the digression has fewer appearances.

In rondos in which the two digressions are of identical material (ABABA) there is usually contrast of key. Very rarely do the two digressions appear in the same key, except for the occasional use of parallel major or minor. Some nineteenth-century examples of key relationships appear below.

Work	Key of first digression	Key of second digression
Beethoven, String Quartet in F, Op. 18, No. 1, second movement (in D minor)	F	D
Schubert, Impromptu in C minor, Op. 90, No. 1	A-flat	G minor
Schubert, Sonata in A minor, Op. 143, final movement	F	C
Schumann, Sonata in G minor, Op. 22, final movement	B-flat	E-flat

In the Schubert Impromptu, the second digression, while restating the theme of the first, introduces a modification in the rhythmic motion, as well as the change of key, as a source of variation.

Ex. 5.18   Schubert, Impromptu in C minor, Op. 90, No. 1.

The second digression as a contrast to the first

The rondo in which the second digression is thematically unlike the first (ABACA) is somewhat less common. Below are listed some key relationships between unlike first and second digressions.

Work	Key of first digression	Key of second digression
Mozart, Quintet in E-flat, K. 407, for horn and strings, final movement	B-flat	C minor, E-flat
Beethoven, Piano Trio in E-flat, Op. 1, No. 1, second movement (in A-flat)	E-flat	A-flat minor, F minor
Beethoven, Sonata in A, Op. 30, No. 1, for violin and piano, second movement (in D)	B minor	B-flat
Beethoven, Rondino in E-flat for wind octet (Op. Posth.)	C minor	E-flat minor
Schubert, Sonata in D, Op. 53, final movement	A	G

The two digressions in the Beethoven Violin Sonata movement are extremely strong contrasts. The first begins at measure 17, the second at measure 44. In the Trio movement, C is more extensive and more digressive than B. In the Mozart, the second digression is a simple ternary form—again a strong contrast to the first, which had been based on motives of the rondo theme. In the Mozart, as well as the Beethoven Rondino and Trio movement, transition is omitted at the point where the second digression enters; in all three examples, however, retransition is used following this section. The Mozart retransition, following the second digression, is a good one for study, having as its motivic basis the final fragment of the second digression. The coda to this movement might also be mentioned as especially worthy of investigation; it begins at measure 143, and includes a little canon on the rondo theme.

Ex. 5.19 quotes a fragment of the first digression and the entire second digression, in outline, from a Haydn Sonata movement. This example is in simple ternary form (period, phrase, period) in the subdominant key, and it is followed by a simple but excellent example of retransition, with dominant prolongation and anticipation of the anacrusis motive of the rondo theme.

Ex. 5.19   Haydn, Sonata in D (Peters No. 7), final movement.

First digression

Second digression

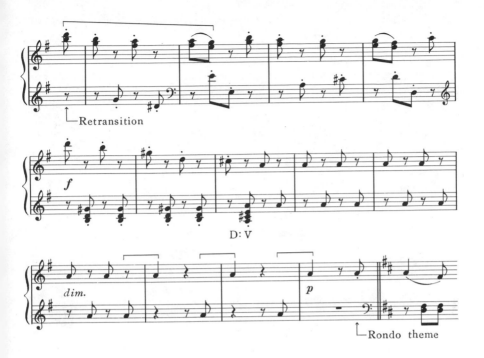

An example of highly unusual and very segmented form in a rondo second digression is that of the Mozart Octet in B-flat, K. 361, for winds, seventh movement (ABACA). This digression, measures 57–88, contains *four* contrasting sections, each repeated, in the keys of E-flat, C minor, G minor, and D minor. The basic key of the movement is B-flat.

Final statement of the rondo theme

Differences in the two retransitions, if any, are usually attributable to the nature of the preceding material. For example, the *adagio* movement (in D) from Beethoven's Sonata in A, Op. 30, No. 1, for violin and piano, has scarcely any retransition after the first digression, which is in the relative minor. Following the second digression, which is in B-flat, there is a lengthy retransition. This also contributes to the heightened psychological effect of the final return of the rondo theme. In the final retransition, the music leads first from B-flat to D minor, wavering around the dominant of that key for the last 8 measures. Hesitations in the rhythmic motion, and the *fermata* at the end, measures 60–63, add to the suspended feeling before the rondo theme enters. The motive of measure 52 (second measure in Ex. 5.20) is from the second measure of the opening theme of the movement.

Ex. 5.20 Beethoven, Sonata in A, Op. 30, No. 1, for violin and piano, second movement.

An example which has *no* retransition after the second digression is the final movement of Beethoven's Sonata in G minor, Op. 49, No. 1. The retransition following the first digression (see measure 65) leads from B-flat, the key of the first digression, through G minor, to G major for the return of the rondo theme. The second digression, however, is in G major and thus requires no modulation into the final appearance of the rondo theme (see measures 135–136). There is direct passage into the theme, which shortly dissolves into a coda.

Ex. 5.21   Beethoven, Sonata in G minor, Op. 49, No. 1, final movement.

End of second—┘   └—Rondo   └—Dissolution by
digression   theme   repetition of motive

The final statement of the rondo theme is in the tonic key, and may again be the subject of variation treatment. Not uncommon is the abbreviation of the final return, as seen in Ex. 5.22, which dissolves at the point indicated into the coda (see also Ex. 5.21).

Ex. 5.22   Haydn, String Quartet in E-flat, Op. 64, No. 6, final movement.

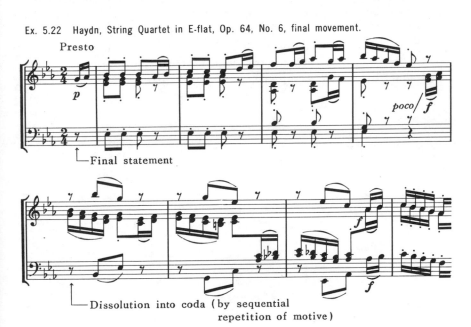

└—Final statement

└—Dissolution into coda (by sequential
repetition of motive)

The codetta; the coda

The codetta or coda begins after the final statement of the rondo theme has reached its cadence, or at the point of its dissolution. Ex. 5.23 shows the beginning of a coda set off by the theme cadence; there is an immediate resumption of the dotted rhythms with which the movement began, and the coda introduces an essentially new theme.

Ex. 5.23   Beethoven, Sonata in A, Op. 30, No. 1, for violin and piano, second movement.

Ex. 5.24 shows the 12-measure codetta of a rondo movement. What might have been the final tonic appears in first inversion at the outset of the codetta, followed by the cadential formula $II_5^6-I_4^6-V_7-I_6$. This progression is repeated and ends finally on the tonic in root position. From this point, a tonic pedal point is used, over which there are progressions involving IV, I, and VII, sometimes dissonant to the pedal and sometimes consonant, all serving to emphasize and elaborate the final tonic harmony over its sustained root.

Ex. 5.24   Mozart, Sonata in D, K. 576, final movement.

A rondo coda which is short (9 measures), at the same time relating to much of the movement's major content, is illustrated as Ex. 5.25 in the reproduction of key fragments. In this movement, the first digression (measure 20) is an inversion of the rondo theme in a new key, while the second digression presents an independent theme. The coda, from measure 77, is set off by a sudden rest (Ex. 5.25a), followed by precipitous, rapid movement. The fourth measure of the coda (measure 80) finds the horn recalling the theme of the second digression (see measure 37), as shown in *b*, below. The measures immediately following recall the motive of the rondo theme (see cello, measure 81). Now the music sweeps to the final cadence, which includes one last statement of the rondo motive in flute and bassoon (*c*).

Ex. 5.25a   Toch, Concerto, Op. 35, for cello and chamber orchestra, second movement.

Ex. 5.25b

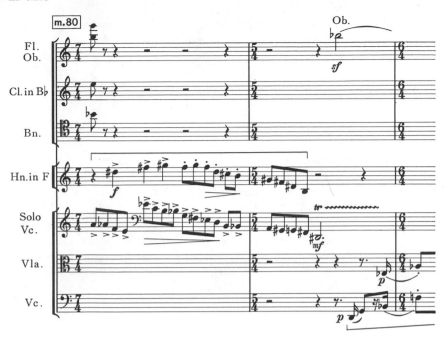

Ex. 5.25c

A rondo movement built on the design ABABA, in which the coda uses materials of both A and B, is the final movement of Schubert's Sonata in A minor, Op. 143. A highly unusual coda concludes the Prokofiev movement cited in Ex. 5.6. In this coda, the theme of the subsequent movement appears prominently just before the end.

Repeats in particular examples

While many examples of rondo form have no repeated sections, it is not difficult to find examples which do contain such repetitions. Any part of a rondo movement may be repeated.

Two examples will illustrate the use of repeat signs following the initial statement of the rondo theme. In the final movement of the Haydn Sonata in C (Peters No. 21), both parts of the incipient ternary theme are repeated at the beginning; no other repeats are used in the movement. Here, the repeats help to establish the theme clearly before the continuation of the movement; a lengthy transition follows immediately.

A similar case is the finale of Schubert's Sonata in D, Op. 53, whose ternary theme is repeated at the outset. Again, no further repeats are used.

In the second movement of Schubert's Sonata in A minor, Op. 164, more repeats are used. Only the second part of the theme is repeated, with each of its appearances, but in addition both digressions are accompanied by repeat signs.

In none of the above examples can the repeats, when practiced, be said to have a significant effect upon the form, except to extend it. In each case, the repeat is immediate and applies only to a single component in the form. An alteration (enlargement) of the basic design would result if, for example, a repeat followed the first digression and applied as well to the rondo theme. In such an instance, AB:||ABA, there would be, with the repeat observed, not a 5-part rondo, but a 7-part form (ABABABA). An example of this kind, which is hypothetical, is mentioned only to re-emphasize that in the Haydn and Schubert examples the repeats do not affect the basic rondo design. Even in the *allegretto* of the Schubert A minor Sonata, ABACA becomes, with the repeats observed, AABBAACCAA. The change is durational rather than structural. Actually, the pattern is somewhat more complex since only part of the rondo theme is repeated.

The rondo principle in da capo forms

In the chapter on compound ternary form, the point was made that the traditional movement with "trio" and *da capo* is sometimes extended to include two trios and a second *da capo*. In this connection certain Beethoven and Schumann works were cited as examples, with the observation that this kind of enlargement of the compound ternary results in a rondo form. (See

Chapter 4, pp. 104–05.) Such a rondo is invariably of the compound type, often with relatively little integration among its several parts.

A further example is the Mozart Serenade in B-flat, K. 361, for winds, which includes two movements (the second and fourth) in which the addition of second trios results in rondo form. In the second movement of this work—*Menuetto*, Trio I, *Menuetto*, Trio II, *Menuetto*—each of the five major parts is a simple ternary; thus, the total movement is a compound rondo. The movement is basically in B-flat, while the two trios are in E-flat and G minor, respectively.

Degrees of integration in rondo form

The subtlety with which music moves from one section to another is a highly important factor in its form, whether or not it is a value to be sought in the composition. Certainly, those rondos which are not strongly sectionalized often have an especially vital effect because of the continuous, even relentless flow through points of cadential punctuation.

A high degree of integration is achieved, as in other forms, by (1) the use of bridging passages—transitions and retransitions, and (2) interrelationships among the materials of the various sections. We have already seen illustrations of both features. A third means by which integration is achieved is that of adept concealment, by rhythmic drive or elision, of the point separating two sections.

Ex. 5.26 shows the point separating the first return of the rondo theme and the second digression: ABA̸BA-Coda. Although there is no transition, a high degree of integration is achieved by the use of a common motive (bracketed) and by elision at the cadence. At this moment, the tonic in C suddenly appears as a minor triad, introducing a new phrase. The *sf* is a further factor in the forward impulse. The effect of the elision becomes even more striking when compared with the pronounced cadence and rest which had separated the opening statement of the rondo theme and the first digression (measure 22).

Ex. 5.26   Haydn, String Quartet in C, Op. 33, No. 3, fourth movement.

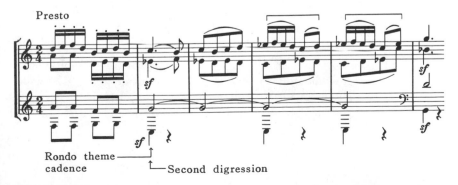

We need not add here to the transition and retransition examples already given. It should be acknowledged, though, that just as there can be high integration without a transitional passage (see Ex. 5.26), there can be transition without complete integration. Thus, in the second movement of the Schubert Sonata in A minor, Op. 164, the theme and both digressions are clearly "closed" units, with transitions *following* their strongly marked cadences.

The movement from the Toch Cello Concerto, referred to in Ex. 5.25, is a good example of a rondo form having very tight integration of its various parts. Another is the finale of the Haydn Symphony in E-flat, No. 103. This movement should be studied with care. Two facts will be apparent at once: (1) the *entire* movement is based on

with digressions formed of motivic development and change of key; and (2) the motion is continued vigorously at every cadence, except for two *fermate* preceding the returns of the rondo theme and another near the end of the movement.

Integration is not impaired by cessations in the rhythmic motion if the interruption is on a point of harmonic instability or dissonance. Such a technique of uneasy hiatus is a common and highly effective means of keeping the listener engaged and his attention drawn through the rest in the music. When the interruption is of indefinite length, the feeling of anxiety is all the more intense.

Ex. 5.27   Haydn, String Quartet in C, Op. 33, No. 3, fourth movement.

In many instances it is clearly the composer's choice that motion should not be constant throughout the greater part of a movement, and that strongly contrasting sections should be sharply delineated. In a lengthy movement, points of clear punctuation—of "breathing"—may seem necessary. In the

Haydn movement cited as Ex. 5.26 and Ex. 5.27, the few real interruptions are significant; in relation to them the general vitality of the music is all the more compelling. And the truth remains that, in the Haydn as in all successful tonal music, interruptions are only rarely on perfect tonal consonances. More often, intensity is built—through harmonic dissonance, rise in pitch, dynamic growth, rhythmic drive, and other devices—and held unresolved through interruptions of the kind seen in Ex. 5.27.

Extensions of rondo form

A traditional seven-part rondo form, much used by composers of the eighteenth and nineteenth centuries, is discussed in Chapter 7, following the chapter on single-movement sonata form, to which it bears certain important resemblances.

Of course, taking the five-part rondo scheme as a standard of the type discussed in this chapter, extension is possible by the addition of theoretically any number of further digressions and rondo returns. The Bach *Gavotte* discussed on page 125 is of this type.

Another example of this type of rondo extension is Schumann's piano work *Faschingsschwank aus Wien,* Op. 26. Its first movement, an *allegro,* has five statements of the rondo theme. The fourth movement of the Ravel String Quartet is a rondo design consisting of four statements of the rondo material (not a theme in the usual sense) : its basic form may be represented as ABABABA.

The compound rondo, in which, for example, the rondo theme is itself a simple ternary form, has been discussed in connection with certain examples cited in the foregoing pages. Theoretically, a rondo in which the digression is a small ternary is also a compound form (Ex. 5.11). A five-part rondo in which the initial theme is a ternary yields a more complex structure which may be represented by the symbol

$$
\begin{array}{ccccc}
\text{A} & \text{B} & \text{A} & \text{B} & \text{A}\,, \\
(aba) & & (aba) & & (aba)
\end{array}
$$

assuming that the rondo theme appears in its entirety each time and that the two digressions are of the same material. The justification for describing this as a five-part rather than an eleven-part rondo is in the tight unity of the opening ternary.

A final illustration of such a rondo theme is shown as Ex. 5.28. Here, *a* is a period in C (with extension by motive repetition), *b*, a brief development of the same motive in G, followed by the original period. The middle part, *b,* is only 7 measures long, including links which attach it to the flanking parts. The brevity of the whole theme, and the use of common material throughout, are factors binding it into a single major unit in the over-all form.

Ex. 5.28   Clementi, Sonata No. 5 in C, final movement.

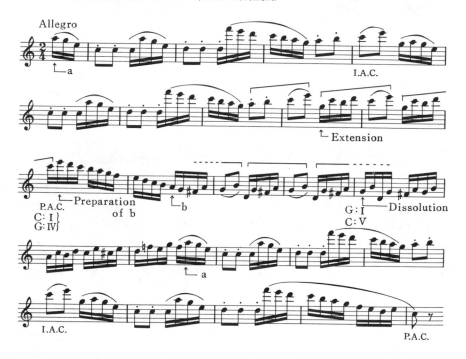

The finale of the Sonata No. 8 in C by Muzio Clementi (1752–1832) also has a simple ternary theme; in this instance the middle part, *b,* is slightly longer than that of Ex. 5.28 but it is without tonal change, remaining on the dominant of the original key (measures 20ff.).

Beethoven, Trio in E-flat, Op. 70, No. 2, for piano, violin, and cello, second movement

For study of a complete movement, the reader is referred to the second movement of the Beethoven Trio in E-flat, Op. 70, No. 2, for piano, violin, and cello. Certain key points in the structure of the movement will be illustrated by direct quotation in the course of the following discussion. The reader should, however, have reference at the same time to the complete score.

The movement begins with the rondo theme, stated without introduction. The theme is a 16-measure enlarged period—enlarged by the repetition and variation of each of the two basic phrases. The variation technique in the repetition of the antecedent and consequent phrases is a redistribution of voices and instrumental parts, with their essential outlines and the harmony preserved. For example, in the repetition of the antecedent phrase (see measure 5), the original violin part is in the piano, an octave higher; the original cello part is in the violin, two octaves higher; and the original melody in the piano is taken by the cello, transposed down an octave.

The half-cadence at the middle of the period is preceded by the dominant of the dominant; the final cadence is a perfect authentic form. Apart from the melody lines and the harmony, the most important identifying aspect of the theme is the characteristic rhythm of the opening motive in the piano. Ex. 5.29a is a reproduction of the entire theme.

Ex. 5.29a   Beethoven, Trio in E-flat, Op. 70, No. 2, for piano, violin, and cello, second movement.

Ex. 5.29a   (continued)

The first digression follows without transition. The key is the parallel minor (Ex. 5.29b) and this time there is a group of three phrases. The first two (measures 17–24) are similar except for their cadences, the second phrase being an ornamental variation of the first (5.29c). During the first digression, which ends at measure 28, the keys of C minor, A-flat, and F minor are touched at the three cadences, in that order. In the first digression, the motive

takes on a special significance; it is later to become

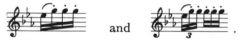   and   .

Its relationship to the original anacrusis motive is clear, although here the characteristic emphasis on the second note is achieved dynamically rather than durationally.

Ex. 5.29b   (piano only).   Ex. 5.29c

In the second half of measure 28 the opening motive returns for retransition to the rondo theme. Throughout the retransition (6 measures) the harmony vacillates between tonic and dominant of F minor. In the last measure, an implied f:I becomes C:IV by chromatic change of A-flat to A-natural (5.29d).

Ex. 5.29d

The second digression, a variation of the first, is similarly entered
In its first return, the rondo theme is repeated, thereby extended to a total length of 32 measures. Several variations are developed, as may be seen by comparing the following fragments with the first measure of the original theme (see also measure 35, above).

Ex. 5.29e

The second digression, a variation of the first, is similarly entered without transition. Structurally, tonally, and harmonically, it is precisely parallel to the first digression. The characteristic motive (see Ex. 5.29b, c) now takes on more rapid rhythmic motion, the precedent for which was set in the variation of the rondo theme which just ended. The technique of ornamental variation applied here can be seen by comparison of fragments (5.29f) with the first measure of the first digression (5.29b, c).

Ex. 5.29f

The retransition is now cut from 6 to 4 measures. Again, it anticipates the anacrusis motive of the theme, although in steady 32nd-note motion as a result of the rhythms developed in the second digression. Just before the theme appears, the cello enters with a descending anacrusis figure of three eighth-notes, helping to prepare the slower motion of the theme (5.29g).

Ex. 5.29g

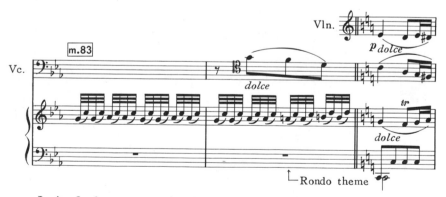

In its final statement, the theme is reduced to two phrases—the basic antecedent and consequent of the original period—and it appears as at the beginning of the movement, without variation (5.29g). It is followed by a transition of 4 measures, based on the original anacrusis motive, introducing a change of mode, and leading to the coda, which is in C minor.

Ex. 5.29h

The coda is 42 measures, unusually long in view of the total length of
the movement, 138 measures. In its key and mode, C minor, it is reminiscent
of the digressions. In thematic material, it is varied. It begins with a repeated
phrase which has only a tenuous relationship to the rondo theme melody
(5.29i). The anacrusis to each of these phrases is the familiar first measure
of the rondo theme. Following the first 8 measures, there is a development of
the opening motive of the first digression, a portion of which (the development) is quoted as Ex. 5.29j.

Ex. 5.29i

Ex. 5.29j

The coda continues in 4-measure phrases, with a perfect authentic cadence in C minor concluding each. The last of these reaches its cadence at measure 120 and is extended by repetition of the tonic and dominant cadential harmonies, stopping on the dominant at measure 123, and prolonging that harmony with a gradual reduction in dynamic level, in texture, and in rhythmic motion over the next 4 measures, at which point the characteristic anacrusis motive of the theme returns again (5.29k).

Ex. 5.29k

There is a brief development of this motive, with a sudden, dramatic *forte* at measure 129, followed by a pause of half a measure. Now the first 2 measures of the theme, first in major, then in minor, make a final appearance (5.29l), with abrupt changes of tempo.

Ex. 5.29l

With a few further, toying appearances of the motive  in a brief dialogue between piano and strings, the music rushes to a final cadence in C minor.

Ex. 5.29m

Exercises and examples for further study

1. Find examples of the following.
   a) An antecedent of the Classical rondo.
   b) A rondo theme of period form.
   c) A transition linking the rondo theme to the first digression.
   d) A retransition preparing the return of the rondo theme.
   e) A highly integrated rondo.
   f) A piece, possibly a song, illustrating the rondo principle in an extended form.

g) A rondo using variation techniques in the restatements of the theme.

2. Select an example cited in connection with the first question, or choose an example from the text of this chapter. Write, in outline form or in an expository paragraph, a brief analytical discussion about the musical form, referring to some of the points discussed in this chapter.

3. Write at least the melody of a theme of your own which might form the basis for a traditional rondo. Show two or three ways in which the theme might be varied in its reappearances.

4. Be prepared to give a complete analysis of the second movement (*adagio*) of Beethoven's Sonata in C minor, Op. 10, No. 1. Give special attention to the following points.

a) Study the retransition preparing the first return of the theme.

b) To what extent does the music fall obviously into sections, and to what extent is it integrated? (For example, the first transition is an integrating factor, but it follows a well-marked cadential division.)

c) How is this movement similar to sonatina form, or single-movement sonata form without development? (Rf. Chapter 6.)

d) How would you justify describing the last eleven bars as a codetta?

5. List some of the advantages of the rondo design with respect to the requirements for a balance of unifying and contrasting elements. What are some examples of possible distortions that might weaken this balance? What is an obvious danger implicit in the form, and how do composers attempt to circumvent it?

6. Find an example of a coda in a rondo movement.

a) What is its length?

b) What is its proportion in relation to the entire movement? To the rondo theme?

c) Can it in any degree be said to be developmental? Explain.

d) From what sources is its thematic material drawn?

e) Is there any departure from, or momentary disturbance of, the basic tonality?

f) Is it sectional? Explain.

g) Is a considerable portion of the coda taken up with repetitions of cadential harmonies in a sort of elaboration and extension of the final cadence?

h) Is there any use of sequence in the coda? Of contrapuntal imitation?

7. Looking over Chapter 5, prepare a list of questions that might be used in an examination on rondo form.

8. How would you characterize the form of the Mozart "Rondo" in D, K. 485?

9. Prepare an analysis of the Concerto in C minor, Op. 26, for clarinet and orchestra, by Louis Spohr (1784–1859). Why is this a compound form? Give special attention to transitions and to the coda, measure 295, produced by the dissolution of the rondo theme. Why are numerous repetitions within each section a likely feature of the concerto?

10. Study the techniques of variation in the restatements of digression and rondo theme (ABA′B′A″) in Haydn's Sonata in D (Peters No. 19).

11. Many specimens of the five-part rondo have been used for illustration or

mentioned in the text of this chapter. A few supplementary works are listed below for further study.

Johann Christian Bach (1735–82), Sonata in E-flat, Op. V, No. 4 (No. 6 in the Landshoff Edition, published by Peters), second movement

Bartók, Concerto No. 3 for piano and orchestra, third movement

Beethoven, *Polonaise,* Op. 89 (introduction and 2 contrasting digressions) Sonata in G, Op. 49, No. 2, final movement

Gabriel Fauré (1845–1924), Prelude No. 3 in G minor for piano

Haydn, Sonata in E-flat (Peters No. 3), third movement Sonata in D (Peters No. 9), final movement Sonata in D (Peters No. 32), final movement Sonata in E (Peters No. 34), final movement

Johann Hummel (1778–1837), Rondo, Op. 11, for piano (interesting transitional passages)

Mendelssohn, Concerto in E minor, Op. 64, for violin and orchestra, final movement

Mozart, Octet in B-flat, K. 361, for winds, second, fourth, and seventh movements Quartet in F, K. 370, for oboe, 2 violins, and cello, final movement Sonata in C, K. 545, third movement *Rondeau* in F, K. 15hh, for piano (Is the *"Rondeau"* in D, K. 15d, really in rondo form?) Rondo in A minor, K. 511, for piano

Rameau, *Air en rondeau* from *Hippolyte et Aricie* *Musette en rondeau* from *Les Indes Galantes*

Schubert, Sonata in C minor (first of *Three Grand Sonatas*), final movement (note extensive and very digressive digressions)

Stravinsky, Concerto in D for strings, third movement

Tchaikovsky, Concerto in D, Op. 35, for violin and orchestra, final movement (rondo theme developed in later appearances)

12. Find examples of extended rondo in piano works of K. P. E. Bach—for example, the Rondos No. 1 in C, and No. 2 in D.

6

SONATA

he term *sonata* has its origin in the Latin verb *sonare,* to sound, and initially referred to a work to be played on an instrument, or group of instruments, as opposed to a vocal work, or *cantata,* from the Latin *cantare,* to sing. In its evolution from this obvious connotation, the word has at various times assumed various meanings. Thus, in addition to medium of performance, it has to do with particular types of multi-movement composition as well as with the specific formal design of certain single movements and single-movement pieces.

In the latter sense, denoting a specific single-movement form, the term applies to many movements of symphonies, quartets, concertos, piano sonatas, and other multi-movement orchestral, chamber, and solo types. Single-movement sonata form occurs often in the overture as well. In the sense of multi-movement composition, the use of the word *sonata* is now usually limited to works for solo instrument, or for piano and another instrument.

This chapter is concerned chiefly with single-movement sonata form as it is commonly represented in at least one of the movements of a multi-movement sonata, whether for orchestra (symphony), chamber ensemble (quintet, quartet, trio, etc.), or solo instrument. There are several terms which relate, with various confusing implications, to this particular form. The simple designation "sonata form," as already stated, refers both to single-movement and multi-movement designs. The term "sonata-allegro form," also in common usage, misleadingly infers tempo, yet the design is often applied in slow movements. Finally, the term "first-movement form" has serious limitations since the form is by no means restricted to opening movements. A solution to the problem of terminology lies in the designation *single-movement sonata form.*

A detailed tracing of the historical development of the sonata does not lie within the scope of the present study, which is concerned with the description and analysis of single-movement sonata form as it ultimately evolved late in the eighteenth century. Moreover, despite its independent history, the symphony is regarded here as an orchestral manifestation of sonata form. The reader will find ample resource for the study of the evolution of the symphony, as well as of the other chamber and solo media in which single-movement and multi-movement sonata forms occur.

While single-movement sonata form is associated in part with the keyboard sonatas of such composers as K. P. E. Bach and J. C. Bach, in whose works it is at least incipient, it was not until the time of Haydn and Mozart that the classic outlines of single-movement sonata form became firmly established in the use of contrasting thematic complexes and increasingly sophisticated thematic development.

The multi-movement sonata

Certain general observations can be made as to the usual movement types in the multi-movement sonata. The first movement, for example, is nearly always in single-movement sonata form. Works like the Mozart Sonata in A, K. 331, and the Beethoven Sonata in A-flat, Op. 26, are exceptions; in each of these works the opening movement is a theme with variations (Chapter 9). Another exception is the Beethoven Sonata in C–sharp minor, Op. 27, No. 2, labelled *quasi una Fantasia.*

The second movement of the four-movement scheme is frequently in a slow tempo. The Sonata, Op. 26, of Beethoven, discussed above in connection with its exceptional first movement, again departs from the norm: its second movement is a scherzo. The standard slow second movement may have any of several forms: theme with variations, three-part form, rondo, binary, single-movement sonata form, or some combination or modification of any of these. The slow movement of the Beethoven String Quartet in E minor, Op. 59, No. 2, is in single-movement sonata form. That of the Haydn Sonata in D (Peters No. 7) is in binary form. Slow variations as the second of three movements may be seen in the Beethoven Sonata, Op. 57, while the slow second movement of the same composer's Sonata, Op. 13, is in rondo form. An example of large ternary form in a slow movement occurs in the Brahms Quintet in F minor, Op. 34, for piano and strings. The slow second movement of Haydn's Symphony No. 104 in D is *monothematic,*[1] deriving its contrasts by tonal change and return and by the use of variation principles. The Haydn slow movement often is a hybrid of two or more types.

---

[1] A *monothematic* work or movement is one based essentially on a single theme (as is any theme with variations, except where there is a double theme). Therefore it relies upon devices of variety other than that of material thematic contrast as afforded by the use of two or more contrasting themes or thematic complexes, usual in rondo and single-movement sonata forms. (In the Haydn movement, compare the first violin in measures 1–2, 42–3, and 60–61.)

The third movement of the four-movement form is very often a minuet (later a scherzo of similar design) with contrasting "trio" followed by re-statement of the first part (Chapter 4). The Beethoven Sonata, Op. 26, is still exceptional: its third movement is a slow funeral march. Haydn and Mozart piano sonatas are not usually in four movements, although the minuet with trio can be found as the second of three movements in these works. This type of movement as the third of four is very common in Classical symphonies. Numbers 1–5 and 8 of the Beethoven Symphonies are examples, although in Nos. 4 and 5 the restatement of the first part is written out with some variation. Piano sonatas having scherzo or minuet with trio as the third of four movements are the Beethoven Sonatas, Op. 7, Op. 10, No. 3, Op. 22, and Op. 28. Further examples may be seen in the Piano Sonatas of Schubert: Op. 42, Op. 53, and Op. 122, to name only a few.

The final movement is commonly very fast, often in rondo form or single-movement sonata form, although other types are to be found. (The final movement of Brahms' Fourth Symphony is a set of variations on an 8-measure harmonic theme.) The last movement is frequently of strong momentum, of relatively simpler texture than the first (although it may contain passages of fugal imitation in rapid tempo, a highly favored finale device), and of expressive force appropriate to its position as conclusion of the over-all work. The finale to the Haydn Symphony in B-flat, No. 102, is in single-movement sonata form with a characteristic fugal passage at measure 188. The final movement of the Beethoven Quartet, Op. 59, No. 2, is a rondo. An example of a fourth movement which is neither is Beethoven's Third Symphony, with its variation finale.

Many sonatas, of course, contain three movements, or fewer than three movements. Generalizations as to the nature of the movements are difficult because of wide variance among examples. Still, the first movement is in most cases in single-movement sonata form, and the second is con-trastingly slow in tempo when it is part of a three-movement work. Three-movement sonatas are so numerous, especially in the solo literature of the Classical period, that specific examples hardly need mention. The Mozart Sonata in F, K. 547a, and Haydn's Sonata in G (Peters No. 10) are examples of two-movement sonatas, as are the Beethoven Sonatas of Op. 49, Op. 53 (whose *adagio* is an introduction to the second movement), Op. 90, and Op. 111.

Relationships among the movements

The question of relationships among the various movements of the multi-movement sonata is troublesome. Of course, there are cases in which the movements are bound together by actual transitional passages and there are numerous examples of multi-movement sonatas in which the movements are related by the employment of common thematic materials. In the former category are such works as the Mendelssohn Piano Concerto in G minor and the Beethoven Violin Concerto, whose second and third movements are bridged by the passage quoted as Ex. 6.1.

Ex. 6.1   Beethoven, Concerto in D, Op. 61, for violin and orchestra.

The technique by which the movements share common materials reaches its most extensive application among French composers of the middle and late nineteenth century, notably in the music of Berlioz and César Franck (1822–90). Both the Debussy and Ravel String Quartets are *cyclical* in this sense, and the technique is to be observed as well in such earlier works as the Schubert Fantasy in C, Op. 15, Beethoven's Fifth Symphony, and the Schumann Piano Quintet. Ex. 6.2 shows the reappearance in the fourth movement of the principal motive of the first movement of the Schumann Quintet.

Ex. 6.2 Schumann, Quintet in E-flat, Op. 44, for piano and strings.

First movement excerpt:

Allegro brillante

Fourth movement excerpt:

Allegro ma non troppo

Another means of relating the several movements is the insertion, without actual integration, of momentary reminders of materials of early movements late in a multi-movement work. Thus, the final movement of Beethoven's Ninth Symphony is preceded by brief reappearances of materials of the first three movements and an anticipation of the theme of the fourth movement. These statements, each of them abruptly abandoned after a few measures, alternate with recitative-like phrases in the low strings.

But in the absence of apparent and palpable relationships of common motives and themes, or the binding of one movement to another through the avoidance of final cadence in favor of a bridge passage, how does one explain the coincidence of two apparently independent movements in the same work? This question is not satisfactorily answered by discussion of "spiritual ties." Given the important aesthetic conditions of surface unity, especially of tonality and style, and those of contrast, especially of tempo, an appropriate balance among these factors, and the obvious requirement that two movements of the same work not be so contradictory as to be mutually defeating, there are certainly many instances in which two movements of similar nature from two multi-movement works of the same style (hence, probably of the same composer) might be convincingly interchanged. This is true, for example, of the third movements of the Haydn Symphonies Nos. 101 and 104, both in D. The relationship that we sense between or among movements of a large work is often nothing more than one of conditioned association.

Smaller and larger exceptions to the multi-movement norm

A few examples of two-movement sonatas are given on p. 170. One-movement sonatas, representing regular or modified single-movement sonata form, or some kind of condensation of multi-movement form, occur prominently in the present century, as one symptom of the modern tendency toward greater compression in musical design. Yet, if we exclude symphonic poems and overtures, one-movement sonatas are relatively uncommon, even in the twentieth century. Examples of recent symphonies in one movement are the Seventh of Jean Sibelius (1865–1957), the Third of Roy Harris (b. 1898), and the Sixth of William Schuman (b. 1915). An example of a one-movement piano sonata is the Op. 1 of Alban Berg (1885–1935).

Sonatas comprising a greater number of movements than the normal three or four are also to be found, although relatively rarely. Examples of these are the Beethoven Quartet in B-flat, Op. 130 (six movements), the Schumann Symphony No. 3 in E-flat (five movements), the Piano Trio in E minor, Op. 90, of Antonin Dvořák (1841–1904), which has five movements, and the Brahms Sonata in F minor, Op. 5 (five movements).

Single-movement sonata form:

The introduction

Our attention now turns to the principal subject of this chapter—the important and common design in music which we have termed *single-movement sonata form*. Basic features of the form are the statement of themes or thematic complexes at contrasting tonal levels (exposition), development of some or all of the exposition material, and its restatement (or recapitulation).

An introductory section, preceding but not necessarily distinctly separated from the main body of the movement, is not unusual, although it is by no means a standard feature of the form. Moreover, its content, size, structure, and other characteristics are unpredictable. Each introductory section has to be studied in terms of its own character, which is largely determined by its function as prefatory material as well as by the nature of what is to follow.

Lengthy, slow introductions are fairly frequent. The First, Second, and Fourth Symphonies of Beethoven have formal introductions, and the Seventh has an especially extensive and elaborate introduction with a well-delineated form of its own. Many symphonies of Mozart have introductions, for example the Symphonies in C, K. 425, in D, K. 504, and E-flat, K. 543. Haydn's symphonic introductions are so common that specific examples need not be cited. Other examples of introductions to first movements of symphonies are the "Great" C major Symphony of Schubert, Brahms' First, and, in the twentieth century, the First Symphony of Sibelius. In the literature of chamber music the following examples may be mentioned: Mozart's Sonata in G, K. 379, for violin and piano, and Quartet in C, K. 465, with its extraordinary chromatic introduction; Beethoven Quartets, Op. 59, No. 3, and Op. 74; the Haydn Quartet in D, Op. 71, No. 2; Schubert's Octet, Op. 166, for winds and strings (whose final movement also has an introduction); the Franck Quartet in F minor for piano and strings, whose slow introduction is worked subtly into the following *allegro* and returned in its original tempo late in the first movement; and, in the twentieth century, the Second Quartet of Walter Piston (b. 1894). Another twentieth-century example of an introduction to the first movement of a large work is found in the Piano Concerto No. 3 by Serge Prokofiev (1891–1953).

Apart from introductory sections of such scope, many movements have brief opening figures which arrest attention prior to the statement of the principal thematic material. Such a work is Beethoven's Third Symphony, with its two full tonic chords introducing the opening theme, or Haydn's Quartet in G, Op. 76, No. 1, with its simple but commanding I-V-I progression at the beginning of the first movement. A further example is quoted as Ex. 6.3, from the opening of Chopin's Sonata in B-flat minor.

Ex. 6.3   Chopin, Sonata in B-flat minor, Op. 35.

It is instructive to look for examples of brief, introductory gestures of this sort and to consider what may be in the nature of the thematic materials of the movement to make such a device appropriate.

The function of the introduction is to "set the stage" for what follows, to prepare the mind and ear for the presentation of the principal materials of the movement. The reason for an introduction may be found in the nature of the opening theme of the exposition: its decided importance in the movement's future course and content, its unpretentious or very active beginning, its tonal ambiguity, or simply the swiftness of its general impression. It is sometimes revealing to subtract the introduction from an example (the first movement of the Beethoven Sonata, Op. 13, and the Schubert Octet mentioned earlier are good illustrations); the beginning of the form proper often appears awkwardly abrupt. It is difficult to plunge into the course of a busy theme without the preparation that an introduction affords.

The above sets forth only the most general circumstances in which introductory material is helpful; other reasons may be cited in particular examples. Although instances of introductions to final movements have been mentioned, the opening movement of a work is, for obvious reasons, more likely to be preceded by an introductory section. Additional examples of introductions to final movements are those of the Beethoven First Symphony (a slow passage of 6 measures), the Brahms Piano Quintet, the Brahms First Symphony, and the Tchaikovsky Fifth Symphony.

Very often, the materials used in the introduction are not used again in the movement proper. This is the case with most introductions of Haydn, Mozart and Beethoven, although some exceptions are noted below.

It may be argued that a greater degree of compactness of form is achieved when materials of the introduction are developed or restated later during the course of the movement, so that the opening section is related in its thematic materials to what follows. An example of this procedure is Beethoven's Sonata, Op. 13, first movement. Here, the theme of the slow introduction is not only returned in rhapsodic fashion in its original form during the movement proper, but the principal motive of the introduction is actually merged with the opening theme of the exposition during the development. The introduction motive is indicated in Ex. 6.4.

Ex. 6.4   Beethoven, Sonata in C minor, Op. 13, first movement.

Other works in which introductory materials are used during the form proper are the Beethoven Quartets, Op. 130 in B-flat and 132 in A minor, the Haydn Symphony No. 103 in E-flat (an exception for Haydn), the Schubert C major Symphony, the Tchaikovsky Fourth and Fifth Symphonies, and the First Symphony of Brahms, whose introduction supplies the chief subject matter of the first movement. Related passages from the introduction and exposition in the Brahms First Symphony are quoted in Ex. 6.5. Many other examples could be cited.

Ex. 6.5 Brahms, Symphony No. 1 in C minor, Op. 68, first movement.

Because it usually introduces fast material, the tempo of the introduction is in most cases slow. The effect of its length, relative to the balance of the movement, is thus greater than it appears to be if one judges by the number of measures involved. No two introductions have quite the same features and it is always interesting to compare different examples with respect to contrasting styles and the demands of each particular work. Sometimes the introduction begins with a brief formula which, in itself, is an attention getter. Thus, in Haydn's Symphony No. 102 in B-flat, the tonic note is sounded throughout the orchestra in unison and octave doublings in the first measure, sustained through a *fermata,* and expanded and reduced dynamically by *crescendo* and *diminuendo.* There is an identical bar five measures later (see Ex. 6.6, and more extensive quotation in Ex.

Ex. 6.6 Haydn, Symphony No. 102 in B-flat, first movement.

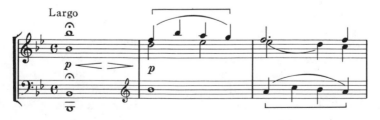

6.44a). These measures add interest to the structure by introducing an element of irregularity opposed to the 4-measure regularity in the phrases of the theme of the introduction. Their indeterminate length, an effect of suspension in the motion, contrasts to the broad, measured pace of the introduction as a whole. The first measure also prepares the ear for the motive of measure 2—the basis for the entire introduction—and serves to establish the tonic note strongly. In short, it introduces the introduction.

The exposition

There are a few things that can be said of the exposition which will apply without exception in single-movement sonata form. In the exposition, the themes and motives are set forth in their most direct form. The terms "principal theme (or subject)" and "subordinate theme (or subject)" have been applied to these materials, which often consist of two major thematic ideas, but it is meaningless to assign any sort of comparative rank of significance to the ideas stated in the exposition. Moreover, the materials are not always melodies of clearly defined form and shape. A group of motives or ideas not having the unity of a single "theme" may be presented. There may, in fact, be strong contrasts within each section of the exposition. The materials of the exposition should therefore be referred to as "groups" or "complexes" of ideas. For example, the first movement of Mozart's Sonata in F, K. 332, begins with a twelve-measure period, followed by a very new and different thematic element in measures 13–22. This second theme is to be considered a part of the first section, or group, because it is in the same key as the opening period theme. The second group (in the key of C) is even more diverse, with individual themes at measures 41, 56, and 71.

The most universally applicable point to be made concerning the traditional exposition is that its content is centered first in one tonality, the principal key of the movement, and then in a second key. On each of these key levels significant activity takes place. There are thus two centers of considerable tonal stability: the first *tonal group* is followed by a passage of modulatory transition, after which there is a settling at the second tonal level for statement of the materials of the second tonal group. Again, exceptions are to be found; either complex may be tonally unsettled as part of its essential character (Beethoven Sonata, Op. 53, first movement, first tonal group).

In traditional eighteenth- and nineteenth-century sonata examples, the two keys of the exposition are normally closely related. The most usual relationship is that of tonic and dominant between major keys. In instances in which the first is of the minor mode, it is likely to be paired with its relative major. Again, the Beethoven *Waldstein Sonata* offers an exception:

the first tonal group is in C (despite its tonal fluctuation, mentioned above), while the second is in the mediant key, E.

Ex. 6.7 Beethoven, Sonata in C, Op. 53, first movement.

Beginning of first tonal group: **Beginning of second tonal group:**

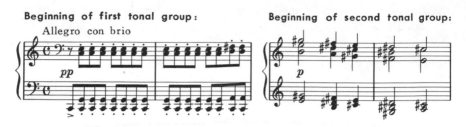

The thematic materials of the first tonal group in the exposition are usually substantially different from those in the second group, but occasionally the same ideas will be the basis for both. Ex. 6.8 illustrates this point with reference to the Haydn Sonata in C-sharp minor.

Ex. 6.8 Haydn, Sonata in C-sharp minor (Peters No. 6), first movement.

First group: **Second group:**

In the relationship between the two complexes, the contrast of tonal levels is basic, but almost always the materials are contrasted in other ways as well—if not in actual motivic derivation, at least in the treatment of the materials, as seen in Ex. 6.8. Each tonal group may have any of a wide variety of structures: there may be a group of phrases, a period form, a small two- or three-part form, or simply a freely-woven or sectional sequence of ideas not conveying the sense and unity of any single specific formal scheme. The occurrence of binary or ternary forms as part of the exposition is not very frequent, because of the customary uniformity of tonality within each complex, although tonal homogeneity is possible, if not usual, in these small forms (Chapters 2 and 3).

It will be useful to list a few examples of the above types. Simple three-part form may be seen within the first tonal group of the first movement of the Schubert Sonata in A, Op. 120 (measures 1–20). The first movement of the Ravel String Quartet begins its first tonal group with a simple ternary followed by a phrase based on a rhythmic permutation of the original motive. This phrase, entering at measure 24, is immediately repeated in sequence. The Mozart Sonata in C, K. 296, for violin and piano, begins with a repeated phrase (measures 1–8), followed by three statements of a two-measure motive (measures 9-14) and an eight-measure period (15-22), ending the first tonal group. The opening of the Piano Quartet, Op. 34, of Brahms is a good example of a phrase group in the first tonal complex: measures 1–11 might be termed introductory gestures, followed in measures 12–26 by a group of phrases, with cadences at measures 17, 22, and 26. Measure 27 begins a new phrase which dissolves into a transition leading into the new key level.

One should dismiss the observation sometimes made that the first complex is more "noble," "masculine," or "rigorous" than the second, or that it is in any expressive quality predictably or commonly distinctive in any particular way. But some form of contrast, apart from tonal, is usual between the two groups.

A characteristic of many early works in single-movement sonata form is the absence of fully developed and confirmed modulation prior to the introduction of material in the key of the second tonal group. This can be seen in numerous Mozart Sonatas (first movements of K. 280, K. 283, K. 284, and K. 311, to list only a few examples) and, sometimes, in Haydn Sonatas. Of the latter, the reader may look into the first movements of the Sonatas in D and G (Peters Nos. 9 and 11, respectively). Here, the transition out of the first tonal group leads only to the dominant harmony of the original key. The second complex, which follows immediately, simply takes up this harmony as its tonic. Ex. 6.9, taken from the first movement of the Mozart Sonata in F, K. 376, for violin and piano, illustrates the absence of real modulation preceding the second group.

Ex. 6.9 Mozart, Sonata in F, K. 376, for violin and piano, first movement.

The technique of modulating even beyond the desired tonal destination, often seen in Haydn and Beethoven, for example, is characteristic of highly developed single-movement sonata form, and is shown in Ex. 6.10,

Ex. 6.10   Beethoven, Sonata in G, Op. 14, No. 2. first movement.

from Beethoven's Sonata in G, Op. 14, No. 2. Here, the reader will observe that the modulation from G to D reaches slightly beyond its destination by the momentary reference to A. This use of a passing G-sharp enhances the effect of the final yielding to the new key.

The passage linking the two tonal complexes is called a "transition" or "bridge." In the exposition, this transition does have the function of effecting modulation to the key of the second tonal group, even though, as we have just observed, this function is not always thoroughly carried out. Even if the modulation is incomplete, the entrance of the second group will have some degree of tonal preparation. The transitional passage may be approached in any of a number of ways: the first complex may be concluded on a strong cadence, followed by the transitional material, as in the following passage from Beethoven's Sonata, Op. 10, No. 1, in C minor (Ex. 6.11); the transition may be started simultaneously with the cadence

Ex. 6.11   Beethoven, Sonata in C minor, Op. 10, No. 1, first movement.

② The symbol in which two harmonic levels are separated by a horizontal line denotes that the upper (here, V/V) occurs *over* and in conjunction with the lower (here, V, represented by its root).

ending the first group (Ex. 6.12); or, the final element of the first group

Ex. 6.12   Schubert, Sonata in E-flat, Op. 122, first movement.

may dissolve in a subtle way into figuration which leads without even a tentative cadence into the transition. An example of this may be observed in the first movement of Beethoven's Second Symphony (see measures 16–22). This transition, a small part of which is quoted as Ex. 6. 13, develops the primary motive of the first group.

Ex. 6.13   Beethoven, Symphony No. 2 in D, Op. 36, first movement.

The transition may, as observed in connection with ternary form, contain ideas of the first tonal group, from which it departs, as well as the second, which it approaches. Thus, in the Beethoven Quartet in C, Op. 59, No. 3, the transition linking the two groups employs, in measures 71–75, a motive of the first, and in measures 65–66, a motive of the second. The reader is urged to seek out these relationships in the score.

Occasionally the transition appears to be entirely freely composed. The transitions in the following Mozart movements bear no relationship of *thematic* consequence to the elements surrounding them: the Sonata in C, K. 309, first movement (measures 21–32); and the final movement of the Sonata in F, K. 332 (measures 36–49).

The transition is frequently built fully or in part on a pattern of harmonic sequence. This technique is illustrated in Ex. 6.14, quoted from the first movement of the Haydn Symphony in B-flat, No. 102. The transi-

Ex. 6.14   Haydn, Symphony No. 102 in B-flat, first movement.

Free sequential repetition ③

tion is in this case built upon two motives of the opening theme of the exposition. The technique of sequence is used again later in the same transition (measures 53–4; Ex. 6.44c). The first movement of the Beethoven Sonata in C minor, Op. 10, No. 1, uses sequence through almost the entire transition between the two tonal groups (measures 32ff.).

Beyond the possibilities mentioned above it is difficult to generalize regarding the material of the transition. It should be remembered that this transition has the function of effecting a smooth change of character, assuming that the two groups are of different character, in addition to that of modulation. The function of transitional modulation, as will be seen in connection with a later division of single-movement sonata form, may be lacking altogether, but even when this is true there is usually some tonal digression within the transitional passage as a source of variety. We have already observed that the transition within the exposition, as in Mozart and Haydn examples cited, often does not modulate. As a further illustration, we may consider the transition linking first and second tonal groups in the first movement of the Beethoven Sonata in D, Op. 28 (measures 40–62). In this example, modulation from D to A is not a function of the transition, since it is entirely in A, with sequential false[4] references to the further dominant, E, according to the following pattern: A-E-A-E-A. This example bears out the observation made earlier that there is normally some tonal fluctuation in a transitional passage even when it begins and ends in the same key. To summarize, the transition most often involves some degree of tonal change as a source of contrast, but it is not necessarily modulatory, in the sense of leading out of one key and into another at its conclusion.

Since the art of joining two areas of diverse characteristics is one of the most challenging aspects of musical composition, the reader should

③ In a *free sequence* the repetition of the basic pattern is in some way modified. In Ex. 6.14, the first harmony of the pattern is changed in repetition; the second harmony remains dominant, but in a different form; and some chord positions are altered, e.g., the first inversion at the end of measure 3 of the excerpt. (See footnote, p. 7.)
  [4] See footnote, p. 37.

examine carefully the nature of transitional passages of many periods and composers.

At the end of the exposition, following the statement of materials at the second key level, there is usually a brief concluding section. This section, a codetta (Chapter 4), has the appearance of an appendage to the main body of the exposition, normally set off by the latest authentic cadence, of which it may be little more than an extension and elaboration (Ex. 6.15). The codetta often includes some motivic material of the first group, or it may derive from any part of the exposition. An example of a codetta taking its motives from the first group is that of the first movement of Mozart's Symphony in D, K. 504, after measure 136.

But as stated above, the codetta is often a mere flourish of cadence chords. This is seen in the excerpt quoted as Ex. 6.15, a two-measure codetta consisting of nothing more than an extension of the final tonic.

Ex. 6.15   J. C. Bach, Sonata in E-flat, Op. 17, No. 3.

Ex. 6.16, the codetta to the exposition of the first movement of the Haydn Quartet in G, Op. 76, No. 1, is a similar flourish of cadential harmonies, in this case both tonic and dominant.

Ex. 6.16   Haydn, String Quartet in G, Op. 76, No. 1, first movement.

In some examples the second tonal group leads into a distinctive new theme, or into a codetta containing such a theme. A thematic entity of this kind, set apart from the main body of the second group by a transitional passage (Mozart Sonata in F, K. 332, measure 71), a cadential punctuation, or by rests, or appearing as part of the codetta, is called a *closing theme.* The "closing theme" of Ex. 6.17 arises in the codetta (measure 82) of the Beethoven Sonata, Op. 31, No. 3. The codetta, not quoted in full, leads into a retransition preparing the return to the key of the beginning of the exposition.

Ex. 6.17   Beethoven, Sonata in E-flat, Op. 31, No. 3, first movement.

In the first movement of the last Haydn Symphony (No. 104, in D) a closing theme affords the only material contrast to the theme of the first group, which is also used at the dominant key level as the basis for the second group. The theme which is shared by the two tonal groups is quoted as Ex. 6.18, together with the closing theme, which occurs as part of the codetta (measure 84).

Ex. 6.18   Haydn, Symphony No. 104 in D, first movement.

Closing theme

In the opening movement of Mozart's "Jupiter" Symphony, K. 551, there is a closing theme of great importance, set apart from the balance of the second group by rests and occurring prior to the codetta. The beginning of this theme, and the approach to it, are illustrated as Ex. 6.19.

Ex. 6.19   Mozart, Symphony in C, K. 551, first movement.

The codetta consists of the final 4 measures of the exposition and is made up of tonic and dominant chords and a recurrent motive from the first group. It will be useful here to consider again the definition of *codetta,* established earlier: it is the final section of the exposition, set off by the latest strong cadence. It has a clear motivic consistency which makes it a unit.

The exposition of Beethoven's Sonata, Op. 7, first movement, may be mentioned as a further example of a work containing a distinctive closing theme, in this case as part of the codetta, the final 10 measures of the exposition. Finally, we may observe a single example of a Mozart codetta of thematic character; simple cadential elaboration is more of a rule in Mozart sonatas. Ex. 6.20 is from the first movement of Mozart's Sonata in C, K. 309. It shows the codetta to the exposition, consisting of a two-measure phrase, immediately followed by its own variation.

Ex. 6.20   Mozart, Sonata in C, K. 309, first movement.

The closing theme is not to be confused with distinctive material occurring as part of the second tonal group and not really separate from it. Of course, the distinction between late elements of the second group and an actual closing theme is often difficult to make. If the theme in question actually closes the section (that is, is part of the codetta), there is no question of the appropriateness of the term *closing theme.* But any thematic substance occurring earlier than the codetta itself should come at the end of the second group, set off by a cadence or rests if not by a transitional passage, to warrant the designation *closing theme.* The relatively restrained and settled character of a closing theme should also be taken into account. Many examples in addition to those cited above should be found and evaluated.

The exposition codetta closes in the related key, the key of the second complex, and there is traditionally a repeat of the entire exposition, especially in eighteenth- and nineteenth-century examples. The codetta is sometimes followed by, or dissolves into, a retransition to the tonal level and material of the first group. Such retransition is normally unnecessary because of the usual relationship of tonic for the first group and dominant for the second. The tonic of the dominant key, in this case, is the final chord of the exposition and is easily followed by the tonic key of the opening, to which it is a dominant. The beginning and conclusion of the exposition of a J. C. Bach Sonata are shown as Ex. 6.21 to illustrate this point.

Ex. 6.21   J. C. Bach, Sonata in D, Op. 5, No. 2.

Beginning of exposition:
Allegro di molto

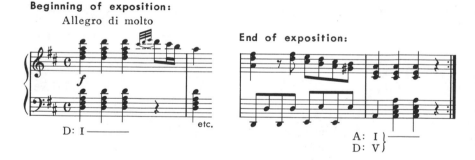

When the exposition opens in a minor key and ends in the relative major, the situation is much the same in early examples, even though the tonic harmony of the relative major is not as functional a common chord as is the tonic of the dominant major. Of course, the original tonic, with which the exposition would most likely begin, is a more useful common chord than that of the relative major, in which the leading-tone of the minor mode is cancelled.

Thus, retransition is not in either case a vital necessity, nor is it commonly found in piano sonatas of Mozart and Haydn, even in movements beginning in the minor mode. Exceptional examples in which retransitions are found at the end of the exposition are the Haydn G minor Sonata (Peters No. 4), first movement, and the Mozart Sonata, K. 457, first movement. The first movement of Mozart's G minor Symphony, K. 550, uses the principal theme of the first group as codetta material at the end of the exposition, followed by a retransition of a single chord to prepare the repeat.

Ex. 6.22   Mozart, Symphony in G minor, K. 550, first movement.

g : V⁷

Retransitions are frequent in later examples beginning in the minor mode, and they are effective because of the relative weakness of harmonic progression[5] when the tonic of the relative major moves directly to the tonic of the opening minor. An elaborate retransition is found at the end of the first movement exposition of the Beethoven Sonata, Op. 13; another can be seen at the corresponding point in the Beethoven Sonata, Op. 31, No. 2. At the end of the exposition of the first movement of Beethoven's Fifth Symphony, there occur two extremely effective measures of silence just preceding the repeat.

Retransitions are found at corresponding points in all of the A minor Sonatas of Schubert; the reader should study the first movements of Op. 42, Op. 143, and Op. 164. In Op. 143, the second tonal group is in the dominant rather than the more usual relative major. There is also a retransition of a single chord, chromatically derived, ending the exposition of the first movement of the Schubert Sonata in C minor; this passage appears in Ex. 6.23.

5 Weakest progressions are those whose roots are a third apart, for in this case two tones are in common: there is a minimum of harmonic change. This is especially true when the root movement is *up* a third, because in this event the root of the second chord is anticipated in the first. Several other factors affect the *qualitative aspect of harmonic rhythm*—among them, the presence of "tendency" tones (chromatic alterations, dissonances), the distance and interval of root movement, the presence of chord inversions, the movement of the highest voice, and the metric positions of the harmonies.

Ex. 6.23 Schubert, Sonata in C minor (No. 1 of Three Grand Sonatas), first movement.

Retransitional passages are also found in many specimens in the major mode. That of the first movement of the Schubert Sonata in E–flat, Op. 122, simply adds the minor 7th to the final tonic in B–flat, rendering it dissonant and strengthening its relationship to the opening E–flat tonic. Another example is the Mozart Quartet in C, K. 465, first movement; this retransition also contains a motivic preparation for the repeat of the first group. Many excellent transitional passages can be seen in the chamber music of Brahms; the rule in many of these works is motivic as well as tonal preparation of the repeat. An excellent example of complete retransitional preparation of the first tonal group can be seen in the String Sextet in G, Op. 36, first movement (measure 213).

A word should be said regarding the usual repeat (repeat sign and double-bar) at the end of the exposition. The composer's use of the repeat sign following the exposition, and sometimes at later points as well, would appear to be an outgrowth of the earlier binary, in which the first and second parts were individually repeated (Chapter 2). The remainder of the form, like the exposition, is often repeated. (See first movements of J. C. Bach and K. P. E. Bach Sonatas; Beethoven Sonatas, Op. 2, No. 2, Op. 10, No. 2, and Op. 79; Mozart Sonatas for violin and piano, K. 301, 302, 304, etc.; most Mozart Piano Sonatas; and the Haydn Quartet in C, Op. 76, No. 3, to name only a few of a multitude of examples from works of the Classical period.)

When the repeats are regarded as a survival of an earlier practice relating to a different formal concept, their relevance to mature single-movement sonata form becomes questionable. They are, in fact, often omitted in actual performance and are not even indicated in more recent examples of the form: Beethoven Ninth Symphony; Beethoven Sonatas, Op. 54, Op. 57, Op. 90, Op. 101, Op. 109, and Op. 110; and most works of the later nineteenth century. The repeat principle does persist through many works of Schumann, Schubert, Chopin, and Brahms. In the Brahms Symphonies the repeat sign begins to disappear at the fourth movement of the Third Symphony.

The often-repeated explanation of this practice, as an important assurance that the themes of the exposition are firmly impressed upon the listener's mind, is of doubtful validity and fails to take into account the matter of the evolution of single-movement sonata form from binary antecedents. Perhaps the only sense in which such repeat is significantly useful is to show the complete interrelationship of the two tonal levels; yet even this has been amply demonstrated in the course of the exposition.

One may well ask what effect such repetition, when practiced, has on the form of the music. In the repetition of the exposition of single-movement sonata form, the relative dimensions of the form are substantially affected. But we have concluded in earlier chapters that repetition has bearing on form, which is shaped by unity *and* diversity, only when it occurs after digression, and especially when it is not literal. Thus, the incessant repetition of a small unit would be perfectly coherent but would not have form without being opposed to contrasting elements. Furthermore, one can immediately see the poor logic of classifying a literal, immediate repeat as a "second part," when it is precisely the same as the first part, following without intervening contrast.

Yet, the repeat of the exposition follows such contrast; there has been a change of tonal level and considerable activity at the new level in the second group. The repeated exposition is not just *AA;* it is *ABAB.* It must then be conceded that the design is indeed altered when the repeat of the exposition, or of any later segment, is practiced. The fundamental characteristics of single-movement sonata form—statement of thematic materials at contrasting key levels followed by their development—are not affected. But the relative proportions and the outline of the design are changed. With the repeat(s) the design becomes more rondo-like (Chapters 5 and 7). (Compare the above with the discussion of repeats in the binary and ternary forms, Chapters 2, 3, and 4.)

The development

The section following the exposition is most often a free manipulation of the ideas presented earlier. Occasionally, however, this section may introduce materials of apparent significance which are not derived from or motivically related to those of the exposition. In the Beethoven Sonata in C minor, Op. 10, No. 1, first movement, the theme occurring and developed sequentially at measures 118ff. is essentially new, even though a minor relationship can be traced to the exposition—namely, the appoggiatura figure with which the theme phrases end. In extreme cases, the entire middle section may be devoted to statement of new material. An example of this is seen in the final movement of the Beethoven Sonata, Op. 2, No. 1. In this movement, the materials of the exposition are avoided completely until the preparation for the recapitulation. The analyst must then be prepared for the possible appearance of materials which are not motivically related to those of the exposition.

What is usually found here, however, is a working out (German *Durchführung*) of the themes and motives of the exposition—not necessarily all of them—in a section which is tonally unstable to a much higher degree than anything which has occurred before, excluding the transition sections, which are normally of much smaller size. Many keys may be traversed in the development, and the range of relationships among them is often wide. The single key which one may expect to be avoided, except possibly at the beginning, is the tonic, since its appearance in the middle section can have the effect of impairing the effectiveness of its return later. The preparation for this return is often the climax of the development and of the movement, commonly featuring arrival on and prolongation of the dominant harmony of the tonic key. Or the climax may occur just earlier, shortly before the end of the development. The frequent sustained dominant at the end of the development creates an impression of suspended dissonance, or tension, often quite lengthy, and relieved only by the return of the first tonal group in the original key at the point of recapitulation. A portion of such a passage is reproduced as Ex. 6.24 taken from the final movement of Mozart's Sonata in F, K. 332. Dominant harmony has

Ex. 6.24   Mozart, Sonata in F, K. 332, final movement.

actually been established several measures earlier, and is continued in figuration, as shown, even beyond the point quoted. A further excellent example of this technique is to be seen in the Schubert Piano Trio in E–flat, Op. 100, first movement. In the preparation for the recapitulation, dominant harmony begins at measure 329 and continues, with only slight interruption at measure 333, to the beginning of the recapitulation at measure 385. After measure 337 the 7th and minor 9th are added to the dominant to make it increasingly dissonant as the tension of its prolongation mounts.

The length of the development cannot be specified, although in mature examples of the form it is of a size fully comparable to and often greater than that of the exposition.

Development is of primary importance in the sonata for in no other traditional form is the free manipulation of musical ideas so emphasized, nor is there in any other conventional form a special, major division in the structure for treatment of this kind. Musical ideas of some kind occur to almost anyone who is musically literate, but the development of such ideas offers the composer one of his foremost challenges. The development section may be very fantasy-like with frequent and abrupt changes of key, of material, even of tempo. The development of the Beethoven Sonata in E–flat, Op. 81a, first movement, is short—only 40 measures long— but it is entirely involved with two motives of very different character, with agitated, erratic change from one to the other. In this same example, there is tempo change at the sudden delivery of a portion of the main theme at measure 91.

The development often contains the movement's most exciting events; it is the scene of conflicting moods, of restlessness, of drama, of the unexpected. It affords important contrast to the more direct and stable presentation of themes which occurs earlier and later. This contrast is afforded by the greater freedom of form and texture, by the mixtures of opposing elements (often merged in fascinating ways, as in Ex. 6.4), and by tonal fluctuation. The middle section has assumed increasing importance during the evolution of the form; witness the insignificance of the developmental principle as applied in very early examples, indistinguishable from simple binary except for possibly greater diversity of ideas (see discussion of sonatina, later in this chapter). In many recent examples, the techniques of development may be operative through the greater part of the movement. Thus, in the Sextet for strings, clarinet, and piano (1937) by Aaron Copland (b. 1900), the materials of the first movement are set forth and developed with very little direct restatement.

The techniques of development are not, of course, restricted to the development section. It has already been observed that transitional passages in the exposition may involve development of earlier motives, and developmental techniques are often applied in other sections of the sonata movement as well, notably in the coda. Furthermore, developmental techniques are not limited to single-movement sonata form. They are basic in some degree, if not as significantly, to all musical composition.

Often, the development begins with a forthright statement, possibly abbreviated, of the opening material of the exposition, as a sort of reminder of what is to be treated in the middle section. This is especially likely when no repeat of the exposition is indicated. When this is done, especially in the tonic key, the form becomes even more closely allied to the so-called "sonata-rondo" or "extended rondo" (Chapter 7). An example of this is the first movement of Brahms' Fourth Symphony, in which the main theme of the first tonal group returns in the development section in its original key (measure 145). Examples in which an abbreviated form of the theme appears at the corresponding point are the first movements of the Beethoven Quartets, Op. 59, No. 2, and Op. 74, and the Haydn Quartets, Op. 64, No. 5, and Op. 76, No. 1. In the first of these Haydn examples, the theme of the first group is stated in the subdominant key (G); in the second, a good share of the opening theme is recalled with a counterpoint added. In the Beethoven examples there are more fragmentary reminders of the original materials.

It is difficult to generalize as to the key of the development's beginning, except that it may be expected to relate closely to the final key of the exposition. Sometimes the development begins by taking up a motive with which the exposition has ended. This is shown in Ex. 6.25.

Ex. 6.25   Brahms, Sextet in B-flat, Op. 18, for strings, first movement.

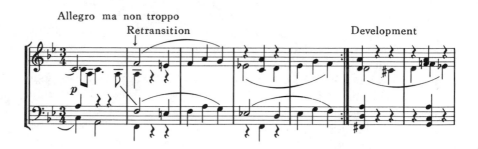

Reference has been made earlier to the end of the development, which is more predictable. At some point, near the end, the development will arrive in the tonic key, which is to be the key of the following section. Ordinarily this will come about on the dominant harmony, as suggested before. The movement of the music onto the dominant of the original key is, more often than not, brought about quite imperceptibly, without any formal end to the development proper—any end, that is, marked by a firm cadence. Ex. 6.26 is quoted from the end of the first movement development and beginning of the recapitulation in the Haydn Quartet in E–flat, Op. 9, No. 2.

Ex. 6.26 Haydn, String Quartet in E-flat, Op. 9, No. 2, first movement.

The prolongation of dominant harmony, usually in an *implicitly dissonant form*,[6] is one of the most basic tension-producing devices in tonal music. It sets up an air of expectancy which is fulfilled by the reprise of the materials of the exposition. Because the tonic key is not likely to occur during the course of active development, its appearance very frequently heralds the end of the development and the preparation for the recapitulation.

Other devices for evoking a feeling of tense expectancy are common at this point. The music may rise in pitch. The dynamics may change radically: either intense *diminuendo* or *crescendo* can serve to build tension. Further, there is often a motivic preparation of the first complex— a tentative repetition, even toying with, the opening motives of the thematic

[6] An *implicit dissonance* is one whose *individual properties,* in a given style, demand resolution—e.g., an augmented triad, or a minor 7th in eighteenth- and most nineteenth-century music. A *tonal dissonance* is one whose need for resolution (also conditioned by style) is determined by its position in a tonal system. For example, the normal dominant triad is not implicitly dissonant; yet, in a tonal context, it is felt as a level of harmonic instability and must resolve. The dominant 7th-chord is dissonant implicitly as well as tonally.

material with which the recapitulation is to begin. In the first movement of Beethoven's Sonata, Op. 53, the development gives way to the recapitulation at measure 156. As early as measure 136 the dominant of the original key (C) begins, and at measure 142 a very intense and increasingly exciting preparation for the recapitulation is underway: there is *crescendo,* a rise in pitch over an insistent, unmoving bass, and a steady recurrence of one of the key motives of the first group in several different forms.

The preparation for the recapitulation, occurring at the end of the development section, is always interesting and should be examined carefully. The analyst will find many additional individual devices by which composers heighten the effectiveness of the retransition. For example, the character of the theme, as well as its tonality and precise motivic content, is likely to be prepared in some way.

Occasional examples show the interpolation of a suggestion, or even complete statement, of the theme of the first group (even in the tonic key) in the midst of development as a sort of "false" entry, which is then abandoned to further development. Haydn was fond of this procedure, as seen, for instance, in the D major Quartet, Op. 64, No. 5. In the first movement of this work the principal theme of the first group is brought into the middle of the development, in complete form and in the tonic key, at measure 105. The actual recapitulation does not occur until 37 measures later. Even when such a false reprise is made in a key other than the tonic, the effect is similar. In the Haydn Symphony in B–flat, No. 102, there is an entry of the complete first theme (Ex. 6.44h), as an interruption of the development, at measure 185, in the key of C, while the recapitulation arrives 42 measures after this point.

It will be useful to list, in summary, some of the techniques of the development section.

1. The simple statement of early materials, even entire phrases and larger units, is a common technique.

2. Another is the segmentation and repetition of thematic fragments, often at changing pitch levels (sequence), seen in Ex. 6.27 from the first movement of Haydn's Sonata in E-flat (Peters No. 3). The repetition of a fragment, especially when extended and supported dynamically, can be a strong tension-building device.

Ex. 6.27   Haydn, Sonata in E-flat (Peters No. 3), first movement.

Source of motive (exposition, first tonal group):

Development of motive in sequential repetition:

(3.) The ideas may be employed contrapuntally, in imitation. The fugato (Chapter 11) is a frequent device in development and, of course, the whole range of contrapuntal techniques—augmentation, inversion, stretto, and others (see Chapter 11)—is available to the composer in this connection. Ex. 6.28 is a quotation of the opening theme of the Quartet No. 2 of Walter Piston, and a later developmental passage on the theme. In the development, the theme is treated in augmentation and in canon between the outer parts.

Ex. 6.28 Piston, String Quartet No. 2, first movement.
Copyright, 1946, by G. Schirmer, Inc. Reprinted by permission.

Original theme:

Canon on augmentation of theme:

Ex. 6.29 illustrates the diminution of an exposition theme in the development section of Prokofiev's Quartet in B minor, Op. 50. Only a portion of the original theme is quoted, followed by its diminution as it appears at measure 127.

Ex. 6.29   Prokofiev, String Quartet in B minor, Op. 50, first movement.
   Reprinted by permission of the copyright owners, Boosey & Hawkes Music
   Publishers Limited.

(4.) The thematic material may be subjected to any of the techniques
of variation (Chapter 9): change of mode, change of rhythm with
melodic outline preserved, change of melodic outline with rhythm preserved,
change of dynamics, change of register or instrumental color, change of
meter, or of any other theme element. The first group theme of the Brahms
Piano Quintet in F minor, Op. 34, first movement, appears in development
with a striking alternation of mode (A–natural, A–flat). Beethoven's
Symphony No. 8 in F, Op. 93, affords another illustration of modal change
in the appearance of the primary motive at measure 161 of the first
movement.

Ex. 6.30   Brahms, Quintet in F minor, Op. 34, for piano and strings, first movement.

Both rhythm and melodic contour may be altered, with some distinctive feature retained. Thus, in the first movement of the Schubert Sonata
in A minor, Op. 42, the use in the opening of the development section of
a characteristic ornamentation of the original theme is enough to recall
the first tonal group. A fragment of the theme is reproduced as Ex. 6.31;
following it is the beginning of the development, in which the ornamental
figure is retained.

Ex. 6.31   Schubert, Sonata in A minor, Op. 42, first movement.

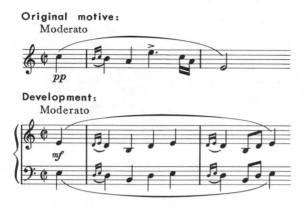

Original motive:
Moderato

Development:
Moderato

(5.) Various motives of different themes or sections may be combined contrapuntally or even merged into the same melodic entity (Ex. 6.4) ; or they may alternate so that one motive is abruptly abandoned for another which is very different.

Ex. 6.32 shows a rapid alternation between two motives, widely separated in pitch location, from the opening measures of the exposition of Beethoven's Sonata, Op. 53, first movement. The developmental passage is preceded in the illustration by measures 3–4 of the first group, to show the source of the motives.

Ex. 6.32   Beethoven, Sonata in C, Op. 53, first movement.

Allegro con brio

(6.) An idea, or a pair of ideas, may be used in a manner of "dialogue" —a kind of imitation—between opposing voices or bodies of sound. This is seen in Ex. 6.33, a passage from the Debussy String Quartet, first movement.

Ex. 6.33   Debussy, Quartet in G minor, Op. 10, first movement.
  Permission for reprint granted by Durand et Cie., Paris, France, copyright
  owners, and Elkan-Vogel Co., Inc., Philadelphia, Pa., agents.

Animé et très decidé

7. A thematic substance may be stated in part and then dissolved
into any kind of figuration—free or motivically related to the theme, or its
continuation simply altered. This technique is clearly apparent in Ex. 6.34.

Ex. 6.34   Haydn, Symphony No. 101 in D, first movement.

Sequence:

Presto

—Free continuation of
 theme motive

(8.) The use of a rapid pace of modulation, often in sequential patterns, is a further resource of development. Tonal contrast is no less important in much current music, in which the traditional key relationships are, of course, often inapplicable.

It is impossible to list all techniques used in the development of musical themes and motives, since the only limit to the possibilities is the composer's imagination. One cannot over-emphasize the importance of sub-jecting a wide selection of development sections to the most careful scrutiny. Such an analysis involves the following questions: Is the material under consideration new or does it derive from the exposition? At the point in question, precisely what is being done with it? The answer to the second question has many parts, having to do with tonality, harmony, dynamics, texture, and all areas of analysis, in addition to the use of specific techniques.

The recapitulation

The recapitulation is the formal return, or restatement, of the materials of the exposition. The presence of a fluctuating and complex development —often a wide departure from the character of the exposition—makes such a return fitting and important. The idea of rounding a structure has been discussed in an earlier chapter as a fundamental element and device of artistic coherence. It is questionable whether convincing form is possible in a work which proceeds tonally, motivically, dynamically, and drama-tically from a certain point and is then simply left in flux, without some reference to the original conditions. The sense of return, of restoration, may of course be achieved in other ways than by the complete and literal restatement of the original themes. Certain other solutions of composers will be discussed presently.

The contrasting middle section is thus usually related to the whole of a work by its position between two like, or clearly related, flanking sections. The long survival of the principle of restatement after digression, discussed in Chapter 3, is good evidence of its validity. It has been argued that the more completely a development section departs from the "attitudes" of the exposition the more impossible a return to the original ideas becomes. On the contrary, an extensive, complex, restless middle section seems to require some kind of reprise—a binding together of the whole. The technique of brief, summary recapitulation is a common solution to the problem of the need for stability at the end as opposed to the danger of redundancy in full restatement.

The entry of the recapitulation is sometimes an element of surprise, although the usual procedure involves the clear tonal, harmonic, and motivic preparation already described. Examples of a surprise recapitula-tion are not hard to find. Two may be mentioned specifically: the first movement of the Beethoven Second Symphony, and the first movement of Haydn's Quartet in C, Op. 33, No. 3, illustrated in Ex. 6.35. In this work the tonic key of C does not arrive until the recapitulation of the first exposition theme is underway. The usual preparation is altogether lacking. In the Beethoven example, the development is in F–sharp minor until the very last moment, the tonic key (D) occurring only one measure before the recapitulation. A further example is the first movement of Brahms' Sonata in A, Op. 100, for violin and piano, whose recapitulation (measure 158) is entered abruptly, through a chromatic progression, without tonal preparation.

Ex. 6.35   Haydn, String Quartet in C, Op. 33, No. 3, first movement.

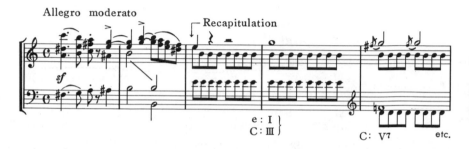

Sometimes, as an element of variation, the entry of the recapitulation may be disguised by a change of harmony, or a change of some other theme characteristic. The recapitulation of the first movement of Mozart's G minor Symphony, K. 550, creeps in so subtly that one is not entirely aware of it until it is underway. Its beginning is submerged under harmonic progressions which to some degree draw attention away from the theme melody.

Ex. 6.36   Mozart, Symphony in G minor, K. 550, first movement.

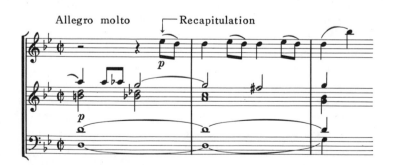

The themes of the exposition are often abbreviated somewhat in the recapitulation. Repetitions, for example, which had occurred initially, are likely to be eliminated. In the first movement of Hadyn's Symphony No. 102 the first theme of the exposition is repeated, but stated only once when it appears in recapitulation.

Movements in which the two groups of materials are motivically related especially require a changed recapitulation, usually shortened or turned here and there into flights of development. The reason is obvious: the movement has already, in exposition and development, seen much of the motive or motives shared by the two tonal groups. In this connection, the reader may review the Haydn example cited in Ex. 6.8, or any comparable movement.

It is probable too that materials much used in the development will be stated only partially in the recapitulation. An extreme case of this is the first movement of the Beethoven Sonata, Op. 31, No. 2, in D minor. In this movement, the principal thematic substance of the first tonal group is thoroughly avoided in the recapitulation because of its extensive use in the development.

Occasionally the first theme of the exposition is stated in a more grandiose manner in the recapitulation, becoming the climax toward which the developmental processes have led. Typical of such cases is a *crescendo* just before the recapitulation begins, followed by the first theme in a delivery which is bigger, dynamically and texturally, than it had been before. The Beethoven Symphonies are interesting to study in this regard, especially the first movements of the Third, Fourth, Fifth and Sixth. In the first movement of the Third, the recapitulation is preceded by a preparation of scope and intensity; however, the most potent delivery of the theme is delayed until later during the recapitulation, which is interrupted several times for passages of prolonged dominant tension followed by repeated theme statements. In the Sixth Symphony, first movement, the recapitulation begins regularly with changed accompaniment patterns and counterpoints and continued developmental attitudes leading toward a *forte,* fully orchestrated appearance of the first theme in the 34th measure of the recapitulation.

A unique and interesting specimen is the first movement of the Mozart Sonata in D, K. 311, in which the materials of the two complexes are reversed in the recapitulation, that of the second tonal group occurring first. Thus, the recapitulation begins in measure 79, but the theme of the first group is withheld until measure 99.

Variation techniques of all kinds can be applied to add interest to the recapitulation, to avoid the possible monotony of literal and full restatement. Principles of variety applied here do not, ordinarily, reach the level of development, except perhaps in transitional passages and rather frequently in the final section, the coda. In the main body of the recapitulation, there is a steadiness of tonality and an integrity of structural units characteristic of the exposition and unlike the typical development.

As implied above, the recapitulation is in a very important sense even more compact and unified than the exposition, for the function of the restatement in bringing secure balance to the over-all form is under-scored by the traditional practice of stating the second thematic complex in the tonic key.

The relative homogeneity of tonality in the recapitulation may neces-sitate a change in the transition connecting the two tonal groups, since its function in the exposition was partially one of modulation. The bridge passage will then be redirected to end in the tonic key. Comparison between this section as it appears in the exposition and as it appears in the recapitula-tion is instructive. Of course, the general character and substance of its motives are not normally altered, since the function of bridging elements of opposing character is just as applicable here as before. Reproduced as Ex. 6.37 is the complete transition in the first movement exposition of the Haydn Sonata in E (Peters No. 30). The first group has reached its cadence in E, the transition beginning in C-sharp minor, modulating to the dominant key (B) in preparation for the second tonal group. Below the example is quoted its counterpart (beginning only) in the recapitula-tion. Here, at the point where the first group ends, again in E, the music is directed into F-sharp minor, which is to E as C-sharp was to B. The tonal adjustment is made very early, so there is a very near identity of the two transitions.

Ex. 6.37   Haydn, Sonata in E (Peters No. 30), first movement.

Corresponding point in
recapitulation:

f♯: V   etc.
                                        (to E)

The only cases in which the transition can be expected to be exactly the same in both parts of the movement are those, already referred to, in which the transition in the exposition does not actually modulate to the dominant key, but simply ends on the dominant harmony of the tonic key. The second group may then enter, more or less convincingly, either in the dominant key, as in the exposition, or in the tonic, as in the recapitulation. (See Ex. 6.9 for an illustration of such a transition.)

Another way in which the transition materials might theoretically remain intact is for the first group, in the recapitulation, to be stated in the subdominant key, with the normal transition then leading back to the tonic. In the Mozart Sonata in C, K. 545, first movement, the first theme appears in the recapitulation in F rather than in C. However, in this movement the transitions are dissimilar in structure, rather than following the obvious procedure of strict transposition up a fourth in the recapitulation. The transition in the recapitulation is four measures longer, in fact, than that of the exposition, and contains a much stronger modulation to the key of the second tonal group. It is an interesting specimen for study.

Often the transition is much abbreviated in the recapitulation—especially when the motives which it contains have been used a great deal in development. In the first movement of Schubert's Sonata in E-flat, Op. 122, the transition in the recapitulation is eliminated entirely. (Compare measures 28–40 with the approach to measure 186.)

In contrast to the above, the transition may in the recapitulation be expanded into a sort of subsidiary development, traversing new key levels, ultimately returning to the tonic. This is the case with the final movement of the Beethoven Sonata, Op. 31, No. 2. In the recapitulation in this movement, the reprise of the first group is dissolved into tonal digression at measure 233. The transitional passage following, leading into the second tonal group, is more than twice as long as the corresponding passage in the exposition, broadened by the application of developmental techniques.

In summary, the recapitulation may be an exact copy of the exposition, apart from change of key, or it may in any of a number of ways be a new version of the materials. It may be a token restatement of the original thematic ideas. It is always important to determine precisely how the two flanking sections of the movement compare in a given case. Some sort of carrying out of the idea of recapitulation will be in evidence, however incomplete. Its function as a release from the fluctuation and turmoil of the development and as a binding, unifying force—a part of the frame within which the development is cast and with reference to which it has meaning—is a vital one in single-movement sonata form.

The coda

The final section is certain to *center* in the tonic key, although a related or even distant key or series of keys may be touched upon during the coda with the effect of intensifying the sense of release at the end. In some way the coda adds emphasis to the close of the movement: by summing up its major thematic content, by a final development of its motives, by increasing the pace of movement, or simply by underscoring the final cadence through repetition of its harmonies. Most often it begins as a restatement of the codetta of the exposition, following the recapitulation of the second tonal group, with the material extended to serve a larger function.

In a movement which is not highly developed there may, however, be nothing more than a repetition, in the tonic key, of the material of the earlier codetta, even if that codetta is simply a brief cadential elaboration. This is the case in many Mozart and Haydn Sonatas and, for example, in the Beethoven Sonatas of Op. 49 and Op. 22. Examples of simple transposition and repetition of the original codetta material at the end of the movement are numerous. When the final section is of such modest proportions and calculated merely to add weight to the final cadence, it is, like the section closing a single division of the form, best termed *codetta* rather than "coda." In nineteenth-century examples there is usually a good deal more than this momentary flourish of cadential chords at the end.

Of whatever scope, the closing section is likely to be set off by a strong cadence. The cadence separating the coda from the main body of the movement may be of any type, sometimes with rests following to enhance the effect of punctuation. The problem of determining, in analysis, where the coda begins is often simply that of locating the recapitulation of the exposition codetta, which follows the statement of the materials of the second tonal group. As stated above, the codetta to the exposition, in reprise, together with whatever is appended in its extension, frequently constitutes the coda. In rare examples in which the original codetta does not return, the coda may be understood to begin after the restatement of the original thematic material, usually following some kind of cadential punctuation.

The term *coda* thus denotes an extensive peroration at the end of the movement, having the quality of being an appendage to the main body of the form, but integral to it. Several examples are given to show cadential punctuation separating recapitulation and coda. The fourth of these (Ex. 6.41) is exceptional because the coda is *not* an extension of the original codetta.

Ex. 6.38   Beethoven, Sonata in E, Op. 14, No. 1, first movement.

Half cadence   Coda

Ex. 6.39   Bruckner, Symphony No. 1 in C minor, first movement.

Elided   Coda
cadence

Ex. 6.40   Mozart, Quartet in A, K. 464, first movement.

Perfect   Coda
authentic
cadence

Ex. 6.41   Haydn, Quartet in D minor, Op. 76, No. 2, first movement.

Deceptive   Coda
cadence

Beethoven is the first composer to be especially associated with the large, developmental coda—sometimes called a *terminal development*. It can be seen as early as the Sonata, Op. 2, No. 3 (measure 211, corresponding to the closing theme of the exposition at measure 77). Other examples of Beethoven codas of important size and significance are those of the Sonata, Op. 53 (both movements), and the Third Symphony, whose first movement has an enormous coda of 145 measures. The final movement of the Sonata, Op. 53, has a very full and complex coda; the movement is a rondo form in which the final statement of the theme merges with and is a part of the coda.

A highly developed coda may give the impression of a fourth major division in the form—a full, new commentary upon what has gone before, even a rival to the development. The coda is then a kind of final view of the materials, cast in a new frame, but having a quality of conclusion and epilogue even when the character is somewhat digressive, episodic, or developmental. In the quality of peroration, or summing up, as well as in the quality of hastening inexorably to the final close, many of the Brahms codas are without equals, although they often subside into quiet conclusion. The student should investigate the Symphonies in this connection. In addition to the codas of the first movements of all four, that of the final movement of the Third Symphony is a splendid example, beginning in measure 217. (The coda, again, should be understood to include the recapitulation of the original codetta.) Occasionally the closing section begins without a pronounced cadential effect, but with some kind of substitute device: the coda to the first movement of the First Symphony is marked by a sudden rhythmic change (measure 430); that of the first movement to the Second Symphony—a big, sectional coda of great momentum—is merged with the return of the first theme of the second group, with a moving triplet accompaniment (measure 424). The closing movement of Beethoven's Sonata, Op. 53, is a further example, as suggested in the preceding paragraph.

Thus, the coda, as it has evolved, especially in nineteenth-century music, adds an exciting new dimension to single-movement sonata form. Even though the coda is often of somewhat developmental character it does not actually, except in very rare instances, seriously contend with the development section itself. It could not, for if it were to constitute a second, restless departure equal to that of the development, it would defeat its purpose, which is, after all, to close the movement, not to lead it into further untraveled regions. A very extensive coda may require a concluding section of its own, and a "coda to the coda" is not uncommon even in closing sections of moderate scope. This is seen in the Schumann Piano Quintet, Op. 44, whose first movement coda begins at measure 314, comes to a very strong cadence at measure 332 (Ex. 6.42), and then continues into a final passage which, in a sense, is to the coda as the coda is to the movement.

Ex. 6.42 Schumann, Quintet in E-flat, Op. 44, for piano and strings, first movement.

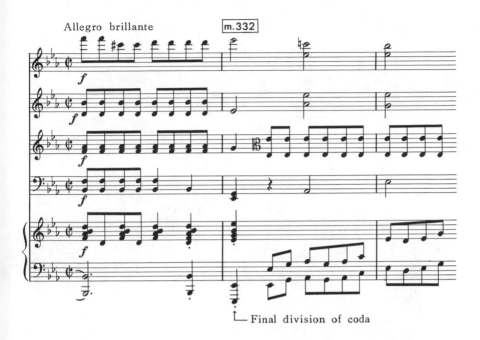

└─ Final division of coda

Rarely does the coda introduce new themes or motives of any distinction. The reason is clear: the introduction of something new here would detract from the direction of the movement toward conclusion. The appearance of significant new material, unless it is quiescent, raises the expectation of some kind of treatment of the new material. The coda loses its meaning when it is that digressive. Often the principal materials of the movement are rather directly stated for a final time during the coda, especially at its beginning. This, too, is illustrated by the coda to the first movement of the Schumann Piano Quintet, cited earlier (Ex. 6.42) in another regard.

Frequently the coda is sectional in structure, each small division adding momentum and drive to the pace of the preceding, and each cadence having more emphatic effect than the preceding, the cumulative effect becoming progressively more resolved and definite. Again the Schumann is a case in point. A further, excellent example is the coda to the first movement of the Mendelssohn Piano Trio in D minor, Op. 49, beginning at measure 479. At first, it is developmental, treating motives of both groups. At measure 530, it reaches a strong tonic cadence, shown as Ex. 6.43a below. There are further strong cadences, of increasing effect, at measures 580 and 596. The first of these is quoted as Ex. 6.43b. After

Ex. 6.43a Mendelssohn, Trio in D minor, Op. 49, for piano, violin, and cello, first movement.

P.A.C.   └ Succeeding section

Ex. 6.43b

Vln.

Vc.

Piano

P.A.C.

measure 596 there occurs a series of rapid dominant-tonic cadential progressions according to the pattern shown below. The harmony in this last section changes first from measure to measure, and then within the measure at a pace of faster *harmonic rhythm*[7] and increasing intensity. The 13 bars remaining after measure 604 are simply an extended animation and elaboration of unchanging tonic harmony.

---

[7] *Harmonic rhythm* refers here to the frequency with which the harmony changes. The rhythmic patterns formed by the changes constitute a further aspect of harmonic rhythm. (See also the footnote on p. 187.)

FINAL MEASURES OF MENDELSSOHN CODA

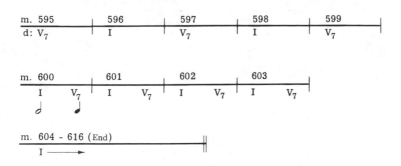

Haydn, Symphony No. 102 in B-flat, first movement

The Haydn movement which is the basis for the following analysis is an individual manifestation of single-movement sonata form. In its broad outlines it is typical of the mature form, but at the same time, as is true of any great work, it is unique in many ways. It is scarcely necessary to underscore the importance of examining many specimens of the form to understand its manifold possibilities.

The slow introduction (measures 1–22) is, except for transitory modulation to F, in B-flat major and minor, and it is dominated by the motive of measure 2, which appears as part of the opening 8-measure period theme. This motive, which is marked in the quotation (Ex. 6.44a), appears in nearly every measure once the theme is stated. The tonic note, stated in indefinite length in measure 1 and measure 6, emphasizes the tonality, and is an effective element of irregularity against the parallel 4-measure phrases of the theme. Our analysis should note that the authentic cadence in F (measure 10) is elided with and countered by the entrance of the basic motive in the bass. The passage which follows (measures 10–20, not fully quoted) is an excellent illustration of the driving power of motive repetition, stimulated by the syncopations and the rising chromatic pitch line above. The thematic material of the introduction is not significantly referred to again in the course of the form proper.

The first tonal group of the exposition extends from measure 23 to measure 38. Its single theme is again a symmetrical period, repeated with changed orchestration. There are three motives that prove to be of profound significance in the later development; they are bracketed in Ex. 6.44b.

Ex. 6.44a Haydn, Symphony No. 102 in B-flat, first movement.

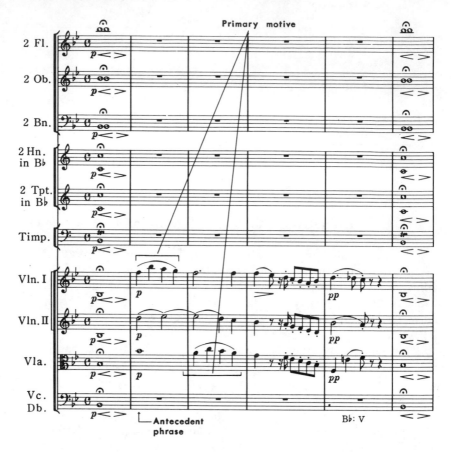

The melodic line of each phrase begins at a high point (toward which the anacrusis is an effective thrust), descends to a mid-point level on f″, and then descends further to the cadence, where it turns up slightly, dropping again. (Compare the first phrase of the *allegro* theme with that of the period which begins the introduction; although the two melodies are of strongly contrasted character, especially because of tempo, they are strikingly similar in line.)

Ex. 6.44a (continued)

Consequent
phrase

F: I

Ex. 6.44b

I └─ **Repetition of period**

213

Ex. 6.44c

The transition begins with a sudden *tutti*, and a strong, *forte* impulse (see Ex. 6.44j, a reproduction of the identical passage in recapitulation). It develops all three of the theme motives cited earlier, occurring here in the order of their initial appearance in the theme itself. They occur in the prominent upper part, alternately soaring and plunging in a highly turbulent, restless manner, at first over a tonic pedal. The use of the typical device of sequence should be noted; that of measures 47–50 is not quoted, but Ex. 6.44c includes measures 53–54, in which sequence is used.

m.60

Mirror of primary
motive

Motive of first theme,
used as source of
accompanimental motion

Fragment of
primary motive

The excerpt also includes the beginning of the second tonal group, in the dominant key. The initial motive of measures 57–58 dominates most of this section (see vln. 1 and vc., one the mirror of the other). Clearly there is no "theme" here in the conventional sense in which we see it in the first group. A development of the motive, and of two of its fragments, leads to a big cadence (7 measures of cadential tonic $\frac{6}{4}$), to be followed by a new theme—part of the present complex.

Ex. 6.44d

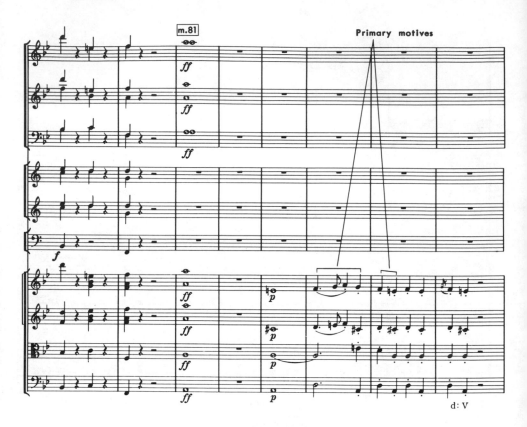

Ex. 6.44d shows the end of the extended cadential formula described in the preceding paragraph. Now, contradicting the deceptive "finality" of the cadence, strings and winds, *fortissimo*, sound A, the dominant of D minor. This bar *looks* like measure 1 but is almost totally unlike it in effect. Functionally it plays a comparable role, introducing the antecedent of a period theme. As in the introduction, the consequent phrase is similarly introduced. A bar of silence (measure 82) emphasizes the contrast between the outburst of measure 81 and the hushed theme, in strings alone.

The period theme takes the second group on a momentary excursion into D minor, its consequent phrase restoring F. The perfect authentic cadence which closes the period is overthrown, as was that of the initial *allegro* theme, by sudden *tutti* and the rush of 8th-notes, now in the bass. The basic motive of the second group returns, making of the total thematic complex a tripartite form. The quotation shows in the bass a motive of the opening *allegro* theme—that of measure 24—here used accompanimentally.

Ex. 6.44e

m.100

Imitative
development
of m.25
motive

(sf)

Codetta on I pedal

The exposition codetta, in F, is set off by cadential punctuation at measure 100. Over a tonic pedal (see Ex. 6.44e), it capriciously develops another motive of the first theme (that of measure 25), in a rapid dialogue between the violin sections. The motive of measure 24 is also used, as indicated in Ex. 6.44e, followed by a very strong tonic cadence at measure 110. Repeat of the exposition is specified without retransition; F:I acts as B-flat:V for the return.

Space permits only a brief *résumé* of the events of the development, one of Haydn's best. All exposition materials are treated, and there is considerable tonal fluctuation, touching the following levels in the order listed: c, E-flat, f, A-flat, b-flat, c, d, g, c, C, c, A-flat, F, B-flat, E-flat, F, g, B-flat.

219

Ex. 6.44f

Development of 2-note fragment
of second group theme

The period theme at the middle of the second group is developed extensively, especially following measure 132. A 2-note fragment is taken down and up the A-flat diatonic scale (Ex. 6.44f). The continuation of this development, in which a 2-measure motive is manipulated imitatively and sequentially, in devious tonal movement, is partly shown above. A bit later, the principal motive of the same theme undergoes extreme variation of intervallic structure—variation in which its identity is clearly preserved:

becomes

Ob.

m.143

Cello

Development of
m.84 motive

A♭: I

bb: V

Sequence pattern, repeated
4 measures later

Ex. 6.44g

The beginning of an extensive canon (Chapter 11) on the first second-group motive (measures 57–58) is reproduced as Ex. 6.44g. Canonic development continues from measure 161 to measure 184, all of it on the same material, after which there is a rest of indefinite length (*fermata*). Now Haydn jests with a "false" return of the opening theme—its complete period—in the "wrong" key of C. The end of that statement, presented by the flute, and succeeding *tutti* development of a motive of the same theme are shown in Ex. 6.44h. The complete score should be consulted concerning the use of sequence and modulation in this phase of the development.

Ex. 6.44h

Conclusion of "false" return

Resumption of development
(m.24 motive, mirror form)

Ex. 6.44i

The end of the development, and the retransition preparing the recapitulation, appear in Ex. 6.44i. The approach to B-flat:V is seen. Once achieved, the harmony is prolonged for 10 measures. The upper voice rises, contributing to the anticipatory feeling, repeating the opening motive of the approaching theme—quietly, whimsically, and with quickly changing colors—over the sustained dominant harmony. The recapitulation enters assertively, *forte*, releasing the tension of the long dominant. The development has been of impressive scope, comprising more than a third of the total form.

The restatement of the original *allegro* theme is without change except for the elimination of the repetition of the period, as may be checked in

Thematic preparation
(continued in oboe and flute)—
concurrent with
reduction in texture

Recapitulation

measures 227–234. The transition linking first and second groups, its original modulatory function no longer valid and its material now exhaustively developed, is considerably reduced in length. It touches the secondary level of E-flat (through the V_7 of IV) but does not significantly digress from the fundamental tonic. It is seen in full as Ex. 6.44j, which includes the beginning of the second group.

The reprise of the second group, which is not quoted (see measures 243–288), is abbreviated in some areas, extended in others. It is fundamentally in B-flat, but its middle theme refers momentarily to G minor, paralleling the corresponding reference to D minor in the exposition. The

Ex. 6.44j

└─Transition, abridged

tonic cadence toward which the second complex seems to move (see Ex. 6.44k) is upset by deceptive progression to VII_7/V (a diminished-seventh chord) in measures 281–282. This leads to half-cadence, and return of the anacrusis motive which opened the exposition, in measures 286–288. The coda follows, as marked in Ex. 6.44k.

The coda does not, as is often the case, begin with the material of the former exposition codetta. Ex. 6.44k shows that it begins with the first group theme. The example does not, however, show the dissolution of the theme, the motive of whose second bar is repeated, haltingly, finally in augmentation (increased note values), coming to a full stop and *fermata*—a last irresolution before the movement rushes to its close:

The dissonance on which the music pauses at this point (VII_7/II) contributes to the uncertainty of the moment, mildly threatening the supremacy of the B-flat tonic.

Ex. 6.44l shows the conclusion of the coda. There is further, limited development of theme motives, some of it over a tonic pedal, *paralleling the content of the earlier codetta.* As before, the imitative toying with the motive of measure 25 and the vacillation of harmony (mostly I, V) over the paradoxically static pedal, drive the music vigorously to its cadence.

One could go on. In the foregoing sketch, we have been able only to cover main outlines of the movement's design, and to point out examples of some of the elements from which *form* is derived in Haydn's music.

Ex. 6.44k

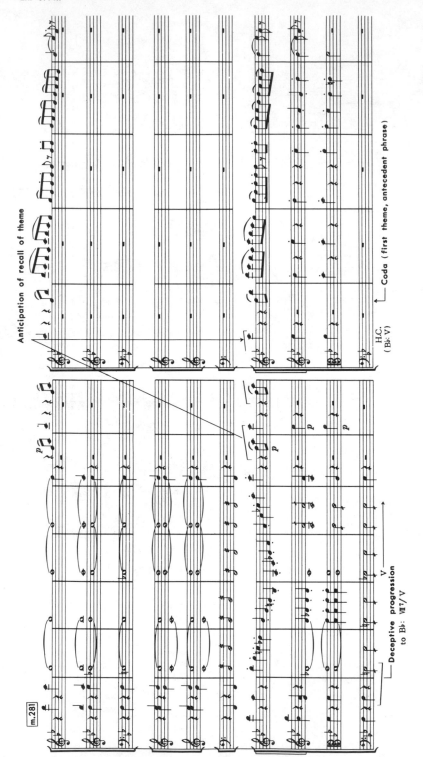

Ex. 6.441

m.300

Tonic pedal

229

A binary or ternary design?

Music theorists often concern themselves with the question of whether single-movement sonata form is basically a two- or three-part structure. The problem is too often treated with regard to an arbitrarily established absolute, without proper consideration of the fact that some examples of the form exhibit more pronounced characteristics in the one direction than the other, and that no clear and universal distinction can be applicable to all examples.

Single-movement sonata form is, as has been suggested, a derivative of binary, or two-part form (above-mentioned sonatas of the pre-Classical composers often represent a clear intermediate stage between the two forms); yet it is idle to insist that the ultimate development has the same two-part form as its ancestor. Even the clear binary, as represented in the majority of eighteenth-century dance movements (Chapter 10), embodies at least one principle of tripartition—i.e., departure and return—despite the fact that the same material is usually employed throughout: this is the technique of modulation away from the tonic key in the first part and back to the tonic key in the second part (Chapter 2). The first part, ending in a related key, corresponds in this sense to the exposition of single-movement sonata form, with its traditional repeat and its conclusion in the dominant or other related key. The second part of the traditional binary corresponds, in the sense of tonal return, to the development and recapitulation of single-movement sonata form. It is because of these parallels that single-movement sonata form is often said to be essentially a two-part, or binary structure.

The argument holds well in single-movement sonatina form, which has only a minuscule development, if any. This is like binary form with a slightly inflated second part. In fact, many early examples of Mozart and Haydn movements in single-movement sonata form (often better termed *sonatina form*), in which the middle section is negligible in scope and importance, can be cited as relating clearly to binary form. The reader may refer to such Mozart first movements as those of the Sonatas in E-flat, K. 282, and C, K. 545. In the latter example, the "development" consists of only 13 measures and it is entirely figurative, not even touching the principal thematic material of the exposition. In addition to the durational inferiority of these middle sections, the movements are, in their over-all proportions, smaller than is the rule in later examples. In many comparable early movements, the relationship to binary form is doubly significant in view of the use, even prevalence, of the same thematic content throughout the exposition; examples have already been listed.

But when, in its mature stages, the form contains strongly contrasting thematic complexes and a highly resourceful and extensive area of development, it is meaningless to insist that it bears the same relationship to binary design. The fully expanded development is a middle section of considerable proportions. It is not correct to ignore this question of relative dimensions of principal sections in considering the matter of two- as opposed to three-part form. In the typical example of single-movement sonata form, the principle of tripartition is expanded considerably. The fact of departure and return is operative here not only with regard to tonality, as in binary form, but with regard to numerous other elements as well. The middle section brings new textures, new attitudes, a new character, and, often, even new materials. The development is an active manipulation of materials, as we have seen—a significant contrast to the relatively straightforward statement of these materials in the exposition and recapitulation. Thus, the recapitulation is a "return," a third major division. It is the rounding out of an essentially tripartite structure.

Thus, for example, the middle section of the first movement of Haydn's Symphony No. 102, outlined in the preceding section of this chapter, is 117 measures long, as compared to a total number of 311 measures in the movement, including the introduction, which is not really an integral part of the form. The development is a thorough contrast in character and in other respects, and there is a pronounced sense of return at measure 227, the beginning of the recapitulation. Obviously it is meaningless to insist that this is binary form. The facts of departure and return constitute the essential substance of tripartite musical structure.

The sonatina and single-movement sonatina form

Movements in which the middle section, if present at all (see Beethoven, Op. 10, No. 1, second movement), is of slight scope and importance, and whose general dimensions are more nearly bipartite than tripartite, have been characterized above as of *single-movement sonatina form*. Similarly, and in correspondence with the foregoing discussion of sonata form, a work of several movements of small proportions, relatively incipient form, and restricted thematic content and development is best described as a *multi-movement sonatina,* or simply *sonatina.*

The two- and three-movement sonatas of J. C. Bach, which include binary, rondo, and variation forms in addition to incipient and even well-developed examples of single-movement sonata form, are, in many cases, appropriately described as sonatinas, as are comparable works of other early Classical composers. Two extremes from the sonatas of J. C. Bach may be mentioned: the Sonata in E, Op. 5, No. 5, first movement, states the reprise of the opening materials immediately at the beginning of the second section; the E-flat Sonata, Op. 5, No. 4, first movement, is, on the other hand, an example of quite developed single-movement sonata form. Certain sonatas of Beethoven—those, for example, of Op. 49, especially the second, are properly identified as sonatinas. Mozart examples have been cited. More recent piano sonatinas have been written by Max Reger (1873–1916), Maurice Ravel, and Béla Bartók. The latter, which consists of Romanian folksongs under a somewhat aribitrary title, does not really employ any of the forms under discussion here. The Ravel first movement has a fairly sizeable midsection, but its over-all proportions are slight, and there is an intimacy and simplicity of content—qualities often mentioned as characteristic of sonatina forms (although irrelevant to many examples, especially slow movements). The dynamic qualities associated with mature sonata form— qualities which are especially manifest in the developmental areas within the form—can scarcely occur within the limited scope of the sonatina.

Thus, even more than the factor of over-all length, the absence of significant development is the earmark of single-movement sonatina form. Sonatina types may contain certain areas of restricted development, but there is little if any of the vigorous wrestling with ideas that one associates with, say, a mature Beethoven example. Slow movements in the Classical and early Romantic sonata often are in single-movement sonatina form, bearing all of the characteristics of single-movement sonata form except for the absence or extreme insignificance of the middle section. Examples are the second movements of the Mozart Sonatas in F, K. 280, and G, K. 283; the second movement of the Beethoven F minor Sonata, Op. 2, No. 1; and the Haydn Sonatas in E minor and C (Peters Nos. 2 and 5), second movements.

It follows that the thematic materials in single-movement sonatina form are not likely to be as involved with developmental possibilities and potentialities. In place of the development, there may be a brief interlude; more often there is only a retransition leading at once into the recapitulation. Thus, in the Haydn Quartet in F, Op. 3, No. 5, second movement, the "development" of eight measures merely serves, by statement of the main theme of the first group around the $\genfrac{}{}{0pt}{}{G:I}{C:V}]$ common chord, to return the tonic key (C) for the recapitulation in measure 42. The "middle section" had begun in measure 34.

Single-movement sonatina form is distinguishable from binary when the "second part" is inflated at its beginning, separating even slightly an "exposition" from a "recapitulation" in the tonic key. Moreover, binary form has greater thematic homogeneity as opposed to some diversity in single-movement sonatina form.

Despite these differences, it is impossible to establish an absolute line of distinction between the sonatina and the sonata, or between either of these and binary form. Thus, it is apparent that many examples fall neatly into none of these categories, and that many works published as "sonatas" are actually closer in form and content to the sonatina. The analytical consideration of *reasons* for classification or non-classification is always valuable.

The vitality and adaptability of single-movement sonata form

Single-movement sonata form is of extraordinary vitality. There has been no period in music history, since the inception of the form, in which it has been significantly neglected, including the present time. Based as it is on the technique of development through transformation and imaginative manipulation of thematic and motivic materials, single-movement sonata form, even when freely applied, presents a substantial challenge to the creative mind.

A good part of the music of the twentieth century has been strongly influenced by Stravinsky, Schönberg, Anton Webern (1883–1945), and, in earlier years, the Impressionists Debussy and Ravel. It is true that the music of these composers shows limited and in some cases no interest in sonata form. Yet one can see continuing strong signs of the vitality of the form even in the present period (see examples cited below). And Debussy and Ravel did not entirely neglect traditional sonata form as may be seen, for example, in their string quartets.

The prevalence of any musical principle over a long period is certain to result at times in its over-use and misuse. Gustave Mahler (1860–1911) and Anton Bruckner (1824–96) attempted to expand the form into something unprecedentedly mammoth, sometimes spreading attractive and even potent materials thinly over immense expanses of time in which the form seems torn into disharmonious parts. Some composers (for example, Reger and Alexander Scriabin, 1872–1915) have been criticized as having forced their music unnaturally and inappropriately into sonata molds.[8]

On the other hand, many twentieth-century composers have made extensive and effective use of the principles of single-movement sonata form, and in some cases interesting variants have appeared. The Sonata, Op. 1, of Berg is a single-movement work applying the principles of the form even to the point of the traditional repeat at the end of the exposition, although there is irregularity in the tonal level of the return of the second group. Works like the Hindemith Second Trio for strings and Second Piano Sonata, first movements, are clear examples of the form. Walter Piston's Quintet for flute and string quartet, first movement, employs even the traditional key

---

[8] See, for example, Aaron Copland's comments on Scriabin in the book, *What to Listen for in Music* (New York: McGraw-Hill Book Company, Inc., 1939), pp 189–90.

relationships, E minor and B minor, for the two tonal groups. Further examples of twentieth-century use of single-movement sonata form are the Quartet in C, Op. 36, of Benjamin Britten (b. 1913); the Symphony No. 4 in F minor of Ralph Vaughan Williams (1872–1958), whose first movement presents interesting changes in the materials in the recapitulation; the Prokofiev Quartet, Op. 50, first movement (keys: B minor, D major), whose recapitulation omits a large portion of the second tonal complex. Many of the symphonic movements of Dmitri Shostakovich (b. 1906) should be included here: for example, first movements of the First and Fifth Symphonies. In the former, the recapitulation states the first theme last, very simply and briefly at the end of the reprise; in the latter, the recapitulation is a vast development with continued vigorous treatment of the themes, much of it canonic and thus long-lined and steady, the conclusion achieved by more static harmonic rhythm and by dynamic and textural reduction.

Bartók's employment of single-movement sonata form, often provocatively unconventional, may be seen in, for example, the first movements of Quartets No. 1, No. 5, and No. 6, Sonata No. 1 for violin and piano, the Sonata for two pianos and percussion, Concerto No. 3 for piano and orchestra, and the exterior movements of the Concerto for violin and orchestra. The reader is referred to Stevens' analyses of these and other sonata movements of Bartók.[9]

The Stravinsky Concerto for piano and winds (1923–24), first movement, brings back in recapitulation the original thematic complexes in their original keys, and restates its broad, introductory material as a closing section at the end of the movement. The idea of rounding out a form by very summary restatement is illustrated by Stravinsky's *Symphony in Three Movements,* first movement. The opening of the movement features a powerful *glissando* motive which is very little used during the middle section. It is returned at the end (Ex. 6.45) in two widely-spaced utterances, abruptly

Ex. 6.45   Stravinsky, Symphony in Three Movements, first movement.
    © 1946 by Schott & Co., Ltd., London. Used by permission.

[9] Halsey Stevens, *The Life and Music of Béla Bartók* (New York: Oxford University Press, 1953), Part II.

abandoned each time; the discretion of this limited reprise seems necessary in view of the strength of the motive, and its prominence (over a distance of 19 bars) at the beginning.

Two earlier examples of Frederick Delius (1862–1934) might be added. The Piano Concerto in C minor contains a slow movement between exposition and recapitulation. The Violin Concerto, a single-movement work, conforms in its broad features to single-movement sonata form but yields to a good deal of apparently extraneous thematic material, especially in the long, digressive coda.

Sibelius, in his symphonies, applied sonata form with great freedom, so that at times, as in much twentieth-century music, only the *techniques* can be observed, while the nineteenth-century structural model is radically altered. Sometimes there is a seeming lack of logic in the succession and evolution of themes (the beginning of the Second Symphony) or an unconvincing grouping of diverse and unrelated, if not incompatible, materials (Fourth Symphony—both in the final movement and the first, whose middle section seems at times to have little to do with the balance of the form). In some works Sibelius uses single-movement sonata form in very regular fashion—for example, in the first movements of the first three symphonies. Occasionally one can observe resourceful, varied treatments of the principles of the form. The first movement of the Fourth Symphony is arch-like, with the original thematic complexes reversed in their restatement at the end, *AB* becoming *BA*. The second movement of the Second Symphony is an example of the form modified in the sense that its modal themes are restated, after exposition, *in* development—a combination, so to speak, of development and recapitulation. Sometimes the recapitulation slights or omits altogether certain themes, as in the first movement of the Sixth and the final movement of the Fourth. While there is, in general, much to question as to Sibelius' achievement of form, it cannot be denied that much of his music is convincingly and interestingly wrought, nor can one fail to recognize the singular power and individuality of many of his thematic concepts.

The above examples taken as a whole, many of them conforming to the outlines of single-movement sonata form very strictly, show that the form has not passed into disuse. If one bases one's observation on the practices of a few important composers, it is a simple matter to find considerable evidence of the neglect of any musical form in any age. In every historical period artists speak and think differently, as a result of the evolutionary change of musical resources as well as the constant transformation of social patterns with its inevitable effect upon human thought and action. Thus it is perfectly understandable that sonata form as it appears in the middle nineteenth-century cannot be a precise reflection of that of the eighteenth, just as the sonata of today shows distinct differences from its earlier prototype.

The contemporary application of single-movement sonata form being freer in concept, with the divisions to which tradition accustoms us less clearly marked, or not marked at all, one is sometimes at a loss to decide whether a particular work is more akin than alien to the principles of the form. In such cases, it is important to consider the question but unnecessary to insist upon a definite answer, in the same sense that it is often futile and without reasonable purpose to insist on a fine line of distinction between the binary form of the late eighteenth century and the emerging single-movement sonata form of the same period. It is important to remember that the cardinal principles implicit in single-movement sonata form are *statement* of thematic materials at contrasting tonal levels and the *development* of these materials. The function of recapitulation is not necessarily impaired when the reprise is radically reduced; often a mere gesture of stability, a simple reminder of the original materials, is adequate for rounding out the form.

Exercises

1. Looking among a variety of works of all relevant periods, find examples to illustrate the following items, discussed in this chapter.
   a) An introduction which is motivically related to the balance of the movement.
   b) A tonal group consisting of two or more distinct thematic entities.
   c) Tonal groups conforming to some of the various structural possibilities mentioned.
   d) Tonal relationships between the two complexes which are not the usual tonic-dominant or relative major and minor.
   e) Two tonal groups unified by the sharing of common motives.
   f) A transition containing no real modulation, ending on dominant harmony in the tonic key.
   g) A transition modulating beyond the actual tonal destination.
   h) Transitions embodying some of the specific techniques mentioned in the chapter.
   i) An exposition codetta which is merely a brief cadential elaboration.
   j) A closing theme.
   k) A codetta returning material of the first group.
   l) Examples of single-movement sonata form containing one repeat, two repeats, and no repeat.
   m) An exposition ending in a retransition into the repeat.
   n) The appearance of new themes or distinctive new motives in the development.
   o) Extended dominant preparation of the recapitulation, and exceptions to this practice.
   p) Statement of the first theme at the beginning of the development.
   q) "False recapitulation" of the first theme during the development.
   r) Examples of the various developmental techniques listed, pp. 194 ff.
   s) The unprepared recapitulation (see pp. 199–200).

t) Irregularities in the recapitulation of the original materials; explain possible bases for these alterations.

u) Use of variation techniques in the recapitulation.

v) Expansion (or reduction) of the transition in the recapitulation.

w) Tonal digression in the coda.

x) Literal repetition of the exposition codetta at the end of the movement.

y) A coda not growing out of the original codetta.

z) A developmental coda.

aa) A sectional coda.

2. Find examples among movements of early sonatas to show (a) binary form, (b) incipient single-movement sonata (sonatina) form, (c) well-developed single-movement sonata form.

3. Discuss some of the implications of the term "sonata."

4. List examples of four-movement sonatas whose arrangement of movements conforms, and does not conform, to the norm discussed.

5. Find additional works whose movements are related in one of the ways described in the chapter.

6. Consider examples of introduction with the purpose of evaluating the necessity for and importance of introductory material preceding the main body of the form.

7. Find examples of slow movements, like those mentioned, which are in single-movement sonatina form.

8. Outline, in the manner shown in relation to the Haydn B-flat Symphony, a movement in single-movement sonata form from one or more of the following groups or categories.

a) K. P. E. Bach or J. C. Bach

b) Haydn or Mozart

c) Beethoven

d) Mendelssohn, Schubert, Schumann or Chopin

e) Brahms or Tchaikovsky

f) Mahler or Bruckner

g) Debussy, Ravel, Fauré, or Franck

h) The twentieth century

9. Answer the following questions concerning one or two examples of single-movement sonata form of your own selection.

a) What is the fundamental key?

b) What is the structure of the first tonal group?

c) How long is the transition? Where is the modulation to the new key? How does the transition begin, in view of the various possibilities discussed in this chapter?

d) How would you describe the structure of the second tonal group?

e) How are the tonal groups contrasted? How related?

f) What is the length of the codetta? What is its content?

g) Is there a retransition preparing the exposition repeat?

h) What are the key levels, motivic materials, techniques of development used in the middle section?

i) How is the recapitulation prepared?

j) How does the recapitulation compare with the exposition? What is eliminated or shortened? What new versions of the materials do you find?

    k) Is the coda an expansion of the codetta? Or is it altogether new? What kind of cadential separation sets it off? Is it developmental? Is it a simple repetition of the earlier codetta?

    l) What irregularities, if any, do you find in the movement as a whole?

10. Outline at least one hypothetical example of single-movement sonata form, including the listing of key levels, to show the basic features of the form as well as some possible irregularities.

11. Try composing original examples of some of the following:

    a) A short, introductory figure or passage.

    b) A transition leading from tonic to dominant keys.

    c) A transition leading from minor to relative major.

    d) Both transitions (2 and 3, above) as they might appear in the recapitulation.

    e) A developmental sequence on a given motive.

    f) Examples of various developmental techniques, as listed in the present chapter.

    g) A codetta of the type that is a simple extension of the cadence.

    h) A typical preparation for the recapitulation of a first theme of vigorous character in the key of E-flat.

12. Prepare an analysis of Schubert's Octet in F, Op. 166, for clarinet, bassoon, horn, and strings, final movement. How would the total effect of the form be amended by repetition of the exposition? Consider the structure of the *andante* and the role its materials play in the movement proper.

13. Carry further the analysis of some of the works cited in this chapter. Find other examples to which one might refer for illustration of single-movement sonata form, and for illustration of its modification in various ways in contemporary and other styles. Specific works for supplementary reference are not given here because of the extreme prevalence of the form in multi-movement sonatas, especially in first movements but in others as well (see, for example, many final movements of Haydn and Mozart Quartets.)

7

SONATA–RONDO

*I*n preceding chapters, we have drawn on large numbers of works to illustrate particular features of each of the forms under consideration. In this chapter, we shall set forth the outlines and characteristics of the sonata-rondo by explanation in the following paragraphs and, on subsequent pages, by analysis of structure in a few complete examples of movements which are in sonata-rondo form. Several quotations will be made from each of these movements.

As its name suggests, the sonata-rondo incorporates features of two major traditional forms—the rondo and single-movement sonata form. It is in that sense a kind of hybrid, and the first in our listing of traditional forms to show the possibilities of combining in a given work characteristics of two or more conventional musical structures.

In the practice of the composers who used the form, the application of the sonata-rondo is limited almost exclusively to final movements in multimovement sonatas, chamber works, symphonies, and concertos. This fact is borne out in the examples cited in the course of this chapter, all of which are finales of such works.

We should recall, in the present connection, certain conditions which have been discussed to distinguish between simple and compound designs. In Chapter 4, pp. 119–20, it was pointed out that the compound ternary, represented as A B A when its first part is a simple ternary, bears a
_(aba) _(aba)
superficial resemblance to the sonata-rondo, represented as ABACABA. The principles postulated in that discussion are not repeated here.

We may, however, further emphasize one of the primary conditions establishing a line of distinction, albeit not an inflexible one, between simple and compound forms: Does the degree of differentiation of materials in, for example, ABACABA, suggest *three* or *seven* parts? Is B more like than unlike A? Stated another way, are the initial parts—ABA—related through compactness, similarity of material, and brevity to the point of constituting a single unit in the over-all form? This and other factors are treated in Chapter 4, cited above, and in Chapter 5, pp. 157–58.

Sonata-rondo form defined

The concept of an arch is more clearly suggested in sonata-rondo design than in any other traditional musical form. The diagrams below demonstrate this, and show further that the concept is not carried out to the same consistency in the distribution of tonal areas. The symbol, *R,* denotes a related key; *D,* the dominant.

DISTRIBUTION OF MATERIALS AND TONAL LEVELS IN SONATA-RONDO FORM

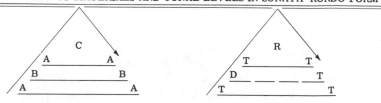

Of the seven chief parts of the design, four are statements of the rondo theme, A. There are three digressions—two of them of like material (B) and the middle one of contrasting character and/or material (C). The full sequence of parts, excluding transitional elements, is thus: rondo theme—first digression—rondo theme—second digression—rondo theme—repetition of first digression—rondo theme.

As discussed with respect to other forms, the structure may include an introduction. Transitions and retransitions are frequent—especially the latter, and a coda is usual.

The key of the first digression is closely related to the basic key of the movement, often the dominant or relative. The key of the second digression is a different related level, possibly the subdominant or parallel key; or the tonality of the second digression, especially when it is developmental, may fluctuate, with rapid, often sequential movement from one tonal level to another. The rondo theme, barring rare exceptions, returns in the tonic key for each of its major appearances. The first digression, in its return near the end of the form, appears in the *tonic* key, as is seen in the diagrams above.

It has by now become clear that recurrences of material may be expected to involve variation techniques, including abbreviation, which may be quite extreme. This is particularly true of a form in which a given element occurs *four* times. In fact, the final statement of the rondo theme in the sonata-rondo is very frequently cut to a simple (but clear) reminder, or omitted altogether, with the coda recalling its principal motives.

It has been implied that the second digression, C, may be of a developmental character; indeed, this is often true. When the middle section is developmental, it may treat materials of A or B, or both. When it is not developmental, it commonly introduces a new theme or complex. In any case, the second digression is generally longer than any of the other parts—a factor which tends to suggest a basic division of three parts even when there is not a total compound organization. Possible form and content in the rondo theme and first digression, as well as introductory, transitional, and closing sections, are analogous to corresponding sections in forms studied heretofore.

Relationships to single-movement sonata form

Two major factors relate the sonata-rondo to single-movement sonata form: (1) the fact that the final appearances of rondo theme and first digression are in the tonic key, corresponding to the recapitulation in single-movement sonata form; and (2) the frequent occurrence of a developmental middle section in which the principal thematic material is taken through paces similar to those which are characteristic of the development section in single-movement sonata form.

Apart from the above, one could cite other obvious characteristics which the two forms share. Both may have introductions, and both very often have codas—sometimes extensive, developmental codas. Both involve contrasting themes and thematic complexes which are exposed at related tonal levels and, often, developed before formal recapitulation. Often the line of distinction is blurred; again, one errs in approaching the problem of classification with rigid preconceptions. Yet the question is always worth considering because it leads to an understanding of the form of the specific work at hand, whatever its deviations from the norm.

The finale of Beethoven's Sonata in F minor, Op. 2, No. 1, is a case in point. The opening material does recur following the first digression (see measure 50), but in the "wrong" key—the dominant, more in the manner of an exposition codetta. Further, the middle section is primarily taken up with a new theme in the relative major—not uncommon in rondo form but an anomaly in single-movement sonata form, where a development is expected. The initial theme does not occur at the end of the movement, although there is reference to it in the coda. (See pp. 189–90, where it is suggested that this movement may best be characterized as a single-movement sonata form without development.)

The distinction sometimes suggested on the basis of a particular character in the rondo theme—that it is "tuneful" or "sprightly" as opposed to the "weightiness" of the related form—is rejected here. The wide disparity among themes of examples cited in this chapter, or among those cited in Chapter 6, will suffice to bear out the point that the character of any given thematic member in any given form is not to be predicted, and not to be the subject of generalization.

Mozart, Trio in B-flat, K.502, for piano, violin, and violoncello, final movement

In the course of the discussions to follow, the student should have scores of the various works at hand. Musical quotations, while carefully selected, are no substitute for a view of the total movement from which they are taken.

The rondo theme in the Mozart finale is 18 measures long, consisting of a double period with the consequent half extended 2 measures by the repetition and inversion of a motive (see Ex. 7.1a). The two parts of the period are in parallel construction, and the antecedent half is made to lean slightly toward the key of F, without actual modulation, by the use of secondary functions around B-flat:V. Nevertheless, the cadence in measure 8 is on the dominant in B-flat. In the example, significant motives are bracketed.

Ex. 7.1a　Mozart, Trio in B-flat, K. 502, for piano, violin and cello, final movement.

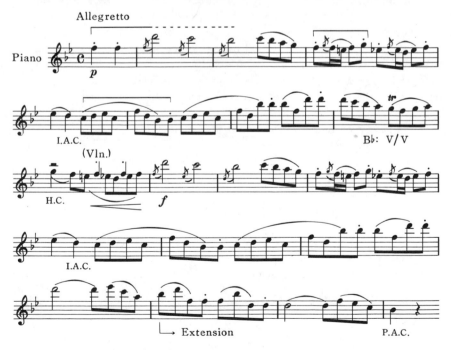

The transition to the first digression immediately establishes the key of F by repeating F:V and F:I (measures 19–20, 22, 24). Using some of the rhythms of the rondo theme (Ex. 7.1b), the transition comes presently to piano figurations repeating F:V and F:V/V—the familiar technique of reaching slightly beyond the actual tonal destination for stronger modulatory effect (c). Near the end of the transition, B-flat is added to the C major triad to turn it clearly back toward the tonic, F, before the first digression appears. The rests convey a sense of tentativeness, of rhythmic (but not harmonic) relaxation in preparation for the new thematic material (d).

Ex. 7.1b

Ex. 7.1c

Ex. 7.1d

Ex. 7.1e

The first digression is, of course, in the dominant key, **F**. It consists of two phrases of irregular lengths (7 and 10 measures) forming a group rather than a period; the second phrase—see measure 45—is extended by varied repetition. There are two half-cadences, one on V, the other on IV. The example shows, in outline, the first phrase in its entirety; the corresponding point and the extension are shown to illustrate how the second phrase is made. Again, characteristic and important motives are bracketed (**Ex. 7.1e**).

The retransition (measures 50–79), which suddenly reintroduces the motive of the rondo theme (f), adheres at first to the key of **F**; although the example shows some tonal digression, it is all secondary, and there is a strong cadence in **F** at measures 56–57 (g). Measures 57–58 are reminiscent of the conclusion of the first digression, after which the rondo material returns in a variation of the opening phrase of the retransition (compare f and h). There is some development of two motives of the rondo theme,

ending on **F:I**, to which E-flat is added (measure 74) to point toward the tonic key and the formal return of the rondo theme (i).

Ex. 7.1f

Ex. 7.1g

Ex. 7.1h

Ex. 7.1i

Bb: I $\frac{6}{4}$ V⁷ —————————————— └─Rondo theme

The second statement of the rondo theme (the first return), measures 80–93, recalls the first three phrases in their original form, the fourth phrase undergoing dissolution by motive repetition in sequence (j).

Ex. 7.1j

└─Dissolution by sequential repetition

The middle section, the second digression (ABA*C*ABA), is developmental. The sequence which dissolved the preceding rondo statement (j) has led to G minor. From this point, the original motive,

takes off at measure 100 in a modulating sequence—g, c, F, B-flat—leading to E-flat at measure 108. Now the theme of the first digression enters in E-flat, its first phrase directed to a cadential modulation into F minor. Here, the phrase begins again (k) in the new key.

Ex. 7.1k

Now the music is led into an elaborate development (l) of the first motive of the first digression,

again in sequence, leading to the C minor tonic at measure 127 (m). Still another sequence on the same motive (m) leads to a cadence in F at measure 131 (n). Note the use of stretto imitation (Chapter 11) during this phase of the development.

Ex. 7.1l

Ex. 7.1m

The retransition which follows brings back motives of the rondo theme, in anticipation, again taking F : I as a dominant in B-flat by the addition of E-flat (measure 139). There is a prolongation of this dominant, as in the previous retransition, leading directly into the return of the opening theme. (Note, at measure 131, the elision in the structure; the piano goes forward before the cadence is completed.)

The third statement of the rondo theme, measures 145–162, has the same form as the original statement.

Ex. 7.1n

F   II   V⁷   I

The transition into the return of the first digression, measures 163–176, is built of the same material as its earlier counterpart (Examples b, c, d) but the tonal arrangement is changed because the first digression will now appear in the tonic key. Where the transition originally pointed to the key of F, it now remains in the tonic key, B-flat, although secondary functions are used for a degree of tonal variety (o). Examples 7.1b and 7.1o should be compared.

Ex. 7.1o

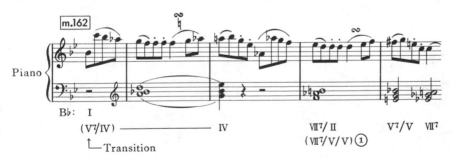

① The dominant to the dominant to the dominant. This would, for instance, describe the function of the A major triad in a context of C major, when that triad functions as a dominant to the D major triad, which is V/V. In Ex. 7.1o, the diminished 7th-chord on B-natural is a dominant (i.e., leading-tone 7th-chord, or "incomplete V_9") to the harmony on C, which is a dominant to the primary dominant on F.

Some of the analyses in this book also extend the principle of secondary function to encompass the *secondary subdominant* (which, in practice, creates a larger secondary tonal region). Thus, C: I-II-V-V₇-I is better analyzed as IV/V-V/V-V-V₇-I, the first 3 harmonies constituting a secondary tonal level on G. (See Ex. 1.19 for illustration of a secondary supertonic.)

While there is some variation in register, the return of the theme of the first digression is essentially unchanged except for the transposition into B-flat. (See measures 177–193.)

Again, there is a retransition (measures 194–213); it begins as before except for the difference of key. Ex. 7.1p should be compared with 7.1f. At measure 208 there is an abrupt change from the course of the earlier retransition. The former developmental passage, which would at this point be somewhat redundant, is sacrificed in favor of a longer, more elaborate cadential affirmation of B-flat (see the chromatic approach to the I_4^6 in Ex. 7.1q).

Ex. 7.1p

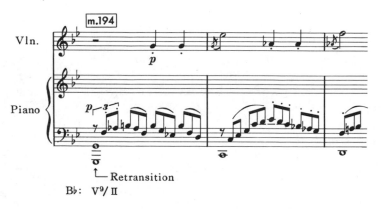

Ex. 7.1q

Bb: I⁶₄

The final statement of the rondo theme begins at measure 214. In keeping with common practice, the theme, having been heard three times previously, is now abbreviated. Its two central motives are treated imitatively without disturbance of the tonic key (r). Again, the imitation is in stretto, comprising a brief development in lieu of a complete final statement. The imitation continues to a strong cadence at measure 230 (Ex. 7.1s).

Ex. 7.1r

Ex. 7.1s

The section from measure 230 to the end is the coda. Here, the motive of the first digression is recalled, while a B-flat:I pedal is sustained under it. There is stretto like that of the second digression (see Examples 7.1t and m). At measure 238 the pedal breaks into a final cadential flourish of tonic and dominant harmonies.

Ex. 7.1t

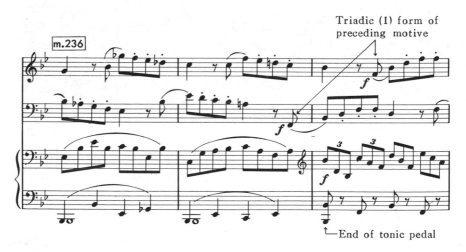

Beethoven, Symphony No. 8 in F, Op. 93, final movement

While it will not be possible to outline the Beethoven movement in detail, we may point out some of its distinctive features. The reader should analyze the structure of this movement further, comparing it with the finale of the Second Symphony. Both are sonata-rondos in which resemblances to single-movement sonata form are to be noted. The rondo theme is cut off in its second appearance, and virtually omitted in its final statement— even occurring in the "wrong" key in the Second Symphony. Mammoth developmental codas, in which the rondo theme is taken up, compensate for the seeming neglect of the theme at the close of the form proper. With the more extended rondo form, involving a larger number of statements of the basic theme, a simple reminder is sufficient prior to further development of the theme in the coda.

The rondo theme, in the finale of the Eighth Symphony, is a small ternary (*aba*, resulting in a compound form) whose middle part, *b*, is over a dominant pedal. Note the unexpected C-sharp at the end of this dominant pedal, just before the return of *a*. The tonic cadence at measure 28 is followed by a transition to the first digression, built on motives of the rondo theme.

Ex. 7.2a Beethoven, Symphony No. 8 in F, Op. 93, final movement.

Allegro vivace

Ex. 7.2a (continued)

A major surprise is the key level of the first digression. The transition reaches C:V (dominant of the *expected* key), which is prolonged for 6 measures. Then the digression theme enters deceptively on A-flat! Ten measures later it has worked its way to the "normal" key of C.

Ex. 7.2b

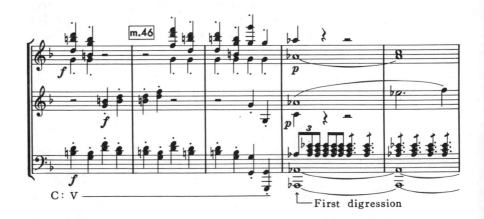

The retransition begins at measure 68, with the tonic key re-established at measure 86. The return of the rondo theme is prefaced by capricious appearances of part of its primary motive.

Ex. 7.2c

The rondo theme is cut off before it is completed, with dissolution into the developmental middle section (second digression). The development

Ex. 7.2d

which follows is based on the rondo theme; in it, Beethoven employs a considerable amount of canonic imitation (see Chapter 11).

The theme is announced again at measure 151, on $A:I_{4}^{6}$, at the outset of the retransition. It is quickly abandoned, to be returned again in the tonic key at measure 161. The complete ternary is stated, as before except for changed orchestration. The succeeding transition is now expanded: the original 19 measures are extended to 34, and it is modified to end on $F:V$ rather than, as before, on $C:V$. Again, the dominant moves, at the conclusion of the transition, unexpectedly to the lowered submediant (D-flat, on which the *B* theme enters), finding its way to the tonic just before measure 236, where the digression theme appears in the fundamental key of F.

The lack of consistent formality in the final statement of the rondo theme is a factor in the movement's resemblance to single-movement sonata form, as explained above. The theme falsely returns in B-flat, falling into dissolution (Ex. 7.2e) a few bars later. Further development features the

Ex. 7.2e

rondo motive,

and a new element,

which appears in various guises. Considerably later, at measure 355, the rondo theme appears in the tonic key. At that point in the ternary at which the unusual C-sharp originally appeared (a b a), Beethoven now writes the enharmonic equivalent, D-flat, which leads into the coda, cutting off the third part of the theme (Ex. 7.2f).

Ex. 7.2f

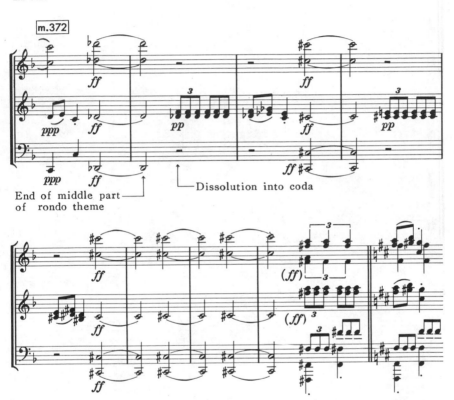

The coda is exceedingly large—123 measures, developing materials of the rondo theme and the first digression (for the development of the latter, see measure 408). Note the brief, *irregular augmentation*[2] of the rondo motive, about half-way through the coda, after the *fermata* in measure 438

---

[2] *Augmentation* is described elsewhere as the reproduction of a musical unit in longer note values. An *irregular augmentation* is one in which the relationship of the augmentation to the original material is not in a consistent ratio (2:1, or 3:1, which is rare). When the original rhythmic values are exactly and consistently multiplied— usually doubled, the technique is described as *regular augmentation*. Irregular augmentation is an interesting type of rhythmic variation.

(see Ex. 7.2g). This is a prelude to the final section of the coda, which is relentless in momentum and powerful in dynamic intensity. Again, the rondo theme is a source of development. There is a very strong affirmation of the tonic, F, as may be seen, for example, in the low string pedal point starting at measure 450, and the insistent timpani part, especially after measure 470.

Ex. 7.2g

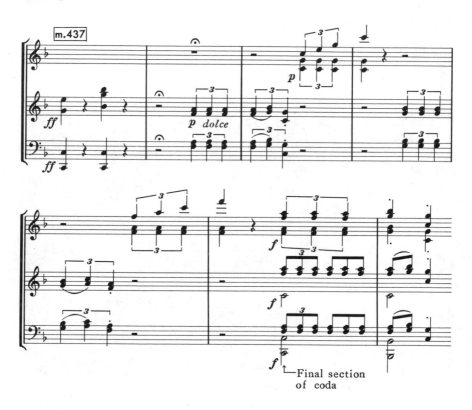

Prokofiev, Sonata No. 4 in C minor, Op. 29, for piano, final movement

The closing movement of the fourth Prokofiev Sonata for piano, written in 1917, is a clear example of twentieth-century application of the form and principles of the sonata-rondo.

The movement begins with a rondo theme of the following basic motives:[3]

The theme, like that of the Mozart movement, is a double period. In the Prokofiev, the consequent part is repeated, ending on a perfect authentic cadence at measure 25. The theme is symmetrical, the first bar being an anacrusis; the antecedent extends to measure 9, consisting of two equal phrases, and the consequent part, also consisting of two phrases, extends to measure 17. Corresponding parts should be compared—for example, measures 2–3 with measures 10–11. These two points—beginnings of the antecedent and consequent parts, respectively—are parallel in rhythm and in general contour. On the other hand, measures 2–3 are *identical* with measures 12–13, while completely dissimilar in *function* in the over-all theme structure. The repetition of the consequent half (measures 18–25) involves only minor changes.

Ex. 7.3a   Prokofiev, Piano Sonata No. 4 in C minor, Op. 29, final movement.
Reprinted by permission of the copyright owners, Boosey & Hawkes Music Publishers Limited.

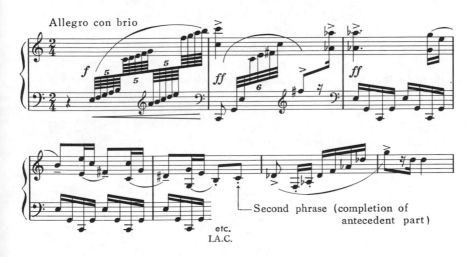

---

[3] Reprinted by permission of the copyright owners, Boosey & Hawkes Music Publishers Limited.

Ex. 7.3a (continued)

The reader who wishes to undertake harmonic analysis of the theme will find that the harmonies are basically clear and strong traditional functions with "foreign" tones, often unprepared, adding to the harmonic color and activity. (For example, measure 2 is C:I with F-sharp and A-flat as non-harmonic tones, both of which resolve to G in measure 3.)

The transition is sequential: a pattern of 4 measures (itself sequential, as is apparent in the bass line, which rises in major thirds) is repeated at a different level. The key of C is cancelled in the process. In Ex. 7.3b, the complete sequential repetition of the pattern is not shown; the student may wish, as an exercise, to continue the quotation without reference to the score.

Ex. 7.3b

⌞ Beginning of
sequential repetition

This leads to an appearance of the motive of measures 6–7, on C-sharp, progressing like f-sharp:V to f-sharp:IV, on the root, B, then to a new root, D, as in $\frac{\text{f-sharp}:\text{IV}}{\text{G}:\text{III}}$] to G:V$_9$ (measures 35–37). The D is prolonged as dominant of the key of the approaching digression, which is to appear, conventionally, in G. The transitional passage has been symmetrical much of the time (see the 4-measure pattern of the original sequence) but it ends with 3-measure segments. Its concluding bars are shown in Ex. 7.3c.

Ex. 7.3c

G: V ⸺

G: I
⌞ First digression

At the outset of the first digression, G:I recurs in almost every other bar, separated by IV- and II-like harmonies. Characteristic elements are the grace-note motive and the continuing trill-like sixteenth-notes carried over from the end of the transition.

Ex. 7.3d

⌐ First digression, first phrase

The first digression is, in structure, a group of phrases of symmetrical organization. The first unit, measures 43–46, quoted as Ex. 7.3d, is itself divisible into two 2-measure motives; the second, measures 47–50, is also divisible into halves, ending with a relatively strong cadence; the third, measures 51–54, corresponds to measures 43–46; and the fourth, measures 55–58, is rhythmically akin to the second phrase, but opposite in shape. Excerpts from the second and fourth phrases, showing the relationship between them, are quoted as Ex. 7.3e.

Ex. 7.3e

⌐ Second phrase

—Fourth phrase

A retransition follows (measure 59), taking up the motive of the first digression and modulating in rising chromatic progressions to the key of C.

Ex. 7.3f

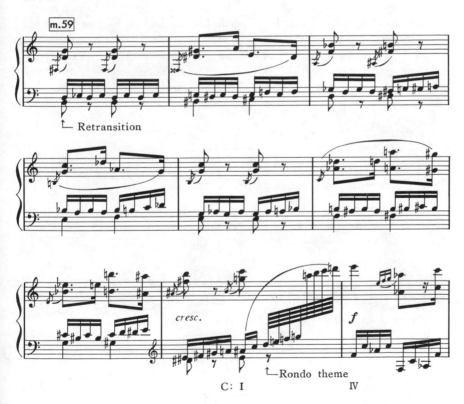

⌐ Retransition

—Rondo theme

C: I   IV

The first restatement of the rondo theme consists of its last 16 measures (the consequent half, repeated) with a more emphatic cadence (Ex. 7.3g). After a rest, there is direct movement into the second digression, which begins in E-flat.

Ex. 7.3g

The middle section in the Prokofiev movement, unlike those of the Mozart and Beethoven examples discussed earlier, is composed of a new, strongly contrasting theme. It has the form of a simple ternary of three nearly equal parts. It is, as expected, the larger of the digressions, 50 measures long. At its close, it moves directly into the second reprise of the rondo theme. In Ex. 7.3h, the thematic material is shown in short excerpts from each of the three parts of the ternary; it will be noted that in the return of the opening phrase (measures 118–122), the accompanimental pattern is varied.

Ex. 7.3h

Again, the rondo theme is limited in restatement to its consequent 8 measures, repeated as before, this time with a further repetition of the last half of the consequent (total length: 20 measures). Here, Prokofiev uses some variation in accompaniment as well as melodic ornamentation.

Ex. 7.3i

└─ Second restatement

The transition is now extended to 24 measures, beginning at the anacrusis to measure 154. It is built of the same material as its earlier counterpart, but at its center there is an unexpected reminiscence of the second digression, quickly abandoned to a sequential repetition of the transition's first 8 measures. The movement is toward C:III, as shown in the diagram of root progression below.

Ex. 7.3j

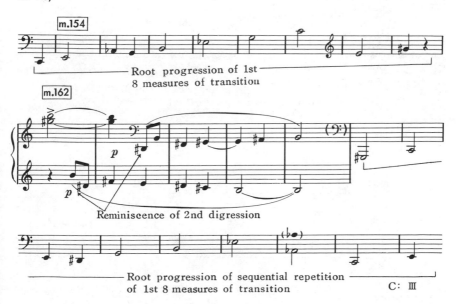

── Root progression of 1st ──
8 measures of transition

Reminiscence of 2nd digression

── Root progression of sequential repetition ──
of 1st 8 measures of transition   C: III

The first digression, B, is now restated with its length unchanged. There is considerable variation, however. Its character is now very full and it is enunciated *fortissimo*. Moreover, the elements are contrapuntally inverted— the former treble is now the bass. And the material is transposed to the tonic key level, according to the traditional formula.

Ex. 7.3k

Restatement of first digression
C: I

The retransition is as before, the only significant change being that its conclusion remains in C. As a prelude to the final statement of the rondo theme, Prokofiev now takes the original motive of measures 2 and 3,

unused since the beginning in its exact form, and develops it in sequence. It is treated very brilliantly, establishing a feeling of climax. The motive is stated twice, moving up by step, the remaining 2 measures repeating only the anacrusis figure. In Ex. 7.3l the elaborate, upward sweep of the anacrusis is indicated by a diagonal dash. The diagram shows melodic and root progression throughout the six-measure passage just described, immediately preceding the final statement of the rondo theme.

Ex. 7.3l

Rondo theme,
final statement

The antecedent of the original theme now appears, vigorously launched by the preparation outlined above; the sixteenth-note accompaniment is dropped to a lower octave, assuming a thunderous, climactic quality. The original period goes on into the consequent half (where, it will be recalled, the earlier restatements had begun) with accompanimental variation and melodic ornamentation of the sort already employed. Into the 15th measure of the theme the music corresponds in form and substance to the initial statement; after this point, the theme cadence is transformed for great emphasis—necessary to its present function as the conclusion of the movement. The basic V-I progression of the final bars is clear.

Ex. 7.3m

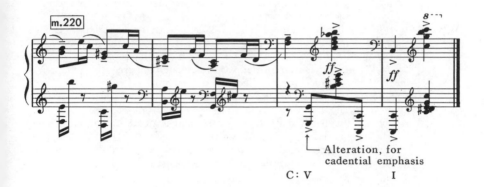

Alteration, for
cadential emphasis

C: V   I

Historical significance of sonata-rondo form

Sonata-rondo form is of great importance in the late eighteenth and early nineteenth centuries, and of diminishing importance thereafter. The extended rondo, including the seven-part form having an exterior resemblance to the sonata-rondo, has a continuing vitality, but the specificities of the traditional form, with its conventional *tonal* implications, are not widely practiced in the music of the twentieth century. Despite this, examples already cited and to be listed below show that the use of sonata-rondo form covers a broad historical range not excluding the present time.[4]

[4] *Extended rondos* in which tonal outlines are relatively free (see the fourth movement of Hindemith's Sinfonietta in E for orchestra, 1949) are excluded from the discussion here and fall more appropriately within the scope of Chapter 5. It is understandable that a form having as one of its primary bases the adherence to a traditional scheme of tonality and tonal relationships would be relatively rare in the present age, even though the principle of extended rondo-like repetition and digression (like that of statement and development in single-movement sonata form) is extremely viable and important.

The strict sonata-rondo, then, is associated especially with the Classical tradition, more particularly with music of Mozart and Beethoven. For this reason, the examples given for reference and supplementary study are concentrated heavily in the Classical Period.

Exercises and examples for further study

1. Find and analyze one or more examples of sonata-rondo. In your analysis, consider the following problems.
   a) Mark the appearances of the rondo theme. How do they compare in form? What variation techniques are used?
   b) Compare the transitions approaching the first digression and its restatement as to (*a*) material used, (*b*) length, (*c*) tonality, and (*d*) degree of correspondence between the two.
   c) In what respects are the rondo theme and the first digression contrasted? In what respects complementary?
   d) Is the middle digression taken up largely with new material? If so, consider it in relation to question c, above. If it is developmental, trace the materials developed and the key levels which are touched.
   e) Look for devices of retransition, as enumerated in preceding chapters, in the passage preceding the second restatement.
   f) Where does the coda begin? If it is entered by dissolution, locate the point in the final rondo statement at which the dissolution begins. If it is set off by a cadence, mark the cadence, and evaluate its harmonic and rhythmic qualities.
   g) What unusual features do you observe? Does the form differ in any of its details from the norm outlined in this chapter?

2. Make an outline of a hypothetical sonata-rondo, showing tonal levels, forms of individual sections, possible techniques of development and variation, and one or two likely and reasonable departures from the Classical norm.

3. The finale of Haydn's Piano Sonata in C (Peters No. 21) was cited as an example in Chapter 5. What features relate it to the sonata-rondo? What is in the nature of the thematic material to render unlikely the use of the formal sonata-rondo plan?

4. On the basis of Beethoven examples cited, what general statement can you make regarding that composer's treatment of the final statement in the sonata-rondo? Give at least one example, written out with analysis, in support of your statement. Can you cite possible reasons for Beethoven's procedure? Does your example seem unrounded, or are there compensatory factors?

5. What key scheme (in the over-all relationship of rondo theme and digressions) do you observe in Beethoven, or is there considerable variation from work to work? Refer to the finales of several of the Piano Sonatas for evidence to support your conclusion.

6. Analyze the finales of Beethoven's first two Sonatas for violin and piano— —Op. 12, No. 1, in D; and Op. 12, No. 2, in A. How many of the remaining violin sonatas of Beethoven have final movements in sonata-rondo form?

7. Look among Viennese Classical concertos for specimens of the sonata-rondo.

8. Study one or more of the following. Make special note of irregularities: unexpected developments, interpolations, extensions, variations—often extremely interesting and provocative bases for study.

Beethoven, Concerto No. 2 in B-flat, Op. 19, for piano and orchestra, final movement

Concerto in D, Op. 61, for violin and orchestra, final movement (Consider liberties of form, key, and character in the final statement. How is the cadenza worked into the form?)

Sonatas in F and G minor, Op. 5, Nos. 1 and 2, for cello and piano, final movements

Sonata in E-flat, Op. 27, No. 1, for piano, final movement (Note interpolation from slow movement.)

Sonata in E minor, Op. 90, for piano, second movement

String Quartet in F, Op. 18, No. 1, final movement

Symphony No. 2 in D, Op. 36, final movement (Consider similarities to single-movement sonata form.)

Brahms, Concertos in D minor and B-flat, Op. 15 and Op. 83, for piano and orchestra, final movements (In each, what compensations do you find for absence of the final formal restatement of the rondo theme? Which movement has a thematic complex as first digression?)

Edvard Grieg (1843–1908), Concerto in A minor, Op. 16, for piano and orchestra, final movement (Note the use of introduction, as well as liberties which in many respects parallel those of the Brahms concertos.)

Mozart, Concerto in G, K. 313, for flute and orchestra, final movement (Note the use of ornamental variation.)

Concerto in G, K. 216, for violin and orchestra, final movement (Note interpolation of *andante* material. Why does Mozart insert an "extra" reminder of the rondo theme at measure 315?)

Concerto in D, K. 218, for violin and orchestra, final movement (Again, note interpolations, and use of introductory material throughout the form.)

Concerto in E-flat, K. 271, for piano and orchestra, final movement

Piston, String Quartet No. 3, third movement (Note Beethoven-like omission of final statement in favor of strong, but brief, reprise of primary motive during coda, at measure 280.)

Schubert, Sonata in A (second of *Three Grand Sonatas*), final movement (Give special attention to the brilliant, developmental second digression.)

9. Consider, in one or more of the following works, *relationships* to traditional sonata-rondo form.

Mozart, String Quartet in D, K. 575, final movement

Haydn, Symphony No. 101 in D, final movement (Why would strict sonata-rondo form be extremely unlikely in this movement?)

Beethoven, Sonata in A, Op. 69, for cello and piano (Compare the finale with the corresponding movements of the two sonatas listed above— Op. 5, Nos. 1 and 2.)

Vincent Persichetti (b. 1915), Symphony No. 4, final movement

8

OSTINATO FORMS

he Italian word *ostinato* means precisely the same as its English cognate, obstinate. And it is in the ostinato forms of music that the principle of repetition is applied in its most direct and uncompromising manner. The technique of ostinato repetition is, while a primitive and obvious means of extending music in time, capable of a high degree of intensity and expressiveness when endowed with subtle control and imaginative means of variety. Ostinato technique is the basis for some of the finest compositions in our musical heritage, as examples cited in the present chapter will show.

The origins and interrelationships of specific ostinato forms (chiefly chaconne and passacaglia) are not well understood, and troubling confusion persists despite considerable research and analysis. The device of ostinato repetition can be traced at least to the thirteenth century, as in the *pes*[1] of the famous *Sumer canon,* but commentators differ widely as to the evolution of the passacaglia and chaconne and the meanings of terms used in reference to them. The reader is best referred to Nelson's *The Technique of Variation*[2] for an excellent account of the confusion that prevails concerning the nomenclature and history of forms built on the ostinato principle, and for a remarkably thorough and perceptive discussion of many examples of those forms.

It is commonly held that both the passacaglia and chaconne are derived from stately Spanish dances of the sixteenth and seventeenth centuries—dances characterized by slow tempo and triple meter. The chaconne is sometimes thought to stem more distantly from a tempestuous Mexican dance *(chacona)* which was taken into Spain in the sixteenth

[1] Literally "foot" in Latin, the word *pes* is used to denote the repeated bass motive, or ostinato, of the example cited.

[2] Robert U. Nelson, *The Technique of Variation* (Los Angeles: University of California Press, 1949).

century. The antecedent dance types are not usually involved with ostinato treatment, however, imparting only certain qualities of meter, tempo, and mode to many (not all) specimens of the later ostinato forms.

The technique of ostinato repetition is extremely important in music of the twentieth century, whether or not it is formalized in passacaglia and chaconne types adhering specifically to traditional models. A number of the examples to be quoted and cited here are drawn from the contemporary literatures. Possibly because of the weakening of tonality as a unifying element in contemporary idioms, and probably because of the non-romantic associations of ostinato literatures of the past, many major twentieth-century composers have adopted the device of ostinato as a basic, insistent approach in composition. This is especially apparent in the music of Stravinsky and Bartók.

The reader must be cautioned against the formation and acceptance of absolute generalization regarding the ostinato forms. The statement that the passacaglia, for instance, is in the minor mode and triple meter, and that it invariably begins with an unaccompanied statement of the ostinato theme—qualities not infrequently cited as explicitly and generally true—is contravened in its entirety by citing a single example, the finale of Brahms' Variations on a Theme of Haydn.

The practice of introduction is not widely observed in ostinato forms, probably because the vast majority of examples begin with uncomplicated, often monophonic statements of the ostinato theme—such a statement comprising in itself an introductory gesture. Similarly, the use of a coda is relatively uncommon in ostinato forms. While the use of codetta-like elaborations and the emphatic broadening of final cadences may be expected, the rigidity of the ostinato technique does not seem to permit an even mildly digressive closing section of major size and importance. (The coda which is appended to the final variation of the Beethoven Thirty-two Variations in C minor is a well-known exception to the above.) Ostinato forms are neither developmental nor built on the principle of digressive contrast of material, and there is little occasion for perorative summation at the end. When an ostinato form reaches considerable dimensions, a separate concluding form, often a fugue, may be attached to the ostinato series.

Characteristics of the ostinato

When it is the basis for an extended form, the ostinato is a theme of at least a complete phrase, usually from four to eight measures in length. It may be of an odd number of measures (Ex. 8.1). In most instances it is in triple meter.

Ex. 8.1 Hindemith, String Quartet No. 4, Op. 32, final movement.
© 1924 B. Schott's Soehne/Mainz, Germany. Renewed 1952. Used by permission.

A useful distinction may be made between an "ostinato motive," an "ostinato phrase," and an "ostinato period." The ostinato motive occurs in some sixteenth- and seventeenth-century examples of ostinato form (early and pre-Baroque; see Ex. 8.9) and in musical works in which ostinato technique is used incidentally and independently of the full, rigid plan of the ostinato form. Ex. 8.2 shows a 3-voice ostinato motive of the latter kind. Unlike the type quoted in Ex. 8.1, the incidental ostinato is not primarily associated with the bass voice.

Ex. 8.2 Bartók, String Quartet No. 3, first part.
Copyright 1929 by Universal Edition. Renewed 1956. Copyright and renewal assigned to Boosey & Hawkes, Inc. for the U.S.A. Copyright for all other countries of the world by Universal Edition (London) Ltd. Reprinted by permission.

Ex. 8.3 is an illustration of an ostinato period. Ex. 8.4 shows an ostinato phrase from the early part of the seventeenth century, as an indication that even quite early ostinati may extend beyond the motive (see also Ex. 8.11).

Ex. 8.3 Bach, Passacaglia in C minor for organ.

└─Consequent phrase

Ex. 8.4 Monteverdi, L'Incoronazione di Poppea (1642).

The ostinato is often rather neutral in character. In a large form it is repeated many times, and intensity must develop in voices other than that containing the ostinato—voices more clearly subject to variation and control.

On the other hand, certain ostinato melodies entered into standard, almost stereotyped usage in music of the seventeenth and early eighteenth centuries, often associated with particular emotional qualities. Chromatic descent was in some instances employed to express intense anguish or despair, as in Ex. 8.5, and in the famous lament of Dido from Purcell's *Dido and Aeneas,* Ex. 8.18. A much used ostinato stereotype of the sixteenth and seventeenth centuries was the *romanesca,* distinguished by an opening descending tetrachord,

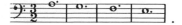

For complete discussion of this and other common ostinati of the period the reader is again referred to Nelson's *The Technique of Variation,* Chapter III.

Ex. 8.5 Bach, Crucifixus from the Mass in B minor (bass ostinato and voice parts).

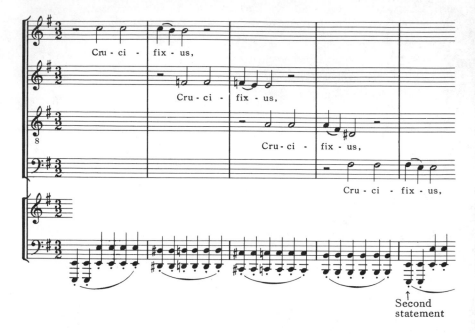

The ostinato theme may end on active or inactive harmony. Ex. 8.5 ends on the dominant. In passacaglia and chaconne forms the theme is repeated in direct contiguity, usually without interruption, at the same tonal level. During most of the time the ostinato is found in the bass voice, but the pitch level may change while the tonality remains constant, and movement of the ostinato into one of the upper voices is a valuable source of change.

If a "passacaglia" treats the theme imitatively and at changing tonal levels, it is closer to fugue than to true ostinato form, despite whatever title is affixed by the composer. (See the first movement of William Schuman's Symphony No. 3, published by G. Schirmer. Here the "ostinato" is presented one half-tone higher with each appearance, and it changes freely from voice to voice.)

Examples of ostinato themes

Further examples of ostinato themes are given below, with brief discussion.

Ex. 8.6 is taken from one of the organ chaconnes of Dietrich Buxtehude (1637–1707). It shows a five-measure ostinato, appearing at the outset in a contrapuntal setting with the harmony fully realized. The harmonic rhythm consists, in the main, of two harmonies in each measure (♩ ♩) and the bass melody describes a progression of one octave, descending from tonic to tonic. It strongly affirms the key of E minor. The second statement has a nearly identical setting, the first real variation coming with the third, at which point dotted rhythms are introduced over the continuing ostinato bass and harmony.

Ex. 8.6   Buxtehude, Chaconne in E minor.

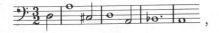

It may be mentioned parenthetically that the same composer's Passacaglia in D minor, on a 4-measure bass theme,

falls into four sections formed by groupings of the ostinato repetitions around the tonal levels d, F, a, and d. Spitta comments that "this subdivision gives rise to the only fault that can be found; the sections might have been welded together in a more imperceptible manner by smoother modulations...."[3] As our study develops, it will become clear that the quality of a continuous impression of smooth progression is one of the chief points of critical analysis in the ostinato forms.

3 Philipp Spitta, *Johann Sebastian Bach,* trans. Clara Bell and J. A. Fuller Maitland (London: Novello and Company, Ltd., 1899), p. 282. Reprinted by permission of the publishers.

Ex. 8.7 is another chaconne theme. Here we have an 8-measure harmonic theme with descending chromatic progression in the bass and with two functional alterations: the V_7/IV in measure 3, and the German sixth chord on IV in measure 5. The theme is a single phrase. Its harmonic rhythm is less active than that of the Buxtehude chaconne, and it is marked by an unexpected syncopation in measures 6 and 7, after a perfect regularity of change at the beginning of each measure. The steady rise of the top voice (C, D, E, F, F-sharp, G, A-flat) is a forceful contrast to the movement of the bass, the contrary motion underscored by the *sforzando* at its conclusion. After this, intensity is abruptly dispelled at the authentic cadence.

Ex. 8.7 Beethoven, Thirty-two Variations in C minor (Kinsky-Halm Wo O 80).

Ex. 8.8 is included to show a more complex, more chromatic ostinato theme, this one from the late nineteenth century. It is like the preceding examples in its mode and meter and, like the Beethoven, it is 8 measures in length. Unlike either of the preceding, it concludes on dominant harmony; this, in addition to its melodic instability and chromatic leanings, contributes to a highly kinetic and restless quality—a quality not appreciably weakened by its moderate tempo.

Ex. 8.8 Reger, Introduction, Passacaglia, and Fugue for two pianos, Op. 96.

The ground

(English music)

Like so many words used in the description of music, the term "ground" is widely current and yet lacking in precision of meaning. It refers sometimes to an ostinato motive, sometimes to an ostinato phrase or period, sometimes to the resultant ostinato form, sometimes to ostinati and ostinato forms of a particular historical period and national style, and sometimes to those of any period.[4]

Often the term is applied specifically to ostinato form in music of the English sixteenth and seventeenth centuries, music which is based on the reiteration of a ground bass (regarded, in this sense, as identical to the bass ostinato). The ground bass is often an ostinato motive of one or more measures, and often of great simplicity. Ex. 8.9, found in the first volume of the *Historical Anthology of Music,* p. 105, is a very early one. In its simplicity and lack of melodic substance, the ground is a motive, even though 4 measures long. A ground of this kind (here a simple reiteration of tonic and dominant notes) is, in effect, rather like the principle of drone bass (see, for example, the *musette* in Bach's English Suite No. 3) or the *bourdon*[5] of French seventeenth-century music, whose bass is similar to bagpipe drones, separated, like the notes of the ground in Ex. 8.9, by the interval of a fifth.

---

[4] "Basso ostinato variations from this period [seventeenth, eighteenth centuries] appear under five chief names: ground, folia, bergamask, passacaglia, and chaconne. Although it is customary to speak of each type as having distinct characteristics, there is considerable overlapping among them. Such ambiguity is especially apparent in the passacaglia and chaconne, whose interconnection is historically very close. It can also be seen in the name *ground,* which is sometimes used generically to include all basso ostinato variations, sometimes to refer to a specific English variation type, sometimes to denote the bass subject itself; when *ground* is used to denote the bass subject itself the word is synonymous with *ground bass,* or *basso ostinato.* All five species, except the English ground, may be traced back to prototypes in dance music. The exact relation between dances and variations is in all species obscure; the most definite connection exists in the folia and bergamask, both of which are constructed upon the basses of the original dances, and sometimes upon the melodies as well.

"The ground, using the name in its more restricted sense to mean a definite English variation type, dates from the sixteenth century." From Robert U. Nelson, *The Technique of Variation* (Berkeley: University of California Press, 1948), p. 66.

[5] The French word *bourdon,* in one of its meanings, is applied to French pieces of the seventeenth century in which there is a recurring, accompanimental bass figure.

Ex. 8.9   My Lady Carey's Dompe (ca. 1525).
> Reprinted by permission of the publishers from Archibald T. Davison and
> Willi Apel, *Historical Anthology of Music: Oriental, Medieval, and Renais-*
> *sance Music* (Cambridge, Mass.: Harvard University Press, copyright 1946,
> 1949, by the President and Fellows of Harvard College).

Ex. 8.10 consists of two excerpts from *A Ground* by Thomas Tomkins, one of the sixteenth-century English composers represented in the *Fitzwilliam Virginal Book* (ca. 1600).[6] The two quotations show wide disparity in harmonization of the ostinato,

The variation employs canon on the ostinato melody between the two upper voices. In this work, the ostinato appears in the upper voices a good part of the time.

Ex. 8.10   Tomkins, A Ground.

[6] The author's source for the Tomkins excerpt is E. W. Taylor's study of the Fitzwilliam manuscript, *An Elizabethan Virginal Book* (London: J. M. Dent and Co., 1905), p. 188.

The literature of the English ground provides some of the most memorable examples of ostinato form, especially in the works of Purcell. Purcell's grounds (ostinati) are often well-developed phrases (Ex. 8.11 and Ex. 8.18). Ex. 8.11 shows an unusually vigorous and disjunct ground, one that is in part a *compound melody*.[7] Purcell's skill in extending the musical motion over the points at which ostinato repetitions end is unsurpassed in any period. This quality is strikingly evident in Ex. 8.18.

Ex. 8.11   Purcell, Ground for harpsichord.

Incidental reference may be made to the seventeenth-century English practice, called "division," in which a solo part was freely extemporized against a reiterated ground bass. There is a clear parallel between division and a fashion of modern jazz—that of the flight of the improvisatory, rhapsodic solo part against a steadily repeated pattern called a "riff."

The passacaglia

The passacaglia, the most important of the ostinato forms, consists of a continuously reiterated bass ostinato, the setting for which is varied with each appearance. The ostinato, which is normally of some melodic distinction, is at least a phrase. Usually, it appears in the bass voice without accompaniment at the beginning of the passacaglia, or with only a meager setting, after which the repetitions of the ostinato follow in direct succession with changing accompanying parts.

It is, of course, mainly in the changes established in the materials accompanying the repeated ostinato that possibilities for contrast lie; such contrast is extremely vital in view of the steadfastness of the repetition. The following example shows varied repetitions of a small segment of the ostinato of a passacaglia by Ernest Bloch (1881–1959). The quotations illustrate changes in the accompanimental fabric as well as in the ostinato itself. The latter is embellished by the addition of notes at measure 18, and at measure 10, moved for variation to an upper voice.

---

[7] In a *compound melody* (see measure 2 of the Purcell bass) the activity is on two levels, each of them progressing, with interruptions, as a kind of counterpoint to the other. The two levels are distinguished by distance of pitch level, and, often, by opposition of direction. The latter is not true in much of the Purcell example, in which the curious effect of parallel octaves is suggested in the progression of the "two voices."

Ex. 8.12   Bloch, String Quartet No. 2.
    Copyright 1947 by Boosey & Hawkes Ltd. Reprinted by permission of Boosey & Hawkes Inc.

Inasmuch as any ostinato theme is brief in its relationship to the entire form, and in order to prevent strong punctuation and segmentation at the many joints separating the repetitions, the composer carefully establishes and controls factors of motion in the form. As in so many facets of music, a paradox arises here—the static quality of the ostinato repetition opposed to devices of motion in the over-all texture. There are several means by which motion is maintained and extreme segmentation avoided.

1. The ostinato itself may, in tonal works, end on the dominant, with the implicit motion of unresolved harmony directing the music into the next ostinato statement. (Ex. 8.5).

2. In an ostinato which ends on the tonic, the final harmony may be avoided or upset by the use of dissonance. (Ex. 8.18d).

3. Rhythmic motion may be kept alive at the ostinato cadence. In Ex. 8.13, the use of suspensions is an important factor in the forward impulse.

Ex. 8.13   Brahms, Variations on a Theme of Haydn, Op. 56a, finale.

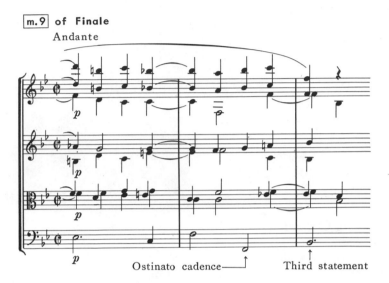

4. Several contiguous statements may be accompanied by corresponding material. This technique of relating adjacent segments thematically tends to establish division into units larger than those defined by the individual ostinato repetitions themselves. This technique can be seen in almost any passacaglia or chaconne example.

5. A sense of over-all progress and contour of motion may be established by the controlled use of gradually faster rhythmic values throughout the course of the form or any major part of it (possibly retarded at the end), or by the use of such devices as syncopation and imitation, especially stretto—devices which have the effect of setting the motion forward. (In this connection, and for illustration of point 4, above, the finale of Brahms' Haydn Variations is an excellent study.)

6. A variation may begin simultaneously with or earlier than the cadence of that preceding, creating an elision joining two adjacent statements of the ostinato. (See Ex. 8.16.)

The tempo, meter, and mode of the passacaglia often correspond to the dance from which its character is thought to be derived; however, as already demonstrated, there is nothing to preclude the occurrence of moderate or fast tempo, duple meter, and major mode in the passacaglia—

especially that of the nineteenth and twentieth centuries. The harmonic rhythm, traditionally, is relatively slow; the texture is often contrapuntal for at least part of the time.

Ex. 8.14   Bach, Passacaglia in C minor for organ.

Fourth statement

Contrapuntal imitation

The Chaconne

The chaconne corresponds closely to the passacaglia in form and technique. There are two perplexing difficulties involved in attempting to draw a distinction between the two forms: (1) composers have often applied the terms indiscriminately, or without regard to any clearly established distinction; and (2) theorists differ widely concerning the possibility and manner of distinction.[8]

The only distinction which is feasible, useful, and significant—one worth establishing for terminological clarity even though not all titles in the ostinato literature conform—defines the chaconne as based upon an ostinato consisting of a series of *harmonic* progressions, as distinguished from the *melodic* ostinato of the passacaglia—the latter normally without harmonization in its first entry. Since such a distinction is indeed a major one, with important ramifications as to the nature of the resultant variations, there is good reason for applying contrasting terms. It is vital, of course, that definition be clearly established in each specific use of the words *passacaglia* and *chaconne*. Ex. 8.15 is added to Examples 8.6 and 8.7; it shows a chaconne ostinato theme at its first appearance.

---

[8] Coeuroy even attempts a distinction on the basis of tonality: "It (chaconne) differs from the passacaglia in that it maintains a single tonality, while the passacaglia involves modulations." From André Coeuroy, *La Musique et Ses Formes* (Paris: Les Editions Denoël, 1951), p. 52, translated by the author.

Ex. 8.15   Brahms, Symphony No. 4, fourth movement.

Because it is the harmonic structure (as well as the bass and other voices) which gives identity to the chaconne ostinato, harmonic change is less likely to be a means of variation in this form. However, the harmony of the ostinato is occasionally subject to modification even in the chaconne, as is seen in Ex. 8.16 in a variation of the ostinato shown in the preceding example.

Ex. 8.16

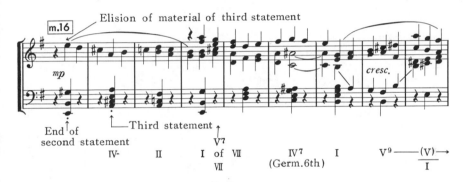

⑨ The accidentals create the feeling of secondary tonal levels, or regions, which do not overthrow the fundamental tonic, e. In measures 5–6, the secondary level is V(B), to which measure 5 is dominant, measure 6 subdominant, the V₇ of measure 5 progressing "deceptively." In measures 7–8, the secondary level is IV (a), to which measure 7 is the French 6th chord on II, measure 8 the dominant (and at the same time the tonic of the primary key level). The secondary tonal levels at the end of the ostinato are, by their irresolution, one of the factors which drive the music forward into the succeeding statement.

As is evident in the Brahms, the harmonic basis of the chaconne ostinato does not preclude the recurrence of any of its voices as a significant melodic entity. (Note, for example, that the upper voice is maintained intact in the supporting harmonies in Ex. 8.16.) It is interesting to compare the Brahms theme with that of the Beethoven Thirty-two Variations in C minor (Ex. 8.7), from which it may have been derived.

Vitality of motion at cadence points is no less important in the chaconne than in the passacaglia, and similar means are employed to counteract the fixed quality of the ostinato repetition.

In both forms, the final statement may be made more emphatic and conclusive by dynamic, rhythmic, or other means. In Ex. 8.17, from a twentieth-century passacaglia, intensity is increased primarily by changes of rhythm and tempo rather than by reliance upon broadening of the final statements or—a possible technique—gradual disintegration and diminuendo toward the conclusion.

Riegger, Symphony No. 3, final movement

The passacaglia from the Third Symphony of Wallingford Riegger (1885–1961) moves with increasing urgency and carefully spaced changes of tempo, meter, rhythm, and texture into a contrasting final section—a fugue. As it progresses, the passacaglia develops in textural richness. It begins with the 5-measure ostinato illustrated in Ex. 8.17a, shown in its first two appearances. At the second appearance, a single upper voice, syncopated, is added.

Ex. 8.17a Riegger, Symphony No. 3, final movement.
© 1957 by Associated Music Publishers, Inc., New York. Used by permission.

At measure 56, the texture has developed further, each measure is thrust into the next by the use of short *crescendi,* the ostinato changes are punctuated by eighth-note doublings, syncopation is continued, and faster note values are introduced.

Ex. 8.17b

At measure 91, the tempo is changed to *allegro,* and the ostinato is broken up into very short, impulsive motives which are highly contrasted dynamically. The absence of upper-voice motion compensates here for the increase in tempo.

Ex. 8.17c

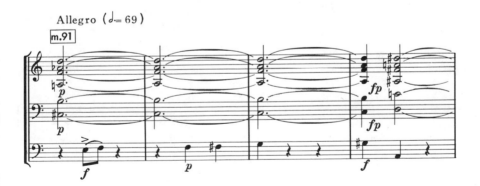

A variation in meter is introduced at measure 109, with the dynamic level reduced but with great urgency of rhythm.

Ex. 8.17d

The fugue subject which emerges (measure 136) is derived from the tone series on which the bass ostinato was built. The fugue constitutes the concluding section in the symphony, and is also a complementary appendage to the passacaglia.

Ex. 8.17e

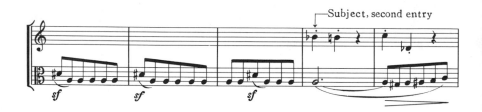

Harmonic fixation in ostinato forms

On the basis of the definition just stated, the ostinato theme in the chaconne is identified mainly as a set of harmonies, even though its bass and soprano lines may well be of distinction and importance at the same time. And although the passacaglia theme is regarded as a bass melody rather than a series of harmonies, it must be recognized that in tonal music of the periods in which these forms are used there is a very close inter-connection and interdependence between bass line and harmony. Thus, even in the passacaglia, the harmony to which the ostinato is set is relatively fixed—restricted in its possibilities of change—in the restatements of the theme. That there are exceptions in both forms to the principle of harmonic fixation goes without saying, and is illustrated by Ex. 8.16.

The considerable degree of harmonic fixation in ostinato variations is a characteristic of important effect. Harmonic change is not a major source of variety in the ostinato forms. This is less true, of course, in passacaglias of the twentieth century, in which there is normally greater independence between bass line and harmony. In contemporary styles, a given bass line is less likely to "dictate" its harmonizations, and thus permits a degree of harmonic freedom not possible in the periods of tonal, functional harmony.

Ostinato forms as variation sets

The term "variation" has been used a number of times in the fore-going discussion of the ostinato forms. Its appropriateness is evident, since the ostinato technique is that of taking a given theme and repeating it with alterations in certain of its elements—textural setting, rhythm, mode, and others. The principle of a variation series on a given theme is thus implicit in the passacaglia and chaconne, and it is important to recognize the ostinato forms as variation series.

Moreover, we should recognize a characteristic of the ostinato variation forms which sets them apart from the vast majority of variation sets of other kinds. This is their *continuous* structure, in which there are no breaks between the statements of the varied theme. Chapter 9 deals with types of variation sets in which there is more often deliberate interruption at the end of the initial theme statement and at the end of each variation. These are described as *sectional* variations.

Purcell, Lament of Dido from Dido and Aeneas

A justly famed passacaglia, and one of the most universally quoted works of its kind, is the lament of Dido from Purcell's opera *Dido and Aeneas*. It is an example that ought to be known to every person who is devoted to music, because of the perfection of its form and because it is one of the most moving expressions in the literature. It represents a structural technique often used by Purcell.

The bass ostinato, or ground, is an intense chromatic phrase of 5 measures, in triple meter and slow tempo. Its steady descent from tonic to tonic is interrupted only briefly in measure 4, before the final drop of a 5th. The first phrase of the voice part overlaps the end of the ostinato.

Ex. 8.18a Purcell, Dido's Lament from Dido and Aeneas.
Reproduced by permission of Novello & Co. Ltd., London, from the version edited by W. H. Cummings.

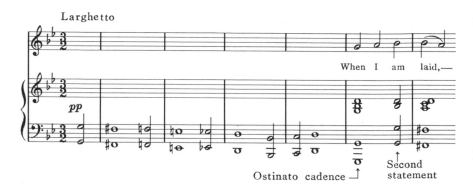

At the next ostinato cadence, the voice part is forcefully drawn into the subsequent statement by the text, whose verb "create" must be joined to the object which follows (see Ex. 8.18b). Further, we may note that a VI_6 is substituted for the usual I beginning of the bass theme.

Ex. 8.18b

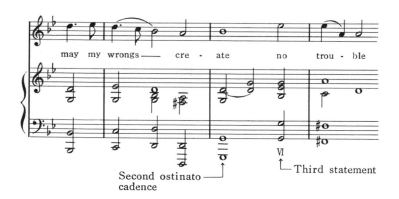

After a repetition of the music of the two ostinato entries just concluded, the voice again enters at the point of the ostinato cadence (*Remember me...*), moving through that cadence and establishing a link with the following statement. The cadence is suppressed, not only by the rhythmic motion of the voice part, but by the voice's entry on the fifth of the tonic harmony, which upsets the otherwise perfect authentic cadence.

Ex. 8.18c

The suspension seen in Ex. 8.18c, at the beginning of the emerging ostinato statement, is the first of a series which helps drive the music toward the approaching climax. The next ostinato cadence finds the tonic harmony overthrown immediately, weakening the cadential effect and supporting the voice part in its rise to the climax note, g″. Again, there is elision between the solo part and the ostinato phrase. Several variations in harmony may be seen in Ex. 8.18d.

Ex. 8.18d

The solo part coincides cadentially with the bass only at its final cadence. Following this, the ostinato has two further appearances (one is shown in Ex. 8.18e), making a total of nine. In the final variations, a great deal of chromaticism and nonharmonic embellishment are used. The final chromatic descent of the top part, a reminiscence of the ostinato melody in a contrasting rhythm, starts *before* the end of the penultimate ostinato phrase. The pull of its descent, often enforced by dissonance in its relationship to the bass, has the effect again of partially concealing the cadence through which it passes.

Ex. 8.18e

Exercises and examples for further study

1. Prepare an analysis of the second movement of the Stravinsky Septet (1953).
   a) There are how many recurrences of the ostinato?
   b) Is the contiguity of the ostinato statements interrupted at any point?
   c) How is the ostinato itself varied? Compare the rhythmic placement of notes in its first and final statements.
   d) Discuss the over-all form from the standpoint of the progress and relaxation of rhythmic intensity.
   e) What correlation do you see between faster motion and simpler texture? Which sections are more contrapuntal? Compare the first and last statements as to texture.
   f) Exceptionally, Stravinsky emphasizes at most points the breaks between ostinato appearances. Where is this not true? Explain. Do you feel that other factors keep the passacaglia from falling into pieces?
   g) What factors contribute to the sense of finality in the last several measures?
   h) Why does the movement seem to center on A?

2. On the basis of research in sources specified by your instructor, write a short paper dealing with suppositions regarding the historical origins of forms based on the ostinato principle.

3. Compose an ostinato theme—harmonic or melodic—and at least one or two varied restatements.

4. Looking among works cited in this chapter, find additional examples of the following.

   a) A device for concealing (bridging) the cadence ending an ostinato statement.

   b) A 4-measure ostinato.

   c) An ostinato of an odd number of measures.

   d) Duple meter.

   e) Use of contrapuntal imitation in an ostinato variation.

   f) Variation in harmony.

5. Which of the following do you feel might serve best as a passacaglia theme? Why? Assume moderate tempi. What advantages, disadvantages, and problems would you foresee in each case?

6. Look over some of the works mentioned in this chapter or select some analysis projects from the following list. How many times does the ostinato appear? Is the work an example of incidental use of ostinato or is a full ostinato form developed? If the latter is true, to which type does the example most closely conform? What are the means by which motion is maintained to counteract the static quality of the ostinato? Does there appear to be a controlled development of acceleration and deceleration in the over-all plan? What are the sources of variation used—the techniques by which the ostinato statements are varied?

John Blow (ca. 1648–1708), *Venus and Adonis,* finale of Act II

Chopin, *Berceuse* for piano

Franck, Chorale No. 2 in B minor for organ

Handel, *Susanna,* opening chorus

Arthur Honegger (1892–1955), Symphony No. 2, second movement

Jean-Baptiste Lully (1632–87), *Amadis,* final chorus

Ravel, Trio in A Minor for piano, violin and cello, third movement

Reger, Introduction and Passacaglia in D minor, Op. 145, for organ

Schönberg, *Pierrot Lunaire*, No. 8, *Nacht*

Stravinsky, *Histoire du Soldat* (To which sections does the present study apply?)

Webern, Passacaglia for orchestra, Op. 1

7. Find in one or more of the following sources examples of ostinato technique and ostinato form.

   a) *Historical Anthology of Music*, Vol. II
   b) Couperin, *Pièces de Clavecin*
   c) Bach, works for solo violin
   d) Handel, *Suites de Pièces*

8. Find a Handel chaconne for harpsichord in which there are 62 variations on the theme. What is the extent of harmonic fixation in these variations?

9. Look up the passacaglia in Act I of the opera *Wozzeck*, by Alban Berg. List the devices by which the composer modifies the ostinato theme in its several appearances.

9

VARIATIONS

*V*ariation styles in major historical periods are characterized significantly by particular techniques relating to fixation and variability of theme elements. Some of these will be discussed presently: fixation of tonality in most variations preceding the late nineteenth century; fixation of structure throughout the same period; introduction of tempo and mode change according to stereotyped patterns in the Classical variation; variation in structure in many works of, roughly, the past century; embellishment of theme melody in melodically-harmonically-fixed variations of the Classical and early Romantic periods; and others. Such generalizations are valuable in any commentary concerning variations of a specific style, so long as it is understood that most variation sets of any period embody a variety of procedures. Thus, it is extremely unlikely that all works of a period and style, any more than all variations in any given set, will strictly conform to any generalization.

For exhaustive analysis of variation techniques in the various periods in which variation forms flourished, the reader is referred again to Nelson's *The Technique of Variation*. A summary classification of these historical periods and the techniques which prevailed in each is found in the opening chapter of that study.

A variation and the theme from which it is derived always share at least one common element, and one of the aims in the analysis of a theme with variations is to identify the theme elements which are retained, with or without modification, in each of the variations of the series. This presupposes a thorough understanding of the theme—its structure, melodic content, harmony, and all other distinguishing, variable features.

A thumbnail sketch of the history of variation techniques, styles, and types, may be found in the *Harvard Dictionary of Music*.[1] The idea and

[1] Willi Apel, *Harvard Dictionary of Music* (Cambridge, Mass.: Harvard University Press, 1947), pp. 784-6.

practice of theme with variations is more than four centuries old—a longer uninterrupted history than that of any other large instrumental form. While even earlier examples are extant, the important beginnings of variation form are seen in the music of the early sixteenth century, especially in the lute and keyboard music of Spain and England, respectively. Spanish variations are called *diferencias*. Many examples of early English variation sets have come to us in the *Fitzwilliam Virginal Book*, to which reference is made in the preceding chapter. Some of the examples included in this chapter are drawn from these literatures.

The techniques of variation are, of course, of enormous significance in virtually all music and all forms, whether or not they have so systematic an organization as that of theme statement with variation series following. The list of musical genres in which variation plays a part is inexhaustible; the following examples are only a reminder of the universality of variation in music.

1. In the mass of the fifteenth and sixteenth centuries, a given plain-song melody is often the basis for all movements, with that melody appearing in varied form in each. This can be studied, for example, in masses and magnificats of Giovanni da Palestrina (1525–94). The technique often involves retention of melodic interval succession with modification of metric structure according to the text to which the music is set.

2. Variation techniques are used in the variation suite (Chapter 10).

3. In a chorale prelude, a given phrase may be repeated with modified setting. Thus, in Bach's organ prelude on *Allein Gott in der Höh' sei Ehr'* (*Clavierübung*, Part III, No. 8) the first phrase of the chorale, appearing initially at the anacrusis to measure 13, is repeated at measure 46 in an inverted contrapuntal setting.

4. Occasionally movements in the Baroque suite are paired, one a variation (Fr. *double*) of the other. An example of this, in all respects a theme with variation or variations, is found in the first of Bach's English Suites. This suite includes two *courantes*, the second of them having two *doubles*—repetitions in variation.

5. A multi-movement work based on a single theme is, in a sense, a set of variations on that theme. Bach's *Art of the Fugue* is an example.

6. A strophic song in which the strophes, while nearly identical, are slightly varied, is an example of the use of variation. An example is the change of mode in the second stanza of Schubert's *Der Wegweiser* from *Die Winterreise;* another is seen in the introductions to the *andante* stanzas of Papageno's song in Act II of Mozart's *Die Zauberflöte*.

7. An orchestral work often involves a modified doubling of an instrumental part, another example of the incidental use of variation. The technique illustrated in Ex. 9.1 is fundamental in the craft of orchestration.

Ex. 9.1   Brahms, Symphony No. 4 in E minor, Op. 98, second movement.

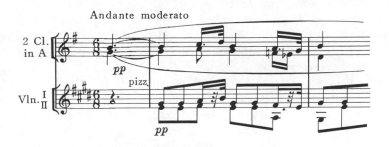

8. In the *da capo* aria (Chapter 4), the return of the first part may be modified. In fact, the ornamentation of the *da capo* by the singer was a common practice in much opera before Christoph Willibald Gluck (1714–87).

9. Indeed, any form in which repetition occurs—especially those, like rondo forms, in which numerous restatements of a theme take place—is likely to employ variation techniques. An excellent illustration of this principle, to supplement those cited in other chapters, is the third movement of Beethoven's String Quartet in A minor, Op. 132; this movement is a five-part rondo with variations of the rondo and digression themes: A B A′ B′ A″ coda.

The variation series, in which several forms of the same basic idea are presented in succession, is, of course, an ideal solution to the requirements for unity and variety, provided that the elements of contrast are of well controlled and balanced assortment and distribution. (Constant and extreme tempo change from variation to variation would be a hypothetical example of poor—jagged, distracting—distribution of, in this case, tempo contrast. Another would be a group of slow statements followed by a cluster of fast statements, with no rounding of the tempo-form. Moreover, a regular alternation between slow and fast throughout a variation series could be wearisome.) The idea of restating several times the basic material of a composition, with changes of various kinds, is a convenient and effective means of extending a musical work in time, especially in periods (sixteenth, seventeenth centuries, for example) in which tonal fluctuation as a source of contrast was not widely practiced. Variation on a given theme is adopted as a solution in much music of today in which tonality as a source of contrast is negated or obscured (see tone series, in the following discussion of the fixed elements of the theme). Moreover, the practice of embroidering a relatively simple thematic proposition with increasingly elaborate figurations is a logical, if obvious, means of exploiting the resources of an instrumental medium, when that is part of the composer's intent. In summary, not only is the systematic form of theme with variations the oldest of all structural procedures in the history of instrumental music, but the principle of variation, restatement with change, is the most universal solution to the fundamental requirement for unity and variety in music. Themes with variations are basic in other arts as well, as, for example, in dance choreography.

It is sometimes argued that variations on a theme are often so far removed from their source that the theme ceases to be apparent in the variation, with the result that the intended unity of the form fails to be perceptible. But while an occasional member of a variation series may depart from its thematic origin to this extent, normally a sufficient number of the variations in any given series clearly recall the theme, perhaps in rondo-like fashion, to lend the series a unity that is both demonstrable and perceptible.

In no area of music theory is confusion of terminology more persistent and widespread. For example, the term "melodic variation" can mean variation in which the melody of the theme is retained in its original form, in which it is retained with embellishment, or in which it is abandoned. A variation which retains theme harmony, structure, and melody, with the latter ornamented, is called "ornamenting variation," "ornamental variation," "embellishing variation," "decorative variation," "melodico-harmonic variation," "figural variation," and "melodic variation"—a partial list of possible terms.

The following discussion attempts to establish a precise terminology, with terms chosen to designate those *basic* elements of the theme—*structure, melody,* and *harmony*—which, in variation, remain fixed. An example of such a term is "melodically-harmonically-fixed variation." Since traditional variations, with few exceptions, involve retention of theme structure, structural fixation is specified in terminology only when it is the sole basic element remaining fixed. The more recent variation, in which structure is quite commonly modified, is called "free variation."

A theme with variations may be one of the movements of a multi-movement work (Beethoven, Piano Sonata in A-flat, Op. 26) or it may constitute the entire structure of an independent single-movement composition. The frequent reference to music of Beethoven and Brahms in the following pages indicates the importance of these masters in the history of variation form, and the vitality and brilliance of their contributions to that history.

The theme

As might be expected, the theme for a variation series is usually stated at the beginning of the composition. However, there are occasional exceptions to this rule. There may, for instance, be a short introduction, or even an extended one if the work is large. Ex. 9.2 shows an introduction to a variation movement. The suggestion of G minor in the opening bars is an ironic twist, since the movement is actually in E-flat. And what follows the introduction is the bass of the theme, which might be called variation 1, followed by two variations on the bass, with the full theme, complete with melody, arriving only after three variations in which its harmony and structure gradually emerge as adumbrations of what is to come.

Ex. 9.2   Beethoven, Symphony No. 3 in E-flat, Op. 55, final movement.

Other introductions to variation sets are the introduction (8 measures) which precedes the *Rapsodie sur un Thème de Paganini,* Op. 43, *pour piano et orchestre* by Sergei Rachmaninov (1873–1943) and, at the other extreme, that of *Don Quixote,* Op. 35, by Richard Strauss (1864–1949). The introduction to the latter work is a gigantic development of one of its themes.

In Ex. 9.3, the theme is first suggested, after the brief introduction, in a nebulous outline consisting of its harmonic roots, somewhat in the manner of the Beethoven example cited as Ex. 9.2. Apel refers to a variation such as that which precedes the theme in this work as a "negative variation"—an excellent characterization.[2] It is a kind of shadow appearing before the complete theme arrives.

Ex. 9.3   Rachmaninov, Rapsodie sur un Thème de Paganini, Op. 43, pour piano et orchestre. Copyright renewed 1962 by Charles Foley, Inc. Used by permission.

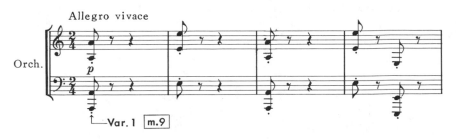

Aaron Copland, in his Piano Variations, "reverses the usual procedure by putting the simplest version of the theme second, naming 'theme' what is, properly speaking, a first variation. The idea was to present the listener with a more striking version of the theme first, which seemed more in keeping with the generally dramatic character of the composition as a whole."[3]

A very unusual specimen, *Istar*, Op. 42, by d'Indy, begins with the variation series in order of diminishing complexity, with the theme appearing at the end.

The theme is normally relatively simple in form and direct in expression, constituting a foundation upon which the variation series is to build.

___

[2] Willi Apel, *Harvard Dictionary of Music* (Cambridge: Harvard University Press, 1947), p. 786.
[3] Aaron Copland, *What to Listen for in Music* (New York: McGraw-Hill Book Company, 1957), p. 159.

It is frequently a period (Brahms, Variations on a Hungarian Song, Op. 21, No. 2), binary (Bach, *Goldberg Variations*), or incipient ternary (Schubert, Impromptu in B-flat, Op. 142, No. 3). But the only general observation that can be made is that it is of small proportions, usually not exceeding 32 measures in length, and often a good deal shorter. Ex. 9.4 is a symmetrical simple ternary, whose third part corresponds to the first in melody, while opposing it in tonal direction.

Ex. 9.4   Brahms, Variations on a Theme by Robert Schumann, Op. 9.

The theme may be composed specifically for variations (Ex. 9.2), or it may be borrowed from a traditional or popular source (Ex. 9.5) or from the music of another composer (Ex. 9.3 and Ex. 9.4). The theme quoted in Ex. 9.5 is from the music of the Roman liturgy.

Ex. 9.5   Norman Dello Joio, Variations, Chaconne and Finale (1947).
    Copyright 1950 by Carl Fischer, Inc., New York. International copyright secured. Used by permission.

A composer may borrow his variation theme from previous works of his own. An example is Schubert's variations on his *lied, Die Forelle,* used as the basis for the fourth movement of his Quintet in A major for piano and strings, Op. 114.

A variation series may be based on two themes (or a "double-theme," as in Ex. 9.6). In the Haydn example the tonic is shared by both parts

Ex. 9.6   Haydn, Variations in F minor.

while one is in major, the other minor. In this work, the two parts of the theme are varied in alternation according to the following pattern: first, second, variation no. 1 on the first, variation no. 1 on the second, variation no. 2 on the first, variation no. 2 on the second, variation no. 3 on the first, and coda. The resemblance to rondo form scarcely needs mention.

Other examples of variation series with two themes are Strauss' *Don Quixote,* in which the themes are intended to represent the knight and Sancho Panza, and the second movement of Beethoven's Piano Trio in E-flat, Op. 70, No. 2, whose two themes are contrasted in mode. The slow movement of Beethoven's Symphony No. 5 in C minor is often described as a variation series on two themes.

Sometimes the theme, in more or less literal form, is recalled in the course of the variation series, or restated at the conclusion. An example of the former technique, again showing parallels to rondo form, is the fourth movement of Mozart's Quintet in A for clarinet and strings, K. 581. The reprise of the theme at the end, in a quasi-ternary design, is seen in Haydn's String Quartet in D, Op. 20, No. 4, second movement. The theme, which is 18 measures long, is recalled up to its seventeenth measure at the conclusion of the series, at which point it dissolves into a coda.

The sectional variation series

Although a few of the works mentioned in this chapter have continuous form, in most specimens of theme with variations the theme and each of the variations are followed by clear cadential breaks of indefinite length, forming sectional series in contrast to the continuous form of ostinato variations. The performer naturally does not exaggerate these breaks, lest the continuity and relationships within the series be impaired. A composer can, of course, indicate that there is to be no break in the form; Aaron Copland does this in his Piano Variations.

A further distinction between ostinato forms and the sectional theme with variations is that in the latter the theme melody is often of greater importance in the variations, even though it is from time to time dismissed. The usual theme for a sectional variation series is of greater length, moreover, than that of the ostinato forms.

We may consider briefly a few works that present problems of classi- fication in the terms outlined above. The *Goldberg Variations* (Ex. 9.26) of Bach lose sight of the theme melody altogether during the variations, which are built on the theme structure, bass line, and harmony, but are sectional rather than continuous in form. Something comparable may be said of the *Diabelli Variations* (Ex. 9.16) of Beethoven, although in this work the composer develops melodic motives of the theme, which is not of distinctive melodic character, in addition to the retention, in most of the series, of the theme structure and harmonic outlines. The Piano Variations of Copland, which are continuous rather than sectional, are an eloquent discourse on the principal motive of the theme,

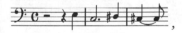

rather than on its bass line or harmony, as would be the case in ostinato forms.[4]

Rarely, transitions are used in the sectional variation series. Thus, there is continuous motion through cadences in the *Diferencias Cavallero* by Antonio de Cabezon (1510–1566), included in the first volume of the

---

[4] A further exception to all of the above may be seen in the *strophic bass* of certain seventeenth-century cantatas and other works. Here, the bass line—as a kind of ostinato theme, but of greater length than that of the usual passacaglia—is repeated with each textual strophe with varied accompaniments, but the over-all structure is sectional rather than continuous. (See among Monteverdi's *scherzi musicali* the aria for soprano, solo instrument, and continuo, *Et è pur dunque vero,* whose strophic bass appears seven times with changes in its superstructure.)

Historical Anthology of Music (pp. 145–6). Despite this, sectionalization is quite pronounced in this work. Transitional passages in variation series whose fabric is frankly continuous are, of course, more usual. (See measures 108 through 116 of Beethoven's variations in the final movement of the Symphony No. 3 in E-flat, Op. 55; this is a transition linking the first complete theme statement with the first of the fugal variations.)

An even rarer feature is the use of an introduction to one of the members of a variation series; such an introduction precedes variation 12 of the *Enigma Variations* of Edward Elgar (1857–1934).

One of the most interesting areas of analysis with respect to the theme with variations is the consideration of the over-all plan which gives a profile and cumulative effect to the total series. The composer may achieve this by gradual increase (and/or subsidence) of motion, of dynamic intensity, of brilliance of color, of textural complexity, and of degrees of submergence of the most recognizable features of the theme. Control of such factors is extremely important in the unity of the total composition—as important as the interrelationships among variations and theme. (See prefatory notes on pp. 295–96, which include discussion of considerations of unity and variety in the variation series.)

A sense of total shape and progress can transcend the cadential interruptions in the musical flow, as in Ex. 9.7, which employs an obvious, yet effective device: the gradual increase in rhythmic motion from variation to variation.

Ex. 9.7   Handel, The Harmonious Blacksmith (Air and variations from the Suite in E).

Examples of theme elements fixed:

Structure; the structurally-fixed variation

While it goes without saying that any element of the theme may, in a variation, remain fixed, it can be observed in the historical practice of variation form that primary significance and systematization attach to the fixation of three basic elements as devices of variation: surface structure, harmony, and melody. Indeed, omitting many examples of about the past century, it is possible to classify virtually all traditional examples of theme with variations as having structural fixation, usually in combination with melodic, harmonic, or melodic-harmonic fixation, although rarely is any combination of fixed elements retained consistently through an entire series of variations. In Romantic, Classical, and pre-Classical variations, theme structure is modified in only isolated instances. The following classification of traditional variations suggests itself:

1. Those having *fixed structure,* with theme harmony and melody decisively altered, or abandoned altogether.
2. Those having *fixed structure and melody,* with theme harmony decisively altered, or abandoned altogether.
3. Those having *fixed structure and harmony,* with theme melody decisively altered, or abandoned altogether.
4. Those having *fixed structure, harmony, and melody,* with any one of these varied slightly[5] or with variation applied to other theme elements.

Or the above may be expressed with letter symbols denoting fixed basic elements in each of the four classifications.

$$
\begin{array}{ll}
\text{S} & \text{(rare)} \\
\text{SM} & \\
\text{SH} & \text{(very common)} \\
\text{SMH} & \text{(very common)}
\end{array}
$$

[5] Obviously, no absolute distinction can be made between the "decisive" and "slight" variation of a musical entity to establish that point at which the element ceases to be "present in variation" and is, in effect, dismissed totally or in "decisive alteration." Some guides for consideration of this point of variation analysis are laid down in this chapter. "Retention" in variation implies the presence of features that bring the original element readily to mind. The feeling of melodic retention in variation can be achieved, for example, by the continued supremacy of its primary motive in a form closely allied to that of its original appearance. The presence of melodic outline, with new embellishments, has the same effect. As to harmony, again "retention" implies the adherence to basic outline and distinguishing features. If the structurally vital points (cadences) are altered, the balance must be clearly reminiscent of the original element or the feeling is that the harmony is dismissed. In many cases, the analyst must judge for himself whether a given theme element is associably preserved in variation or, in effect, extinguished altogether. The rationale behind the judgment is important. Examples and analytical discussions in this chapter will help to clarify this aspect of variation analysis.

When we consider the theme as a composite of many elements, of which the above are the most basic in traditional variation treatment, we avoid the mistake of equating "theme" with "melody." Morris commits this error in discussing Bach's *Goldberg Variations:* "This work is a masterpiece of its kind, but I confess it seems to me somewhat of a strain on terminology to speak of it as a 'theme and variations.' The theme itself—a highly rococo little dance in binary form—is completely ignored; all that is kept is the binary structure and the basic harmonic progressions."[6] Thus, Morris recognizes Bach's retention of theme structure and harmony (together, it is assumed, with its bass line), but considers that with the dismissal of the upper-voice melody the "theme" is "completely ignored."

The reader may question the apparent exclusion of rhythm in the above delineation of three "basic elements"; certainly rhythm is one of the vital distinguishing elements of any theme. But rhythm in music is primarily associated with melody, harmony, and structure (meter, both *mensural* and *intermensural*[7]), and the above outline understands it to be a vital part of each of the three fundamental elements which are the basis for the classification suggested.

Since structural fixation is a feature of nearly all variations until the late nineteenth century, despite exceptions which will be noted, we define the *structurally-fixed variation* as that in which structure is the *only* basic element to remain fixed, with harmony and melody of the theme abandoned in their identifying outlines.

Minor traces of theme harmony or melody, or both, are nearly always present in the structurally-fixed variation. It would be impossible, as so often in theoretical discussion of music, to establish a clear line of distinction between "alteration" and "dismissal" of a given theme element. In Ex. 9.8, the theme structure is clearly the principal tie between theme and variation —the chief basic element of the theme remaining fixed. Harmony conforms in some degree at phrase beginnings and endings but is otherwise reduced to b-flat:I in measures 1–2 and D-flat:I in measures 3–4, with uncertain

---

6 R. O. Morris, *The Structure of Music,* p. 71.

7 As implied earlier, *mensural meter* is here understood to be the organizational principle within the measure, the unit of which is the beat. Meter is also viewed at higher levels, levels in which groupings are formed of measures or even larger units; this is *intermensural meter.* Viewed thus, a phrase of 5 temporally equal measures is a sort of magnification of the 5-beat measure. (To feel meter at various levels —mensural and intermensural—the reader may try "conducting" a very simple theme, like that of the Haydn Symphony analyzed in Chapter 6, equating "beat" with a half-measure—i.e., making one bar of two, then gesturing a full measure per "beat," and finally two measures per "beat," so that the entire period feels like a magnification of the 4-beat measure. It then becomes clear that measures and groups of measures —phrases and larger units—have weak-strong organization which is analogous to that of the measure.)

movement to b-flat:V at the very end of the variation phrase. Of the theme melody, primarily the sixteenth-note motive,

is woven into the canon.

Ex. 9.8   Brahms, Variations and Fugue on a Theme by Handel, Op. 24.

Another example that may be described as a structurally-fixed variation is number 6 of the Brahms Variations on a Theme of Haydn, Op. 56a. Here, theme melody and harmony are retained at phrase beginnings but radically altered at cadences. Furthermore, the middle section (third and fourth phrases) of this variation violates the theme melody and harmony so severely that for all practical purposes neither element, despite the presence of traces, remains fixed. (See also the later sections on melody and harmony as variable elements.)

Structure and melody; the melodically-fixed variation

The term *melodically-fixed variation* refers to that procedure in which, of the three basic elements, melody and structure are retained while harmony is abandoned or at least decisively altered in its essential outlines. The melodically-fixed variation is also known as the *cantus firmus* type. Ex. 9.9 is among the earliest examples of theme with variations, taken from a lute book of 1538. The complete piece can be seen in the *Historical Anthology of Music,* first volume, pp. 130–32.

Ex. 9.9   Luis de Narvaez, Diferencias sobra O Gloriosa Domina.
  Reprinted by permission of the publishers from Archibald T. Davison and Willi Apel, *Historical Anthology of Music: Oriental, Medieval, and Renaissance Music* (Cambridge, Mass.: Harvard University Press, copyright 1946, 1949, by the President and Fellows of Harvard College).

For further study of the melodically-fixed variation, another example of the same period may be suggested. It is Cabezon's *Versos del sexto tono,* also included in the *Historical Anthology* (pp. 144–5). In the four sections of this composition, the *cantus firmus* moves through the four voices of the texture, starting in the soprano and ending in the bass. A later example of melodically-fixed variation is the second movement of Haydn's String Quartet in C, Op. 76, No. 3.

Structure and harmony; the harmonically-fixed variation

The *harmonically-fixed variation* is vastly more common than the structurally- or melodically-fixed types. We have learned that harmonic fixation is a feature of many ostinato variations. Harmonic fixation, with dismissal of the upper-voice theme melody, is a feature of many individual variations of the Classical period, and of many earlier works, including Bach's *Goldberg Variations,* as well as of most variations of the nineteenth century through Brahms. The majority of nineteenth-century character variations are of this type. It must be understood that harmonic fixation permits occasional minor variation in harmony, but with the "essential harmonic outlines"—the focal points of intra-phrase and cadential harmony—preserved. Inevitably, changes in such elements as texture and tempo involve adjustment in harmonic rhythm, occasional simplification of the harmony, and other comparable alterations.

An example of the harmonically-fixed variation is shown as Ex. 9.10. It will be seen that the theme melody is dismissed. (As in the preceding paragraph, reference is to the upper-voice melody, an obvious thematic focal point in homophonic styles; it is understood that in the harmonically-fixed variation the bass "melody" is usually retained along with the theme harmony.) Harmonic fixation is maintained, although in measure 3 of the variation a new augmented-sixth chord is used to introduce the cadential dominant. The use of this chromatic harmony is encouraged by the slower tempo, and by its higher accessibility in the minor mode.

Ex. 9.10   Mozart, Ten Variations, K. 460, on Come un agnello by Sarti.

Further examples are the *Abegg Variations* in F, Op. 1, of Schumann and the variation movement of Beethoven's String Quartet in C-sharp minor, Op. 131, in which the composer displays extraordinary fantasy and ingenuity. These are highly resourceful and expressive variations on a theme which, in its opening four measures, is a simple progression from tonic to dominant and dominant to tonic.

Structure, melody and harmony; the melodically-harmonically-fixed variation

The rather cumbersome designation *melodically-harmonically-fixed variation* is adopted here in preference to Nelson's "melodico-harmonic" only because implicit in the former term is the specification that all the basic elements remain *fixed,* with variation dependent upon minor alterations in these elements or in variation upon other theme elements.

Like the preceding category, the melodically-harmonically-fixed variation is of great importance in view of the sheer volume of works (especially eighteenth and early nineteenth centuries) composed according to this principle. Many of the variations of Mozart, Haydn, Beethoven, and Schubert—to mention only the most significant names of the Classical and early Romantic periods—involve melodic-harmonic fixation.

In the melodically-harmonically-fixed variation, the theme melody, fixed at its chief points, is rarely retained in its original form. In some cases a nearly new ("transformed") melody is built upon the original outlines. But more often than not the retention of the theme melody in this type of variation involves its embellishment by the addition of new note-groups around its essential outlines. It is for this reason that this category is often designated "ornamental variation." Melodic ornamentation is a fundamental characteristic of the melodically-harmonically-fixed variation. (See Ex. 9.11, as well as Ex. 9.7.)

Ex. 9.11   Mozart, String Quartet in A, K. 464, third movement.

Retention of the melody may involve its fragmentation, often with contrapuntal or other developmental treatment of its important motives. In Ex. 9.12, minor variation in the structure results from such fragmentation,

Ex. 9.12   Bach, Chorale Variations on Sei gegrüsset, Jesu gütig.

which causes a delay in the otherwise straightforward statement of the embellished chorale melody.

Other examples of the melodically-harmonically-fixed variation are found in the variation movements of Schubert's *Trout Quintet,* cited earlier, Beethoven's Quartets in A, Op. 18, No. 5 (see variations 1 and 3) and C-sharp minor, Op. 131 (see variation 3), as well as Haydn's Quartet in B-flat, Op. 55, No. 3, in which variation 2 treats the primary motive of the theme melody imitatively.

Motive as a fixed element; the free variation

In all four categories of variation just discussed, structure is a constant element. It is in the free variation of the late nineteenth and twentieth centuries that all three basic elements—structure, melody, harmony—are often largely dismissed, with the only commonly practiced link between theme and variations that of a theme motive or theme motives, retained as a source of free development or as a point of departure in the variations.

Examples of earlier free variation are found in the final movement of Beethoven's Symphony No. 3. A motive derived from the theme bass,

becomes the basis for free development (see measure 211) which can be regarded as a free variation rather than an "episode" or interruption in the course of the series; and the fugal variations (measure 117 and measure 278) on the above motive and its inversion are similarly free.

Ex. 9.13 is included to illustrate the use of a theme motive taken as a point of departure for a twentieth-century variation whose structure represents an alteration upon that of the theme. In this work, the theme (see Ex. 9.3) is an enlarged period of 24 measures (repeated antecedent phrase of 4 measures, repeated consequent phrase of 8 measures) ; the variation from which the quotation is drawn is 42 measures long. Its form may be outlined as follows: introduction, 2 measures; antecedent group with half-cadence, 11 measures; consequent group with perfect authentic cadence, 11 measures; second consequent group with perfect authentic cadence, 9 measures; codetta (an extension leading to a stronger cadence), 9 measures. In the variation, the motive which constitutes the entire theme, becomes the springboard which gives rise to a variation of totally contrasting character. As seen in Ex. 9.13, the motive is inverted.

Ex. 9.13   Rachmaninov, Rapsodie sur un Thème de Paganini, Op. 43, pour piano et orchestre. Copyright renewed 1962 by Charles Foley, Inc. Used by permission.

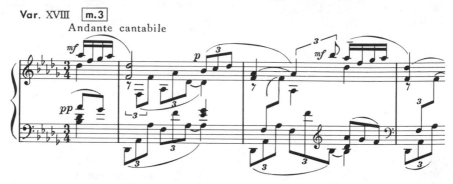

An excellent work for further study of variations freely deriving from theme motives is the colorful, sensitive *Variaciones Concertantes* for chamber orchestra, by the Argentine composer Alberto Ginastera (b. 1916).

The tone series as a fixed element in the free variation

In some works of the twentieth century the link between theme and variation series, sectional or continuous, consists of nothing more than the succession or coincidence of the tones used; indeed, the theme may be simply a prescribed sequence of the 12 notes, which becomes a basis for pitch succession and coincidence in the variations. (For supplementary study, the student may refer to writings on the 12-tone technique by Schönberg, Josef Rufer, Egon Wellesz, and Křenek in sources specified by his instructor.)

Ex. 9.14   Dallapiccola, Quaderno Musicale di Annalibera for piano (later issued as variations in an orchestration by the composer).
© 1953 by Edizioni Suvini Zerboni, Milan, Italy. Used by permission.

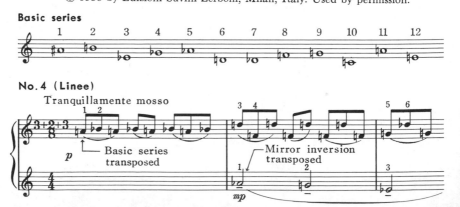

No. 7 (Canon cancrizans)

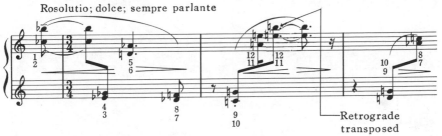

Ex. 9.14 is taken from a composition by Luigi Dallapiccola (b. 1904) in which the fixed element uniting the variations is a 12-note series. The degree to which this relationship contributes to perceptible unity in the total work is doubtful, and unity and contrast are dependent rather upon other form-building devices (imitation, motive repetition, dynamic and tempo contrasts) and factors of balance and distribution as among the several movements of any multi-movement work. In most works of this type, tonality is relinquished or of only minimal importance as a basis of structural unity and variety.

Other fixed elements in theory and practice

A particular fact has been cited as the rationale behind the classification of variation techniques based on fixation or non-fixation of the three basic thematic elements: it is that melody, harmony, and structure (with rhythm understood to be a component of all three), unlike other theme elements, are treated with a considerable degree of consistency within given styles and periods of traditional music.

(An example cited by Eschman[8] as one in which "the rhythm is maintained and the melody varied" assumes a definition of melody as pitch succession independent of rhythm. If melody is rather made of both pitch succession *and* rhythm, the example must be analyzed as one in which melody is fixed in one of its aspects, varied in another [see Ex. 9.15]. Similarly, harmony involves rhythmic distribution and emphasis as well as root progression and chromatic alteration; and structure is not just a product of plan and shape, but of meter and relative proportions as well.)

8 Karl Eschman, *Changing Forms in Modern Music,* pp. 118, 121. Copyright, 1945, by E. C. Schirmer Music Company, Boston, Massachusetts, and reprinted with their permission.

Ex. 9.15   Philipp Jarnach, Kleine Klavierstücke.

In any of the foregoing traditional classifications, other elements of the theme may of course remain fixed. Some normally are, except in the free variation. An example is tonality, which is constant throughout an entire series in many examples of traditional variation form. At the opposite extreme, certain elements may be fixed only rarely—for example, the theme color, which is likely to change in subtle ways in nearly every variation, even when the medium of execution is a solo instrument. Other theme elements—meter, mode, tempo, texture—may be fixed or not and in nearly all cases change considerably during the course of a variation series, but without any predictable stylistic regularity. The following sections of this chapter will refer to examples from many works in illustration of ways in which any of the theme elements may be subjected to variation while certain others remain fixed.

Examples of theme elements in variation:

Structure

The foregoing section (Ex. 9.13) dealing with theme motive as a fixed element refers as well to variation in structure, for when structure is altered a motive of the theme often becomes the sole or principal binding factor between theme and variation. Variation in structure, the exception in most traditional styles, becomes the rule in more recent variations.

Variation in structure can be of two kinds: the form of the theme may be altered in its relative proportions, e.g. in the introduction of asymmetry or in the abandonment of or modification of the degree of asymmetry (Ex. 9.13) ; or the *kind* of form represented by the theme may be changed—binary to ternary, or period to *fugato,* for instance, as in the *Eroica* examples cited; or what was a set form may become a fantasy-like free form. With respect to the first of these points, we are speaking not of total length (a product of tempo as well as metric structure) but of *relationships* of parts; if these relationships are altered in the variation so that, for example, what was originally symmetrical loses its symmetry, even while the type of form is preserved, it is incorrect to say that the structure is unchanged. Thus, an 8-measure period of equal phrases is unchanged in structure when it becomes a 16-measure period of equal phrases, but is modified significantly when it is adjusted to consist of, say, 4- and 6-measure phrases.

Ex. 9.16   Beethoven, Thirty-three Variations on a Waltz by Diabelli, Op. 120.

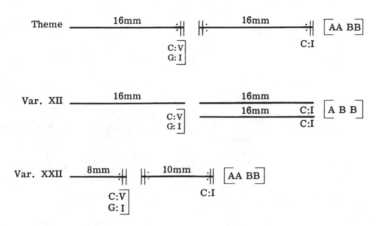

In Ex. 9.16, variations 12 and 22 are made asymmetrical, the former by the omission of the repeat of the first part of the original binary, the latter by the extension of the second part. An example of actual change in the kind of form—in this case, binary to fugue—may be seen in the penultimate variation of the same series.

The form of the final variation in a traditional series is often extended or otherwise modified to allow for coda or codetta, another instance of structural variation. In the last variation of Mozart's Twelve Variations on *Je suis Lindor*, K. 354, the conclusion of the original form is dissolved into a codetta with cadenza. The means by which such freedoms are taken with theme structure are relevant in the development toward the later free variation.

Later examples of free variation may be studied in the *Enigma Variations* of Elgar, in which, for example, variations 2, 6, 7, and 9 may be compared with the theme of that series. Ex. 9.23 is a contemporary specimen.

Eschman, in his discussion of the modern variation, closes his chapter with a succinct, summary statement: "In short, the form has been added to the possible 'variables' in modern variations."[9]

9 Eschman, *Changing Forms in Modern Music*, p. 129.

Harmony

Just as the theme melody may be a fixed element and at the same time be ornamented without disruption of its outline (Ex. 9.11), the harmony of the theme may, in a variation, be changed slightly (in Ex. 9.17, embellished) while its chief progressions are retained. Ex. 9.17 illustrates one kind of harmonic variation—embellishment; it is from a set of variations by Carl Maria von Weber (1786–1826) on a theme by a German contemporary.

Ex. 9.17   Weber, Eight Variations on an air de ballet from Vogler's Castor and Pollux.

However, we have suggested that harmony ceases to be felt as a fixed element when severe alteration takes place—alteration at points of structural significance, like beginnings and cadences, or such extreme alteration within structural units that identification with the original theme harmony is significantly obscured (Ex. 9.8).

Melody

Ex. 9.11 shows melodic embellishment, perhaps the most frequent kind of variation in theme melody, and Ex. 9.12 illustrates melodic fragmentation and imitative treatment. In such instances, primary identifying features of the melody—its characteristic motives, its basic profile, or both—are preserved.

There are, of course, many other means of varying the theme melody. For instance, the line may be presented in altered rhythm or altered pitch succession (Ex. 9.15), or in augmentation or diminution, or it may be stated in mirror inversion. An example of the latter technique is quoted as Ex. 9.18;

Ex. 9.18   Ginastera, Variaciones Concertantes.
Copyright 1954 by Hawkes & Son (London) Ltd. Reprinted by permission of Boosey & Hawkes, Inc.

another which is suggested for study is variation 2 of Schönberg's *Variations for Orchestra*, Op. 31; this variation begins as a canon between solo violin and oboe on an inversion of the theme melody, rhythmically altered.

When the theme melody is omitted from the variation (see Ex. 9.10), a new melody may be introduced over the original harmonic-structural framework. Further examples of this technique are seen in the opening variation of the third movement of Beethoven's Piano Sonata in E, Op. 109, and in variation 7 of Brahms' *Haydn Variations* (Ex. 9.29). Moreover, a melodic variation in which broad original outlines are preserved but other basic changes take place—tempo, mode, meter—may have the effect of new melody where in fact a profound transformation has occurred without abandonment of the bases of the original line (Brahms, *Haydn Variations,* variation 4). Thematic transformation on the original melodic motives and profile is a very important resource, to be distinguished from ornamentation in which the original melody is simply adorned with figurations which, subtracted, leave the original line essentially intact.

Meter

Variation in such elements as meter, mode, tempo, and dynamics may, especially when treated collectively, change the theme character very radically. Total transformation of the theme appears with regularity for the first time in the variations of Beethoven, whose works in many respects predict the broad latitude of later techniques. Ex. 9.19, an illustration of variation in meter, is a sixteenth-century example, in at least one basic sense a transformation of theme character. The *saltarello*, a lively Italian dance of the period, often appears as an after-dance (German, *Nachtanz*) in alliance with the *passamezzo*, a dance in duple meter.

Ex. 9.19   Nicolaus Ammerbach, Passamezzo antico.
> Reprinted by permission of the publishers from Archibald T. Davison and Willi Apel, *Historical Anthology of Music: Oriental, Medieval, and Renaissance Music* (Cambridge, Mass.: Harvard University Press, copyright 1946, 1949, by the President and Fellows of Harvard College).

Passamezzo

Saltarello

Rhythm

The interdependence of theme elements (e.g., texture and color, harmony and modality), rendering somewhat deceptive and often difficult their separate consideration, is most pronounced with respect to rhythm. Rhythm is an aspect of virtually all elements, each element suggesting and representing a specific feature of rhythmic effect. Thus, rhythm is an aspect of tempo, tempo of rhythm; rhythm is an aspect of meter, meter of rhythm. Rhythm as a feature of structure and structural proportion has been important in consideration of all the forms we have treated.

Short of a study devoted specifically and extensively to rhythm, we can only suggest some of the areas in which rhythmic fixation (Ex. 9.15) and variation enter into variation technique. We have referred often to rhythmic motion as a basic character determinant in music—the degree of melodic, accompanimental, contrapuntal, and harmonic activity which determines the pace of music. Rhythmic motion (which is also conceived and perceived as *tempo*[10]) can be lessened, as in the so-called negative variation (Ex. 9.3), or increased, as in Ex. 9.7 and Ex. 9.9, as a source of variation.

Ex. 9.20   Munday, Variations on Goe from my window.
Reprinted by permission of the publishers from Archibald T. Davison and Willi Apel, *Historical Anthology of Music: Oriental, Medieval, and Renaissance Music* (Cambridge, Mass.: Harvard University Press, copyright 1946, by the President and Fellows of Harvard College).

No. 7

In Ex. 9.20 by John Munday (d. 1630), the rate of beat-succession[10] is unchanged, as are harmony, form, mode, meter, color, and dynamics. The melody (a folksong) is varied only slightly. The principal alterations are in the simplificaion of texture and the transformation of rhythmic motion— the introduction of sixteenth-notes in the accompaniment. This is felt as a considerable change.

The interrelationship of harmony and rhythm, with modification of

---

[10] *Tempo* is, in one sense, the rate or frequency of beat-succession—the "tempo" which is indicated by metronomic figures. In another sense, tempo is related to the degree of internal motion, the *activity* interspersed among the beats. Thus, a piece at $\quarternote = 96$ in which the motion is primarily in quarter-notes has the effect of being "slower" in tempo than a piece at $\quarternote = 96$ in which the primary unit of motion is the sixteenth-note.

harmonic rhythm as a variation device, is seen in Ex. 9.8 and Ex. 9.17. Textural change, often a product of rhythmic differentiation among voices, can be described as a kind of rhythmic variation (Ex. 9.26). Melodic ornamentation represents an alteration of melodic rhythm (Ex. 9.11 and Ex. 9.12). Variation in characteristic *patterns* of melodic rhythm in a theme can be seen in Ex. 9.18, where the difference of long-short is lessened, with a "smoothing out" effect in the variation. A specimen like Ex. 9.19 is often called "rhythmic variation" rather than the more correct "metric variation," but clearly meter and rhythm, as musical elements, are largely interdependent. Another type of variation in rhythmic effect is the modification or elimination of anacrusis (Ex. 9.22 and Ex. 9.27). In summary, the alteration of any rhythmic feature lending a distinctive quality to a musical idea is rhythmic variation of a kind.

Color

We can state simply, without going into acoustical properties of musical sound, that color is associated with and is a product of timbre of instrumental or vocal medium. When the medium is a relatively homogeneous one, a solo instrument or ensemble of like instruments, color change is produced by differences of register, by changes in the manner of articulation, or by the use of muted or other special effects. Color and dynamics are, of course, impossible to set apart, since changes in dynamics are certain to have an effect upon the color, and the opposite is equally true.

Color change is obviously of the greatest significance in a medium of broad palette such as a chamber ensemble of unlike instruments, or the orchestra. But striking resources are at the composer's disposal in a homogeneous medium. Attention is called, for example, to the unforgettable *pizzicato* statement of the theme in the cello, against sustained accompanying chords in the upper voices, in the sixth variation of Brahms' String Quartet in B-flat, Op. 67, final movement.

Ex. 9.21 shows the theme of Don Quixote in Strauss' tone poem as it appears in variation 7. Programmatically suggesting the Don's flight through air, the theme is thrust in brilliant eruptions through the strings (supported by harp and winds) into the highest violin octave.

Ex. 9.21 Strauss, Don Quixote.

Theme

etc.

Tonality

Tonality is not generally used as a variable element until after the middle of the nineteenth century. And it is one of the neo-Classical features of the variations of Brahms that tonality generally remains a fixed element through his variation series. Tonal change as a means of variation is exploited more in works of the late nineteenth and twentieth centuries except, of course, in atonal music.

Again it is Beethoven who frequently breaks away from the principle adhered to in the traditions which preceded him. In the *Diabelli* series, variation 5 modulates to the mediant minor rather than to the dominant or relative; and the fugal variation is in the key of E-flat while the theme is in C. The *Eroica* variations, basically in E-flat, traverse such tonal levels as D, C, and G minor. Moreover, the composer's Variations in F, Op. 34, includes variations in D, B-flat, G, E-flat, and C minor, with the final variation returning to the original tonic.

Ex. 9.13 shows a twentieth-century excerpt in which a key distantly opposed to that of the theme is employed in variation.

Mode

Variations 15, 21 and 25 of Bach's *Goldberg* set employ change of mode, being in G minor rather than G major, while the variations in Handel's Suite in E (Ex. 9.7) eschew change of mode entirely. In the late eighteenth and early nineteenth centuries it became a general rule that a variation series included one variation in mode. The term "minor variation," often applied to this practice of modal change, is inappropriate in view of the fact that major variation upon a minor theme is not infrequently found. An example is shown as Ex. 9.22; another is to be seen in Mozart's String Quartet in D minor, K. 421, final movement, variation 4. (See also Ex. 9.32e.)

Ex. 9.22   Brahms, Sextet in G, Op. 36, for strings, third movement.

In more recent styles, modal scales other than the conventional major-minor are occasionally significant as a source of variation. In Ex. 9.23, the

Ex. 9.23   Britten, The Turn of the Screw (opera, Op. 54; piano reduction by Imogen Holst)
Copyright 1955 by Hawkes & Son (London) Ltd. Reprinted by permission.

Theme motive

principal theme motive is quoted; it constitutes the primary link between theme and free variations in this work. As a variation technique, the composer sometimes inverts[11] the intervals; thus, the motive appears very early in the work in the following form:

In variation 5, which is partly mixolydian, a changed motive derives from the theme: the note succession ADBE occurs in the permutation ABED, transposed to an F tonic (thus, FGCB-flat, as in the opening of the variation, quoted in Ex. 9.23), the A in the revised motive having a nonharmonic character.

This variation also has the motive in the bass of measure 5: here, it is a mirror inversion (as well as a retrograde—see Chapter 11, p. 397) of the four notes of the theme. The reader will note that there is further modal treatment in the use of the phrygian scale at the approach to G minor at the end of the quoted excerpt.

---

[11] Interval inversion, in which a sixth becomes a third, a fifth a fourth, etc., should not be confused with mirror inversion, in which an interval is duplicated in size but moved in the opposite direction.

Tempo

Tempo change is a vital facet of variation technique in all styles of music. It is difficult to imagine that any single theme element, substantially altered, can have so profound an effect upon the expressive character of the theme. The variation literature shows that tempo variation is decisive in its mutative action upon the theme even when other elements remain relatively stable (see Ex. 9.24).

For the fifth variation in the final movement of Mozart's Quartet in D minor, K. 421, all theme elements are fixed except structure and tempo. After 8 measures, the theme submits to brief development and coda.

Ex. 9.24   Mozart, String Quartet in D minor, K. 421, final movement.

In variation sets of the melodically-harmonically-fixed category of the Classical period, there is almost inevitably an *adagio* variation around the middle of the series, and a concluding *allegro* variation, often quite brilliant. Examples are easily found.

Dynamic levels

The effect and frequency of dynamic change as a source of variation are so apparent that an example is hardly necessary. Change of dynamic quality is, of course, usually accompanied by other changes, although reduction or intensification of dynamics alone would drastically affect the original theme character. Like that of other variable elements (for example, tonality) the variation in dynamics may be a total one (in which, for instance, *piano* becomes *forte*) or it may be one in which only certain dynamic directions and contrasts of the theme are, in variation, changed or suppressed. In Ex. 9.25, the most telling variation techniques are those of meter, color (strings in theme, *tutti* in variation), tempo, and dynamics, the latter clearly allied to changes in articulation of performance.

Ex. 9.25   Elgar, Variations in G minor on an Original Theme, Op. 36.
            Reproduced by permission of Novello & Co., Ltd.

Texture

The principal means of variation in texture is the adoption of contrapuntal techniques: fugal imitation, canonic imitation, inverted counterpoint, and the like. Another way of expressing this would be to say that the homophony of the theme often becomes polyphony in the variation, sometimes simply by the introduction of free accompanying counterpoints. Variation of this kind is often called "contrapuntal variation" with obvious reason. Famous examples are found in the *Goldberg Variations* of Bach, in which every third member of the series, beginning with variation 3, is a canon. Alteration in the nature and complexity of texture is a very important and fundamental variation technique.

A single example is given as Ex. 9.26. In it, the harmonies and bass of the theme are fixed while the texture is modified to include 2 voices in canon at the unison, with an accompanying bass which is not a part of the canon.

Ex. 9.26   Bach, Aria with Thirty Variations.

Further reference may be made to Ex. 9.8, Ex. 9.12, Ex. 9.14, and Ex. 9.18, as well as to variation 5 of the sixteenth-century *Diferencias* of Luis de Narvaez cited in Ex. 9.9.

Textural variation may also involve modification of the accompanying fabric within a prevailing homophonic style to introduce varying degrees of internal motion and density or a higher or lower complexity of pattern in inner voices.

The variation shown in Ex. 9.27 preserves the homophonic character of the theme, but reduces its texture to 3 voices. The theme pedal point is abandoned, as are the original inner voices of more than harmonic significance.

Ex. 9.27   Brahms, Variations in D on an Original Theme, Op. 21, No. 1.

Theme

Poco larghetto

Var. II

Character

The theme character is the product of all its elements with the exception of tonality, although the relative employment or absence of tonal fluctuation (not usually a feature of brief variations) would also have an effect upon the expressive character of the music.

It is the most pervasive elements—tempo, dynamics, meter, mode, rhythmic pattern—that have the strongest effect upon the theme character. Extreme change of one or more of these may totally alter the expression of the theme. In Ex. 9.28, there is little or no variation in tempo, mode, harmony, melody (as pitch succession), texture, and structure. But the meter is changed and the rhythms are "spread out," with syncopations of the theme eliminated and constant motion introduced. The changes in dynamics and the color effect of the warm, high cello register opposed to the dark accompaniment are also factors in the character change, as is the introduction of conjunct motion in the theme melody.

Ex. 9.28   Brahms, Piano Trio in C, Op. 87, second movement.

Ex. 9.28 (continued)

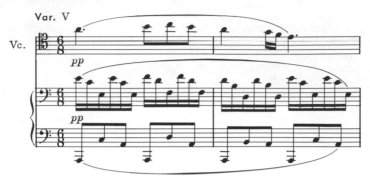

The term "character variation" frequently means that theme character-istics are radically modified so as to give the variation the character of a specific musical genre, such as a type of dance. This type of variation is especially a feature of the Romantic tradition, although the label "character variation" is often applied to such earlier works as the Bach *Goldberg Variations.* (See Nelson's *Technique of Variation,* p. 6, which also refers in this connection to the *Partite sopra l'aria della Romanesca* of Girolamo Frescobaldi [1583–1643]. See also Ex. 9.19 in the present chapter.)

Ex. 9.29, from Brahms' *Haydn Variations,* shows the adoption in varia-tion of the qualities of a *siciliano* (a seventeenth-century Sicilian dance in rather slow tempo and compound meter, often featuring dotted rhythms). In the same series, variation 5 is a scherzo—also a character variation.

Ex. 9.29   Brahms, Variations on a Theme of Haydn, Op. 56a, for orchestra.

Treatment of the variable elements in the practice of variation

It is clear that any given variation series is concerned with not one but a variety of techniques, ranging from fixation of all three basic elements to modification of all of them. Similarly, any single variation of any period acts upon the theme in a number of ways, usually transforming several of its elements. Thus, a combination of variable elements is treated in each variation; and some elements, like texture and color, are altered to some degree in nearly all variations.

Ex. 9.30   Schumann, Symphonic Studies, Op. 13.

Theme

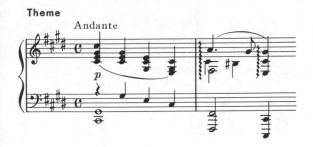

Etude IV   Allegro marcato

In Ex. 9.30, structure, meter, tonality, and mode are fixed elements in Etude IV. The harmony corresponds with that of the theme although displaced here and there by the requirements of the canon. Varied elements are melody, rhythmic pattern, color, tempo, dynamic levels, and texture. Articulation seems in this case to require separate mention as a varied element, although it can be viewed as an aspect of melody, rhythm, dynamics, color, and texture—in a sense integral in each of these.

Occasionally, material appearing prominently in a particular variation is drawn, not from the theme, but from an earlier variation. This technique, frequent in Brahms, tends to draw the variations of a series into larger units, further interconnecting the individual segments in the over-all variation form.

Ex. 9.31 Brahms, Variations on a Theme of Haydn, Op. 56a.

Coda; appendage of separate structure

"A free fugue is a favorite solution of the problem of the coda in a set of variations. The momentum produced by the revolution of true variations in the orbit of the theme gives the key to the whole problem. A fugue solves it by flying off at a tangent. Very sublime is the way in which Beethoven [in the *Diabelli Variations*], after letting his fugue run its torrential course, returns to the orbit of his theme in an ethereal little minuet with a short coda of its own which, sixteen bars before the end, shows signs of beginning to revolve again."[12] The fugue with which Beethoven ends this work is based on a subject extracted from the opening bars of the theme melody.

Another example of a fugal finale to a set of variations may be studied in Brahms' Variations on a Theme of Handel, Op. 24. We have seen in Chapter 8 that Brahms ended his *Haydn Variations* with a passacaglia, whose bass ostinato is derived from the Haydn theme. This series is also a good illustration of the reprise of the original theme at the end—in this instance a major portion of the theme—in its original form but in a much more emphatic, climactic delivery and with the original theme codetta expanded at the end. The reprise of the theme is an extremely useful, rounding device; it is a reminder of the material out of which the variation series, in this case a monumental one, emerged.

The fugue is particularly appropriate as a conclusion to variations. The form of the fugue (see Chapter 11), in its textural accumulation toward climax, may be interpreted as a reflection of an analogous, if structurally disparate, accumulation of intensity and complexity in the variation set itself. The fugue thus presents the composer with the opportunity to withdraw after climactic development to a minimal beginning in his fugal

---

[12] Sir Donald Tovey, *The Forms of Music* (London: Oxford University Press, 1957), p. 244.

exposition, and to progress again, in a different manner, toward a new climactic culmination within a condensed span of time.

A theme with variations may close with the appendage of a free finale, related or unrelated to the theme, like that which provides so spirited a conclusion to the Schumann *Symphonic Etudes,* Op. 13, or the same composer's *Abegg Variations,* Op. 1, with their finale *alla fantasia.*

Another technique, mentioned earlier in connection with variation in structure, involves the enlargement of the final variation by the addition of a short codetta, a cadenza-like concluding section, or a big and expansive coda which develops theme material. The first of these may be seen at the conclusion of Schubert's Impromptu in B-flat, Op. 142, No. 3, where the codetta consists mainly of abbreviated theme restatement and cadence repetitions; in the variation movement of Haydn's "Emperor" Quartet in C, Op. 76, No. 3, where a 4½ measure codetta is appended to variation 4; or in the variations of John Munday from which Ex. 9.20 is drawn. The use of a cadenza in the concluding section is associated especially with Mozart's keyboard variations (see p. 313) and can be observed in his Twelve Variations on an *Allegretto,* K. 500; here, variation 12 is extended by avoidance of cadence, and by the addition of a cadenza and theme reprise. The literature is replete with examples of the big coda. Brahms' Variations on a Hungarian Song, Op. 21, No. 2, has its 13th variation dissolve into such a coda, with a precise theme reprise in the final bars, extended from 8 to 9 measures for slight cadential broadening. The coda to Beethoven's *Eroica Variations* incorporates material of the introduction as well as the theme, putting both to extremely powerful use.

Brahms, Quintet in B minor, Op. 115, for clarinet and string quartet, final movement

Generally speaking, the Brahms movement is a series of harmonically-fixed variations, but as we have by now learned to expect, so general a statement is unlikely to apply to the entire group. Thus, certain of the variations retain major points of the theme melody in transformation or ornamentation and belong in the category of the melodically-harmonically-fixed type; this applies to variation 3 and, especially, to variation 5.

The theme is in two parts. The first is a period of 2 parallel phrases of 8 measures each; melodically they are nearly identical but the first moves to b:V, the second to D:I. Part II has the same form, but its consequent matches the opening phrase of Part I—the earmark of incipient ternary form. The total length is 32 measures, the second part repeated. The total incipient ternary might also be regarded as a double period, the final cadence being stronger than the middle one. In Ex. 9.32a, which shows key instrumental parts only, harmonic analysis of the antecedent of Part II is given at both primary (D) and secondary (G) levels.

Ex. 9.32a Brahms, Quintet in B minor, Op. 115, for clarinet and strings, final movement.

The first variation is harmonically (and, of course, structurally) fixed, even though there are minor changes at certain points such as measures 36, 44, and 48. Often, the cello alone, as at the beginning of the variation, outlines traces of the theme bass and melody and represents the theme harmony. The "linking motives" of the theme, originally in the clarinet and having the function of setting the motion ahead at points of punctuation, are present in an expanded form. The harmony of the middle section is rigidly fixed; that of the reprise is retained but again with minor alterations.

The first variation increases texturally as it develops. Brahms plays upon two motives, as he often does in variations: one of them is in the violin and clarinet parts in the quotation (the clarinet, imitating the cello, has the motive in a more disjunct form) ; the other is in the viola—a two-note anacrusis figure which has a vital part in the motion of the music.

Ex. 9.32b

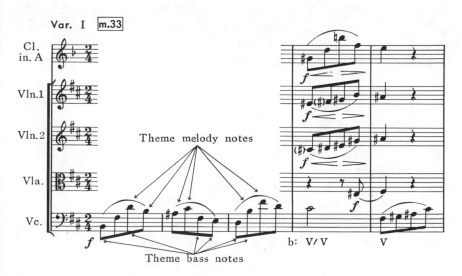

There is important rhythmic change in variation 2, with syncopation in the accompanying inner parts, part of it created by the dynamic accents in measures 2, 4, etc. The music is more dramatic than the preceding as a result of these rhythmic qualities as well as the falling, surging motives heard first in clarinet and cello. Melodically, the variation presents essentially new lines built on the structural-harmonic basis of the theme. Motion is increased (even with stability of tempo) by the syncopations, the rising and falling motives, and the unbroken steadiness of sixteenth-note articulation.

Variation 2 is harmonically fixed despite such minor changes as the substitution of VII$_7$ for V and V$_7$—a change not in tonal-harmonic function but in the degree of dissonance. The stability of the bass line at cadential points should be noted.

Ex. 9.32c

In variation 3, the sixteenth-note motion continues in the same tempo, but the urgency of variation 2, with its irregular accents and syncopations, is subdued. Despite reduced intensity, there are anacrusis rhythms both in the sixteenth-note motives,

and the figuration of the accompaniment,

The fidelity of the bass line should again be marked. The device of melodic ornamentation is apparent in Ex. 9.32d, in which notes of the original theme melody are indicated in the first violin part. It is not unusual that the middle variation should thus recall the theme melody, as does the final one.

The harmony of variation 3 is especially close to that of the theme. Only the most minor changes can be found, as at measure 124, which may be compared with measure 28 of the theme.

Ex. 9.32d

Notes of original cl. motive

Var. III m.97

Notes of theme melody

Outer voices

p

Notes of theme bass

Variation 4 is a change in mode. The opening motive of the theme melody is transformed to become

,

and it is used imitatively, together with another form of the same motive, creating the first significant change in texture, complemented by the contrapuntal association of second violin and viola. In a metronomic sense, the tempo is still constant. The sixteenth-note motion continues but there are steadying factors: the dismissal of anacrusis rhythms and syncopations, and the increased prominence of eighth-note and dotted-quarter-note motives. Thus, the relaxation after variation 2 continues, suggesting that the intensity of the series is highest at variation 2. The dynamic-rhythmic contour

of the complete movement might be represented thus:

It can be seen in the quotation of the opening of Part II that the syncopation of variation 2 is recalled, but without comparable force—a kind of ripple in the subsiding motion.

While the harmony and bass are again in general correspondence with the theme, we should note, for example, two significant changes: (1) the dominant pedal introduced at measures 133–136, which does not affect the theme harmony except at measure 135; and (2) the middle cadence on the dominant of d-sharp, caused by the use of the major mode and the increased distance of D, the original relative major. Still, the harmony clings to the original theme patterns remarkably closely. Where the theme harmony revolved around a secondary center of G, we now have g-sharp (measures 17–20 compared with 145–148); just before the reprise the music leads back to the dominant of B. Details should be studied carefully, as should the movement of the bass line in relation to that of the theme.

Ex. 9.32e

Now the higher textural density of variation 4 is relinquished, and the minor mode is restored. The tempo continues to be stable, but variation 5 introduces the first change in meter, and the most significant variation in color, with a new form of the melody in the richest register of the viola and a pizzicato elaboration of the theme bass in the cello. It is in this variation that the nearest approach to character variation is achieved, largely through the alteration in meter.

Ex. 9.32f

In Ex. 9.32f, notes of the original theme melody and bass are pointed out. The clarinet motive is developed as a diminution of the opening notes of the viola melody; both, of course, refer to the theme.

As stated before, this variation is the one that is most definitely in the melodically-harmonically-fixed category. The transformation of the theme melody continues into Part II, but with reduced fidelity. It is worth noting again that the theme melody is most conspicuously recalled in the middle and final variations.

It is a good plan for the analyst to think through the melody of the theme (which should be committed to memory) against the bass line of the variation, or at least to compare the bass line of the variation with that of the theme. It will be found again that the harmony is generally fixed. Changes that should be noted occur at the cadence to Part I, and at the point of variation of measures 23–24 of the theme, where harmonic direction is preserved but with alteration in the harmonic rhythm and in the root progression itself.

Double variation (see discussion following) is exemplified in these variations, especially clearly in variation 5; the second half of Part II is, as usual, a reprise of the opening, but it is much enriched in color and texture.

The repetition of Part II of variation 5 concludes in a half-cadence for direct motion into the coda. The tempo is slightly relaxed, and the meter changes to 6/8—in a sense a product of the original 2/4 and the 3/8 of variation 5, preserving both the duple measure of the former and the triple divisions of the latter; it is also a return of the meter of the first movement.

The coda dwells mainly on theme motives of the first movement of the Quintet, but it includes reference to the opening of the variation theme melody:

This motive, clearly allied to the variation theme (compare the viola part in variation 5), bears a striking resemblance to one of the motives of the first movement,

now recalled.

Variation principles freely applied

We have referred to the combination of variation principles with other procedures of form in music, as for example the use of variation in theme restatements in the rondo, or in strophic forms, to which instrumental variations are very closely allied (see pp. 54–5, as well as p. 294 in this chapter).

Similarly, variation is commonly used in free forms. A famous example is the final movement of Beethoven's Ninth Symphony, in which the familiar theme and its variations are intermingled with introductory and transitional passages, recitative-like statements in the low strings, recollections of themes of other movements, contrasting themes, and many dramatic episodes, including fugal sections on subjects derived from the theme, in effect free variations (as at measure 101).

Many other examples can be found. As a further illustration, consider the slow movement of Haydn's Symphony No. 95 in C minor. Haydn's symphonic slow movements are often rather freely constructed, often monothematic, sometimes composite or hybrid forms, with variation techniques appearing conspicuously in theme restatements in rondo-like or ternary forms. In the movement cited above, the theme (Ex. 9.33) is followed

Ex. 9.33   Haydn, Symphony No. 95 in C minor, second movement.

immediately by variation, with the melody transferred to the cellos. This is followed by a digression in the parallel minor, based on the theme and characterized by silences and a sense of uncertainty. Now the theme returns in part, unadorned, after which there is a complete variation in shorter rhythmic values. A coda, also based on the theme, closes the movement.

Double variation: variation on variation

Variation themes are often in binary and small ternary forms, with customary repeats. This presents the opportunity for repeated sections to be written out in further variation (Ex. 9.32 and Ex. 9.34). Nelson describes the "double variation" as the "use, within a single variation, of varied restatements to take the place of literal repetition in the theme"[13]—variation on variation. The principle of double variation can apply to any theme units which appear in the theme more than once, whether literally and contiguously or not, and of whatever size. Thus, further alteration in the reprise in a variation on a ternary theme is a form of double variation. Ex. 9.34 shows a theme repeat written out in double variation.

Ex. 9.34   Brahms, Variations on a Theme of Paganini, Op. 35, Vol. I.

Theme (first 4 measures repeated literally)

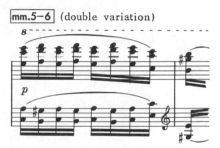

mm.5–6 (double variation)

Exercises and examples for further study

1. Prepare an analysis of a work in the form of theme with variations, giving particular attention to the theme elements which might be varied. How would you characterize the form of the theme? If you feel it is a good theme for variation, explain why. What theme elements are fixed in each of the variations? With reference to the variable elements of the theme, list the techniques actually used by the composer. What over-all shape (in rhythmic motion, dynamic intensity, textural growth, etc.) can be observed? Are the variations of increasing complexity? Does the theme return in its original form at any point? How is the series concluded?

   You may use as the basis for study one of the many works cited in this chapter, or you may select one of the compositions listed below.

[13] Nelson, *The Technique of Variation,* p. 8.

Bach, English Suite No. 6 in D minor, *sarabande* with *double*
    Chorale variations and partitas on *Christ, der du bist der helle Tag; O*
        Gott, du frommer Gott; and *Ach, was soll ich Sünder machen*
    Five canons on *Vom Himmel hoch*

Bartók, Concerto for violin and orchestra, second movement

Beethoven, Piano Sonata in F minor, Op. 57, second movement
    Sonata in G, Op. 96, for violin and piano, final movement
    String Quartet in E-flat, Op. 74, fourth movement
    String Quartet in E-flat, Op. 127, second movement

Boris Blacher (b. 1903), Variations, Op. 26, on a Theme by Paganini

Luigi Boccherini (1743–1805), Quintet No. 6 in C, Op. 30, for strings,
    final movement

Britten, Variations, Op. 10, on a Theme by Frank Bridge, for strings
    Young People's Guide to the Orchestra

William Byrd (b. 1543), *The Carman's Whistle* and other virginal
    variations

Elliott Carter (b. 1908), Variations for orchestra

Chopin, Variations, Op. 2, on *Là ci darem la mano* from Mozart's
    Don Giovanni, for piano and orchestra
    Variations, Op. 12, on a Theme from Halévy's *Ludovic*

Delius, *Appalachia*

Dvořák, Symphonic Variations, Op. 78

Fauré, Theme and Variations in C-sharp minor, Op. 73, for piano

Ross Lee Finney (b. 1906), Variations for orchestra

Franck, Symphonic Variations in F-sharp minor for piano and orchestra

Harris, String Quartet No. 2

d'Indy, Piano Sonata in E, Op. 63, first movement

Kodály, Variations on a Hungarian Folksong, for orchestra

Mendelssohn, *Andante con Variazioni* in E-flat, Op. 82, for piano
    Variations in B-flat, Op. 83, for piano
    Variations in D, Op. 17, for piano and cello
    Variations Sérieuses in D minor, Op. 54, for piano

Mozart, Serenade in B-flat, K. 361, sixth movement

Luigi Nono (b. 1924), *Variazioni Canoniche* on the row of Schönberg's
    Ode to Napoleon, for orchestra

Giovanni Pergolesi (1710–36), Suite No. 3 in D, final movement
    (*Gavotta con variazioni*)

Rachmaninov, Variations on a Theme by Chopin, Op. 22, for piano
    Variations on a Theme by Corelli, Op. 42, for piano

Ravel, *Bolero*

Reger, Variations and Fugue, Op. 134, on a Theme by Telemann, for piano,
    4 hands

Schubert, String Quartet in D minor, second movement

Stravinsky, Octet for flute, clarinet, 2 bassoons, 2 trumpets, and 2 trombones,
    second movement

Tchaikovsky, Six Pieces on a Single Theme, Op. 21, for piano
    Variations on a Rococo Theme, Op. 33, for cello and orchestra (variations
    separated by a recurring *ritornello*)

Vaughan Williams, Fantasy on a Theme by Thomas Tallis, for double
    string orchestra

Webern, Piano Variations, Op. 27

2. Make an outline of the first chapter of Nelson's *The Technique of Variation*.

3. Find as many examples of sectional variation form as you can in each of
the following sources.
   a) The piano sonatas of Beethoven
   b) The string quartets of Haydn (for example, the first movements of
   Op. 2, No. 6; and Op. 3, No. 2)
   c) The piano sonatas of Haydn (for example, Nos. 11, 12, and 27 in the
   Peters edition)
   d) Works of Franck
   e) Harpsichord pieces with *doubles* by Rameau
   f) Keyboard music in the twentieth century
   g) The chorale variations of the seventeenth and eighteenth centuries, including works of Johann Pachelbel (1653–1706) and Buxtehude
   h) The *Tabulatura Nova* of Samuel Scheidt (1587–1654)
   i) The *Fitzwilliam Virginal Book*

4. Write your own variation on a Mozart theme of your choosing.

5. Find an example of variations by Schubert on a binary theme. Take one
of the variations in which repeat signs are used and write out the repetition
as it might occur in a double variation.

6. Find examples of the following.
   a) A structurally-fixed variation (as defined in this chapter)
   b) A melodically-harmonically-fixed variation
   c) Variation in meter
   d) Variation in tonality
   e) Variation in texture involving use of contrapuntal imitation
   f) Free variation
   g) Character variation
   h) A variation in which the fixed element is a 12-note series

7. With regard to some of the quoted excerpts in this chapter, list and discuss
variation techniques illustrated but not discussed in the text.

8. Compare rondo form and theme with variations as seen in the *Allegretto
con variazioni* of Mozart's Quintet in A for clarinet and strings, K. 581.

9. Select one of the leading motives (German *Leitmotive*) from Wagner's *Der
Ring des Nibelungen* and trace some of its varied appearances. What variation techniques do you find to be especially important?

10

THE SUITE

his is the only chapter devoted primarily to a multi-movement form, although Chapter 6 deals in part with the multi-movement sonata. The forms and techniques observed in individual movements of the suite are treated at length in other parts of this book.

The suite and the sonata are the two chief multi-movement types in the history of instrumental music. They are, as might be expected, not firmly separable; for example, the minuet which occurs in many sonatas is a suite derivative, and the suite sometimes includes movements of abstract character which would not be out of place in the symphony or other sonata medium. Again, there is overlapping among forms: a given work may be called by some analysts a suite, by others a multi-movement sonata, by still others a hybrid combining elements of both. Despite this, it is important that criteria of consideration of classification be understood.

It is sometimes held that the real sonata emerges only in the later eighteenth century with the distinguishing features of strong intra-movement contrast of theme and key. In this view, all pre-Classical "sonatas" are suites.

The suite is the major multi-movement form of older instrumental music, having its highest manifestation in keyboard music of the century before 1750. No discussion of traditional approaches in the structure of music is complete without reference to the suite; yet an essay of this kind is problematic since the suite is a standardized form only to a very limited degree. Even in the Baroque period there is much variation in the structure and ordering of the suite from composer to composer and national style to national style. Moreover, the suite of more recent styles is of such diversity that it resists all but the most general commentary.

A consequence of the rise of dance forms in the secular music of the Medieval and Renaissance periods, the suite may be described as an aggregation of dances and dance-like movements, often highly idealized, interspersed with occasional contrasting movements which are not dances or dance-derived but which usually reflect the general lightness and brevity of expression which characterize the suite. That dance forms should enter so significantly into the history of art music is not surprising in view of the inevitability and universality of the alliance of dance and music.

The inter-movement arrangement of the suite is, broadly viewed, extremely free. Within the Baroque, the most significant standardization of movement sequence is found in the suites of J. S. Bach, and even among these there is considerable disparity in inter-movement structure.

The intra-movement form in the suite is usually binary, as pointed out in Chapter 2. The discussion of binary form should be reviewed in connection with the suite. In those rare instances in which the form of the dance movement is not binary, it is most often periodic or ternary. The use of compound ternary form in dances paired in *alternativo* style has been treated in Chapter 4. All of these forms are found in symmetrical and asymmetrical proportions.

As in the multi-movement sonata, the problem of inter-movement unity in the suite (apart from that which is a consequence of homogeneity of harmonic style, parity of forms used, and the like) is one of considerable difficulty. Many examples would suffer no impairment by the exchange of, say, the *allemande* of one with that of another of the same style and tonality. In the evolution of the suite, however, certain significant efforts toward inter-movement unity can be discerned: (1) the use of the same key for all of the movements; (2) the occasional use of the same theme or motive, as in the variation suite; and (3) unity of extra-musical subject, as in suites of a programmatic character. Of course, the optimum arrangement of movements for balance and contrast in the total work is also a vital factor in unity by imparting to the full sequence of movements a total tempo-, mood-, and dynamic-contour. Many of the points made with respect to inter-movement unity in the multi-movement sonata (Chapter 6) are relevant here.

Contrast of all kinds—of tempo, of dynamic level, of rhythmic pattern— is particularly vital among the movements of the suite in view of the absence of strong contrast within movements in binary form.

Origins of the suite

It is impossible to deal conclusively with the history of the suite in this chapter, and the student is referred for a more complete tracing of that history to sources suggested by his instructor. One that may be mentioned here is the fourth chapter of Ulrich's *Chamber Music*.[1] An interesting and useful historical summary is found in Apel's *Harvard Dictionary of Music*.

---

[1] Homer Ulrich, *Chamber Music: The Growth and Practice of an Intimate Art* (New York: Columbia University Press, 1948).

Dances are included in many sixteenth- and seventeenth-century collections of lute and keyboard music. In Chapter 9 reference was made to the sixteenth-century custom of joining dances in pairs, with contrast of meter (often the first duple, the second triple), contrast of tempo (usually the second dance at a faster pace), and affinity of theme. The second dance is sometimes called by the German word *Nachtanz*, literally "after-dance," or designated *proportio*, from *proportio tripla*—a reference to its usual triple meter. (See Ex. 9.19, a quotation from a *passamezzo-saltarello* pair.)

Other dances frequently paired in the sixteenth century are the *pavane* and *gaillarde*—the former a slow, stately dance in duple meter, probably of Italian origin, and the latter a very lively triple-meter dance. Later the *allemande* and *courante* form a dance pair which was ultimately incorporated into the mature suite. The concept of the dance pair of the late fifteenth and sixteenth centuries is extremely important in the evolution of the suite. The pairing of dances of common theme but opposing character "was common to all countries of western Europe in the early sixteenth century, and was the germ out of which the seventeenth-century dance suite grew."[2]

Some early sixteenth-century European publications of lute and keyboard music contain, in addition to dance pairs, "suites" of three or more dances grouped together, although it is not always clear whether the intention was that the group should in performance constitute a suite. One of the earliest of these, a publication of 1508 by the Venetian printer Ottaviano dei Petrucci, contains dances for lute in sets of three. Another lute collection, published in France in 1529 by Pierre Attaingnant, contains dances in groups of three or more. A German clavichord tablature of 1571 by Elias Ammerbach has, in addition to dance pairs, a "suite" of three movements. (See the *Historical Anthology of Music*, Vol. I, No. 137.)

English virginal books of the sixteenth century include dances, sometimes of polyphonic texture and occasionally with variations; an example of the latter is Byrd's Five Variations on a Galliard in the *Fitzwilliam Virginal Book*. Ensemble suites for viols, called "lessons," are found in late sixteenth-century and early seventeenth-century English sources; examples are *Consort Lessons for Six Instruments* (1599) by Thomas Morley and *Lessons for Consorts* (1609) by Phillip Rosseter, both significant items in a movement that culminates in the suites of Purcell in the late seventeenth century.

Thus, instrumental collections in the sixteenth century often included dances, dance pairs, and occasional larger groups of dances leading toward the late seventeenth-century maturation of the dance suite.

The extraction of excerpts from stage works to be strung together with the prelude or overture at the head, the whole forming a kind of suite, is

---

2 Ulrich, *Chamber Music: The Growth and Practice of an Intimate Art*, p. 69.

a practice of considerable age which enjoyed much vogue in seventeenth-century France, notably in the works of Lully. Many of the types of dances occurring in operas and ballets of Lully, dances of both peasant and court origin, assumed important places among the *Galanterien* (optional dance group of lightest character) of the Baroque suite.

As the suite evolved and became an established, highly popular form in late seventeenth-century music, dance components tended to become more and more stylized, although those of the optional group—*bourrée, passepied,* etc.—retained more of the original dance character and simplicity of texture than the basic group of the *allemande, courante, sarabande,* and *gigue,* which in the high Baroque achieved a level of refinement and sophistication sometimes obscuring their dance origins.

During the late seventeenth century the suite spread rapidly over Europe, becoming the vehicle for a large share of the instrumental art music of the time. In this period there is standardization neither of movement sequence nor of the number of movements included in the suite. Qualities that appear relatively universal are the unity of key among the movements and, to a lesser but significant extent, a prevailing homophonic style with a clearly edged surface of melody which is at times ornamented. In the later Baroque, the style becomes more polyphonic, especially in certain movements, notably the *allemande* and *gigue.*

Apel comments on the various national contributions in the development of the suite: "The development leading to the suites of Bach presents an interesting picture of international cooperation. Briefly stated, Italy contributed the early development (sixteenth century), England the *gigue,* Spain the *sarabande,* France the great wealth of dance types (early seventeenth century), and Germany the conception of the suite as a unified and definite musical form."[3] While the foregoing is obviously too simple a statement, it is an interesting general observation. It is true that French dance groups, called *ordres,* often seem somewhat arbitrarily arranged as to identity of key and dance type (Jacques Chambonnières, 1602–72; Louis Couperin, 1626–61; and later composers as well), while German suites of the seventeenth century more often appear carefully organized for group unity, contrast, balance, and suitable performance length in the arrangement of the movement sequence (for example, suites of Johann Hermann Schein, 1586–1630).

The principal figure in the seventeenth-century establishment of the suite is the German composer Johann Jacob Froberger (1616–67), whose significant keyboard suites are marked by an elegance, a textural richness, and an expressiveness which bring into a carefully ordered and balanced form the outstanding qualities of the several national styles to which they are contemporary.

[3] Apel, *Harvard Dictionary of Music,* p. 716.

The Baroque suite

The antecedents of the suite as well as its later developments are best viewed from the period in which it became established in its most definitive form and most universal acceptance, the late seventeenth and early eighteenth centuries. The formation of dance suites, sometimes by the addition of a second dance pair to the first, became gradually more widespread in Italy, Germany, France, and England during this period.

The following is a summary of characteristics of the Baroque suite, most of them bearing significantly upon its importance as a musical form.

1. The individual movements continue to be commonly in binary form, although some are incipient or periodic, some are ternaries, and the occasional non-dance movements are often free in structure.

2. The inclusion of non-dance movements is an important technique of contrast of form and style. Among the types to be found are *airs, intermezzi,* pieces with suggestive titles (as in many of the French *ordres,* including those of François Couperin), *rondos, fugues,* ostinato forms, and preludes of varying types.

3. The unity of key throughout a suite continues to be a prevailing structural feature, although there are occasional exceptions such as the use of relative keys in dance pairs and, for further example, early *sonate da camera* of Arcangelo Corelli (1653–1713), in which the slow movement is occasionally in a different key.

4. The contrast of tempo and meter is vital in the inter-movement ordering of the suite. A typical arrangement is *allemande-courante-sarabande-gigue,* having a metric sequence of duple-triple-triple-duple, and a tempo sequence of, for example, moderate-fast-slow-fast.

5. More often than not suites are for keyboard, but important examples were written for chamber ensemble (for example, English works of such composers as Matthew Locke, c. 1630–1677, and, later, Purcell, in continuation of the tradition of the English ensemble suite) and orchestra, culminating in the brilliant orchestra suites of Bach.

6. Thematic unity, or cyclic treatment, is not a common feature of the suite except in *doubles* within the inter-movement structure (Chapter 9) and in the variation suite.

7. The number of movements varies widely from as few as three to very many in some of the French *ordres.* Most suites of the Baroque consist of four to six movements, and the movements are usually quite brief.

8. The *allemande, courante, sarabande,* and *gigue,* in whatever order, gradually become established as a basic nucleus in the Baroque suite. They form an ideally balanced distribution of expressive elements, with the *sarabande* fulfilling the function of slow movement. In addition to the basic

group, optional dances are inserted *ad libitum,* many of them from French
opera and ballet sources. The dances of the optional group constitute another
important element of contrast, tending to be less stylized, more primitive,
more symmetrical, more sectional in form, simpler in texture, more straightforward in expression, and lighter in quality.

The order of the basic group varies considerably in the Baroque suite.
In Froberger the sequence is often *allemande-courante-sarabande* (ACS),
with the *gigue* (G) appearing as an optional movement before or after the
courante, and the *sarabande* concluding the suite. Ultimately, in the later
Baroque, the *gigue* and the *sarabande* exchanged positions, as in the suites
of Georg Böhm (1661–1733) and Bach. Still, the location of the optional
group (O) varies: in Pachelbel, for example, the order is commonly
ACOSG; in Bach, it is ACSOG, with an introductory movement often
added at the beginning of the suite. Further variation in the order of the
basic group is seen in Corelli: for example, prelude, A or C (sometimes
both), S, and G or *gavotte.*

A later section of this chapter considers specifically the suite of Bach
and Handel, in whose art the form has its highest flowering.

The introductory movement

There is, of course, an endless range of possible styles and structural
techniques which may be incorporated into the introductory movement.
Such a movement, whatever it is called, is frequently assembled of many
contrasting and corresponding sections. In the Baroque suite, introductory
movements, especially for keyboard works, are frequently freer in rhythm
as well as in form—sometimes of an improvisatory, rhapsodic style which
contrasts strikingly with the dance movements of the suite proper. The
casual sound of many preludes of improvisatory character is sometimes
traced to the functional role of the lute prelude as a series of offhand
gestures in which the tuning is checked, the key established, and the
performer allowed to get the feel of his instrument and put his fingers
in motion.

Ex. 10.1 is the sort of prelude that conveys the impression of playing
extempore, in a free and tentative manner, with a good deal of idiomatic
passage-work and with the tonality strongly affirmed.

Ex. 10.1   Handel, Suite No. 1 in A.

Ex. 10.1 (continued)

The prelude may command attention with brilliant and arresting, sudden force, as in Ex 10.2, which, after a potent opening statement of the tonic root and the dominant ninth-chord, settles into a more relaxed style, *senza rigore*.

Ex. 10.2   Debussy, Suite Bergamasque for piano.
Permission for reprint granted by Editions Jean Jobert, Paris, France, copyright owners, and Elkan-Vogel Co., Inc., Philadelphia, Pa., agents.

Specific types of introductory movement occurring in suites of Bach, with somewhat detailed description of form in those of the Partitas, are discussed in a later section.

Some important components of the Baroque suite

The movement types listed below are some of the most basic of the Baroque suite; they include the four (ACSG) which constitute the relatively fixed nucleus of the suite as well as numerous less universal dances used among the *Galanterien*. All of the listed dances are found in suites of Bach, although not all dances used by Bach are listed here (e. g., the *siciliano*). The reader may easily find descriptions and examples of dance forms other than those included below; he is urged in this connection to consult Apel's *Harvard Dictionary*.

The descriptions given here are generally based upon the appearances of the dances in the Baroque suite. It must be understood, however, that many dances underwent extreme evolutionary changes from nascence, whether peasant or aristocratic, to extreme sophistication in the art music of major composers. For instance, the *sarabande,* which is a movement of dignity and slow tempo in the Baroque suite, is sometimes thought to have been a very tumultuous dance in its early history. It must be acknowledged, finally, that there is little that can be said in general descrip= tion of any given dance form that cannot be contradicted by citing an unorthodox example.

Air[4]

The *air* (*aria*) is, as might be assumed, a movement of lyric style: melody of often vocal or song-like character against a relatively simple background, the whole usually of homophonic texture. Although often designed to accompany choreographic movement in seventeenth and eighteenth-century French opera and ballet, the *air* as it appears in the suite is not a dance form.

Frequently in the Baroque, the melody of the *air* is ornamented. A movement of this kind, often intense and even poignant, is of great importance as a source of variety in the suite. Ex. 10.3, from a modern suite for violin, shows the slow, *cantabile* character of the *air*. Another attractive contemporary example, one that illustrates the features outlined above, is the fourth movement of the Suite for violoncello and harp by Lou Harrison (b. 1917).

Ex. 10.3   Stevens, Suite for solo violin, third movement.
       © 1958 by Halsey Stevens. International copyright secured. Used by permission.

Ornamented reprise (measure 56):

---

[4] French forms are adopted here except in the case of the minuet (Fr. *menuet*), with little-used English forms like *jig* and *saraband* avoided.

A very famous Baroque example is the *air* from Bach's Orchestra Suite No. 3 in D, whose movement sequence is that of French overture, *air, gavotte* I, *gavotte* II and *da capo* of the first, *bourrée,* and *gigue.* The second movement is best known as *Air for the G-string* in a much played transcription for the violin. Another *air* was quoted in excerpt as Ex. 2.3.

Allemande

One of the key dances of the Baroque suite, usually the opening movement when there is no prelude, the *allemande* is moderate in tempo, and it is in simple duple meter[5], sometimes of a sumptuous, flowing quality. It has an anacrusis which varies in length—a single 16th-note in the *allemande* of Bach's Partita in B-flat, but often as many as three notes. (It is not difficult to find *allemandes* without anacrusis: the example of Claude Gervaise, sixteenth century, included in the *Historical Anthology,* Vol. I, is a case in point, as is the *allemande* of Pergolesi's Suite in E, a very highly stylized example.)

Ex. 10.4   Pergolesi, Suite in D, first movement.

In addition to Ex. 10.4, reference may be made to Ex. 2.7, Ex. 2.14, and Ex. 2.15.

In English sources, like the *Fitzwilliam Virginal Book,* the name appears in such forms as *alman* and *almagne.* While it is known to be of German origin, it is not certain that the *allemande* of the Baroque suite has a basis in actual dance.

In the Baroque suite, the *allemande* is more usually polyphonic in texture than any of the other movements except the *gigue.*

---

[5] Simple meter is that in which the beat is divided into two parts, compound meter that in which the beat is divided into three. Duple meter is that in which the measure falls into two parts, triple meter that in which it is in three parts. Examples: simple duple meter, 2/4, 4/4; compound duple meter, 6/8, 12/8; simple triple meter, 3/4, 3/2; compound triple meter, 9/8.

Anglaise

Anglaise is a French word for "English dance" (called *française* in Germany), but the relationship of the *anglaise* to England is uncertain; it may be based on the English country dance, to which it corresponds in meter and character. It is found in seventeenth-century French ballets and it is from this source that the *anglaise* passed into the optional group of the Baroque suite.

It is in simple duple meter, without anacrusis, and the tempo is moderately sprightly. A Bach example is found in the third French Suite. A suggestion of contrapuntal imitation is indicated in the quotation, Ex. 10.5.

Ex. 10.5   Bach, French Suite No. 3 in B minor, fourth movement.

Bourrée

A French dance, apparently from the Auvergne, the *bourrée* is another example of an optional dance which entered the Baroque suite from stage works of Lully. It is comparable in some respects to the *gavotte*, but has an anacrusis of only a quarter-bar and is somewhat more animated. It is in simple duple meter; rhythms like ♩ ♫♩ ♩ are characteristic.

Found in the French and English Suites of Bach, the *bourrée* is sometimes followed by a second with *da capo*.

Ex. 10.6   Bach, Suite (Ouvertüre) in F.

Courante

This dance movement is of two types in the Baroque suite—one of them French (*courante*), the other Italian (*corrente*). Both types emerged in the seventeenth century and were taken into the basic dance group of the suite.

The *courante* has an anacrusis of 1 to 3 notes, is in simple triple meter (often 3/2), more moderate in tempo than its Italian counterpart, somewhat more contrapuntal in texture, and often characterized by dotted rhythms. Ex. 10.7 shows a typical feature: the use of *hemiola* (the mixing of simple triple and compound duple meters, 3/2 and 6/4 in this case), a rhythmic device which occurs often at cadential points in the *courante* and occasionally within the phrase as well. (See also Ex. 2.11.)

Ex. 10.7   Creston, Pre-Classic Suite, Op. 71, for orchestra, first movement (reduction).
Copyright 1958 by G. Ricordi & Co., New York. Used by permission of Franco Colombo, Inc.

The *corrente,* as its Italian name suggests, is a dance of running motion, its meter usually 3/4 or 3/8 and its tempo quite lively. As might be expected in view of its faster motion, the texture is often simpler, more homophonic than that of the *courante,* although many examples contain contrapuntal imitation (see Bach's fifth French Suite). The anacrusis, when present, is comparable to that of the *courante*. Ex. 10.8 (in a realization by F. David) is testimony to the fact that many "sonatas" of the period include dance movements. There is a *gigue* in the same work.

Ex. 10.8 Vivaldi, Sonata in A, Op. 2, No. 2, for violin and figured bass, third movement.

The name given by the composer (or editor) is not always in accord with the actual character of the music. In the fourth French Suite, Bach uses the title *courante* for a movement whose texture, motion, and meter suggest the *corrente,* although the dotted rhythms and somewhat steady tempo might be considered features of the *courante.* There is, of course, no reason why a movement cannot combine features of both forms.

Excellent examples of the *courante* can be found in the suites of Frescobaldi. Bach's English Suites include examples of the French type; the Italian form is seen in the French Suites 2, 4, 5, and 6 and the first, third, fifth, and sixth Partitas. The use of the *courante* in the second and fourth Partitas (the others use the term *corrente* in appropriate designation of the Italian form) is one of the difficulties encountered in the repeated argument that Bach called these suites *partitas* (It. *partite*) because of their Italian features.

Gavotte

The *gavotte* is a graceful French dance, moderate in tempo, and of simple duple meter. Its most distinctive feature is the presence, except in very early examples, of a half-bar anacrusis which is often repeated with every phrase. The phrases are typically short, often of 2 measures. Ex. 10.9 illustrates these features and also shows the French practice of titling dance movements. (See also Ex. 10.17.)

Ex. 10.9   F. Couperin, La Bourbonnoise, gavotte from Premier Ordre.

Here again is a dance of the optional group which came into fashion with the stage works of such French composers as Lully and Rameau. Actually, the *gavotte* continued to flourish in French opera of the later eighteenth century and beyond. Leichtentritt quotes from André-Ernest-Modeste Grétry (1741–1813), in addition to giving several other *gavotte* examples.[6]

This dance is often paired with a second, *à la musette. Musette,* like *loure,* is originally the name of a French instrument of the bagpipe type, and the *musette* as a dance form occurring in association with the *gavotte* is characterized by a drone. Usually the *gavotte* is repeated following the *musette,* the total form being a compound ternary. Bach's third English Suite is an example; in the sixth English Suite the second *gavotte* is also of *musette* character, although simply titled *Gavotte* II. In the first of these the drone is a sustained note; in the second, it is repeated in remarkable animation on the second half of every beat.

Ex. 10.10 shows a twentieth-century composer's use of the Baroque form of the *gavotte-musette* pair with *da capo.* In Ex. 10.10, the drone (on *g*) and the *gavotte*-like features of the *musette* are clearly apparent.

---

[6] Leichtentritt, *Musical Form,* p. 90.

Ex. 10.10   Schönberg, Suite for piano, Op. 25, second movement.

Gigue

Another of the basic group, the *gigue* (It. *giga*) is of sixteenth-century English or Irish origin. Its distinctive features are quick tempo, compound meter (usually duple, occasionally triple), frequent wide leaps, and, in the Baroque suite, imitative texture. In addition to Ex. 10.11, the reader may consult Ex. 2.8 and Ex. 2.13 in the chapter on binary form. Ex. 10.11 shows the beginnings of Parts I and II of a Bach *gigue*.

Part II of the *gigue* binary, as seen below, often starts with a new exposition of the motive using a mirror inversion of the original.

Ex. 10.11   Bach, English Suite No. 4 in F, final movement.

Exceptions to the principle of compound meter are found in Bach's first French Suite and sixth Partita. In the former, the meter is 4/4; in the latter, 4/2. In both there is a prevalence of dotted rhythms in a context of more moderate tempo than is usual, although both of these anomalous examples conform in the use of imitation and inversion in the second half. In general, metric irregularities in the harpsichord suites of Bach are more apparent than real: where the meter is 3/8 (*gigues* of the fifth English Suite and the second and third French Suites) each pair of measures is, to the ear, obviously analogous to a single compound duple measure, and the beat division in quick tempo is, in effect, that of the measure—i.e., triple. In the first Partita, the apparent meter is simple (4/4) but triplets are used throughout.

The Italian *giga* of such composers as Giovanni Battista Vitali (c. 1644–92), Corelli, and their contemporaries is sometimes set apart as a distinct genre, having faster motion and simpler, less imitative texture. Most of Bach's *gigues,* like those of Froberger and Handel, are of the "French" type, with fugal texture, but this is not invariably true; in this respect too the *gigue* of Bach's first Partita is markedly exceptional.

The *gigue* is usually the final movement of the Baroque suite, despite such exceptions as Bach's second Partita and many of the suites of Froberger.

Loure

The *loure,* like the *musette,* is associated with a bagpipe instrument of the same name (from Normandy) and is traced to the sixteenth century. An early example occurs in Lully's opera *Alceste.*

Ex. 10.12   Lully, Alceste (Prologue).

Realization by Raymond Moulaert. Reprinted by permission of the publisher, Michel Prunières.

The tempo is moderate, and the meter compound duple, often 6/4. Its rhythmic patterns are frequently dotted, and the anacrusis is frequent; both of these qualities are seen in Bach's fifth French Suite and his Sonata No. 6 (Partita No. 3) for violin alone:

Minuet

The minuet is perhaps the most familiar of all the dances of the Baroque suite, probably because of its survival in later chamber music, symphonies, and solo sonatas, and because of its common association with courtly ceremonial music of the seventeenth and eighteenth centuries. Again, the works of Lully were an important instrument for the popularization of the dance form.

It is rather slow, very stately, of simple triple meter, and its expression, sometimes superficial, is often associated with courts like that of the *Roi Soleil*, even though the dance may well have peasant origin. It is, in the Baroque, characteristically without upbeat, although anacrusis is often used in minuets of later multi-movement sonatas and, indeed, in the works of Lully.

The minuet is often paired with a second, followed by *da capo*. (The term *trio* appears in connection with the second of the pair, as in Bach's third French Suite; see again the chapter on compound ternary form.) The practice of minuet in *alternativo* form is seen even in the early Baroque. Ex. 10.13 is from a twentieth-century example; it, too, is followed by "trio" and *da capo*.

Ex. 10.13   Piston, Suite for oboe and piano, third movement.
Copyright 1934 by E. C. Schirmer Music Company, Boston, Massachusetts, and reprinted with their permission.

Allegretto

Numerous minuet examples are cited in early portions of this book; a few that may be recalled are Ex. 3.21, Ex. 4.9, and Ex. 4.23. It is the only dance of those under discussion here to have highly significant survival in later styles.

Passepied (pass the foot)

Recent examples, like the *passepied* of Debussy's *Suite Bergamasque*, often depart from the particulars of the traditional dance form to retain only the real or imagined spirit of the dance. Traditionally, the *passepied* is a dance of simple triple meter (3/4 or 3/8), with an anacrusis of one beat. The fact that *passepieds* are found in 6/8 meter is another indication of the correspondence between quick 3/8 (viewed in paired measures) and 6/8.

Originally a dance of Brittany, it is of brisk, lively character. The *passepied* is another dance which enjoyed great popularity in the courts of the French monarchs Louis XIV and XV. A Bach example may be found paired with a second in *alternativo* form in the fifth English Suite. Another is cited as Ex. 10.14; the *passepied* which follows it is three-voiced and in the parallel major.

Ex. 10.14 Bach, Partita (Französische Ouvertüre) in B minor, from Vol. II of the Clavierübung

Polonaise

Polish

A *polonaise* with *double* occurs as one of the movements in Bach's Orchestra Suite No. 2 in B minor. Despite its frequently earthy character, the dance is thought to be derived from sixteenth-century courtly practice. It assumed great favor in the middle of the eighteenth century, and is well-known for its survival in a more grandiose manner in the piano music of the nineteenth century (Beethoven, Chopin).

Its meter is simple triple, and its phrases often conclude with cadences on the second beat of the measure—"feminine" endings. The music often features crisply delineated, short motives, and the tempo is broad and steady —qualities that are exaggerated in many nineteenth-century examples. Ex. 10.15 is an excerpt from Part II of an example of Bach. Another *polonaise* movement is found in Bach's sixth French Suite.

Ex. 10.15   Bach, Brandenburg Concerto No. 1 in F, final movement (polacca).

Sarabande

Conceivably of oriental or Near Eastern origin, the *sarabande* may have come into Europe through Spain in the early sixteenth century, and thence into vogue in France and England a century later.[7] It is of slow tempo (hence a very important element in the basic group of the Baroque suite), and simple triple meter, usually 3/2 or 3/4. It begins without anacrusis.

♩ ♩. ♩ | ♩ 𝅝 is a typical rhythm; the slight cessation of motion and consequent agogic accent on the second beat are characteristic of the *sarabande*. (An exception may be seen in the *sarabande* of Bach's third French Suite.)

The *sarabande* of Bach's sixth Partita shows an especially high degree of idealization and refinement. The memorable *sarabande* illustrated in Ex. 10.16 was written in the first year of the twentieth century.

Ex. 10.16   Debussy, Suite Pour le Piano, second movement.
            Permission for reprint granted by Editions Jean Jobert, Paris, France, copyright owners, and Elkan-Vogel Co., Inc., Philadelphia, Pa., agents.

Avec une élégance grave et lente

[7] A strong case for the Mexican origin of the *sarabande* is made by Robert Stevenson in *The Sarabande, a Dance of American Descent* (*Inter-American Music Bulletin,* July 1962, pp. 1–13).

The suite of Bach and Handel

It is in the suite of Bach and Handel, the two giants of the Baroque, and especially in that of Bach, that the form is seen in its zenith, enjoying a degree of importance and universality characteristic of no other age.

In many of the suites of these two composers the basic group, ACSG, occurs in that order, although this is less true in Handel than in Bach. A prelude or other introductory movement is used in some of the suites of both, and the most usual place for one or more of the optional dances is between *sarabande* and *gigue*.

The orchestra suites of Bach begin with overtures of the French type associated with Lully—opening *grave,* rather fast fugal section, and sometimes a brief concluding passage, again *grave,* with dotted rhythms normally dominant in the slow sections. In the four orchestra suites there is no fixed order of even a basic group, as there is in the harpsichord suites. The movement sequence of the third of these works, in D, is given in connection with the discussion of the *air* on an earlier page. Another example, the Orchestra Suite in C, has the following movements: French overture, *courante, gavotte, forlana* (a Venetian dance of spirited character in duple compound meter, often compared to the *gigue*), minuet, *bourrée,* and concluding *passepied.* Some of the movements have seconds, often in three voices and occasionally in related keys, with *da capo* (the *gavotte,* minuet, *bourrée* and *passepied* of the C major Suite). A *double* follows the fifth movement, *polonaise,* of the second Suite. Some of the movements in the orchestra suites are uncommon; there is, for example, a *badinerie*—a dance-like movement of humorous quality—as finale of the Suite in B minor. The Suite No. 4 in D concludes with a *réjouissance,* a piece of vigorous motion in triple meter.

Inevitably, attention ultimately focuses on the six French and six English Suites, and the six Partitas. In the summary of movement sequence, given below, upper-case letters (ACSG) are used to represent the basic group. Dances and other movement-types of the *Galanterien* are represented as follows: a, *air*; ang, *anglaise*; b, *bourrée*; bur, *burlesca*; c, *capriccio*; g, *gavotte*; 1, *loure*; m, minuet; p, *passepied*; pol, *polonaise*; pr, introductory movement (prelude or other) ; r, *rondeau*; and s, *scherzo*. Definitions of all of these terms are given in the *Harvard Dictionary.*

French Suites	Key	Movement Sequence
No. I	d	A, C, S, m-1, m-2, G
No. II	c	A, C, S, a, m, G
No. III	b	A, C, S, ang, m, trio, G
No. IV	E-flat	A, C, S, g, m, a, G
No. V	G	A, C, S, g, b, l, G
No. VI	E	A, C, S, g, pol, b, m, G

English Suites

No. I	A	pr, A, C-1, C-2 with 2 *doubles,* S, b-1, b-2, G
No. II	a	pr, A, C, S with *double,* b-1, b-2, G
No. III	g	pr, A, C, S with *double,* g-1, g-2 *a la musette,* G
No. IV	F	pr, A, C, S, m-1, m-2, G
No. V	e	pr, A, C, S, p-1 *en rondeau,* p-2, G
No. VI	d	pr, A, C, S with *double,* g-1, g-2, G

Partitas

No. I	B-flat	pr, A, C, S, m-1, m-2, G
No. II	c	pr (*sinfonia*), A, C, S, r, c
No. III	a	pr (*fantasia*), A, C, S, bur, s, G
No. IV	D	pr (overture), A, C, a, S, m, G
No. V	G	pr, A, C, S, m, p, G
No. VI	e	pr (toccata), A, C, a, S, g, G

We may draw certain conclusions regarding the types of movements used in these suites and the sequence in which they appear. The basic group appears consistently in the order ACSG and is complete except in the second Partita, which has no *gigue.* The optional group is placed between *sarabande* and *gigue* except in the fourth and sixth Partitas, where a non-dance movement titled *air* or *aria* is inserted between *courante* (or *corrente*) and *sarabande.* The number of movements in the optional group varies from two to four, the larger number in the sixth French Suite.

Twelve of the suites, the Partitas and English Suites, have introductory movements. The study of form in these preludes is extremely rewarding—a fact that is re-emphasized in Chapter 12, and the reader is urged to subject each of these twelve preludes to the most careful analysis. The prelude is in some cases the longest and most challenging movement of the entire suite; these are not mere "loosening-up exercises" or "curtain raisers." We shall study carefully the structural outlines observed in the preludes to the Partitas, leaving the corresponding movements of the English Suites for the reader's independent research. The reader will follow these notes to maximum benefit if the music of the Partitas is at hand.

The opening movement of the first Partita is called by Bach *praeludium.* It is formed very much like an invention (Chapter 11) ; in fact, comparison might be made with Bach's Two-Voice Invention in the same key. Like the inventions it is sectionalized by cadential arrival points in related keys—in this case the relative minor and the dominant. The short (three-measure) codetta at the end contains the only thickening of texture; otherwise, the piece is consistently in three voices. The basic motivic material which unifies the entire piece is stated at the outset and is treated in typical Baroque developmental fashion, fragmented and repeated in sequence, returning in the concluding bars, first at the dominant and then at the tonic—a kind of mirroring of the first two entries.

The prelude of the second Partita, called *sinfonia,* is in three sections. The first, in strong dotted rhythms, is homophonic in texture, ending on the dominant. The second section, *andante,* is in two voices, again invention-like. In the failure of the opening motive to recur strictly, the music is free, but it is welded together by the firm consistency of rhythmic pattern and motion, and by other factors such as the recurrence of characteristic devices —for example, that of tying a note into the following beat, sometimes as a suspension. The "walking" eighth-notes of the bass and the over-all tonal plan are additional factors which unite this section. There are cadences in c, f, and g, and the music is directed toward the latter tonic at the end of this section in preparation for the next. In the third section there is abrupt change to triple meter. The music is now strictly imitative, but the subject is answered in the fourth bar at the fifth below, unlike the normal intervals of imitation in invention and fugue. (The reason is the unusual beginning of the piece on the dominant harmony, the subject being contrived to lead back to the tonic.) But for this, and the length of the subject, this section too is like an invention. There are strict subject recurrences, an extended middle section featuring sequential progression, and a dominant pedal near the end (measure 80ff.), which helps to prepare the eight-bar codetta. At the conclusion, a final subject statement is given in the tonic key.

A *fantasia* opens the third Partita. This movement is an invention in two voices: the two-measure subject is canonically imitated in invention-like fashion at the octave, the two-voice texture is consistent, there is sequential development on the subject motive and its fragments, and the music is typically sectionalized by cadential punctuation in related keys. (After a cadence in the dominant key, the subject resumes in measure 31 with imitation at the octave as at the beginning but for opposition of voices.) A single "free" element is the failure of the subject to have its expected reappearance in original form at the end, but there is much reference to its component motives.

The introductory movement to the fourth Partita is a French overture, its opening section slow, with dotted rhythms, homophonic texture, and brilliant style. This section ends on the dominant. Because of the dominant opening of the subsequent fugal section (in compound triple meter) the subject, of 2 measures, is (as seen in the second Partita) answered at the tonic, i.e., at the 5th below (or 4th above). The third entry, at measure 25, is again on the dominant. As the lengthy form unfolds, there is again much sequence on subject motives and other typical devices of Baroque counterpoint (see the b:V pedal at measure 62). The "fugue" contains two important contrasting sections in which the texture is thinned, suddenly more homophonic, and in which the subject in its full form is relinquished temporarily; these are at measure 33 and at measure 72. Each time, the subject re-emerges strongly (at measure 48, bass, and measure 104, bass). The return of the subject at the end, measure 104, is especially powerful because of its protracted absence just before in the second and longer of the two contrasting sections, and because of the strong reaffirmation of the tonic key. There is constant allusion to the subject by development of its fragmented components in a very tightly unified movement.

The movement which begins the fifth Partita, in G, is titled *praeambulum*. Like some of the preludes of the *Well-Tempered Clavier,* it is mainly homophonic. Its character is unpretentious and uncomplicated; often it is improvisational in style, as in the sections which correspond to that beginning at measure 5. It consists of scales and chords based upon a scheme of easy, fluent, diatonic harmonic and tonal progressions; unity derives from motive repetition and, again, from the tonal plan, in which modulations orbit in closely related tonal areas around the G tonic. Another important factor in the unity, vital in Baroque music, is the regularity of motion, which is in sixteenth-notes except for the characteristic stops of the theme. Occasional sections in two-voice counterpoint contrast with the pure homophony of the theme (see measure 21). The latter recurs in strict form at measures 17–20 in D, 41–44 in e, and 65–68 in C. Curiously, it does not reappear at the end, probably because it would tend to contradict the powerful momentum Bach develops in the final 27 bars. He could not have reintroduced the theme, with its rather unassuming rhetoric and comparatively static quality, without weakening the dynamic emphasis of the conclusion as he chose to mold it. There is almost unceasing sixteenth-note motion, except for the *fermata* over the V_2^4 at measure 86, and intensity is increased by the powerful force of dissonance in the music of the final page.

The toccata of the last Partita is a brilliantly wrought ternary design, with the flanking sections (measure 1 and measure 89) of relatively homophonic, improvisational quality. Within the first section, motive repetition is again a factor in over-all unity: the motive of measure 1 reappears several times and there are other correspondences as well, as between measure 9 and measure 21. There are interesting relationships in double counterpoint (as between measure 9 and measure 11). (One of these forms a striking parallel to contemporary serial techniques: the material of measure 22 is contrapuntally inverted at measure 23; in the inversion the notes are strictly repeated in their original sequence, but the octave positions, and consequently the melodic intervals, are radically transformed!) The middle section, starting with the upbeat to measure 27, is a fugue in three voices. There is a full I-V-I exposition of the three-measure subject and the fugal development which follows, often obsessed with the subject's opening motive of three eighth-notes, is relentless in motion and compelling in effect. Its single irregular feature is that, adjusting to the material which surrounds it, it begins in E minor and ends in B minor.

In these eighteen suites, the optional movement appearing most frequently, excluding preludes, is the minuet, which occurs in nine of the suites. The *gavotte* is second in frequency, appearing in six of the suites. Four of the suites have *airs,* and four have *bourrées,* while the *passepied* is used twice. Other optional movements—the *anglaise, loure, polonaise*—have one appearance each, as do non-dance movements titled *scherzo, rondeau, capriccio,* and *burlesca.* All of the latter four types are found in the Partitas, which are in many ways the most anomalous of the harpsichord suites.

The Handel keyboard suites are not as well-known as those of Bach, with the exception of the fifth, in E, containing the variations referred to in the preceding chapter, and the ninth, in B-flat, which contains the *aria* theme used for a brilliant set of piano variations by Brahms. The composer called the suites "lessons" in the English tradition, publishing the first eight in 1720 and the second eight in 1733. The basic group order ACSG is observed for the greater part in No. IX through No. XVI, which, like the French Suites of Bach, are written without introductory movements.

Of the first eight suites, only No. IV has the four basic movements together in the sequence characteristic of Bach. In some, no more than half of the basic group is present and in No. II no dance movements occur at all (*adagio, allegro, adagio,* fugue). The seventh, in G minor, includes a passacaglia in addition to an *andante,* an *allegro,* and a *sarabande.* There are several fugues among the movements of the sixteen suites of these two volumes. The Suites I through VIII have preludes. Because of the frequency and even occasional predominance of non-dance movements, the suites of Handel are often regarded as hybrids, some of them as sonatas rather than suites. In any event, many of the movements are captivating, and all of the works are valuable objects for the study of multi-movement form.

Except for the occasional compound ternary formed by paired movements with *da capo,* simple ternary (see the second minuet of Bach's fourth English Suite), or movement in rondo form, the components of the suite of Bach and Handel are in binary form. This excludes the preludes, which we have seen to be of a wide variety of styles, types, and forms, and some of the many non-dance movements of the Handel suites. But for exceptions already suggested, unity of key is the rule. (See the two minuets of the fourth English Suite of Bach.)

Even the optional dances lose something of their original innocence in the later development of the Baroque suite. For comparison, a *gavotte* by Lully is shown in brief excerpt together with the opening of the *gavotte* from Bach's fourth French Suite (Ex. 10.17a and b), over whose expected fundamental rhythms Bach weaves a fabric of tight motivic unity, with imitation at the octave. The Lully example is rhythmically simpler, clearly of dance character and intended to accompany dance, utterly homophonic, and without such sophistications as unifying motivic repetition and development within the *gavotte* framework—in all of these features the extreme opposite of Bach's *gavotte*.

Ex. 10.17a   Lully, Cadmus et Hermione, gavotte from Act V.
  Realization by Matthys Vermeulen. Reprinted by permission of the publisher, Michel Prunières.

Ex. 10.17b   Bach, French Suite No. 4 in E-flat, fourth movement.

Further comparison could be made between the *sarabande* of Lully's *Le Ballet de l'Amour Malade* (*première entrée*)—texturally uncomplicated, unadorned, of danceable quality—with, say, that of Bach's third English Suite.

The later suite

After the Baroque the suite loses its vitality, eclipsed by the emerging multi-movement sonata form of Classical keyboard, chamber, and symphonic music. The existence of the suite does not, however, come to an end: vestigial traces of the form are important factors in a multitude of later forms, including that of the sonata itself, although the suite ceases after the mid-eighteenth century to have the reasonably definitive form it had known in the Baroque. Moreover, the suite is an important vehicle of expression in the twentieth century.

Definition of the later suite is necessarily very general. "The later uses of the word 'suite' comprise almost all sets of pieces mainly in forms smaller than those of the sonata, especially such pieces as have been selected from ballets or from incidental music to plays."[8] "On the whole, the suite in the nineteenth century no longer had as fixed and definite a form as in the eighteenth. Any series of loosely connected pieces of entirely different types (with the exception of the sonata form) could now be linked together in a suite."[9]

"The modern suite is an instrumental form of an optional number of movements, unified by being related to some central subject. Unlike its Baroque counterpart, its movements do not necessarily consist of dances, are not all in the same key, and are generally not in binary form.

"The term 'suite' is also used for a three- or four-movement abstract work, often in sonata form, in which the individual movements are not sufficiently integrated into a larger unit to allow the work to be called a sonata or a symphony."[10]

The third of the above quotations raises problems. We have seen that non-dance movements are common in the Baroque suite, eliminating this factor as a point of distinction. And while it is true that many nineteenth- and twentieth-century suites have unity in extra-musical associations with a "central subject," the type of suite in which the movements are not related in this way still exists and in fact shows considerable viability. (See contemporary suites cited in these pages, as well as numerous examples listed for study at the end of this chapter.) Moreover, it is doubtful that the degree of integration among movements can be established as a tenable basis of distinction between the suite and the sonata.

Dance forms, ancient and modern, continue to have an important part in the suite; where non-dance movements are involved distinction can be made only on the basis of *relative movement length* and *relative lightness or weightiness of content*. Certainly the presence or absence of pronounced *thematic contrast and development* within movements is a factor in both of these criteria.

Thus, while the suite after the Baroque loses much of its vitality, it continues in related forms (see later section) and in recent periods comes back into practice much less universally but with importance as a multi-movement work of light, sometimes dance-based or dance-like character, consisting of movements which lack the expansive and vigorous thematic manipulations and tonal fluctuations of the sonata.

Certain nineteenth-century composers sought consciously to bring about a recrudescence of the Baroque type of suite, but their works are virtually

---

[8] Tovey, *The Forms of Music,* p. 235.

[9] Leichtentritt, *Musical Form,* p. 94.

[10] From *Structure and Style* (p. 160) by Leon Stein, copyright © 1962, Summy-Birchard Company, Evanston, Illinois. Reprinted by permission.

unknown today. We may mention Franz Lachner (1803–90), who wrote orchestra suites, and Julius Otto Grimm (1827–1903), whose *Suite in Canon Form* for strings seems worthy of more than a passing glance.

Brief quotations are made below from the *Suite Modale* for flute and piano by Ernest Bloch. As the title implies, the composer uses modal scales as a source of harmonic and melodic novelty in this work. These modes are freely alternated, but the basic scales for the first three movements are phrygian on E, dorian on A, and lydian on C, respectively; the fourth movement, the most variable, adds the mixolydian on C and G. The work is short, its total duration about 12 minutes.

In the first movement, *moderato,* there is alternation between brief appearances of two motives,

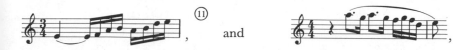

and

in a rondo-like fashion but with extremely short sections and no substantial contrast of motion and character.

The second movement, also *moderato,* is similar in construction, alternating between

used imitatively, and

in the sequence ABABA, with an unmistakable reminiscence of the second motive of the first movement interjected before the final section.

The third movement is *gigue*-like (*allegro deciso*), and ternary in design. Part I features the motive

⑪ Excerpts reprinted by permission of Broude Brothers Music Publishers, New York.

in both *rectus* and *inversus* forms (see measure 7), restated at the end. The contrasting middle section, dorian on G, brings a new theme in a contrasting meter—

possibly derived from the inversion of the original motive. There is a short coda at the end.

The final movement is the least compact, containing a larger number of more diverse sections. There are significant returns of motives of earlier movements: that of the first movement at rehearsal No. 23, the third movement at No. 24, and that of the second movement at No. 25. The material of the *adagio* which opens this movement is recalled in the midst of the coda (see between rehearsal Nos. 24 and 25). The form of the fourth movement may be represented thus: A (*adagio*) ; B—in two parts, both *allegro*, the second featuring the motive

A; B; coda, with the above-mentioned theme restatements, which include a reprise of the *adagio* material. Except for the diversity within B, the greater length and more variegated materials, and the recapitulative role of the coda, the movement is not unlike the first and second in general design.

The work is interesting as an example of the modern suite. The old binary principle is abandoned and we see non-dance forms of unpretentious character in which motives are rapidly alternated in small quasi-rondo or ternary designs, and in which certain devices are adopted toward the goal of inter-movement integration.

The practice of assembling pieces from stage works into suites usually preceded by the original prelude or overture is still a vital practice (*L'Arlésienne,* incidental music to a play of A. Daudet later molded into an orchestra suite by its composer, Georges Bizet [1838–75]; Tchaikovsky, Suite, Op. 71a, from the *Nutcracker Ballet,* Op. 71; Stravinsky, Suite from the ballet *Firebird*; Elliott Carter, Suite from the ballet *The Minotaur*). Such suites often are compounded of movements of rather extensive form, sometimes with substantial, tonally fluctuant thematic development. But the term "suite" is appropriate here in view of the objective, non-abstract quality of the music—its programmatic or descriptive intent, and its consequent avoidance of purely musical profundity and significance. (The same might be said of a work like Berlioz's *Symphonie Fantastique,* despite its massive, sonorous effect.) Often strict dance forms are included, especially in suites extracted from ballets. A suite of this kind naturally involves recasting of the original music with appropriate cuts, bridges, rearrangement of sequence, changed endings, and the like.

While in modern suites the Baroque concept of unity of key is commonly abandoned, the unity of related keys orbiting about a central tonic remains an important factor. Effective contrast is still a vital factor in the ordering of the movements, and unity is less problematic only where it involves a central relationship of subject as the prime basis of coherence (Nicolai Rimsky-Korsakov, 1844–1908, *Scheherezade*) or the cyclic use of common thematic elements among the movements (Alexander Borodin, 1833–87, *Polovtzian Dances* from *Prince Igor*). The latter also affords an example of the occasional use of national dances and folk materials in suites of strongly national character in the later nineteenth century. An American example is seen in the *Indian Suite*, Op. 48, of Edward MacDowell (1861–1908).

Many recent suites incorporate the rhythms and character of Baroque and pre-Baroque dances in new tonal-harmonic styles: Ravel's *Le Tombeau de Couperin;* d'Indy's *Suite dans le Style Ancien* (two of whose movements are *sarabande* and *menuet*) ; Debussy's *Petite Suite,* which includes a *menuet* and a *cortège*—a solemn march—as well as a titled piece, *En bateau,* in the manner of early French *ordres;* Schönberg's Suite for piano, Op. 26; and Bartók's *Dance Suite* for orchestra.

We have mentioned that the recent dance suite finds the repertory of dances greatly broadened. Examples are the polka movement of Dvořák's Suite for orchestra, Op. 39, and the fox-trot of Alfredo Casella's (1883–1947) Five Pieces for string quartet (1920). Walter Piston's Suite from *The Incredible Flutist* includes old (minuet, *siciliano*) and new (tango—free, in 5/8 meter), and Gunther Schuller's (b. 1925) Suite for woodwind quintet has a "blues" movement between the opening prelude and concluding toccata.

In summary, the later suite consists of relatively short, light, often descriptive movements, sometimes fancifully titled, freely assembled for balance and contrast as well as, in some cases, for unity of narrative or subject. The movements are often but not always dance forms or dance-like pieces. The medium of the suite, unlike that of, for example, the Baroque *sonata da camera,* is relatively rarely for chamber ensemble; more often the suite is written for orchestra or for keyboard or some other solo instrument. This is not surprising considering the depth and intimacy commonly associated with chamber music since the late eighteenth century.

The variation suite

The variation suite is a series of dances and other suite movements built on a common theme—a procedure related to that of the dance with *double,* or of the sixteenth-century dance pair, except of course in the degree of rigidity to which the theme is adhered in variation. In some variation suites there are movements which are independent of the otherwise common theme.

The variation suite has significance as an effective solution to the problem of inter-movement unity. Tonal as well as thematic unity generally prevails in the variation suite and the result is a multi-movement form in which the individual components are tightly bound together, with contrasting elements lending necessary interest as in any multi-movement work.

Bach's closest approach to this principle is in the second Sonata for solo violin (first Partita, in B minor), in which five of eight movements are related by the use of the harmonically-fixed variation technique. The sequence ACS is followed by a *bourrée* with four *doubles*.

Ex. 10.18   Bach, Sonata No. 2 in B minor for solo violin, fourth movement with doubles.

Thus, a series of variations on a dance movement (as seen also in the Byrd Five Variations on a Galliard, mentioned earlier) may be judged a kind of variation suite, although what is usually meant by the term is a series of disparate dance types united by the use in all or most of related thematic material.

The variation suite is as old as the suite itself. The German composer Paul Peuerl published suites in 1611 in which the movements are related by common motives. Some of the suites of Schein's *Banchetto musicale* (1617) show a degree of inter-movement motivic correspondence. Other composers who wrote variation suites for orchestra in the tradition of Peuerl and Schein were Andreas Hammerschmidt (1612–75) and Johann

Kuhnau (1660–1722). An unusual specimen in this tradition is Buxtehude's Suite (*sarabande, courante, gigue*) on the chorale *Auf meinen lieben Gott.*

A nineteenth-century example is the piano work *Six Pieces on a Single Theme,* Op. 21, by Tchaikovsky; this set was listed in Chapter 9 for the study of variation.

The suite by other names; related multi-movement forms

In all periods in which the suite has existed it has been known by other names in various national styles, and some of its features have often been incorporated into coexisting related forms.

In the seventeenth and eighteenth centuries the Italian word *partita* (German *Parthie, Partie*) sometimes means suite, although its more proper meaning is variation. Bach uses it in both senses: the chorale variations for organ are sometimes called *partite;* and the application of the word to the suite is seen not only in the six of that name for harpsichord but in the second, fourth, and sixth of the solo violin "sonatas" as well. We have seen the use of the word *lesson* with respect to the early English suite and *ordre* for the corresponding French form.

In the Baroque, both the chamber form *sonata da camera* and the *concerto grosso* (as in Corelli) often contain dance movements. The distinction between the *sonata da camera* and *da chiesa* is often oversimplified in music histories; for example, the latter may have a *gigue*-like movement as its conclusion and the former sometimes has *chiesa* movements in addition to those in the domain of the strict suite.

Dance movements in the *concerto grosso* are found also in, for example, works of Giuseppe Torelli (1658–1709) and Georg Muffat (1645–1704). *Concerti grossi* in which dance movements are prominent are sometimes called *concerti da camera.* (See also, in this connection, Ex. 10.15.)

In the late seventeenth and early eighteenth centuries, suites preceded by the French overture type of prelude were frequently called by the German name *ouvertüre* (Muffat and Georg Philipp Telemann, 1681–1767). We have noted this practice in Bach's designation of the Partita in B minor from the *Clavierübung,* Vol. II, as *Französische Ouvertüre.*

In the Classical Period there came into fashion multi-movement works for chamber ensembles of string and wind instruments consisting of as many as 8 and 10 movements, some of them suite-like and most of them of small forms and rather light, diverting character. These works were variously called *divertimento* (Fr. *divertissement*), *notturno* (not to be confused with the nineteenth-century piano salon piece), serenade (It. *serenata*), and cassation. The relationship of these genres to the earlier suite is less on the basis of prevalence of dance movements (witness the minuet of the symphony) then the multiplicity of short movements of relaxed character.

The *divertimenti* of Haydn and Mozart, which often contain two minuets, tell of a popularity never again achieved by this type of multi-movement work, although chamber pieces like Schubert's Octet in F, Op. 166, are in the same line of descent. Mozart wrote three cassations—K. 62, 63, and 99 (each of the latter two having a march and two minuets). Haydn's *Feldpartiten* and *notturni* (2 *lire*, 2 clarinets, 2 horns, 2 violas, and double-bass) are specimens of the same type of piece. Mozart's Serenade in D (*Haffner*), K. 250, has three minuets, and his *Eine kleine Nachtmusik*, K. 525, is an extremely well-known *notturno* of the same species. Beethoven wrote serenades (in D, Op. 8 and 25) ; Brahms wrote serenades for orchestra, the one in D, Op. 11, containing two minuets; and later comparable works are Dvořák's Serenade in E, Op. 22, for strings, and Serenade in D minor, Op. 44, for mixed ensemble, as well as Elgar's Serenade in E minor, Op. 20, for strings.

Exercises and examples for further study

1. In addition to the works cited in this chapter, make a study of one or more of the following. Try to see and hear a variety of types, without necessarily reviewing all of the music in detail.

Bach, Suites for solo cello

Bartók, Orchestra Suites, Op. 3 and 4
  Suite, Op. 14, for piano

Berg, *Lyric Suite* for string quartet

Bizet, *Petite Suite* for orchestra (from *Jeux d'Enfants* for piano duet)

Bloch, *Suite Symphonique*

Ferruccio Busoni (1866–1924), Suite, Op. 41, from *Turandot* (opera by Busoni)

Casella, Concerto for string quartet (1923–24)

Dallapiccola, *Tre Studi* for soprano and chamber orchestra
  Partita for orchestra

Irving Fine (b. 1914), Partita for wind quintet

Charles Griffes (1884–1920), *Roman Sketches,* Op. 7, for piano

Handel, Suites No. 4 in E minor and No. 13 in E minor for harpsichord

Harrison, *Suite for Symphonic Strings*

Historical Anthology of Music, Vol. II, examples of suite

Gustav Holst (1874–1934), *The Planets*

Alan Hovhaness (b. 1911), *Divertimento,* Op. 61, No. 5, for four winds

André Jolivet (b. 1905), *Suite Delphique,* for winds, *ondes Martenot,* harp, and percussion

Ulysses Kay (b. 1917), Suite for orchestra

Křenek, Two Suites, Op. 26, for piano

Darius Milhaud (b. 1892), *Suite Provençale*

Mussorgsky, *Pictures at an Exhibition*

Persichetti, Serenade No. 5, Op. 43, for orchestra

Piston, Partita for violin, viola, and organ (1944)

Ravel, *Ma Mère l'Oye* (orchestral or 4-hand piano version)

Riegger, *Suite for Younger Orchestras,* Op. 56

Albert Roussel (1869–1937), Piano Suite, Op. 14
   Suite in F, Op. 33, for orchestra
   Petite Suite, Op. 39, for orchestra
   Concert suite extracted from the ballet *Le Festin de l'Araignée*

Schuller, *Contours* for small orchestra

Schumann, *Papillons,* Op. 2, for piano

Halsey Stevens (b. 1908), Suite for clarinet (or viola) and piano

Stravinsky, *March, Waltz, Polka* and *Galop* for small orchestra (1919)
   Suites from the ballets, e.g., *Petrushka, L'Histoire du Soldat, Pulcinella*

Tchaikovsky, Suites Nos. 1, 2, and 3 in D minor, C, and G, Op. 43, 53, and 55, for orchestra

2. Make an extensive list of dance forms not described in this chapter but used in suites of the Baroque and other periods. Include a brief statement of defining characteristics of each as found in the *Harvard Dictionary* or a source suggested to you.

3. Write an analytical statement concerning inter-movement contrast and unity and such factors as over-all tempo-dynamic shape in a suite of your choosing.

4. Prepare an examination on the suite.

5. Prepare a bibliography of sources in which the suite is discussed. Which seem to be of greatest value? Why?

6. Study one of the following groups of suites to determine (1) which movements are in binary form, (2) to what extent unity of key prevails, and (3) to what extent dance movements are used.
   a) Bach's suites for solo cello
   b) The eight suites of Handel's first book
   c) The solo violin and cello suites of Bloch
   d) Any two of the *ordres* of F. Couperin

7. Find an example of variation suite and make a study of variation techniques used.

8. Compare form, rhythm, texture, and general character in four or five *sarabandes* of different composers and periods (for example: Frescobaldi, Bach, Roussel, and Dallapiccola).

9. Make the above comparison with a group of *gigues,* including an example by Goffredo Petrassi (b. 1904).

10. Why is the aria *Lascia ch'io pianga* from Handel's opera *Rinaldo* characterized as a *sarabande?*

11. Study and listen to Schönberg's *Fünf Orchesterstücke,* Op. 16. Do you feel that this work could be called a suite? Give reasons for your opinion. Find other examples that seem comparable in multi-movement form, considering movement size, expressive character, internal diversity, manner of development and other features in relation to the traditional nature of the suite.

12. Do you feel that Bloch's Suite for viola and piano or orchestra (1919) is appropriately titled? Give reasons for your answer.

11

FUGUE AND OTHER

CONTRAPUNTAL FORMS

*A*nyone writing on fugue (It. *fuga,* flight) has im-
bedded in his consciousness the question concerning which every theorist
feels he must take a position: Is the fugue a form? Certainly the fugue as
practiced for some three hundred years exhibits important common *structural* features—exposition of a thematic subject at the beginning, recurrence
of the theme throughout, episodic development and tonal flux in the middle
areas, and tonic return in the final stage.

These are form-defining characteristics in any traditional musical design;
they are features of *form,* not just of texture, if we consider that form has
as one of its bases the architectural plan that determines the general course
of a composition.

Obviously all forms vary in realization. The schematic definition of the
prototype is always fictional, yet always true. The features listed above are
as nearly invariable as anything that can be said of any form; the subject
exposition and recurrence, combined with total tonal shape, in themselves
define fugal form.

There are usually distinct sections—two, three, or more—in a fugue.
If we recall that tripartition in music implies three sections, the third of
which recalls in material, key, and structure the content of Part I (ABA),
it will be clear that the often-mentioned ternary concept of fugal form in
three sections is not supportable.

Tonally, however, the fugue does have a rounded form. Moreover, it
is reasonable to regard the form as consisting of three *stages* of events: (1)
the exposition of the subject material; (2) tonal variation with subject
recurrence in single entries or groups, usually interspersed with episodes
developing subject fragments; and (3) the return to the tonic, with the
subject recurring at that level at least once.

Such stages may involve more than three sections and are defined less
by cadential breaks than by contrasts of content and procedure. The tonic

372

return in fugue, for example, is not always delineated by a punctuative formula, but this is equally true of the passage from development into recapitulation in single-movement sonata form, or between rondo theme and digression.

The Baroque is a period of unsurpassed quality in fugue, and the form is, like the suite, best viewed from that vantage point, the period of its highest craft and greatest universality. Alive but somewhat receded in the nineteenth century, the fugue assumes a renewed vitality in the twentieth; yet, the dominant association of eighteenth-century practice of fugue is seen in modern tendencies to regard fugue-writing as "neo-Baroque."

The following chapter attempts to outline in detail the organization and anatomy of fugue as seen in the major periods of its existence. Specific problems of counterpoint, of fugue-writing, have their place in counterpoint treatises and are not considered in these pages.

Before proceeding, we may quote a few words from Eschman, who expresses well a view that sees in the three primary forms of music three basic processes of musical development, "three fundamental procedures which may be used, if a form of some type is to result: (1) we may repeat the idea with a difference (variation); (2) we may develop some part or all of the idea in a process of germination, induced by its inherent potentiality acting within its environment (the environment in the Sonata-form is in part, at least, furnished by conflict and contrast with other musical ideas), and (3) we may imitate it and extend its ramifications in a horizontal structure of more than one stratum; that is, we may present the idea in contrapuntal 'flight' or fugue."[1]

Origins of the fugue

Although much remains to be learned about the historical evolution of contrapuntal forms, it is likely that that evolution would be traced from the polyphony of the thirteenth century (Perotinus) and would include such fourteenth-century canonic forms as the *rota* and *rondellus* (types of medieval round), and *caccia* (It. for chase; see for example No. 52 in the *Historical Anthology*, Vol. I). An important place in that history would be occupied by the great fifteenth-century Flemish polyphonic school of such composers as Johannes Ockeghem (1430–1495) and Jacob Obrecht (1430–1505), examples of whose works will be found in the *Historical Anthology*. The reader should consult these examples, as well as the commentary that accompanies them.

Josquin des Prez, whose sacred and secular vocal works represent the

[1] Eschman, *Changing Forms in Modern Music*, p. 150. Copyright 1945 by E. C. Schirmer Music Company, Boston, Massachusetts, and reprinted with their permission.

culmination of the fifteenth-century Flemish school, may have been the first highly significant composer of polyphonic music. A common form in Josquin's motets is sectional, with each section exposing its own subject, a technique later seen in the direct predecessors of the fugue.

The immediate background of the Baroque fugue lies, of course, in the sixteenth and early seventeenth centuries. Motets, *chansons,* madrigals, and masses of this radiant period of modal polyphony exemplify many of the techniques of contrapuntal imitation and development which found their way into the fugue and canon of the eighteenth century. The structural techniques of the motet and *chanson* found new expression in instrumental forms like the *fantasia, canzona,* and *ricercar* for organ by such composers as J. P. Sweelinck (c. 1562–1621), Frescobaldi, and Froberger, as well as in the English ensemble fantasy which found ultimate expression in Purcell.

The above-mentioned instrumental forms were, like the vocal forms which preceded them, multi-sectional, their several parts varied in subject and texture. Ultimately, the monothematic *ricercar*[2] became a direct precursor of the Baroque fugue, and the term *ricercar* was in certain Baroque literatures used interchangeably with fugue (see Bach's *Musical Offering*). The example by Andrea Gabrieli (1510–1586), No. 136 in the *Historical Anthology,* Vol. I, illustrates the imitative, multi-sectional form.

The immediate development toward the Baroque fugue is best seen in German fugal literatures of the late seventeenth and early eighteenth centuries, those preceding and contemporary to the young Bach (see, for example, Nos. 215, 234, and 236 in the *Historical Anthology,* Vol. II). Many of these, including some of the "fugues" of Buxtehude, are sectional forms like the earlier *canzona* and *ricercar,* with contrasting themes and textures.

A majority of the examples in this chapter are culled from the fugues of Bach. It is in Bach, of course, that instrumental contrapuntal development reaches its highest level; canons, fugues, and chorale settings of that composer exploit the means of imitative polyphony within a framework of tonal architecture and balance as never before or since. The typical Bach fugue grows out of the subject-germ, finding variety in an endless resource of variation and development, consummately controlled in a perfect equilibrium of horizontality and verticality, of interdependence and independence of voices, of the ebbing and rising movement of line, and the infallible direction of tonal-harmonic progression.

The significance of imitative counterpoint as a form-producing technique

While in imitative counterpoint the separate strata or voices are in

---

2 Apel, in the *Harvard Dictionary,* refers to the composer Luzzascho Luzzaschi (1545–1607) in connection with the monothematic *ricercar,* citing for illustration of his music Vol. II of *Antologia di Musica Antica e Moderna per Pianoforte* (1931–2), G. Tagliapietra, editor, G. Ricordi and Co., Milan, publishers.

their concurrence usually opposed in rhythm, direction of line, color, coincident materials, and in the occasional withdrawal of one or another, they are at the same time often related thematically in imitation at varying distances. Thus, in the midst of contrasting elements, there is parity among the voices in the use of similar or identical motives separated in time.

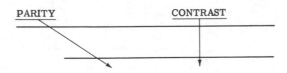

The use and importance of imitative counterpoint is vital in many forms, some of which, like the *concerto grosso,* mass, and oratorio, are treated here only to the extent that their component movements exemplify the principles of fugue or another of the major traditional forms. We have observed the importance of imitative devices as resources of development in largely homophonic forms like those of the sonata and the suite.

Fugue

Except for wider tonal latitudes (such as the dismissal of the principle of subject response at the fifth, the fluctuation of tonality beyond the traditional range of closely related levels, and occasional atonality) most of the characteristics uniting fugues of various periods are applicable to contemporary literatures as well as to the eighteenth and nineteenth centuries. Some of these characteristics are summarized in the following paragraphs.

Although in certain literatures (the organ fugues of Bach, or orchestral fugues, such as the final movement of the *Brandenburg Concerto* No. 2 in F) textural freedoms are more common than in others, the texture is, by and large, fixed throughout a fugue. For textural contrast, individual voices drop out from time to time, and are accounted for by rests. (An example of a 4-voice fugue, Bach's WTC II, 5 in D^3, has all voices in play through about 39 of 50 measures, and it is a "dense" fugue; during these 39 measures there are, of course, shorter rests from time to time in one voice or another.) This principle is expressed with characteristic wit when Morris says that "it is well to open a window occasionally and let a little air in."[4]

Although there may be moments of homophony (Ex. 11.1), again as a source of contrast, or of harmonic emphasis, fugal texture is polyphonic. In some fugues, notably those of such nineteenth-century composers as Mendelssohn and Schumann, chordal texture is naturally more common than in eighteenth-century styles. And in Ex. 11.1, the middle voices are devoted

---

[3] *Well-Tempered Clavier*, Vol. II, fugue No. 5.
[4] R. O. Morris, *The Structure of Music,* p. 96.

to straightforward harmonic progression as homophonic accompaniment to the top voice, which is doubled in 3rds and 6ths; the entire movement occurs over the fixed pedal *A*.

Ex. 11.1   Bach, Prelude and Fugue in D minor for organ (III, 4)[5].

Although occasionally capricious in expression, the fugue is concentrated and intensely active in form, and usually relatively brief. Its intensity is without doubt one reason for its brevity; another is its compactness—the fact that generally all of its motivic material emanates from a single, minuscule source.

The fugue begins with an exposition of the subject. Throughout the fugue, the subject is recalled at intervals, sometimes in changing forms. Occasionally, but rarely, contrasting material may intervene among subject statements, as is sometimes true in Bach's organ fugues, or in the fugues of his orchestral works. The fugal movements of the *Brandenburg Concertos* are sometimes described as "fugal rondos," but can also be conceived as fugues having wider thematic and textural freedom (the finale of No. 2 has a 29-measure middle passage lacking reference to the subject, and those of Nos. 4 and 5 have digressive sections based on subject-derived themes).

There is tonal flux in the modulatory episodes and in the practice of subject statement at changing tonal levels. In most cases, there is relative tonic stability at beginning and end, with greater modulation in the internal parts. The statement of the subject in the tonic at the end of the fugue is a nearly universal feature of the form, and a coda or codetta is sometimes appended.

The romantic spirit of the nineteenth century approached the fugue more freely, without submission to its rigorous disciplines, creating the possibility of its adaptation to a new environment in the *free fugue*, more consistent with the subjective, dramatic impulses of the Romantic tradition.

5 Bach, Organ Works, Peters edition, Vol. III, No. 4.

The following features characterize the free fugue: less fixation of texture; use of chordal strata in place of single lines (a technique seen, too, in the final movement of the Stravinsky *Concerto for Two Solo Pianos*); big, chordal harmonizations of subject material (as in the Franck Prelude, Chorale and Fugue, just before the B major section near the end) and, in general, more frequent concession to homophonic thought; introduction of contrasting thematic materials in sonata- or rondo-fashion; increased total length; and complete interruptions, including tempo changes, with or without resumption of the fugue. An example is the Fugue in E minor, No. 1 of Mendelssohn's Op. 35, which among many of the above features incorporates a chorale in chordal style just before the final section of the fugue. Freedoms of other kinds are to be seen in modern fugues; for example, the first movement of William Schuman's String Quartet No. 3 includes the augmented form of the subject in the initial exposition.

Many of the typical devices which have importance in fugal styles—invertible counterpoint, stretto, subject permutations, sequence, and other devices that lend interest as well as variety in unity—are explained in the following pages.

The Subject

The subject determines the character of the fugue; in the subject reside in essence the expressive qualities that are to unfold in the fugal development. Be it somber, majestic, jocose, or whatever, the subject radiates through the fugal texture as a microcosmic reflection of the personality of the entire work.

The subject is generally short—one or two measures, but its length can vary from a few notes to several bars (Ex. 11.2).

Ex. 11.2a Bach, WTC I, 4 in C-sharp minor.

Ex. 11.2b Bach, Chromatic Fantasy and Fugue.

To bear repetition, and to catch attention through the densities of the fugal texture, the subject must be striking and distinctive in melody and rhythm. Sometimes it is asymmetrical in the distribution of its separate units (WTC I, 14; II, 14).

The subject is frequently self-propulsive, without strong cadential ending, in order to enter best into the horizontal motion (unlike many themes of homophonic forms). Its internal unity may be the product of unbroken motion (Ex. 11.3a) or of the relationship among individual motives (11.3b). Limited in the range of harmonic implications and in the compass of its pitches, its highest and lowest points are rarely separated by more than a tenth.

Ex. 11.3a   Bach, Toccata and Fugue in D minor for organ (III, 3).

Ex. 11.3b   Stravinsky, Symphony of Psalms, second movement.
Copyright 1941 by Russischer Musikverlag; renewed 1958. Copyright & renewal assigned to Boosey & Hawkes, Inc. Revised version copyright 1948 by Boosey & Hawkes, Inc. Reprinted by permission.

In Ex. 11.3a, the subject forms a perfectly arched rise and fall, and is kept in motion by consequent factors of gravity, and by the use of suspensions and syncopations. There is no internal punctuation, and its cadence, as often, is suppressed by the overlapping entry of the answer.

In the Stravinsky subject, the notes C-E♭-B-D occur four times, after which there is a transposition and re-ordering of the same note-series. Or, considering the natural punctuation points in the subject (see brackets), the first bar constitutes a basic motive which is varied by diminution and extension. The final bar is a repetition, transposed, of the preceding motive from its first B-natural.

Still another structural principle is at work in the final bar of the Stravinsky subject. If we count the number of half-steps in each of the six intervals, the result reveals an ordering of graduated interval sizes: 9–10–11, 8–9–10, and the end of the subject forms an augmented sixth whose natural (traditional) resolution is to G, the first note of the answer.

In traditional examples, the tonic and dominant scale degrees and, to a lesser extent, the notes of the tonic and dominant triads, are pivotal and vitally important. Traditional subjects often begin and end on tonic-dominant factors. In Ex. 11.4, tonal uncertainty is countered by the occurrence of tonic factors at metrically strong points.

Ex. 11.4   Franck, Chorale, Prelude and Fugue for piano.

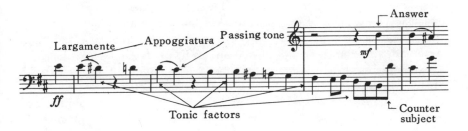

Traditional subjects vary in modulatory character, degree of conjunct motion, extent of chromaticism, and in over-all shape as to direction toward and recession from a climactic point, if there is one. A climactic point may be the product of dynamic or metric stress, duration, pitch level, approach by leap, implied harmonic dissonance, approach by melodic dissonance—

its function as the point toward which motion is strongly directed (Ex. 11.5), or of any combination of these factors. In Ex. 11.5, the designated note is the culmination point of the preceding harmonic-melodic "wedge"; it is also the highest pitch, and is approached by the widest leap.

Ex. 11.5   Bach, Prelude and Fugue in E minor for organ (II, 9).

e: I   V   V/IV   IV   IV(A⁶)   V————————————— I

In a particular fugue, the precise subject length is determined, as far as possible, by considering that it ends in the area in which the answer enters, by looking for a point of mild cadential feeling (a point of metric prominence, a note of the tonic, or a point of hesitation in the motion), and, most importantly, by comparison of all the entries in the fugue to find the point to which most are in conformity. The determination of subject length can be extremely problematic (WTC I, 9).

The many subject quotations in this chapter will serve to illustrate further the above points, some of which clearly apply more precisely to traditional fugue, specifically Baroque fugue, than to that of modern styles. It must be said, finally, that the superiority of Bach in the literature of the fugue is in the captivating charm and nobility, not to mention the persuasive power, of his fugue subjects as much as in the nearly inerrant craft of contrapuntal manipulation and development in his works.

The answer

The first statement of the subject may be in any one of the voices, with its imitation, the answer, appearing in another. The answer may follow immediately after the conclusion of the subject (Ex. 11.7), may enter with the final note of the subject (Examples 11.3a, 11.6), or may follow after a "link" of one or more notes has intervened (Ex. 11.2b).

Ex. 11.6   Hindemith, Ludus Tonalis, Fugue No. 9 in B-flat.
© 1943 by Associated Music Publishers, Inc., New York. Used by permission.

The traditional interval of imitation is the 5th (or 4th below)—the dominant level, and the answer is frequently an exact transposition of the subject at that level. When this is the case, it is called a *real answer* (WTC I, 1).

If the imitation at the fifth is to any degree not consistent, for whatever reason adjustment is made, the answer is called *tonal*. Textbooks often strive over the "why?" and "how?" of tonal answers, sometimes provocatively, as does Oldroyd in his study of Bach fugues.[6] In some cases, either a tonal or real answer is clearly possible, and the composer made an arbitrary choice. In Ex. 11.7, Bach set out on what appears to be a real answer, suddenly shifting to avoid modulation (the subject progression

answered by   ). He could, in a real answer,

have submitted to modulation, as is often done, quickly cutting it off in a transitional episode to prepare the third entry, as seen below.

Ex. 11.7   Bach, Fugue in A minor for harpsichord (Keyboard Works, Peters ed., Vol. IX, No. 15).

6 George Oldroyd, *The Technique and Spirit of Fugue* (London: Oxford University Press, 1948), Ch. V.

Ex. 11.7 (continued)

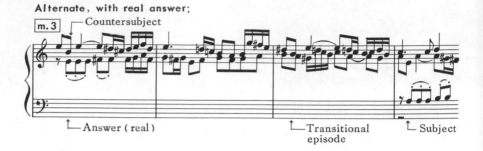

Alternate, with real answer:

It is important to observe the *effect* of the traditional tonal answer: it is almost invariably *the strengthened affirmation of the tonic key and the tonic harmony* as the focal point of the exposition. The exposition may (and, indeed, usually does) include secondary tonal regions, but it always asserts and revolves around the tonic; transitory modulation moves back to the tonic, reaffirming the principal center. What is sought is the prolongation of the tonic center and the tonic harmony into the answer, even though secondary modulation often occurs before the answer is concluded.

When the subject ends on a note of the tonic harmony, suggesting harmonic conformity in the answer, with appropriate intervallic adjustment, the dominant note is often answered by the tonic (a fourth above) rather than by the alien supertonic, the "real" imitation. By no means is this an absolute formula, but it is an exceedingly common procedure for a certain kind of tonal answer.

⑦ Bach, chorus *Sei gegrüsset,* from the *St. John Passion.*
⑧ Bach, cantata *Allein zu dir, Herr Jesu Christ.*

Thus, the gravitational pull of the tonic center is not compromised by imitation at the dominant level, and premature, exaggerated prominence of the dominant tonal level is avoided.[11]

Another way of regarding the tonal answer would be to consider that the tonic and dominant, representing the pivotal points and the standard interval of imitation, split the scale unevenly. To proceed with imitation at the fifth without disturbing the hegemony of the tonic scale, with its unequal "halves," requires the pattern 1–5, 5–8 and consequent unequal intervals in the adjustment which theory characterizes by the term *tonal answer*. In summary, the tonal unity of the exposition, and the avoidance of indecision or wavering of tonality at the point where subject and answer are joined, are a vital traditional principle.

Two examples follow. In 11.8a, the subject (derived from the first phrase of the chorale) is built on the notes

,

which affirm tonic harmony by progressing from 1 to 5; the answer is made to progress from 5 to 1 (cf. Ex. 11.7), with the interval of a fourth responding to that of a fifth in the manner described above. Ex. 11.8b represents still another type of tonal answer. Here, the subject progresses harmonically from I to V, without modulation; the answer is made to move harmonically from V to I, automatically preparing the next entry, by the single intervallic adjustment to which attention is directed in the quotation. (Minor disparity between major and minor seconds is occasioned by the firm retention of the original leading-tone, D-sharp.)

⑨ Bach, WTC I, 22.
⑩ Bach, *The Art of the Fugue.*
11 The practice of tonal answer of this type is often traced to the modal past in which a subject centering on the final and dominant of a mode (for example, d-a in the dorian), answered at the 5th, would in the consequent plagal range center on the low point of the plagal ambitus (here, a) and the *final* of the plagal form (here, d).

Ex. 11.8a   Bach, Fughetta on Allein Gott in der Höh' sei Ehr' (Organ Works, Peters ed., Vol. VI, No. 10).

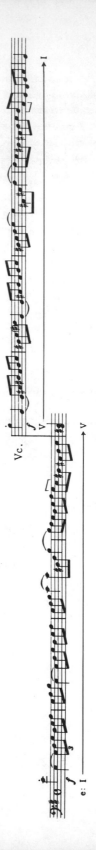

Ex. 11.8b   Brahms, Sonata in E minor, Op. 38, for cello and piano, final movement.

Similarly, a tonal answer may be necessary to restore the tonic *key* after a modulating subject. A common solution would answer a subject going from tonic to dominant key levels with an imitation going equidistantly to the tonic from the subdominant level: 4–1 as a response to 1–5. (See Ex. 11.9, as well as Bach's Organ Fugue in C, II, 7.) In Ex. 11.9, only the first note of the answer is at the fifth. Rarely is Bach's answer at the

Ex. 11.9   Bach, Fugue in G-sharp minor, WTC I, 18.

subdominant level throughout; an illustration of response entirely at that level is seen in Ex. 11.14.

Tonal and real answers may be mixed, even within the initial exposition.

Ex. 11.10   Bach, Prelude and Fugue in G for organ (II, 2).

Within internal expositions during later stages in the fugue, tonal stability is less crucial and tonal response less likely. The form of an answer within such groups is governed by the harmonic environment of the moment.

In modern fugues, and to some extent in those of the nineteenth century, the concept of the tonal answer is weakened along with tonal orientation in general. The answer occurs at any interval and is, more often, real.

Ex. 11.11   Hindemith, Sonata No. 2 for organ, third movement.
            © 1937 B. Schott's Soehne/Mainz, Germany. Used by permission.

Real answer at 3rd

The term *answer* applies only to immediate response within an exposition. Thus, single subject entries corresponding in interval structure to an original tonal answer are *tonal entries,* not "answers" (Ex. 11.19). The practice of labeling the entire fugue according to the use of tonal or real answer ("tonal fugue," "real fugue") has little point.

In the final analysis, every tonal answer requires study on its own terms; each case suggests its own reasons and methods, and only a few of the more usual circumstances have been outlined above. (Some examples make for extremely interesting and instructive speculation. In the A minor fugue, WTC II, 20, Bach might have used a real answer except for the desirability of using the tonic note, which has only slight appearance in the subject, and the unorthodox occurrence of a V_4^6 which would have been caused by strict imitation at the fifth.)

Efforts to characterize composers or periods with respect to partiality toward tonal or real imitation usually come to naught. In Bach's WTC, 27 of 48 answers are tonal.

The countersubject; the free contrapuntal associate; invertible counterpoint

The originating voice continues after the subject is stated, forming a counterpoint to the answer. If this counterpoint appears more than once in association with the subject entries in the course of the fugue, it is called a *countersubject.* (Otherwise, it is simply a *free contrapuntal associate* or *free counterpoint*—the latter a term applied to any fragment of line not derived from subject or countersubject.) The countersubject is usually a contrast to the subject in rhythm and direction, although the two may be motivically and otherwise related (Examples 11.4; 11.12).

Ex. 11.12   Bach, Fugue in G minor, WTC I, 16.

Theoretically, a four-voice fugue may have two or three counter-subjects, the first appearing with the answer to the first subject statement, the second with the following subject entry, and the third with the second answer; but this is unusual. WTC I, 2 has two countersubjects, as does the fugue cited in Ex. 11.13.

Ex. 11.13   Bach, Fugue in A-flat, WTC II, 17.

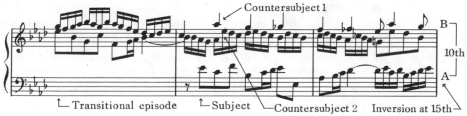

Since it cannot always appear in the same relationship, a counter-subject must function either above or below the subject—must be *contrapuntally invertible* (or *interchangeable*) with the subject.[12]

While space does not permit a full exploration of this subject, we may explain briefly that the *interval of contrapuntal inversion* is determined by adding the distances between the voices in the two versions: if the voices are originally a sixth apart and, in inversion, a third apart *at the corresponding point,* the inversion is said to be "at the octave"—the sum of the

sixth and third: . In eighteenth-century counterpoint

inversion is most often at the octave or fifteenth (double-octave), twelfth, or more rarely, at the tenth. Inversion at intervals other than the octave or octave-multiple (fifteenth, twenty-second) produces significant change of harmonic implications (e. g., in inversion at the twelfth a sixth becomes a dissonant seventh); thus, contrapuntal inversion, when practicable, is a useful source of harmonic variety. Inversion at the fifteenth is indicated in Ex. 11.13. In WTC II, 16, the reader may compare measure 60 with measure 5 to see inverted counterpoint (two voices, thus *double counterpoint*) at the octave, tenth, and twelfth. Inversion at other intervals, extremely rare in traditional counterpoint, is a mark of freer styles and would be common in contemporary polyphony.

The fugal exposition

The *exposition* is the first part of the fugue; it consists of subject statements, in tonal or real form, once in each voice with, occasionally, an added entry in the originating voice. A cadence is usual at the conclusion of the exposition, or following a subsequent episode, but whether or not there is such cadential punctuation, the exposition is regarded as a distinct structural entity because of its unique function. The usual traditional pattern is tonic level to dominant level (T-D), or subject-answer (S-A), in a two-voice fugue, T-D-T (S-A-S) in a three-voice fugue, and T-D-T-D (S-A-S-A) where there are four voices. But occasionally such regularity is violated, as in Ex. 11.14, whose pattern is SAASS.

---

[12] For detailed discussion of invertible counterpoint, the reader is advised to consult Walter Piston, *Counterpoint* (New York: W. W. Norton and Company, Inc., 1947), pp. 167–87, and Kent Kennan, *Counterpoint* (Englewood Cliffs, New Jersey: Prentice-Hall, Inc., 1959), pp. 135–45.

Ex. 11.14   Bach, Prelude and Fugue in D minor for organ (III, 4).

Between answer and subject, for tonal-harmonic adjustment and preparation of the tonic entry, there may be a brief *transitional episode* (called "codetta" in some texts) of the kind pointed out in Ex. 11.14.

While it is nearly universal that a fugue begins with the single-voice statement and subsequent systematic exposition of the subject, freer examples may preface the exposition with an introduction, or some kind of irregularity to offset what may be an unwanted predictability in the fugue opening. Beethoven's *Grosse Fuge* in B-flat, Op. 133, for string quartet, is a free fugue with an introduction in several parts. Other introductions occur preceding the fugues of William Schuman's String Quartets Nos. 2 and 3, and in the fifth of the author's Five Pieces for Small Orchestra. The fourth fugue of Roy Harris' String Quartet No. 3 begins with a statement and brief development of the subject by all instruments, after which a normal exposition occurs. The unusual beginning of the fugue of Stravinsky's *Concerto for Two Solo Pianos* is a further case in point.

The counterexposition

The *counterexposition* is a subsequent pair or group of entries of subject and answer, often separated from the initial exposition by an episode, and remaining within the original tonic-dominant sphere. The counterexposition may be partial—SA, SAS, or any irregular subject-answer combination, or complete, with all voices participating. The final movement of Bach's *Brandenburg Concerto* No. 5 in D completes its exposition (SASA, with a 4-measure episode between subject and second answer) at measure 13, after which a cadential episode leads to the dominant key and an entry in A at measure 17. Now a longer episode precedes a full counterexposition at measure 29 (SASS, with, again, a 4-measure episode separating the third and fourth entries). There may be a series of counterexpositions, as in Bach's Organ Fugue in C (II, 7).

As may be seen in either of the above examples, the counterexposition does not begin again with a single voice, but represents a continuation and maintenance of the developing intensity, density, and motion which are characteristic of fugue.

The use of episode; techniques of development

Where no subject entry is in progress, there is an *episode.* When not merely cadence-forming *(cadential episode),* or brief and simply transitional (within the exposition, the transitional episode), an episode is an area of tonal movement, of free manipulation of subject or countersubject motives. Ex. 11.15 illustrates subject fragmentation and sequence, the most fundamental traditional techniques of episodic development.

Ex. 11.15   Bach, Fantasy and Fugue in G minor (II, 4).

Another technique of episode is a kind of discourse among the voices. Two fugal episodes sometimes match, being built of the same material, possibly inverted contrapuntally. These qualities are seen in Ex. 11.16.

Ex. 11.16   Bach, Fugue in C-sharp major, WTC I, 3.

Voices B,C not inverted.
Inversion of A–C, A–B at 15th (6th+10th).

A subject-centered fugue may be virtually devoid of episodes. Thus, in WTC I, 1, the subject is relinquished only for the formation of cadence at measure 14, measure 23 and the end; there are no real episodes. On the other hand, episodes may be very extensive and occasionally even introduce distinctive material unrelated to that of the exposition. An example is Bach's Organ Fugue in E minor (II, 9), whose subject was quoted as Ex. 11.5; at measure 59 there begins a long episode of new figurations— an episode which only briefly recalls the subject at widely-spaced intervals. Another example appears in Ex. 11.17.

Ex. 11.17   Bach, Fugue in E minor, WTC I, 10.

Subject

Ex. 11.17 (continued)

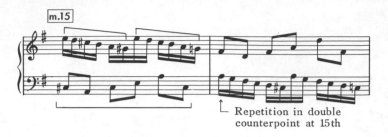

Repetition in double
counterpoint at 15th

Rarely, when not derived from subject or countersubject material, episodes may be built upon other motives of the exposition, as in WTC I, 15. In this fugue, the transitional episode within the exposition, measures 9–10, furnishes material for later episodes.

Episodes should not be confused with actual interruptions in which the fugal motion and progress cease and are later resumed. Such interruptions, common in the post-Baroque free fugue, have been mentioned in connection with Mendelssohn's Op. 35. They are characterized by such departures as radical textural change, or change of tempo, character, and material. A further example of such non-episodic interruption may be seen in Franck's Prelude, Chorale, and Fugue for piano. In measure 154 of the fugue, a homophonic, cadenza-like section brings in a development of the second movement theme, which continues to measure 178, at which point the fugue subject re-enters in combination with the second movement theme. Measures 154–178 can hardly be said to constitute an episode in the fugue.

Successive entries and entry groups

As the fugue unfolds beyond the exposition and counterexposition, if any, it begins to move tonally, and to alternate between episodes and subject statements or groups of statements and answers; or, further counterexpositions might occur, as in Bach's "Leipzig" Organ Fugue (II, 7), to some extent restricting the form to the tonic-dominant tonal sphere.

The subject-answer entry group shown in Ex. 11.18 has imitation at the fourth, the interval established in the initial exposition. It is surrounded by episodes, the preceding one, largely sequential, 14 measures long. The internal entry group quoted occurs at measure 54 of the fugue. Another example of subject-answer internal entry group (re-exposition or internal exposition) may be seen at measures 12–16 of WTC I, 16, where tonal answer is used.

Ex. 11.18   Hindemith, Ludus Tonalis, Fugue No. 2 in G.

We may in summary distinguish among (1) internal expositions, like that in Ex 11.18 with answers at the interval established in the fugue beginning; (2) internal entry groups, lacking such answers; and (3) single entries. Subject entries, whether single or within groups or expositions, conforming in interval structure to an established tonal answer, are called *tonal entries;* others are *real entries.* Ex. 11.19 illustrates a single internal tonal entry. It is preceded and followed by an episode.

Ex. 11.19   Bach, Fugue in C minor, WTC I, 2.

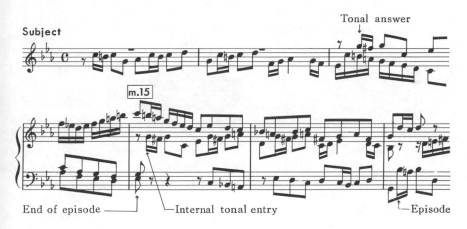

The analyst must be prepared for unanticipated events in the middle sections of the fugue. In Bach's Organ Fugue in C minor (II, 7), unusual developments occur at measure 59, where a new, one-measure "subject"

appears in imitation at the octave, later to be extended and combined with the original subject (see measures 86ff., or measures 92ff.) in the manner of a double fugue. It is, in fact, a kind of double fugue, whose second subject has an irregular exposition and evolution, its full shape emerging only when it is joined to the original subject. Another irregularity would be the statement of the full subject in sequence, repeated contiguously in a single voice, rather than in more usual imitation (WTC I, 3).

Subject variations

Given the monothematic character of the single fugue, and the procedure of subject repetition as a basis of fugue form, it is clear that means of varying the subject are of great importance. The transposition of the subject is useful and requires no explanation.

Mirror inversion is practiced a great deal, sometimes strictly (with precise fidelity to original interval sizes) and sometimes freely. Ex. 11.20 illustrates mirror inversion, as well as homophonic composition of the accompanying figuration—characteristic of the free fugue.

Ex. 11.20   Brahms, Variations and Fugue on a Theme by Handel, Op. 24.

Ex. 11.21 shows two subject forms in stretto (p. 399): the first is a rhythmic alteration and mirror, the second a rhythmic alteration of the

Ex. 11.21   Hindemith, Ludus Tonalis, Fugue No. 3 in F.

rectus form. An exceedingly powerful use of the technique of rhythmic alteration is seen in the second movement of Stravinsky's *Symphony of Psalms,* rehearsal No. 14.

The fugue section of the prelude to Bach's Partita No. 6 uses melodic (intervallic and rhythmic) alteration in ornamentation of the subject at measures 69–71. The reverse of ornamentation may be seen in Bach's Prelude and Fugue in G for organ (II, 2), where the subject end,

,

is often reduced to

.

Another type of melodic alteration may be occasioned by unorthodox approaches to internal entries of the subject (Oldroyd, pp. 128–9). Intervallic variation of a fugue subject, without rhythmic change, is illustrated by Ex. 11.22.

Ex. 11.22   Schumann, Six Fugues on the Name of Bach, No. 2 in B-flat.

Regular *augmentation* is the doubling of the original notes in durational value; regular *diminution* is the reverse. Irregular augmentation or diminution, resulting in a kind of free rhythmic variation (Ex. 11.21), is corresponding increase or decrease not in a consistent 2:1 ratio. The Dallapiccola fugue from which Ex. 11.23 is taken includes mirror (vln., measure 128) and augmented (vln., measure 146) subject forms. The reader may also refer to WTC II, 2, measure 19, and WTC II, 9, measure 26. In Ex. 11.23, there is progressive diminution of the subject's head-motive for increasing intensity; the process is abruptly steadied on a D-sharp pedal (measure 193), at which point the coda begins.

Ex. 11.23   Dallapiccola, Due Studi for violin and piano, second movement.
       © 1950 Edizioni Suvini Zerboni, Milan, Italy. Used by permission.

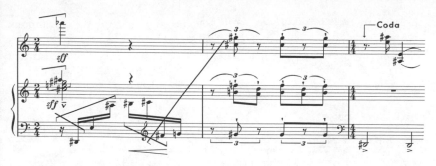

Retrograde and retrograde mirror forms are extremely rare. Examples of retrograde, the appearance of the notes in reverse order, are found in the fugue of Beethovens' Sonata, Op. 106, for piano and Bach's *Musical Offering* (retrograde canon). Examples are also found in Hindemith's *Ludus Tonalis:* the second half of Fugue No. 3 in F is a retrograde of the first (see measure 30, the turning point), and much use of retrograde and retrograde mirror is made in Fugue No. 9 in B-flat. Since retrograde heavily obscures the relationship to the original form of the theme, and may impair unity, its most effective use is in the transformation of small motives.

Ex. 11.24   Bach, Two-Voice Invention in B minor.

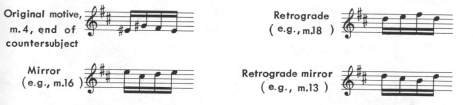

The changed harmonic meaning of a subject entry suggests a further resource of variation. Thus, the fugue of Bach's Prelude and Fugue in B minor for organ (II, 10) has a subject which usually, at its opening, bears tonic harmony; at measure 40, the bass entry is varied to suggest f-sharp: V.

A given fugue may, of course, employ a striking assortment of variational techniques. Bach's "Leipzig" Organ Fugue (II, 7) uses mirror and augmented subject forms with great ingenuity. A fascinating fugue from the standpoint of subject variation is the finale of Stravinsky's *Concerto for Two Solo Pianos*, whose second part sets forth the subject in rhythmic alteration in mirror form. Ex. 11.25 shows an excerpt from a Bach fugue in which the subject appears in three forms concurrently.

Ex. 11.25   Bach, Fugue in D-sharp minor, WTC I, 8.

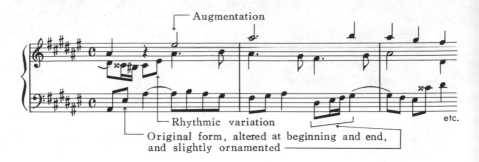

Tonal range; cadential divisions in the form

The basic tonal range of traditional fugue, using symbols T for tonic, D for dominant, SD for subdominant, and R for relative keys, may be expressed as shown below. Arrows indicate overlapping identities (for example, T is the same as D of SD).

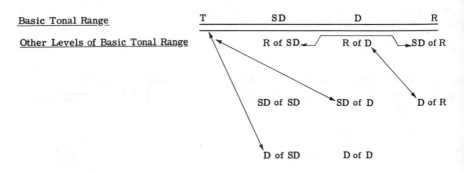

Only rarely would a single eighteenth-century fugue exploit the entire basic tonal range (8 levels) or exceed that range. Typical Bach examples are T–D–SD–R–SD of R (third movement, *Brandenburg Concerto* No. 2 in F), T–D–R–SD–SD of R–SD of SD (WTC II, 8 in D-sharp minor) and T–D–R–SD–D of R–SD of R (fugue of Toccata and Fugue in F for organ, III, 2).

Tonal range is one of the most relevant features of style, and it is to be expected that greater scope of modulation will be found in nineteenth- and twentieth-century fugues. (The fugue of Hindemith's Organ Sonata No. 2, basically in A, freely settles on such tonal levels as B-flat and A-flat.)

The apparently natural principle that the middle parts would avoid the original tonic and even its dominant, to establish a basis for fresh return of the fundamental key level at the end, is not always observed (see for example measure 39 of WTC II, 1). Still, in over-all tonal shape, the concept of tripartition in fugue has significant meaning in departure from and ultimate return to the original tonic.

The fugue is, generally viewed, a sectional form in which clear but often inconspicuous cadences in related keys reveal a bisectional (WTC II, 2: two sections plus coda) or multisectional plan (WTC II, 5: authentic cadences in T, D, SD, and R of D). In addition to being consummated harmonically, cadences are frequently marked by a drop-off in textural density and a renewal of the accumulative process. It is usual that rhythmic motion continues to avoid too pronounced an interruption in the flow. In Ex. 11.26, an ornamented subject entry has just ended, and an episode begins. The suspension and the B-flat dissonance add to the forward movement.

Ex. 11.26   Bach, Partita No. 6 in E minor, first movement.

Stretto

Stretto is the overlapping of subject entries, the statement of the subject in canon with itself. Often, stretto involves an abbreviated form of the subject, presenting enough of the original, including its vital head motives, to make it clearly identifiable as a subject entry. Ex. 11.27 is a stretto on the abbreviated second subject of a double fugue.

Ex. 11.27   Mozart, Requiem in D minor, K. 626, Part II, Kyrie eleison.

Subject 2

Ex. 11.27 (continued)

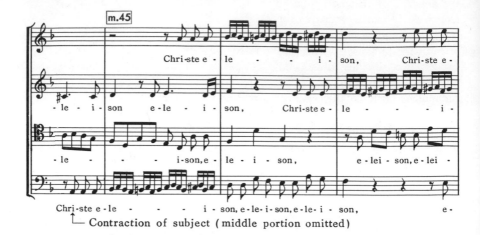

└─ Contraction of subject (middle portion omitted)

Stretto, a climactic device usually of intense effect, is associated primarily with the later stages in a fugal form. However, some fugues have stretto as a more-or-less constant feature of early appearance. Examples of the latter are the Fugue No. 2 in G from Hindemith's *Ludus Tonalis,* with stretto beginning at measure 24—hardly a third of the way through— and WTC I, 1, which has stretto immediately after the initial exposition. Rarely, a subject may even be in stretto with its first answer; see the fugato *Hosanna* which follows the *Sanctus of* Mozart's Requiem, where the answer enters on the fifth note before the end of the subject. (However, stretto is sometimes defined as overlapping *in excess of* any occurring in the exposition.)

Distinction is made between a *total stretto,* involving all the voices, and a *partial stretto.* In traditional styles, the composer must consider the problem of a subject's being combined with itself in stretto; in freer styles, the problem is less one of harmonic fitness than of maintaining counterpoint by the avoidance of unwanted coincidences of notes and rhythms.

The closer the distance of imitation, the tighter, more intense the stretto. In Ex. 11.28, the tight stretto on an extension of the subject head-motive is intensified by the orchestration.

Ex. 11.28   Schuman, Symphony No. 3, Part I, second movement.
Copyright 1941, 1942 by G. Schirmer, Inc. Reprinted by permission.

An example of tight stretto involving the entire fugal texture is seen in WTC I, 22. The subject appears in imitations at the time interval of a half-measure in the passage following measure 67.

Pedal point

Theoretically, a pedal point may occur anywhere after the exposition, but, like stretto, it is associated with the later stages, even the coda itself, as in WTC I, 2. The pedal point is usually on the tonic or dominant (commonly but not necessarily of the fundamental key), forming a dramatic conflict in its rigidly fixed quality, with harmonic and rhythmic motion over it. Examples of pedals in related keys may be seen in the first and sixth of Schumann's Six Fugues on the name of Bach, Op. 60. The first of these, at measure 32, has a c:V pedal, and a g:V pedal at measure 25; its fundamental key is B-flat.

A dominant pedal progressing to a tonic pedal, viewed telescopically, may be regarded as forming a mammoth authentic cadence—a concept that has much to do with the structural function of many pedal points. This function is seen in Ex. 11.29, an excerpt from a tonal 12-tone work. The V pedal is broken by reiteration of the motive B-A-C-H; sequential movement of shrinking pattern repetitions occurs over it (see brackets), descending in whole-tones. The motive, harmonized, continues over the tonic pedal which follows.

Ex. 11.29   Piston, Chromatic Study on the Name of Bach.
            Copyright 1941 by The H. W. Gray Co., Inc. Used by permission.

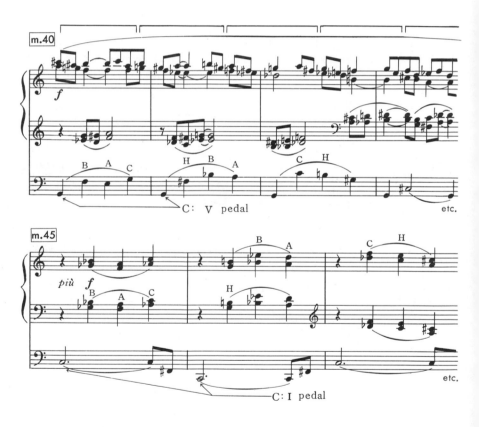

Many pedal points will be found in the WTC—for example, the 8-measure, ornamented V pedal of II, 10. An example of striking length is the V pedal of the fugue of Brahms' *Handel Variations,* beginning at measure 76; here the pedal point, rather than being sustained, is broken and reiterated.

The final stage

The fugue's final stage is marked by the return of the tonic key— its final re-emergence, after which point there is only minor, secondary tonal deviation, if any. Frequently it is set off by a half- or authentic cadence in the tonic, featuring a final subject entry or entry group at the tonic key level. At this point in the fugue, episodes (Ex. 11.32) or final entries touching non-tonic, secondary tonal levels do so without significant disruption of the tonic key feeling.

In the fugue from which Ex. 11.30 is drawn there is a perfect authentic cadence in A minor at measure 63, followed by a vacillating episode of secondary fluctuations ending in a strong half-cadence in the tonic key, with *fermata,* at measure 71. This cadence sets off the final stage of the fugue. Several tonic entries follow, some in stretto. Later, there is a compound tonic pedal[13] with typical harmonic use of the V_7/IV in the final bars (see also Ex. 11.31), and a single entry at the subdominant (harmonic, not tonal) level, appropriate in the harmonic environment of the cadence.

Ex. 11.30   Bach, Prelude and Fugue in G for organ (II, 2).

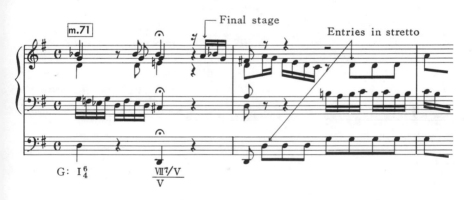

---

13 A *compound pedal point* occurs in more than one voice. In the **Bach organ** fugue under discussion here the bass pedal is doubled in the uppermost voice—a combination of the normal pedal with the *inverted pedal.*

Ex. 11.30 (continued)

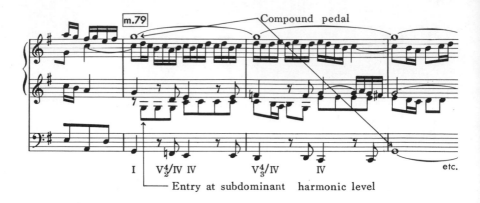

Entry at subdominant   harmonic level

The coda

The end of the fugue is almost always emphatic, never an indifferent subsidence of energy. Sometimes the texture thickens for harmonic fullness and greater strength of the final cadence (Ex. 11.30).

When there is a coda or codetta, it is a concluding appendage *to the final stage,* set off by a clear, premature cadence, sometimes deceptive, in the tonic key, after the re-establishment of that level in the final stage. Thus, distinction must be made between the coda, an appendage, and the integral final stage itself, with the important activity described above.

The coda may include a last subject entry, as in WTC I, 2. An excellently definitive specimen is that of WTC II, 8 (final 3-1/2 bars), whose coda, set off by a perfect authentic cadence in d-sharp, contains two simultaneous subject entries, one the mirror of the other.

Some fugues have closing sections with cadenza figurations—a feature of several of Bach's organ fugues, including the A minor Prelude and Fugue (II, 8), which includes a brilliant cadenza within the framework of an inflated authentic cadence: $VII_7/V–V_9–I_4^6–V_7–I$, in the final six bars. This example, lacking real thematic substance and consisting fundamentally of an inflated cadential progression, is best described as a codetta.

Important in the Baroque fugue, especially that of Bach, is the device of embellishing and extending the final tonic harmony with the dominant to the subdominant (an altered form of the tonic, almost always with the dissonant dominant 7th), the subdominant, and, unless the cadence is plagal as in Ex. 11.31, the ultimate V-I progression. We have seen that this is sometimes carried to the extreme of including a subject entry at the subdominant level (Ex. 11.30, or WTC II, 2, measure 25).

Ex. 11.31   Bach, Brandenburg Concerto No. 2 in F, final movement.

F: V   I   V⁷/IV   IV   I   —   V⁷/IV   IV   I

As Ex. 11.31 indicates, the coda is often primarily or entirely homo-phonic. A final example, Bach's C major "Leipzig" Organ Fugue (II, 7), includes, preceding the coda, augmentations of the inverted subject at the tonic and subdominant levels; its coda, distinctly marked by a perfect authentic cadence, contains stretto on the subject *rectus* and mirror over a 6-measure tonic pedal.

Handel, chorus, He trusted in God, from Messiah

An example from *Messiah,* although less interesting than, for example, a keyboard fugue of Bach, will illustrate fugal function in a universally familiar context and medium. The reader will find other examples of choral fugue in masses, oratorios, and requiems of such composers as Bach, Handel (see also the final chorus of *Messiah*), Haydn, Mozart, Beethoven, Mendelssohn, and Brahms. The following discussion of tech-niques in a Handel choral fugue is of necessity cursory and, while brief excerpts are quoted, the complete fugue should be available for reference.

The opening tonic chord affirms the key, "introduces" the fugue and catches the listener's attention, and by its sharp, emphatic delivery sets the subject in motion. The subject itself is longer than average (nearly five measures) but it is a tight unit, with its dramatic rise and fall over an octave's range. The type of melodic curve displayed here, with its high point occurring after the middle of its length, is very common. Its most likely and basic harmonic implications are I-IV-I; thus, after the first reference to tonic harmony, the subject's secondary high points—marked by duration, approach by skip, and prominence of pitch level—outline the subdominant: F, A-flat, C, after which the subject's cadence restores tonic harmonic reference. The first two notes, dropping from dominant to tonic,

suggest immediately that the answer will probably be tonal, responding
with a descent from tonic to dominant,

Motivic unity is achieved by repetition of the motive

in various forms, as bracketed in the quotation.

Ex. 11.32a   Handel, He trusted in God, from Messiah.

    The tonal answer, from the second note, is consistently at the 5th,
submitting to transitory modulation to the dominant key, a modulation
that is cancelled abruptly by the lowering of the F-sharp leading-tone (see
example) just before the third entry; thus, a transitional episode, usual in
situations of this kind, is avoided. The originating voice continues with a
counterpoint to the answer—a counterpoint designated here as countersubject because of its recurrence in the fugue.

Ex. 11.32b

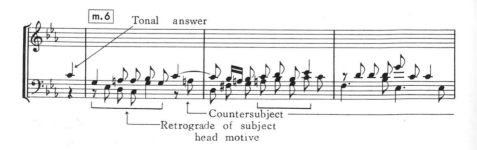

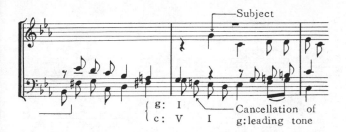

It is interesting that the first notes of the bass, under the tonal answer, are a retrograde of the motive with which the subject began (see above) —

The countersubject affords useful, if not pronounced, contrast to the subject: there is relatively little rhythmic parallelism between the two, although considerable similar motion. The motive which had been repeated in the subject is worked into the countersubject, along with the characteristic skips of a 5th, as seen in Ex. 11.32b.

The exposition proceeds with perfect regularity, with the voices entering from bottom up. After the originating voice has completed the countersubject it continues with free counterpoint. The third entry, with countersubject in the tenor, and the fourth, with the countersubject stated freely in the bass, are quoted in Ex. 11.32c to give a picture of the conclusion of the exposition. An interesting feature is a false entry of the subject at measure 14, just before the appearance of the second tonal answer in the soprano. In the conclusion of the exposition, measure 19, the music again leans toward the dominant key. But at the cadence a B-natural arises suddenly and the g:I moves as a dominant back to the original tonic, c. Orchestra parts are omitted in the quotations, since they duplicate the singing voices most of the time.

Ex. 11.32c

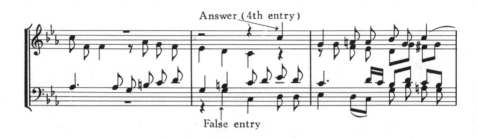

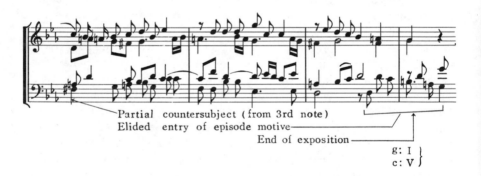

There is no counterexposition. Measure 19 sets the pattern for the fugal episodes, which are based on the motive

,

a rhythmic variation, inverted, of the subject's head-motive. The episode has all the most standard qualities: its derivation (although somewhat far removed) from the subject, the colloquy among voices, the tonal flux, and the sequential repetition of pattern (see Ex. 11.32d). At its conclusion, in B-flat, there is another false entry of the subject, which materializes fully in the alto, together with part of the countersubject, a measure later.

Ex. 11.32d

In the later entries, the subject is varied a good deal by changes of line and rhythm, and by contraction, without impairing its associable features or cutting it so short, as in the false entries cited above, as to obliterate its function as an "entry." The forms are summarized in Ex. 11.32e.

Ex. 11.32e

Original form

Tonal form

Ex. 11.32e (continued)

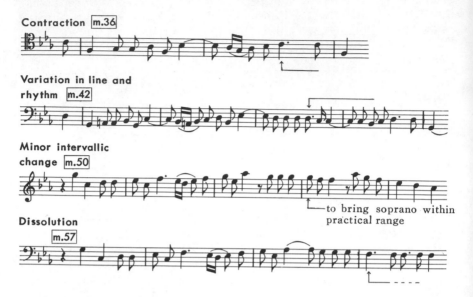

The fugal development includes no stretto, no pedal, and very little inverted counterpoint, since the countersubject recurs with determined consistency below the subject. However, a fragment occurs above the subject at measure 43, forming double counterpoint at the 15th (in Ex. 11.32f, the actual countersubject is shown along with its variation—the

Ex. 11.32f

former in small notes). Slight double counterpoint is also seen in the episodes (e. g., measure 19). Both, as well as the computation of the intervals of inversion—15th and octave, are illustrated in Ex. 11.32f.

The technique of episodic dialogue is even more pronounced in the episodes at measure 33 and measure 46. After the first episode, there are subject entries, all of them single, at measure 23 (B-flat, alto), measure 29 (E-flat, soprano), measure 36 (f, tenor), measure 42 (g, bass), measure 50 (c, soprano), and measure 57 (c, bass). It is interesting to observe the manner in which Handel introduces countersubject fragments in bass and alto under the subject entry in measure 50, and the same may be seen in the alto counterpoint to the entry in measure 29. But the countersubject as a whole is dismissed early in the fugue. The device of false entry, as mentioned in two instances above, is exploited again in measure 28, where the tenor anticipates the soprano entry of the following bar.

Episodes are constructed consistently of the motive seen in Ex. 11.32d, and it is sometimes used sequentially, as in the episode beginning at measure 46 (see also Ex. 11.32d).

The tonal range is of usual traditional scope. Unusually, the subject itself moves to an emphatic cadence, with alternating formulae at tonic and dominant key levels throughout the exposition. Cadences of significant value are at measure 22 (Ex. 11.32d), in B-flat; measure 27, where cadential feeling is effectively lessened by the early entry of the episode motive; measure 33, an imperfect cadence in E-flat, which tonal level gives way immediately to f; measure 38, cadence in f, which is checked by the early entry of the episode motive, as before, by the alteration of f:I to function as B-flat:V, and by the uninterrupted rhythmic drive; measure 41, half-cadence in g; measure 46, whose cadence in g is put down by the devices mentioned above; measure 50, weak half-cadence in c, ending the preceding episode and setting off the final stage; and measure 54, where the tonic key is strongly confirmed, having been established in preparation for the tonic entry 5 measures earlier. The tonal range may be summarized as T–D–R of D–R of T–SD, and there are subject entries at all of these levels.

The final stage of the fugue brings back the subject at the tonic level (measure 50). This is followed by a last episode, end of measure 54, where the music turns slightly toward the relative major, and still another tonic entry, dissolved as shown in Ex. 11.32e, at measure 57. Here, the fugue is led to a half-cadence on $c:V_2^4$. The 3-measure homophonic codetta is of a style characteristic of many choral fugues (see the *Kyrie* movement from Mozart's Requiem).

Ex. 11.32g

Although many of the sophisticated techniques of fugue are ignored in this example of Handel, important lessons of structure are to be observed in the unity deriving from common elements in subject, countersubject, and episodes; unity and contrast in the control of tonal movement from, around, and to the central tonic; the interest of variation in subject modifications; textural contrast achieved by frequent dropping-off at cadential points, and by the use of episodes in which movement of the voices, rather than constant, is taken up with responsorial exchange of short motive repetitions; the interest of the deceptive effect of false subject entries; the systematic recalling of the subject after episodes of moderate length; the frequent suppression of cadence in favor of directed musical motion; and innumerable other factors explicit or implicit in what has been said in these paragraphs.

Multiple fugue

A fugue with two subjects is a *double fugue*. A second subject is distinguished from a countersubject, with which it has much in common, in that it does not appear initially as an accompaniment to the first answer, and usually has some degree of independent existence, occurring alone as well as in association with the first subject. An example to which we may again refer is the *Kyrie* from the Mozart Requiem; its second subject, on the words *Christe eleison,* appears concurrently with the first subject at the outset, entering a bar later, and arises independently, in stretto, later in the fugue (Ex. 11.27).

When a fugue has two themes appearing together at the beginning, each of them recurring exclusively in association with the other, it can scarcely be insisted that the example is either a double fugue or a single fugue with countersubject. The eighth-note associate to the passacaglia ostinato theme in the fugue of Bach's Passacaglia and Fugue in C minor for organ seems of secondary importance—a countersubject to the theme which prevails throughout—and it does not appear independently; yet, this fugue is often characterized as a double fugue.

A second subject must be capable of combination with the first, since the two are always combined at some point; yet it must also be strongly contrasted. Thus, in the Mozart, one is disjunct, the other conjunct; one features relatively long rhythmic values and dotted rhythms, the other is fast-moving and smooth. Some double fugues begin with two separate expositions, one for each subject, later combining them. This is vividly clear in Fugue No. 4 in A of Hindemith's *Ludus Tonalis*, the exposition of whose second subject is at a changed tempo.

Another example, Bach's Toccata and Fugue in F for organ (III, 2), contains an exposition (SAAS) of a second subject at measure 71; the two subjects are combined at, for example, measure 134. Another of the type with separate expositions is the Mendelssohn Fugue No. 4 in A-flat, Op. 35. A final example of the opposite type, in which two subjects are exposed concurrently, is seen in the thirty-second variation of the Beethoven *Diabelli* set.

A triple fugue is, of course, a fugue with three subjects, and a quadruple fugue one with four. The latter is extremely rare, as, indeed, are full forms (separate expositions, later combinations) of either of these. Ex. 11.33 is taken from a triple fugue in which subjects two and three have a concurrent exposition separate from that of subject one. Subject three differs from a countersubject in its independent appearance (as at measure 133) as well as in its initial presentation with subject two rather than as accompaniment to an answer. The example quotes excerpts from each of the two expositions, and from the combination of all three subjects at measure 203. Note the intervals of imitation in the expositions.

Ex. 11.33   Hindemith, String Quartet No. 4, Op. 32, first movement.
© 1924 B. Schott's Soehne/Mainz, Germany. Renewed 1952. Used by permission.

Ex. 11.33 (continued)

The reader should consult the multiple fugues of Bach's *Art of the Fugue*, VIII and XI of which are triple fugues, the latter using mirror forms of the three subjects of the former. IX and X are double fugues, and the final fugue, unfinished, was intended to be a quadruple fugue. The finale of Haydn's String Quartet in A, Op. 20, No. 6 is a further example of triple fugue.

Fughetta

It is incorrect to consider the *fughetta* and *fugato* as synonymous. The former term is the diminutive of "fugue" (actually of the Italian *fuga*) and it denotes a small fugue. The brevity of the fughetta may be the consequence of a very short subject, or of the absence or severe reduction of the usual extensive fugal development between exposition and conclusion. Obviously, the fughetta is far more limited than the fugue in the range of modulation and in the application of developmental and variational techniques.

Examples are variations 10 of Bach's *Goldberg* series and 24 of Beethoven's *Diabelli,* both of these fughettas within binary theme framework. The Bach Fantasies with Fughettas (in B-flat and D) and Preludes with Fughettas (in F, G, d, and e) are further examples. A modern fughetta occurs as variation 3 in the second movement of Stravinsky's Sonata for two pianos.

Fugato

Fugato, used either as a noun or adjective, refers to a passage involving fugal texture and imitation in a work or movement which is otherwise primarily non-fugal; frequently the fugato consists of a fugal exposition only, as may be seen in such examples as the second movement of Beethoven's Symphony No. 7 in A, Op. 92, beginning at measure 183, the opening of Puccini's opera *Madame Butterfly,* whose 8-measure subject is set out in a 32-measure exposition (TDTD), and the Beethoven Quartets, Op. 59, No. 3 in C and Op. 131 in C-sharp minor—the finale of the former and the opening of the latter. The fugatos in Mozart's Requiem, following *Sanctus* and *Benedictus,* have been mentioned. Examples are extremely numerous.

Invention

The term *invention* was used only rarely and inconsistently before Bach (for example, as synonymous with suite), and the current understanding of the word is associated almost exclusively with the well-known 30 harpsichord pieces by Bach, even though half of them, those in three voices, he called *sinfoniae*. It is further testimony to Bach's genius that even in this limited frame of reference, the invention must be regarded as an important contrapuntal genre because of the supreme quality of these works. An invention may be characterized very generally as a study in contrapuntal techniques.

The Bach inventions are sectional, falling into two or more parts, and are based on a unifying recurring motive stated and imitated at the outset, and very often restated with imitation at the beginning of the second section. The inventions are short, remarkably constant in motion, pattern, and tempo. Often the subject-motive is accompanied at the outset. The interval of imitation is most often an octave in the 2-voice inventions, a fifth in the others. Sometimes an invention is devoted more or less exclusively to a primary technique—for example, canon in the C minor 2-voice invention. More prevalent techniques are double and triple counterpoint, sequence, pedal, and motive variation. Systematic binary and ternary forms are exceptional (see the 2-voice invention in E, cited in the chapter on simple ternary form). Sometimes a counter-motive assumes significance in recurrence, like the countersubject in a fugue, or the subject-motive may appear initially with a counterpoint of equal importance (again, the E major 2-voice invention). A coda or codetta is sometimes added.

While the 3-voice invention, with imitation at the fifth, is sometimes distinguished from fugue on the basis of over-all brevity, lesser importance of devices like stretto, accompaniment of initial subject-motive statement, and more restricted development and tonal movement, it is unlikely that any absolute distinction can be made, even though most fugues are bigger in size and concept and most inventions do not have single-voice beginnings like usual fugal expositions. The problem is that any attempt to establish firm distinction between fugues and inventions must face such questions as: How short is a fugue? How short is a fugue subject? What integral and important devices are consistently associated with fugue and not with invention, or the reverse? Indeed, some inventions are fugue-like (Bach's 2-voice in G), albeit on a small scale, and some fugues invention-like (WTC I, 10).

All subject-motives of the 3-voice inventions are accompanied, although not always with material of more than momentary harmonic significance, and only six of the 2-voice inventions begin with unaccompanied motives. Tonal range varies from simply T–D (2-voice invention in G) to T–D–R–D of R –SD of R (for example, 3-voice in f). Some inventions have as few as two sections (2-voice in B-flat), some as many as five (3-voice in E-flat) ; a few virtually avoid cadential sectionalization (like the 2-voice in A) ; some have closing sections (see 2-voice in d or D), others do not. Ten of the 2-voice inventions begin with imitation at the octave, but a few (e.g., the one in b) answer at the fifth. All of the 3-voice inventions answer at the fifth—sometimes tonally (the one in F)—except those in c and b. Subject-motive length, usually short, varies from a half-bar (2-voice in C) to 4 bars (3-voice in a) ; eight have one-measure subject motives. In some, certain techniques predominate: canon in the 2-voice inventions in c and F, and to a lesser extent in the one in B-flat; pedal in the 2-voice invention in e and 3-voice in g, among others; sequence (practiced in all) in 2-voice in a and 3-voice in D, whose subject itself is sequential; mirror inversion in the

3-voice inventions in C and E. The 3-voice invention in f is especially interesting as a specimen of the techniques of motive ornamentation and triple counterpoint (4 of 6 possible contrapuntal inversions are used).

Co-equal, very significant, counterpoints to the opening motives are seen, for example, in 2-voice inventions in E-flat and g, and the 3-voice invention in f. While diatonicism is usual in the inventions, a few are extraordinary in chromaticism of line or harmony, as may be seen in the 2-voice invention in a, and the 3-voice inventions in d and G. The inventions constitute an exceedingly rewarding body of material for study, and the above are only very broad, summary suggestions as to their nature.

An invention beginning is shown in Ex. 11.34, with some of the typical features marked.

Ex. 11.34   Bach, Two-Voice Invention in D minor.

The practice of invention appears under other names (see Chapter 10). Thus, certain of the partita preludes of Bach were described as inventions or invention-like. Additional examples may be found among the WTC preludes—for example, Nos. 13 and 18 in the first book. Inventions are occasionally written in the twentieth century as well (Bartók, *Mikrokosmos,* contrapuntal studies in, for example, Volumes V and VI).

Canon

Canon might easily be the subject for an entire chapter, or even an entire book, and can be dealt with in only the most summary fashion here. Originally, the word (from *kanōn,* Gr. for rule) referred to the rule for realization of imitation not written out. The importance of canonic forms in the fourteenth century has been suggested.[14]

Canon is a contrapuntal type consisting of usually strict, prolonged imitation between two or more voices. A round is a kind of canon. The voice which begins the canon is called the leader (*dux, proposta,* initiating voice) and the second voice the follower (*comes, risposta,* imitating voice). In the terminology of canon analysis, the distance in measures, in measure-fractions, or pulses separating the leader from the follower is called the *time interval.* The *harmonic interval* is the harmonic distance between the first note of the leader and the corresponding note of the follower, a distance which usually, but not always, remains constant throughout the canon. One might thus speak of a canon at the octave, at the time interval of a measure and a half.

A *simple canon* may have any number of voices. In addition to those actually in canon, there may be one or more free, accompanying voices (*accompanied canon*), as in the *Goldberg* canons of Bach. Ex. 11.35 illustrates a particular kind of accompanied canon in which the leader has a homophonic setting which also accompanies the follower.

---

[14] One of these, the *caccia,* achieved great popularity in Shakespeare's England as the "catch." Often, in the catch, the placement of the syllables of the text in the contrapuntal setting was such that hidden meanings came out in performance, some of them very bawdy—a unique approach to the problem of text intelligibility in vocal polyphony.

Ex. 11.35 Franck, Sonata in A for violin and piano, final movement.

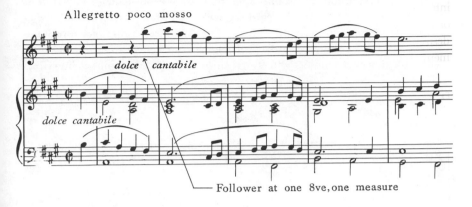

A *double canon* has at least four voices, and consists of two canons progressing simultaneously. The principle can be extended to *triple canon,* an example of which is quoted by Leichtentritt from a *chanson* of Josquin des Prez.[15]

Ex. 11.36 Mozart, Double Canon, K. 228, for four voices.

[15] Leichtentritt, *Musical Form,* p. 81.

In *canon in augmentation* the follower is an augmentation of the leader; a *canon in diminution* is the opposite. Increasing discrepancies in the time interval have to be made up by holding back the faster moving voice by rests or passages of free counterpoint to bring the time interval into conformity as desired. Ex. 11.37 shows canonic imitation of a fugue subject by its augmentation; later, the subject enters in a third voice in a free mirror inversion.

Ex. 11.37   Bach. Fugue In C minor, WTC II, 2.

Like many of the more esoteric forms of canon, the *retrograde canon* (crab canon, canon cancrizans), in which the follower is the retrograde of the leader, is extremely rare, as attested by the fact that reference is made again and again to the same examples, especially that of Bach's *Musical Offering*. Usually the retrograde canon is at a time interval of zero. Theoretically, such unlikely types as retrograde mirror canon are possible. The following is from a retrograde canon of contemporary vintage.

Ex. 11.38   Dallapiccola, Quaderno Musicale di Annalibera for piano, No. 7.
            © 1953 by Edizioni Suvini Zerboni, Milan, Italy. Used by permission.

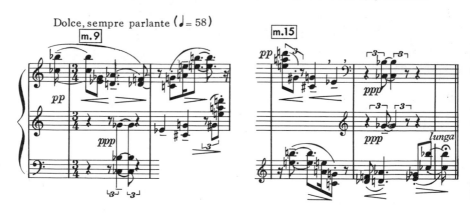

A *mirror canon* is one in which the follower is the mirror of the leader, a canon in contrary motion. (See the Bach *Goldberg Variations*, Nos. 12 and 15.)

Ex. 11.39 Schönberg, Suite, Op. 25, for piano, trio of minuet.
Copyright renewal 1952 by Mrs. Arnold Schönberg. Used by permission of Mrs. Schönberg for the U.S.A. and Canada and Universal Edition (Alfred A. Kalmus Ltd.) for other countries.

The *Harvard Dictionary* discussion of the *enigma canon* (riddle canon, puzzle canon) is well worth consulting. In an enigma canon, the imitation is omitted, with clues to the realization given in the form of clef signs, entry signs, and even literary inscriptions. The solutions for the enigma canons are discussed in the *Bach Reader*.[16] Excerpts from two of them are quoted in Ex. 11.40. In the first, the upper voice (the subject of the entire work) is not part of the canon. The follower for the canonic imitation of the second voice is indicated by the second clef sign (an F clef, placing F on the top line) to begin on A-flat, and the location of its entry is indicated by the symbol $\cdot\mathcal{S}$. The second enigma canon is more difficult, since the time interval is not given and has to be discovered. Moreover, the inversion of the clef sign for the follower means that it is to be a mirror of the leader. (It begins

in the fourth measure.) Such puzzles can be fascinating, confounding, and, in the case of Bach, musically rewarding as well. An example of literary inscription is seen in the second canon: *Seek, and find*—i.e., the time interval.

---

[16] Hans T. David and Arthur Mendel, *Bach Reader* (New York: W. W. Norton & Company, Inc., 1945).

Ex. 11.40 Bach, The Musical Offering.

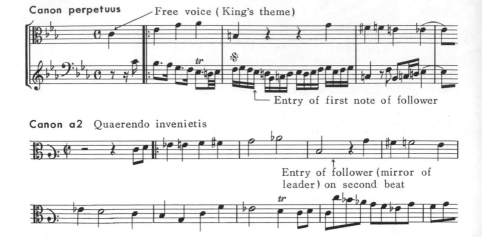

In a multi-voiced canon, the harmonic and/or time intervals may vary. In Ex. 11.41, which has a free bass, the second violin imitates at the fifth, the first violin at a tritone, while the time interval is consistent.

Ex. 11.41 Bartók, String Quartet No. 4, first movement.
> Copyright 1929 by Universal Edition; renewed 1956. Copyright & renewal assigned to Boosey & Hawkes, Inc. for the U. S. A. Copyright for all other countries of the world by Universal Edition (London) Ltd. Reprinted by permission.

There are several types of *free canon*. In one, only a note series is imitated—a method often associated with the 12-tone technique. Conformity of melodic interval succession or rhythmic pattern is not necessarily observed, and the series is freely transposed. A clear example can be seen in the third movement of the second Webern Cantata, Op. 31. Here the voices are imitative rhythmically, but often the relationship of leader-follower is imperceptible when a note series is the only factor of imitation.

Ex. 11.42 illustrates free canons. The first has a follower which imitates melodic intervals, but not rhythms (*rhythmically free canon*); the second imitates rhythms, but not melodic intervals (*intervallically free canon, or rhythmic canon*). In each, the element which is imitated constitutes a significant and perceptible unity in the music, and the implication is clear that other musical elements, e.g., dynamics, might be subjected, in isolation, to canonic imitation. In the quotations below, accompanying voices are omitted.[17]

Ex. 11.42   Schönberg, Variations for Orchestra, Op. 31, variations 2 and 8.

> Copyright renewal 1957 by Mrs. Arnold Schönberg. Used by permission of Mrs. Schönberg for the U.S.A. and Canada and Universal Edition (Alfred A. Kalmus Ltd.) for other countries.

A free canon may, finally, exercise liberties of varying kinds, avoiding rigid imitation of melodic intervals, sequence of notes, rhythms, and other musical factors, but maintaining sufficient imitation to convey the impression of canon. In addition to Ex. 11.43, the opening of Bartók's String Quartet No. 1, as well as measures 6–11 of his Quartet No. 3, might be cited.

---

[17] The second quotation shows the beginning (two principal voices only) of Schönberg's Variation 8. In the rhythmic canon, the roles of oboes and bassoons as leader-group and follower-group, respectively, are clear. Interval relationships, in which for an instant the "leader" imitates the "follower" in mirror inversion (cf. bassoons, measure 2, from D, with oboes, measure 3, from E-flat), are produced by application of the same *row* in both voices and are distinctly secondary to the effect of rhythmic imitation, which, unlike the mirror intervallic correspondence, continues well beyond the quoted passage.

Ex. 11.43   Berry, Duo for violin and piano.

Free voice

If predictability is unwanted, a canonic follower may begin with free counterpoint, subsequently taking up the strict imitation of the leader.

Unless the follower is to continue alone, as in a round, the imitation must be interrupted in order to end the canon. Frequently, the imitation is abandoned to free counterpoint at a convenient point, after which the voices are joined in cadential progression, possibly with a codetta or coda. In an *infinite canon* (e.g., a *round*), the imitation goes on without interruption, repeating to the beginning in apparently endless succession (rarely, changing tonal level each time, as in the ascending *spiral canon* of Bach's *Musical Offering*), possibly with an alternate ending provided to bring the exercise to a close. An infinite canon may be a part of a large form, with the second ending so formed as to lead the canon into the following section.

Examples of canons are easy to find. A few of special interest and quality, other than those cited, are Bach's Five Canonic Variations on *Vom Himmel hoch* for organ; the quartet *Mir ist so wunderbar,* from Beethoven's opera *Fidelio* (free voices enter after measure 40, with dissolution into the coda); the quartet *E nel tuo, nel mio bicchiero* from Mozart's opera *Così fan Tutte*—a canon in three voices with an accompanying bass; and all the canons of the *Goldberg Variations* of Bach. Many sixteenth-century choral works contain canons. Examples of very tight canons—i.e., canons at short time intervals—are seen in the last movement of Bartók's Quartet No. 4 (measure 285, for instance), measures 27–33 of the first movement of Mozart's Sonata in D, K. 576, measure 35 of Piston's *Chromatic Study on the Name of Bach* for organ, and the opening of Bach's *Brandenburg Concerto* No. 6 in B-flat, where, as is not rarely the case, the time interval occasions a changed metric structure in the follower.

The adjective *canonic* is applied to passages in canon during the course of a fugue, or sonata development, or more comprehensive form, as well as to a piece like the Bach 2-Voice Invention in C minor, in which canonic imitation is freely interrupted and resumed. In fact, several of the examples quoted to illustrate various types of canon are canonic passages within large forms which are not primarily canonic.

All kinds of combinations of canon types are theoretically possible in the execution of a single imitation, from section to section of a work, or among the several strata of the polyphonic texture.

The organ chorale

The principles of the chorale prelude, chorale fugue, and other types of organ chorale, while associated especially with the organ, are applicable to other media as well (see, for example, the chorus of Bach's cantata *Jesus nun sei gepreiset*).

The literature of the organ chorale, written on Protestant chorale melodies of a tradition from the time of Luther, is one of the most sublime in all polyphony, and the works of Bach in this medium should be known to all who profess serious interest in music. The history of the organ chorale goes back to the *Tabulatura Nova* (1624) of Samuel Scheidt, and includes the works of such composers as Buxtehude, Pachelbel, Bach, and in the nineteenth century, Brahms. The second volume of the *Historical Anthology* (see No. 190) contains organ chorales of Scheidt, Buxtehude, Pachelbel and Bach on the same chorale melody.

As in all classifications of musical form, each specimen makes its own laws and creates its own problems and unique solutions, but it is possible to list certain fundamental principles in the treatment of the chorale melody, all of them visible in the works of Bach.

One type is only a step removed from the Bach chorale harmonization, known to every music student, with the setting of the chorale activated by rhythmic independence—counterpoint—among the voices, the chorale tune usually in the soprano. Many examples are found in Bach's *Orgelbüchlein*, some of whose chorale melodies are ornamented in the relatively simple setting that has been described.

Ex. 11.44   Bach, Chorale Prelude on Vom Himmel hoch.

First notes of chorale

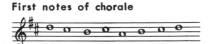

What might be described as a standard *chorale prelude* has imitative introductory, transitional, and concluding passages derived from the chorale melody. With the chorale phrases separated by interludes of this sort, the melody appears in longer notes, often remaining in one voice, accompanied by continued counterpoint in one, two, or more voices. Sometimes the same basic material is used for introductory section, interludes, and concluding section, as in No. 4 of Brahms' Chorale Preludes, Op. 122. Ex. 11.45 is an example of this type, even including, as often in Bach, a tonic pedal at the end; however, its opening counterpoint, while derived from the chorale, is not imitative, as it commonly is in Bach.

Ex. 11.45   Hindemith, Sonata No. 3 for organ, second movement (on Wach auf, mein Hort).
© 1940 B. Schott's Soehne/Mainz, Germany. Used by permission.

It will be convenient to draw further illustrations of the organ chorale from a single, broadly representative source, Vol. VI of the Peters edition of Bach's works for organ. Numbers which follow will relate to numerical ordering in that volume.

Within the classification of chorale prelude represented by Ex. 11.45, No. 1 of the Peters volume is a short, very clear example. No. 2 is an unusual specimen within the same category. This work, on *Ach bleib bei uns,*

Herr Jesu Christ, includes a theme,

derived from the first notes of the chorale melody,

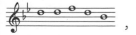

carried in the accompanying voices throughout without the usual imitative treatment. A *da capo,* in which the introductory material functions as concluding section, makes an over-all ternary. No. 3, a further example of chorale prelude, is in only two voices—the chorale and a single accompanying counterpoint; hence, its introductory, intervening, and concluding sections are single-voiced. No. 6, on the same chorale, *Allein Gott in der Höh' sei Ehr',* has an introductory section formed of a free bass and two voices in canonic relationship, with a middle voice assigned to statement of the chorale melody, beginning at the end of measure 12. Sometimes the upper voice takes the chorale, and sometimes the chorale phrase is articulated in canon with itself, as is the third phrase, at measure 78.

No. 9, still of the same general category, has the chorale melody,

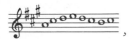

in elaborate ornamentation,

and illustrates as well the common prolongation of the final tonic note into a pedal point (here, inverted) with the use of the V_7/IV under it—a technique characteristic of the style. No. 30, on *Jesus Christus, unser Heiland,* is incomparably striking in its use of canon, invertible counterpoint, and motive variation:

with the chorale in the pedal voice. Many others could be mentioned. No. 16, even though it is titled *Fantasia sopra Christ lag in Todesbanden,* is perfectly regular in the approaches outlined above: introductory section, chorale phrases in sequence with contrapuntal accompaniments and separated by imitative interludes, and concluding section, also of imitative counterpoint.

No. 19, on *Dies sind die heil'gen Zehn Gebot',* represents a classification slightly apart from the standard chorale prelude in that the chorale melody is presented consistently in canon with itself.

Opening and concluding passages in the chorale prelude (*introductory section, concluding section;* first part, last part; or beginning, conclusion) are in nearly all cases integral to the total form. Examples show that the form is characterized by *spaced* appearances of the chorale phrases, with surrounding and intervening passages that are largely *parallel in texture and material.* Only an arbitrary analysis could describe opening and concluding passages as essentially preparatory (like the introduction, usually distinct in tempo, to a Classical symphonic movement) and adjunctive (like a fugal coda or codetta *following* the events of the final stage and set off by a strong cadence in the tonic key). The concluding section in a chorale prelude— that which follows the final chorale phrase—is generally an unbroken progression over (or under, or around) the final chorale note, which is sustained as a pedal point. Because of the intervening passages which separate the chorale phrases, the form seems unfulfilled at the point where the final phrase ends.

Only rarely is there an appendage, occurring *after* the final phrase and confirmation of the tonic key, and set off from it by cadential punctuation. No. 2 of the Peters Volume, *Ach bleib bei uns, Herr Jesu Christ,* comes closer than any example we have considered to having a real introduction (ending with the cadence, with *fermata,* at measure 15) and coda (identical here to the "introduction," beginning with the cadence at measure 46, just before the repeat *dal segno*).

Another type of organ chorale, represented by No. 18 of the Peters edition, on *Christ, unser Herr, zum Jordan kam,* takes a bit of the chorale melody,

and weaves out of it a free contrapuntal study, or invention.

Ex. 11.46   Bach, Organ Chorale on Christ, unser Herr, zum Jordan kam.

From chorale second phrase

From chorale first phrase   Mirror of chorale first phrase

We have referred to that kind of organ chorale which is a fugue (or fughetta), taking its subject from the chorale melody (Ex. 11.8a). No. 33, a fugue on *Jesus Christus, unser Heiland,* draws its subject,

from the chorale's first phrase,

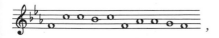

and, strangely, uses mirror canon episodically in the course of the exposition. No. 11 uses the first phrase of *Allein Gott in der Höh' sei Ehr'* as its subject, and later brings in the second phrase as well, using both in augmentation in the pedal voice in the final 19 measures.

Ex. 11.47   Bach, Fugue on Allein Gott in der Höh' sei Ehr'.

Real answer

Canonic transitional episode

Ex. 11.47 (continued)

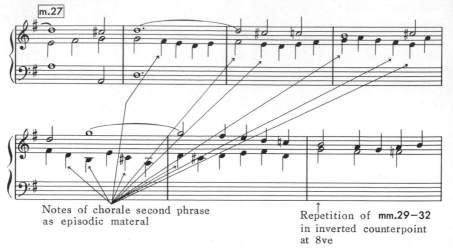

Notes of chorale second phrase
as episodic materal

Repetition of **mm.29–32**
in inverted counterpoint
at 8ve

A good example of the *chorale fantasy* is No. 15, on *Christ lag in Todes-banden*. One of its free features is the extensive, rhapsodic development on the opening notes of the fifth phrase of the chorale melody (Ex. 11.48).

Ex. 11.48   Bach, Organ Chorale on Christ lag in Todesbanden.

Chorale fifth phrase

etc.

Another is No. 29, on *Jesu, meine Freude,* which begins in the most usual fashion of the chorale prelude, breaking away at measure 54 into a section of contrasting meter, in which motives of several of the chorale phrases are freely developed. No. 22, on *Ein' feste Burg,* is often described as a fantasy because of the free movement of the chorale melody from voice to voice, the fact that it is sometimes embellished and sometimes not, and the multiplicity of motives in the accompanying voices, which have the effect of breaking the form into diverse sections, often non-imitative.

The *chorale trio* (Nos. 7, 27) is a three-voice organ chorale which freely derives the voices of its contrapuntal fabric from parts of the chorale, whose melody is not stated directly, although parts or all may be brought in during the final section. This is the case in both of the two cited examples, the first of which concludes with a statement in the pedal of the first two chorale phrases. No. 27, a trio on *Herr Jesu Christ, dich zu uns wend'*, states the chorale in the pedal in the concluding 22 bars, with brief, imitative introductory, interlude, and concluding material precisely as in the most standard type of chorale prelude; hence, it represents a merger of the two approaches.

The *chorale partita,* a further type of organ chorale, is a series of variations on the chorale melody; it was referred to briefly in Chapter 9.

No. 21, the "fugue" on *Durch Adams Fall ist ganz verderbt,* is not a strict fugue. It consists of a series of sections in which chorale phrases and chorale-derived subjects—successively and recapitulatively—form the basis for canonic and fugal imitation. This is the form which is properly described by the term *chorale motet,* still another classification of organ chorale. Finally, No. 14, on *Aus tiefer Noth schrei' ich zu dir,* is worth special note as an illustration of the chorale motet type, conforming generally to the techniques outlined above. In this work, each phrase of the chorale is preceded by introductory or interlude material derived *from that phrase,* as in No. 23. No. 14 takes the first phrase,

in diminution,

imitating it in mirror inversion,

and then in *rectus* form, as the basis for its introductory section. A similar procedure is followed for material preceeding each of the subsequent chorale phrases.

There is an infinite variety of technique and detail of approach in the organ chorales of Bach and other composers. The above statements should be interpreted as illustrations of methods often repeated in broad outlines rather than as exhaustive classifications of stereotypes.

Exercises and examples for further study

1. Consulting several sources suggested by your instructor, write a short paper on the history of the organ chorale.
2. Find examples of each of the following.
   a) Fugato
   b) Second countersubject
   c) Real answer in a choral fugue
   d) Episode restated in inverted counterpoint
   e) Subject variations of several kinds
   f) Total stretto
   g) Coda containing I pedal point
   h) Mirror canon
   i) Canon at the third
   j) Chorale fughetta
3. Check as many as possible of the musical examples of Chapter 11 and find other examples to illustrate the same points.
4. Prepare an analysis of one work from any or each of the following sources.
   a) Chorale preludes of Brahms
   b) Bach, Two-Voice Inventions
   c) Bach, *The Art of the Fugue*
   d) Mozart canons—e.g., K. 89a, 229, 230–4, 347–8, 553–62
   e) Hindemith, fugues from *Ludus Tonalis*
5. Find examples of fugal techniques in the eighteenth-century *concerto grosso,* especially in works of Handel.
6. Find examples of each of the following in motets, madrigals, and masses of the sixteenth century.
   a) Double counterpoint at the twelfth
   b) Imitation at the fourth
   c) Mirror inversion
7. Assemble what information you can on the *mensuration canon.*
8. Answer the following questions with respect to a fugue of your choosing. Depending on the style of the work you choose, certain questions may of course be irrelevant.
   a) Define the subject as to its specific length.
   b) Does the subject modulate? How and where?
   c) What is the range of the subject?
   d) To what extent does the subject move conjunctly?
   e) Is the subject divisible into parts? If it is divisible into individual motives, are they related or contrasting, or both?
   f) The subject begins on what note of the tonic scale?
   g) The final note of the subject is what degree in the tonic or dominant scale?
   h) What are the most obvious harmonic implications of the subject?

   i) The subject has what distinctive melodic or rhythmic features?

   j) How would you describe the character of the subject as determined by its melodic movement, its rhythmic structure, its range, its tempo, etc.?

   k) What do you feel to be the climactic point, if any, in the subject? Why?

   l) The fugal texture involves how many voices?

  m) How frequently are all of the voices brought into play?

   n) Is the first answer real or tonal? If tonal, where are the adjustments made?

   o) If the answer is real, how and where is a return made to the tonic in preparation for the third entry?

   p) Is the answer accompanied by free counterpoint or by a countersubject? Is the countersubject related motivically to the subject?

   q) Is there an additional countersubject?

   r) How is the countersubject a complement to, or contrast to, the subject and its answer?

   s) In counterpoints to subject entries, trace the origin of the motives to subject or countersubject material, or characterize the material as "new."

   t) Where does the exposition end? Is there an additional entry in the starting voice?

  u) What is the order of voice entries in the exposition?

  v) Is there a transitional episode during the exposition?

  w) Is there a full or partial counterexposition?

   x) Mark all subsequent subject entries as "real" and "tonal" entries.

   y) Are there subject groups or internal expositions in related keys?

   z) Mark all episodes and determine how and where they modulate, and to what keys.

 aa) In the episodes, find an example of sequence, analyzing its basic pattern and the series and number of repetitions of the pattern.

 bb) Are there examples of melodic sequence where no total (harmonic) sequence is involved?

 cc) Determine the source(s) of motives developed in the episodes.

 dd) What is the tonal range?

 ee) Is there any use of pedal? Tonic or dominant? Where?

 ff) Are there stretti? Where? What is the pattern of voice entries in the stretto and what is the degree of overlapping (time interval)?

 gg) Is it a total or partial stretto?

 hh) In subject recurrences, look for examples of augmentation, diminution, mirror inversion, rhythmic alterations, retrograde, etc.

  ii) Find examples of double and multiple counterpoint. The inversion is at what interval?

  jj) Is there canonic imitation at any point? At what harmonic and time intervals?

 kk) Does the fugue fall into clear sections? Locate principal cadences and evaluate them as to their relative strengths.

  ll) How fully and concentratedly is the fugue taken up with subject material? With full subject entries? How large and frequent are the episodes?

 mm) Locate the final entry or entries of the subject in the tonic key.

 nn) Is there a coda?

434 FUGUE AND OTHER CONTRAPUNTAL FORMS

oo) If there is a coda, what does it contain? Subject? Pedal? Reduction or thickening of texture? Use of the dominant to the subdominant?

pp) Is the fugue anomalous in any way? What particularly striking, unusual characteristics do you observe in the fugue as a whole?

9. Find an example of the use of canon in an art song.

10. Study the use of canonic techniques in the Stravinsky *Cantata* (1952), *Ricercar* II, including the use of retrograde in what the composer labels *cantus cancrizans* and in, for example, the canon between cello and voice at rehearsal No. 10.

11. Many works have been cited in this chapter, and others are not difficult to find. Listed below are some suggestions for further study and analysis.

Bach, *Brandenburg Concerto* No. 5 in D, third movement
    Goldberg Variations, variations in canon
    Mass in B minor, *Kyrie eleison, Credo* and other movements
    Organ Chorales (Organ Works, Peters ed., Volumes V, VI, VII)
    Eight Short Preludes and Fugues for organ (Peters Vol. VIII)
Samuel Barber (b. 1910), Piano Sonata, Op. 26, fourth movement
Bartók, *Music for Strings, Percussion and Celesta,* first movement
Beethoven, Mass in C, *Cum Sancto Spiritu*
    Mass in D, *Et vitam venturi*
    Piano Sonatas in B-flat, Op. 106, and A-flat, Op. 110, fugal movements
Berg, *Wozzeck,* Act II, Scene 2 and Act III, Scene I
Bloch, *Concerto Grosso* No. 2 for strings, first movement
    String Quartet No. 3, fourth movement fugue
Brahms, Requiem, *Der gerechten Seelen sind in Gottes Hand* (end of Part III)
    Thirteen Canons, Op. 113, for women's voices
    Chorale Preludes, Op. 122
Ingolf Dahl (b. 1912), Music for Brass Instruments, first and third movements
Fauré, Eight Short Pieces, Op. 84, Nos. 3 and 6, for piano
Franck, Prelude, Fugue and Variation, Op. 18, for organ
    Quartet in D, first movement, measure 173ff.
Handel, *Concerto Grosso* in F, Op. 6, No. 9, fourth movement
    Israel in Egypt, chorus, *Egypt was glad*
    Six Fugues for harpsichord (*Handel Gesellschaft* edition, Vol. 2, pp. 161–74)
    Six Short Fugues (*H. G.* edition, Vol. 48, pp. 183–90)
    Suite No. 2 in F for harpsichord (fugue)
Haydn, *The Creation,* chorus, *Glory to His name forever*
    String Quartets in F minor, Op. 20, No. 5, and C, Op. 20, No. 2, final movements
Harris, Quintet for piano and strings, third movement
Hindemith, Piano Sonata No. 3, final movement
    String Trio, Op. 34, fourth movement
    Symphony *Mathis der Maler,* first movement (*Engelkonzert*), following rehearsal No. 12
Mendelssohn, *Elijah,* chorus, *Lord our creator*

Mozart, *Adagio in Canon* in F, K. 410, for 2 basset horns and bassoon
   Adagio and Fugue in C, K. 546, for string quartet
   Fantasy and Fugue in C, K. 394, for piano
   Fugue in C minor, K. 426, for 2 pianos
   Fugue in G minor, K. 401, for piano, 4 hands
Ravel, *Le Tombeau de Couperin,* second movement
Riegger, Canon and Fugue, Op. 33b, for organ
Schumann, Four Fugues, Op. 72, for piano
Shostakovich, 24 Preludes and Fugues for piano
Stevens, Quintet for flute, violin, viola, cello and piano, fourth movement
   Symphonic Dances, third movement
Stravinsky, Septet (1953), final movement (*gigue*)
Vaughan Williams, Prelude and Fugue in C minor for organ or orchestra
Verdi, *Falstaff,* finale, ensemble *Tutto nel mondo è burla*

12

FREE APPROACHES TO

MUSICAL FORM

hat class of works which music theory describes
as structurally "free" is, of course, no less carefully formed than more conventional designs, although in such works the problems of coherence are
treated, and the principles of form realized, without reliance upon any of
the total, standard schemes with which we have been concerned in this book.
It is in their relative independence of established conventional molds like the
rondo or the variation series that such forms are "free," although in another
sense no form is really free, since a plan which gives order and coherence to
a musical work must incorporate many of those concepts and principles
which are at the roots of all of the traditional forms of music.

It could be argued that the study and analysis of free forms is the most
valuable study of all. For while the application of a standard design by no
means *solves* the problems of form, it does suggest and often determines the
nature of many of these solutions. The fascination of studying free forms is the
discovery and analysis of factors which are independent of standard methods,
even though many of the most vital secrets of any form lie in the variable
details of motivation, transition, development and distribution of musical
materials—whether the design is standard or free.

At a few points in this book, free forms have been the subject of brief,
parenthetical reference, as in the section *Other types of multiple segmentation* in Chapter 3, or in the discussion of the preludes to the Partitas of Bach
in Chapter 10. The latter illustrate the use of free forms in multi-movement
works; other examples, along with single-movement works in free form, are
listed at the end of this chapter for supplementary reference. Free *sections*
of otherwise standard forms have been cited from time to time—as in the
concluding parts of certain organ fugues, which have flights of fancy in
cadenza-like passages, or the cadenza sections of concertos, or, for that matter, the development section in single-movement sonata form or the episodes
in fugue.

While it does not result in a free form, the composer's use of license in constructing a standard form is important to recall here. The enlargement or contraction of these forms, the use of hybrid approaches (rondo-like disgressions in fugue; sonata-rondo; or the use of a new theme in rondo-like manner in place of the expected development in single-movement sonata form, as in the third movement of Beethoven's Sonata, Op. 2, No. 1), the practice of establishing thematic likeness between usually contrasted groups in the rondo or the sonata movement—these and many other free approaches to standard forms have been discussed, and have often constituted the most exciting and provocative aspects of the forms in question.

Certain musical types are often, although not always, free in form. Where a text is employed, or a scenario or program—as in vocal media, stage pieces, and symphonic poems—form is often free, relying to some degree upon the order of the text or program to bind it into a comprehensive unit. But the application of a program does not necessarily mean free form (Beethoven's Symphony No. 6 is descriptive in considerable part, and Strauss's *Don Quixote,* for instance, is a variation set) any more than the use of free form means that there are necessarily extra-musical connotations. And even where events and narrative condition the over-all formal design, the procedures which bring coherence to the music—thematic and motivic development, variation, and reprise, for example—are still relevant and basic.

Reference should be made to two books to which we have pointed in other connections—books in which many useful points are made concerning the achievement of form which is independent of over-all conventional design. Chapter XI of Leichtentritt's *Musical Form* discusses many of the factors which enter into the musical organism in determination of its form. And Part III (Chapters X—XIII) of Toch's *The Shaping Forces in Music* presents, with respect to form, the observations of a man who is profoundly musical in his thought and analysis. Toch's analysis of the Wagner Prelude to *Die Meistersinger,* like Leichtentritt's discussion of the Prelude to *Tristan,* reveals and illuminates many vital factors in a context of free form, and Toch's lucid and ardent treatment of such factors as asymmetry, means of joining sections, motive generation and development, and problems of beginning and ending are recommended most highly to the student interested in acquiring every possible insight into the nature of musical form.

Following are analyses of two short works which illustrate free approaches to form. In over-all design they are independent of the standard traditional forms, while the techniques by which they are built parallel those of art music of all kinds, whether free or conventional in total shape.

K. P. E. Bach, Fantasy in D minor

The fantasy is one of many musical genres in which total form is often free of structural stereotype. We have marked this freedom as a feature of, for example, the chorale fantasy (Chapter 11), a genre in which, as its name suggests, the composer's fancy often takes precedence over conventions of form in setting the course of the music. Other musical types in which this is sometimes true, besides the programmatic or descriptive works to which we have referred, are the overture, when it is not in single-movement sonata form, the toccata, the rhapsody, the prelude, and a host of others. But it is important to repeat that, as many examples in this book have shown, works whose titles fall into these and similar classifications are frequently cast in one of the standard traditional forms, as is true, for example, of the nine-teenth-century prelude.

For explicit discussion in this chapter, our subjects must be few and brief, but the implication that free form necessarily implies brevity is not to be drawn (see Bach's *Chromatic Fantasy*). One type is quoted in full as Ex. 12.2—a fantasy of K. P. E. Bach which, despite the recapitulative character of some aspects of its final cadence, is free in form. It is, in style, typical of the Baroque improvisatory fantasy, a kind of written statement by the composer of approaches characteristic of his improvisational practices at the keyboard. The chords would be arpeggiated in realization, possibly as suggested in Ex. 12.1, with considerable freedom of tempo and meter. Not all of the notes of the chords would be assigned equal length; the per-former might choose, for example, to emphasize the rise and fall of the uppermost voice by dwelling slightly on the highest note of each chord. Very probably, the contrasting second part would begin somewhat deliberate-ly, increasing in tempo and pulling back into steadier motion before the final cadence.

Ex. 12.1.

While the fantasy does not state and recall thematic material in the usual manner of ternary form, it is significant that the return in the final cadential harmonies to the texture and manner of the beginning contributes importantly to the shape of the total piece. (It is thus "ternary" in a limited sense, as are most fugues in the return of the original tonal level after flux.)

In further contradiction of the ternary idea, the piece can be viewed as a nearly continuous progression of harmonies interrupted by the dash of descending 32nd-note figures—a passage that is, in a sense, parenthetical to the main course of the music. This view is underscored by the precise identity, even in position and distribution, of the two tonic six-fours on either side of the 32nd-note passage.

The chief single factor in the form is the tonal-harmonic progression, detailed in the quotation. While we cannot discuss all its implications, note should be taken of its most basic elements: the establishment of tonic feeling by pedal point at beginning and end (through, in each case, four harmonies); the repetition of the dominant root through the four harmonies which end the first section and the first two of the cadential progression at the end (see preceding paragraph); the series of thirty-second-note figures in the second section, driving toward G-sharp in preparation for the $I_4^6 - V_7$ harmonies (whose bass resolves the G-sharp) which open the cadential progression; the nearly unbroken plunge of thirty-second-notes, which turn upward only occasionally *toward the tonic note;* and the abundance of *chromatic harmonic progression*[1], much of it unorthodox and highly dramatic, prevailing especially in the fluctuant middle harmonies of the first section, with *diatonic progression* on either side. In this same area of the first section two vital factors, to which the above-mentioned chromaticism is allied, contribute to the forward surge of the musical progression—the emphasis upon harmonic dissonance (minor sevenths, diminished sevenths, augmented sixth, etc.) often "resolving" to further dissonance, and the extraordinarily jagged contour of the bass line between the more stable points already noted. Chromaticism and dissonance in the second section are indicated in the quotation, as is the use of chromatic secondary function around the subdominant in the final cadence, over a tonic pedal. Thus, while the piece includes no modulation, tonal variety is achieved by the use of secondary regions within the fundamental tonal system.

The tonal-harmonic motion is stimulated further by the use of a few nonharmonic devices (anticipation and suspension) as indicated in the quotation.

The following elements of unity and variety are self-evident: rhythmic pattern, connecting the chords of the opening and concluding progressions, interrelating the figures of the second section, and contrasting the two; rhythmic motion; texture—all of it homophonic, but of strikingly contrasted density in the thirty-second-note section, with minor changes of distribution and density in other areas; tempo, as suggested earlier in the possibilities of performance realization; color, especially in the broad compass of the second section; and dynamics.

The subtle joining of disparate sections is accomplished mainly by tonal-harmonic means; thus, harmonic stability or cadential settling are

---

[1] In Ex. 12.2, chromatic progressions (see p. 109) are indicated by the symbol *C*, while *Dec.* denotes *deceptive progression*—movement of a dominant to something other than its tonic. The augmented-sixth chords are indicated by the symbol *A6*.

avoided by harmonic dissonance and harmonic inversion until the final cadence. The final cadence is itself imperfect, although a high degree of finality is possible in the entirely plausible realization suggested in Ex. 12.1. The rest before the descent of the second section is important. It is the only rest; it represents a suspension of energy—a kind of inhalation before the vigorous, inexorable movement of the thirty-second-note figures.

Represented graphically in the illustration is the rising-falling curve of the upper voice of the opening harmonic progression—a curve that reaches its high point, B-natural, at almost exactly the mid-point. The curve corresponds, in the rising intensity of rising pitch, to the increase in chromaticism, erratic bass movement, and harmonic tension and flux in the middle of this section, and is thus an important factor in the motion-intensity contour with which our analysis has been concerned. The melodic fall in the final cadence is also marked.

The entire piece can be said, in summary, to move toward the dominant pedal at the end of the first series of chords, and thence toward the final tonic.

Ex. 12.2 K. P. E. Bach, Fantasy in D minor.

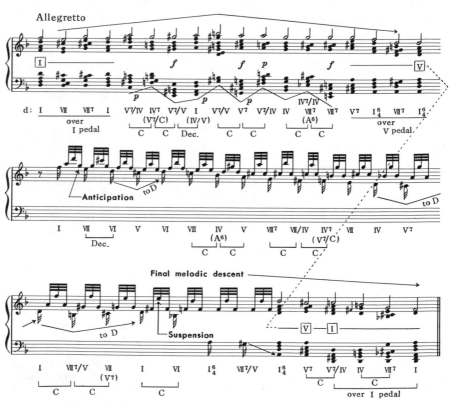

We have noted that there is lacking, as is not unreasonable in a piece of this length, anything of a *thematic* nature—any motive of strong melodic-rhythmic identity. Another fantasy of K. P. E. Bach, in G minor, contrasts with the above work in this and a number of ways, and a few of its important features may be mentioned. In this piece[2], which is longer and of more varied substance, motive repetition and variation are an important factor, as may be seen in the exerpts shown as Ex. 12.3a.

Ex. 12.3a K. P. E. Bach, Fantasy in G minor.

> Reprinted by permission of the publishers from Archibald T. Davison and Willi Apel, *Historical Anthology of Music: Baroque, Rococo, and Pre-Classical Music* (Cambridge, Mass.: Harvard University Press, copyright 1946, 1949, by the President and Fellows of Harvard College).

Recurrences of short, arpeggiated sections play a similar role in the form, as does the recurrence of sections of bravura passage work, notably at the beginning and end.

Ex. 12.3b

---

[2] Reproduced as No. 296 in the *Historical Anthology,* Vol. II.

Ex. 12.3b (continued)

Conclusion:

This longer fantasy contains bold and extreme tonal flux, which is lacking in the D minor Fantasy. Thus, there is internal modulation to such remote key levels as B minor, A-flat minor, F-sharp minor, and B-flat minor, much of it through chromatic progression. For example, the key of B minor is approached by the use of the dominant seventh-chord on the g:tonic as a German augmented-sixth chord in B minor.

Ex. 12.3c

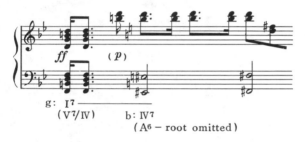

g: I⁷ ————————
    (V⁷/IV)   b: IV⁷
             (A⁶ – root omitted)

The above accounts illustrate some of the chief factors which may contribute coherence, unity, and interest in a free form.

Wolf, Blumengruss (Goethe)

Partly because the unity (of meter, rhyme, meaning) of a literary text imparts a degree of unity to its musical setting, vocal music is frequently written without recourse to the standard procedures of the traditional forms. That this is not always true is seen in the many vocal works quoted in the foregoing chapters (see, for example, the illustration from Schubert's *Der Musensohn* in Chapter 5).

In recitative styles especially, the effort to match in the music the inflections of the text governs the direction of the vocal line more than any other single factor except, perhaps, tonality in music which is tonally organized. This is not as true of composers who, like Stravinsky, often intentionally resist the demands of the textual prosody.

Whether or not the total musical form is free, the text is certain to wield a strong influence upon the details of its elements and motion, its climaxes and points of repose. A perfect unity of text and music was achieved by Hugo Wolf in many of his songs, which are among the precious gems of the literature. One of the most beautiful, *Anakreons Grab,* uses simple ternary form, although the form is somewhat concealed by the fact that the voice part is free, with the reprise in the piano only (compare measures 1 and 15).

Like Wagner, whom he admired profoundly, Wolf often relied heavily upon textual expression and meaning in the development of musical form, and upon persistent motive repetition as a counterbalance to non-recapitulative design and great tonal flux, often abrupt and often through rapidly fluctuant chromatic progression. These qualities may be seen in *Und willst du deinen Liebsten sterben sehen* (from the *Italienisches Liederbuch*), a poignant and moving song on a text of Paul Heyse—one that is for many twentieth-century minds excessive, but in which no one would deny the supreme fidelity of Wolf's setting. The tonal adventures of the music—from A-flat into such levels as F-sharp and G—make for stunning contrast in the musical from, while the accompanimental motive of measure 1 is repeated fixedly with changes as subtle and gentle as those of the breezes to which the text refers (*Wie gold'ne Fäden, die der Wind bewegt*).

Ex. 12.4   Wolf, Und willst du deinen Liebsten sterben sehen.

Ex. 12.4 (continued)

End

The same qualities may be seen in even deeper microcosm in Wolf's *Blumengruss,* to which we now turn. It is quoted in full as Ex. 12.5.

Ex. 12.5 Wolf, Blumengruss.

The first occurrence of the vocal high point, F, coincides with that of Goethe's text[3] on the word *ach;* and this point is intensified by the skip of an octave which precedes it, and by its length. It becomes a dissonance at the middle of the bar, and leads into the most disjunct of the vocal phrases. Other indications of the fidelity of music to textual inflection are the slight lengthening and metric emphasis on the second syllable of *gepflücket* (and its rhymes, *gebücket* and *gedrücket*) as well as on the first syllable of *tausendmal* each time that word appears. The expression of the text, in fact, is an important factor in all of the points of musical analysis which follow.

It is interesting to observe the change of rhythmic pattern and technique as the song unfolds. Against the obstinate rhythm of the piano part, the voice line features off-beat entries, syncopations, and dotted rhythms, settling into an unperturbed progression of quarter-notes only in the resigned setting of the last two phrases. The repose achieved by this and other means pours into the piano part of the final four bars, which are, in the perspective of the entire song, almost motionless.

The motivic repetition in the piano part,

is a primary factor in the form—perhaps the most obvious of all. Despite variations in melodic direction, harmonic setting, and harmonic rhythm, it is steadfast until the end. The upper-voice line of the accompaniment, outlined by the repetitions of this motive, reaches its highest pitch and climax in measure 11, later than that of the voice part, settling (*subito piano*) into unbroken chromatic descent thereafter. It forms a subtle contrast to the

---

[3] The German text may be freely translated as follows, with the title rendered as *Floral Greeting:*

The bouquet which I gathered—let it greet you many thousand times!
I have often bent down—ah, indeed a thousand times,
And pressed it to my heart, as a hundred thousand times.
As a hundred thousand times.

over-all shape of the vocal part, whose strongest intensity is in the fourth phrase.

The tonal-harmonic form of the song as a whole can be seen most strikingly in the prevalence of tonal stability and diatonic harmony in the more reposeful beginning and end, opposed to chromatic, fluctuant tonal movement, through secondary functions as well as modulation, in the internal bars. The analysis given, in which chromatic progressions are again noted by the symbol C, should be checked thoroughly in illustration of this. A vital part of the means of building intensity toward climactic points in measures 7 and 11 is that of harmonic dissonance and chromatic "leaning." It is noteworthy that after the relatively mild chromaticism of the second phrase, there is a withdrawal in every sense to prepare the rebuilding of intensity. The strong assertions of F at beginning and end are pillars which support the vacillating motion of the interior, which reaches its peak in measures 9–11. The sudden interjection of dissonance at the middle of measure 12 is important as a minor thrust which averts a premature subsidence in the tonal-harmonic motion.

Unity is achieved, in part, by artful correspondences of linear motion and direction, intervallic structure, and disjunct-conjunct features among the phrases of the vocal part. (Compare phrases 1 and 5, or 6 and 7, for example.) The second phrase is a complement to the first, but more intense (fall-rise, weaker-stronger: ‿ ——) ; the third and fourth are in a similar relationship (‿ ——) ; the final phrases, logically, have the reverse effect: phrases 5–6–7 convey the impression of rise-fall-fall (strong-weak-weaker, or intense-somewhat resigned-resigned: —— ‿ ‿). The first two groups move away from the tonic, the third toward it.

We can observe a concise illustration of variety within unity by noting the harmonizations of repeated notes in phrases 1, 3, and 5. In the first instance, the repeated C has 3 harmonic meanings (5th of I, root of V, 7th of VI) ; in phrase 3, the same note has 4 meanings, including that of un-resolved 7th to the D-flat harmony of measure 6; in the fifth phrase, the repeated E-flat has 3 harmonizations in a rapidly changing context, and then appears nonharmonically against the B-flat minor harmony of measure 10.

Many other factors could be mentioned—the use of syncopation in the vocal part as a motivating element, other instances of the use of nonharmonic dissonance, the complementary function of dynamics to fit the intensity-contour of the total form. One factor of joining (hence, of motion) should be detailed. The fourth phrase of the voice part descends more radically than any other, and comes to rest on a note of duration and very relaxed pitch level. To compensate, and to impel the music forward toward an approaching climax, Wolf for the first (and only) time interrupts the fixed idea of the accompaniment with a sudden, nonharmonically dissonant A-flat, initiating a syncopated motive which leads gently but insistently into the following phrase.

The elements of musical form

In this book, we have examined the nature of certain conventional forms of music in their broad outlines, referred parenthetically to others, and considered in all of them certain respects in which they provide a framework for unity and variety. We have studied many specific works, embodying an infinite spectrum of demands and conditions, in consideration of the technical means by which a skillful composer establishes, maintains, purposefully interrupts or suspends, changes, and ends a coherently motivated musical work. It may be that we have also caught some glimpses of the factors which are the basis for music's expressive appeal, and for the seemingly inscrutable power of the musical language of great composers.

The reader may find useful here a summary statement of the elements and principles of form discussed in this book. Such a summary, provided in the chart on page 448, must not be viewed as a source of information, but as a focusing, in the most cursory review, of principles to which constant reference has been made in this study. Obviously, only some of these principles are at work in any single piece of music. That no absolute value statements are possible is again apparent in the use in the chart of expressions like "too much diversity" and "effective beginning"; if the studies in this book demonstrate nothing else, they show that we can approach the capacity for sound critical judgment only in the penetrating perusal of the achievements of men who have produced great music.

We have made exhaustive and repeated reference to the element of *motion,* taking the position that little if anything is more vital in musical form than the controlled maintenance, and effective change, subsidence, and direction of motion. Failure to move with conviction and direction is one of the most common and crippling defects of ineffective music. The musical events should, of course, be sufficiently varied, while united to what precedes and proceeds from those of any given moment; but this can never overlook the primary requirement for directed motion, with tension released at fitting points.

> Stagnation is the worst enemy of form; and since form and inspiration are so intimately interrelated, we may well say that stagnation is the worst enemy of inspiration. If inspiration dies, form is doomed to die with it. What keeps them alive, is essentially *movement.* Movement is far more than just a sign of life; indeed, it is *"the very essence of life."*
>
> It is a blessed wisdom of the English and French languages to call a complete division of a sonata or symphony a "movement." Thus in a terse way the product is identified with its most essential source.[4]

---

[4] Toch, *The Shaping Forces in Music,* p. 194, copyright 1958 by Criterion Music Corp.

ELEMENTS OF MOTION AND INTENSITY

UNITY-CONTRAST	COMPATIBILITY OF DIVERSE MATERIALS	MOTION AND INTENSITY	RELAXATION	OTHER FACTORS
Of tonality and harmonic function	Relationship of harmonic and melodic vocabulary	Direction toward and from carefully-spaced climactic, secondary climactic, and cadential points	Internal punctuation (sectional organization of materials of form) through cadence:	Vigor, power, expressive effect, usefulness of ideas (striking, identifiable features of melodic-rhythmic materials—the music's most tangible, most accessible elements)
Of rhythmic pattern	Relationship among tonal levels	Effective beginning; thrust, or quiet ease from which intensity develops		Drama (unexpected twists; fantasy style; sudden change of character; asymmetry)
Of internal structural proportion		Tonal-harmonic function (dissonance: one possibility of "active" silence; chromaticism)	harmonic-melodic formula, relative cessation of motion for appropriate degree of finality	Text and program (extra-musical factors in addition to purely musical structural techniques)
Of melodic-rhythmic theme (reprise, development, ostinato, digression, imitation)	Homogeneity in such basic elements as meter, tempo (affinity of character)	Dissonance apart from tonal function		
Of harmonic color	Actual motivic affinity	Basic pulse (higher stimulation of irregular meters, inconsistency of pulse frequency)	Dynamic subsidence	Interest of total dynamic contour (the "profile" resulting from mounting, receding intensity)
Of pitch levels	Effective bridging and preparation	Rhythm (recurrence of pattern relating sound events; drive, maintenance of pace; devices of propulsion—syncopation, anacrusis, dotted patterns)	Relaxation of low pitch	Best length to contain the musical substance without introduction of too much diversity
Of meter and tempo			Relaxation of mild color	Principle of compensation (e.g., linear settling against continuing contrapuntal or accompanimental motion; imperfect cadence—punctuation without finality; repetition of one element against variation of another)
Of color (the concerto the prime medium of color contrast)		Linear rise and fall ("gravity" drawing or resisting linear motion)	Consonance; diatonicism	
Of mode		Intensity of high pitch	Linear settling	
Of dynamics		Motion across seams (transition; degrees of suppression of internal cadence; elision)	Passivity of rhythm	
Of texture, and among textural strata		Extension of small units	Constancy of meter, tempo	
Of character, the sum of the elements		Nonharmonic dissonance	Simplicity of texture (absence of differentiation of voices)	
		Contrapuntal life (imitation; pursuit of one voice by another)		
		Support of motion by dynamic intensity		
		Intensity of severe, incisive color		

If we have been concerned at length with the question *"How* musical form?," what of the question *"Why* musical form?" To this inquiry, much more than a rhetorical one in our time, no ultimate, incontestable answer is possible. Form in art is a choice one makes, but that it is the choice made by every great musical mind of the distant and recent past is a powerful fact. The value of artistic *order* is a potent one if we choose to view what music *is* with even indifferent respect to what it has been in all of the rich literatures which are today's heritage. Even improvisatory styles traditionally concede to the performer certain freedoms of execution and approach only within a composed or understood, rigidly disciplined framework of structure-producing forces.

Moreover, the perception of organic unity and vitality in a musical form is a fundamental part of the aesthetic experience of listening (or performing), and we have seen that many of the ineffable qualities underlying the *what* and *how* of musical expression are illuminated by the study of form in all of its aspects. The power of a musical statement lies partly in the strength of the musical ideas it sets forth, and partly in the weaving of those ideas into a fabric that convinces as their most appropriate development; in these two factors reside whatever "meaning" the music has, and they are indissolubly linked. The erection of the best-ordered framework for his ideas is a challenge a truly creative and responsible mind cannot easily reject, and it is a challenge that extends to the performer and the listener in each of their roles in the musical experience.

A strong idea demands an enriching, illuminating context—one in which it becomes something that can be perceived as important and rational. The coherence of a syntactic order is of special importance in an expressive language whose structural units do not, as in literature and often in graphic design, achieve inner relationship in their common reference to objective experience.

It is the disciplined restraint implicit in the development of form, as we have defined and observed it, which holds the creative mind to a direct, intensely channeled purpose. Without order, the musical material, however sound and vigorous, may be reduced through its aimless diffusion to an impotent stammer whose impression dissolves as it is issued, lacking the exercise of whatever potential may exist in it for assimilable unity, and renouncing all possibility of *intellectual* appeal.

The above are some of the reasons that have impelled great composers to cultivate form in music. If order is valued, we can dismiss the aesthetic philosophy that would leave the responsibility of formulation to the listener (or spectator); it is clear that order in art is not so glibly achieved.

The attenuation of tonality as a structural force in later styles

To deal with techniques unique to twentieth-century music, with all of their ramifications regarding the *treatment* of the elements of musical form, and to do so in any meaningful way beyond the mere recital of methods and superficial appearances, would be to extend our discussion through another book. It is a fact that most of the *principles* which underlie structural coherence in traditional music remain decisive.[5]

Yet, in view of our emphasis upon tonality in the foregoing studies, it is wise to turn our attention briefly to the diminishing significance of that musical element in certain styles of the past century. We have seen that tonality, tonal-harmonic function, and all attendant principles (for example, nonharmonic dissonance) constitute as much as any single factor a *sine qua non* of traditional musical form. (We may recall the early definition of the period as having its basis in cadential relationships rooted in tonal-harmonic function, and the extension of this and similar principles in the binary and all larger forms.) The obscuration and denial of tonality in many twentieth-century styles is now an established fact, and it is appropriate to consider certain manifestations and implications of the negation of tonality in musical form.

We cannot enter fully into the study of developments of the past century, but will be content in the present context to review the appearance of tonality in the crucial idioms of Wagner and Debussy, with a view to the significance of the musical language of those composers for the current state of tonal function and nonfunction in music.

In much of the music of Wagner, like that of a number of other later nineteenth-century composers, notably Strauss, tonality is often in a state of constant, rapid flux, moving freely (usually chromatically) into the remotest tonal regions within very brief time intervals. In such a state, the importance of tonality as a structural force comes into question; in fact, certain twentieth-century composers, especially Schönberg, viewed this as the beginning of the end of tonality as a meaningful element in musical form. Wagner's *Tristan und Isolde* is the work most often cited to illustrate rapidly, widely fluctuant tonality. It is possible, even in a brief excerpt from Wagner's music, to see the compensatory factors upon which form depends in his style: constant motive repetition, incessant motion of all kinds, and,

---

[5] The dismissal of the principle of melodic-rhythmic "theme" in twentieth-century *athematic* music does not, in itself, pose structural problems new to the tradition of musical form, as seen in such a work as the Bach Fantasy discussed in this chapter, although athematic procedures, especially in the medium of electronic music, are vastly more common today.

particularly, the alliance of the music to a textual-dramatic form. While Wagner is studied for such extremes in his style (see Ex. 12.6), much of his music—for example the prelude to *Das Rheingold,* or *Lohengrin*—is very strongly anchored tonally. In addition to Ex. 12.6, the reader should refer to the dynamic, undulant Prelude and *Liebestod* from *Tristan.*

Ex. 12.6   Wagner, Prelude to Parsifal.

A comparable example from Strauss occurs in the Act III trio, *Hab mir's gelobt,* from *Der Rosenkavalier,* a particularly well-known excerpt. Here, the music moves within a space of 40 measures through the keys of D-flat, A, C, (D-flat), F, G-flat, e-flat, and, again, D-flat, whose recurrence is not without structural significance despite the fluctuant quality of the whole. Another case in point may be seen after the G major duet, quite contrasting in its diatonicism and tonal stability, from 4 bars before No. 299 to No. 300, where there is tonal change in every measure or two.

Debussy's *impressionism* is a sensitive reaction to the passionate, deeply subjective, unbridled *expressionism* of the German composers whose tradition stems from Wagner. Debussy, whose musical language is one of restraint and understatement, often reflecting "impressions" of the physical world, contributed in another way to the weakening of tonality.

If functional harmony is harmonic progression which supports the sense of a key center, Debussy's harmonic progression is sometimes *nonfunctional*. In nonfunctional progression (Ex. 12.7), the possibility of tonal identification is not obliterated—each harmony having certain specific tonal implications— but, in the unorthodox movement of one to another, the feeling of a *relating* tonal center is obscured or extinguished altogether. (See Act II, No. 65, of Puccini's *Madame Butterfly* for a comparable passage.) Nonfunction arises in part from the impressionist's interest in the chord as a color value rather than for its function in a tonal scheme. In the music of Debussy, as in Wagner, compensatory factors are at work: the music is often vocal-dramatic or descriptive, or of dance derivation, its form conditioned in part by extra-musical associations; motive repetition, even ostinato, is an important element in this style, too; and those works and passages of Debussy which are most independent of tonality are often extremely brief.

Ex. 12.7   Debussy, Pelléas et Mélisande, Act I, Scene I.
Permission for reprint granted by Durand et Cie., Paris, France, copyright owners, and Elkan-Vogel Co., Inc., Philadelphia, Pa., agents.

But often strong and simple tonal-harmonic elements are at work beneath the surface of apparently nonfunctional progression. Thus, in Ex. 12.8, a basic progression from I to V, etc., is ornamented by auxiliary augmented triads, moving as *escape chords* and *passing chords*.[6] (See also the firmly sustained d:V embellished by auxiliary harmonies in parallel motion, in the approach to the second tonal complex of the first movement of Ravel's String Quartet.)

Ex. 12.8   Debussy, Suite pour le Piano, first movement.
Permission for reprint granted by Editions Jean Jobert, Paris, France, copyright owners, and Elkan-Vogel Co., Inc., Philadelphia, Pa., agents.

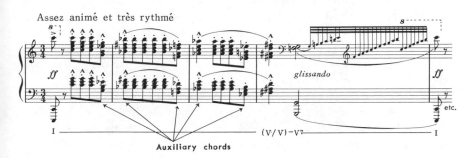

Auxiliary chords

In our own time, while in the styles of many major composers tonality remains a highly important and viable element in musical form,[7] some have felt that its usefulness, in serious question in the late nineteenth-century styles to which we have referred, is spent. Thus, a persistent movement of atonality is current, regarding tonal function as an effete method, and posing new questions with respect to musical form. While tonality can scarcely be argued to be indispensable to form—it is one element of many in traditional music—there can be no question that its denial brings forth problems of singular difficulty, occasioned by the long conditioning of the response to tonal relationships. A widely-used technique in the emerging tradition of atonal music

___

[6] The *escape chord* and *passing chord* are chordal manifestations and extensions of the escape tone and passing tone, respectively. The former leap to "resolution"; the latter are derived and resolved by step.

[7] For discussion of new appearances of tonality (bitonality, etc.) and new theories of tonal function in contemporary idioms, the reader must be referred to other sources. For the moment, twentieth-century theory is scant and uncertain, but a few texts of particular interest are Hindemith's *The Craft of Musical Composition* (New York: Associated Music Publishers, 1945), Vincent Persichetti's *Twentieth-Century Harmony* (New York: W. W. Norton & Company, Inc., 1961), and Adele Katz's *Challenge to Musical Tradition* (New York, Alfred A. Knopf, Inc., 1945), which applies the analytical principles of Heinrich Schenker to certain contemporary and recent styles.

is that of serialization of the independent 12 notes (and, recently, rhythms, dynamics, colors, and other musical elements); yet, it is possible that form in atonal music, to whatever extent it is achieved, derives not from the often imperceptible disposition of ordered 12-note sequences in the musical texture, but from the application at the same time of the ancient principles (tonality excluded or radically diminished) which have brought life and unity to the music of the past. New idioms alter the means of application rather than the principles themselves.

We thus affirm that no persuasive tradition of special solutions to the special problems of atonal musical form has emerged. Form in a Webern cantata or a Dallapiccola variation series, to mention only two composers of assured significance, is the product more of the application of traditional, perhaps largely immutable and integral principles, than of the serial methods by which the composer controls the idioms and vocabulary of his language. In fact, when the repetitions of the 12-note sequence bring about a perceptible unity, the function of the sequence is *exactly analogous to that of melodic-rhythmic theme in traditional music.*

There are those who insist that the emergence of a tonal center—a product of rhythmic and other relationships as well as those of harmonic function—is inevitable in music and cannot be suppressed. However that may be, literatures that resist tonality rely upon many of the compensations for its loss or attenuation which we have observed in styles of the late nineteenth century: motive development and reprise, extreme concision and brevity of expression, and the use of text and scenario. Indeed, many of the most compelling atonal works are written for the stage.

The indisputable fact that principles of musical motion, and of contrast in unity, are pertinent to all music, although postulated in different ways, is powerful testimony to their artistic value and effect. The advancing musical language affords to the creative mind, requiring as it does new modes of address, the fresh stimulation of new possibilities of harmonic function through the control of dissonance-consonance in a context of nontertian harmonic structures; of an infinite range of new colors, some of them derived by mechanical means, requiring their full comprehension *by composers as well as listeners* for credible and convincing employment in art works; of an endless spectrum of rhythmic differentiation and pattern, limited only by the boundaries of human powers to perceive and comprehend; and of incalculable gradations of pitch, which cease to have structural meaning only at that undetermined point where their audible distinctions elude the human consciousness. Yet, whether tonal functions are observed or denied, it remains to be shown that traditional means for binding sound materials into formal units which are at once communicative, interesting, and moving, are not at their basis universal to all musical experience in which expressive statement is directed and ordered within cogent structures—structures which are the fruit of that intellectual discipline which is the most potent resource of man.

Exercises and examples for further study

1. Study, and discuss in an analysis of your own, the means by which climax is prepared and achieved in the Prelude to Wagner's *Tristan*. (You may wish to refer, in your study, to the analysis given in Leichtentritt's *Musical Form*.)

2. Find a piece of music, possibly contemporary, in which the form seems to you to be unsuccessful. Develop a case to support your view.

3. Make a comparative study of three examples from one of the following sources.
   a) Later Haydn symphonic slow movements
   b) Preludes of Bach's *Well-Tempered Clavier*
   c) Debussy preludes for piano
   d) Twentieth-century toccatas

4. Isolating a passage of 3 or 4 measures from a musical work of your selection, try to identify all factors of musical motion which are at work.

5. What principles of purely musical form do you see applied in a movement of Berlioz's *Romeo and Juliet*, or Strauss's *Ein Heldenleben?* Make an outline of structural features deriving from extra-musical associations, and features which are independent of such associations.

6. The following is a list of works, to be added to those referred to in Chapter 12, from which you may select subjects for further study and analysis.

   Bach, Fantasies and Toccatas for organ
      Preludes from the WTC (for example, 1, 2, 3, and 5 in Book I, and 1 and 3 in Book II)
   Bartók, Suite for piano, Op. 14, first movement
   Beethoven, Sonata in C-sharp minor, Op. 27, No. 2, first movement
   Berg, Four Pieces, Op. 5, for clarinet and piano
   Brahms, *Von ewiger Liebe,* and other songs
   Carter, *Recitative and Improvisation* from Six Pieces for kettledrums
      Eight Etudes and a Fantasy for woodwind quartet
   Copland, Piano Fantasy
   Debussy, Preludes for piano (for example, 1 and 2 of Book I)
   Dallapiccola, *Quaderno Musicale di Annalibera* for piano (for example, 1, 2, 4, 8, 9 and 11)
   Franck, Fantasy in A for organ
   Hindemith, Sonata for viola and piano (1939), third movement
   Leon Kirchner (b. 1919), String Quartet No. 1, fourth movement
   Liszt, *Les Préludes*
   Mozart, Fantasies for piano
   Francis Poulenc (1899–1963), *Mouvements perpétuels* for piano
   Prokofiev, Sonata No. 2 for piano, slow movement
   Ravel, *Schéhérezade*
   Schönberg, Piano Pieces, Op. 19
      Fantasy for violin and piano, Op. 47
   Verdi, *Macbeth,* Act IV, Scene 3
   Webern, Four Pieces for violin and piano, Op. 7

INDEX

Regular augmentation, 257n.

Réjouissance, 358

Relaxation as element in musical form, 448 (*Chart*)

Repeated phrase, 17-18 (*Ex.*)

Repeats: in binary form, 47-48; in ternary with *da capo,* 105-6 (*Ex.*); in rondo, 154; of exposition in single-movement sonata form, 188-89

Repetition, 1, 51; of the phrase, 17-18 (*Ex.*); of phrases in single period, 23 (*Ex.*); of the period, 26 (*Ex.*); of motive in period, 51; of motive in binary form, 51; after digression, in ternary form, 51-52; in ostinato forms, 270, 271; use of variation techniques in, 295; of subject as basis of fugal form, 394

Retransition, 47n.; in ending of second part of ternary form, 69-70 (*Ex.*); preparation involved in, 70-71 (*Ex.*); in integrated compound ternary, 112-14 (*Ex.*); in rondo, 138-41 (*Ex.*), 155, 161 (*Ex.*), 162 (*Ex.*); in single-movement sonata form, 186-88 (*Ex.*), 224 (*Ex.*); preceding recapitulation in single-movement sonata-form, 194; in sonata-rondo, 240, 245 (*Ex.*), 248 (*Ex.*), 250 (*Ex.*), 255 (*Ex.*), 263 (*Ex.*)

Retrograde canon, 420 (*Ex.*)

Retrograde and retrograde mirror as subject variations in fugue, 397 (*Ex.*), 407 (*Ex.*)

Rhapsody, free form in, 438

Rhythm: definition of, 7n.; as aspect of all variable elements, 316-17

Rhythmic alteration of fugue subject, 394 (*Ex.*), 395 (*Ex.*), 396

Rhythmic fixation and variation in variation technique, 316-18 (*Ex.*)

Rhythmic motion, 317, *see* Motion

Rhythmic patterns, as factors in musical coherence, 2

Rhythmic variation, 286 (*Ex.*), 316-18 (*Ex.*), 331 (*Ex.*), 333-34 (*Ex.*), 394-96

Rhythmically free canon, 423

Ricercar, 374

Riddle canon, 421

Rieger, Symphony No. 3, final movement, analysis of ostinato form in, 284-86 (*Ex.*)

"Riff" in jazz improvisation, 279

Romanesca, 273

Rondeau: as medieval precursor of the rondo, 123-25; in the suite, 358-59

Rondellus, 373

Rondo, 122-67 (*Ex.*); as expansion of ternary form, 78; relationships of compound ternary form to, 119-20; use of, as final movement of multi-movement

form, 122; historical backgrounds of rondo principle, 123-25; form defined, 125-27 (*Ex.*); diagrammatic symbol for five-part rondo, 125; sections of five-part rondo, 125-27 (*Ex.*); examples of parts of rondo design, discussion of, 127-54 (*Ex.*); introduction, 127-30 (*Ex.*); compound form, 130, 137; rondo theme, 130-32 (*Ex.*); 138-41 (*Ex.*), 147-49 (*Ex.*); transition to first digression, 132-35 (*Ex.*); first digression, 135-37 (*Ex.*); retransition, restatement of rondo theme, 138-41 (*Ex.*); second transition, 141-44 (*Ex.*); second digression as repetition of first, 144 (*Ex.*); second digression as contrast to first, 145-47 (*Ex.*); final statement of rondo theme, 147-49 (*Ex.*); codetta, or coda, 150-54 (*Ex.*); repeats in, 154; rondo principle in *da capo* forms, 154-55; degrees of integration in, 155-57 (*Ex.*); extensions of rondo form, 157-58 (*Ex.*), 267n.; seven-part form, 157; compound, 157-58 (*Ex.*); analysis of Beethoven, Trio in E-flat, Op. 70, No. 2, for piano, violin, and cello, second movement, 158-65 (*Ex.*); *see also* Sonata-rondo

Rota, 373

Round, 373, 418, 424

Rounded binary form, 42, 48 (*Ex.*), 56

Rufer, Josef, 310

S

Saltarello, 316, 342

Sarabande, 343, 344, 345, 347, 357 (*Ex.*); origin of, 357n.

Sarabande, a Dance of American Descent (Stevenson), 357n.

Scherzo: with trio, 103; evolution of, from minuet, 103

Second part of binary form, 39-42; tonal range and modulation in, 39, 40-41 (*Ex.*); symmetrical binary, 39; asymmetrical binary, 39, 40; structure of, 39, 40 (*Ex.*); use of inverted form of motive in parallel construction, 41, 142 (*Ex.*)

Second part of compound ternary form, 88-94 (*Ex.*); contrast as primary function, 88-89 (*Ex.*); relationship to first part, 89-90 (*Ex.*), 92; modulations, 90 (*Ex.*); structure, 91 (*Ex.*); length, 92; development of motives of Part I, 92-93 (*Ex.*); trio, followed by *da capo,* 102-3 (*Ex.*)

Second part of simple ternary form, 65-71 (*Ex.*); contrast in, 65-66 (*Ex.*); key relationships in, 66-67 (*Ex.*); introduction

INDEX OF COMPOSERS